Conservative Brain Trust

Conservative Brain Trust

The Rise, Fall, and Rise Again of the American Enterprise Institute

Howard J. Wiarda

LEXINGTON BOOKS

A division of
ROWMAN & LITTLEFIELD PUBLISHERS, INC.
Lanham • Boulder • New York • Toronto • Plymouth, UK

LEXINGTON BOOKS

A division of Rowman & Littlefield Publishers, Inc.
A wholly owned subsidiary of The Rowman & Littlefield Publishing Group, Inc.
4501 Forbes Boulevard, Suite 200
Lanham, MD 20706

Estover Road
Plymouth PL6 7PY
United Kingdom

British Library Cataloguing in Publication Information Available

Library of Congress Cataloging-in-Publication Data

Wiarda, Howard J., 1939-
Conservative brain trust : the rise, fall, and rise again of the American Enterprise Institute / Howard J. Wiarda.
p. cm.
Includes bibliographical references and index.
ISBN-13: 978-0-7391-2883-1 (hardcover : alk. paper)
ISBN-10: 0-7391-2883-3 (hardcover : alk. paper)
ISBN-13: 978-0-7391-2884-8 (pbk. : alk. paper)
ISBN-10: 0-7391-2884-1 (pbk. : alk. paper)
ISBN-13: 978-0-7391-3305-7 (electronic)
ISBN-10: 0-7391-3305-5 (electronic)
[etc.]
1. American Enterprise Institute for Public Policy Research. 2. Policy sciences. 3. Economics—Research—United States. 4. Wiarda, Howard J., 1939- I. Title.
H62.5.U5W534 2009
320.60973—dc22 2008040887

Printed in the United States of America

∞™ The paper used in this publication meets the minimum requirements of American National Standard for Information Sciences—Permanence of Paper for Printed Library Materials, ANSI/NISO Z39.48-1992.

Contents

Preface

Until 1980 I had been mainly an academic political scientist. I had been a sometimes policy adviser during both the Dominican Republic revolution and U.S. intervention of 1965 and the Portuguese revolution and its aftermath in 1974. I'd been involved, albeit on the periphery, in the 1968, 1972, and 1976 presidential elections. But these were mainly sideline activities; my main work to that point had been as a university professor of comparative politics, specializing in Latin America and Western Europe. I'd written several books by then, taught courses on those areas, and climbed the academic ladder to tenure and a full professorship at age thirty-seven. At the moment that the call came that changed my life, I was happily situated as a research scholar at Harvard University's Center for International Affairs (CFIA—later the Weatherhead Center).

The call, whose contents are detailed in Chapter 1, was from Jeane Kirkpatrick. She had just been named UN ambassador by President-elect Ronald Reagan and she wanted me to accompany her to New York as a top-ranking aide. My position would also carry the title of ambassador. Wow! But as my family (wife Iêda, children Kristy, Howard, and Jonathan) contemplated life in New York, a follow-up call came in from Jeane. She was terribly sorry but she had offered more UN ambassadorships than the State Department had available. My heart sank. But then Jeane offered an alternative: come to AEI as a foreign policy analyst and work on UN things for me from my Washington office.

So that's how I got to Washington and AEI, the American Enterprise Institute for Public Policy Research. That's how I became a denizen of one of Washington's leading think tanks and idea factories. That's how I joined the Reagan Revolution and, for a time, the "neocon" (neo-conservative) community. That's how I became a Washington insider, what we call a "mover 'n' shaker," a policy wonk. And that's how my life changed forever, no longer "merely" an academic political scientist but now engaged in policy analysis and advocacy.

Thus begins my memoir of the Reagan Revolution and the think tank that was the brains behind it all—AEI. AEI came to be known as "the thinking man's think tank," the source of all the great ideas—privatization, state downsizing, social security reform, health care reform, welfare reform, supply-side economics, the Democracy Initiative, winning the Cold War—that constituted the core of President Reagan's far-reaching revolution. AEI was the source of the reform agenda that was enacted into policy and is still with us today. AEI and its core group of scholars and intellectuals were instrumental in designing and fashioning all these policies. For most of the 1980s I was a part of this group; though my work focused on foreign policy, I also saw, up close and personal, all the major domestic policy proposals that constituted the Reagan reform agenda.

AEI's sterling reputation as the source of Reagan Administration policy disguised the fact that all was not well within the think tank. There were many policy arguments, ideological and personal rivalries, and bitter disputes over the future of the institute. AEI was a veritable "Peyton Place" of subsurface political fights, internecine battles, and a neocon coup d'etat. Then, in the midst of these political and ideological wars, AEI went belly-up financially. Its president began secretly dipping into the private endowments that supported his most prestigious and high-powered scholars, AEI verged on the edge of bankruptcy, and in a major upheaval the trustees had to come galloping in like John Wayne (or maybe Butch Cassidy and the Sundance Kid) to fire the president and bail out the institute. Only in recent years with its neocon ideologies and closeness to the George W. Bush Administration has AEI begun to recover both its financial health and its policy influence.

All this is analyzed in this stirring and personal story of the rise, fall, and rise again of this hothouse of intellectual inquiry and policy ideas. Hard though it is for outsiders to believe, the government, even with its $3 trillion budget, doesn't think anymore; that has passed to the think tanks, AEI and others, which do the government's thinking for it. And not just thinking but policy formulation, speech-writing, budget analyses to say nothing of (largely illegal) political campaigning and policy advocacy. AEI is at the heart of it all and serves up a hearty brew.

In this evocative memoir, we try to capture all this and more. We tell the story of my recruitment at AEI and my initial meetings (and often stormy confrontations) with the then big guns of the neocon movement: Jeane Kirkpatrick, Arthur Burns, Michael Novak, Herb Stein, Irving Kristol, James Miller, Walter Berns, Ben Wattenberg, Howard Penniman, and many others.

The book analyzes the hot 'n' heavy social life of Washington, D.C., its political machinations, and AEI's strong role in Washington policy-making. The book is full of insider stories, tales of how things work above and beyond the textbook accounts, and the role of AEI at the heart of all this. Because, as we tell the story, "everyone" in Washington knew that Ronald Reagan lacked the brains to be president; AEI, it was assumed, had to be running the government for him as Reagan's behind-the-scenes *eminence grise*.

In this book we provide an insider's view of what the author saw and heard at the Conservative Revolution. Of all he experienced at AEI. Here are fascinating insights on the policy process, on how the White House works, on Congress, the CIA, State and Defense departments. And on the key individuals involved: President Reagan, Ollie North, Michael Deaver, Nancy Reagan, Ed Meese, Jeane Kirkpatrick, Al Haig, Henry Kissinger, George Shultz, Bill Casey, Cap Weinberger, Margaret Thatcher, and many more. For the author (and the detailed journals he kept during this period) is a walking storehouse of insider stories and gossip, as well as a shrewd analyst of the policy process.

In this book we not only chronicle the rise, fall, and rise again of AEI, its internal battles, and its policy influences; but we also provide in-depth analysis of some of the major issues of the time: the crisis in Central America, the Kissinger Commission efforts to solve it, the Cold War, the "great" Third World debt crisis, the U.S. campaign to promote democracy abroad, the crisis of American policy-making. For I was something of an insider, a participant in many of these great events, a "policy influential" as well as an observer of how the process works. In one chapter I write, "The first time I went down to the White House for a policy briefing, I covered my eyes with my hands in mock agony; it was so nutty and ideological that I couldn't believe what I was hearing. After that, I started writing it all down."

And now we have the full story in book form, full of what I think are fascinating tales, analyses of the policy process, portraits of key personalities, and my own political, social, and policy adventures and misadventures along the way. This is not a tell-all book, let alone a "kiss 'n' tell," but it is a book about Washington and policy-making from a semi-insider, as well as a personal story of my own role and position within AEI and in the broader foreign policy community. I think it's a fun and provocative read with numerous insights on Washington, the Reagan and Bush administrations, and the policy process.

In the preparation of this book I have incurred a large number of debts. Ray Vernon and Sam Huntington were responsible for recruiting me at Harvard's CFIA; without that affiliation and the use of Harvard stationery, I doubt if I'd ever gotten the call to Washington and AEI. Above all, I owe a large debt of gratitude to Jeane Kirkpatrick for bringing me to AEI and thereby changing the course of my life. At AEI, I want to especially thank such colleagues as former President Bill Baroody Jr., and fellow scholars Denis Doyle, Evron Kirkpatrick, Marvin Kosters, Margaret McAuliff, Michael Novak, Norm Ornstein, Howard Penniman, and Austin Ramney, who not only welcomed me to Washington but also helped teach me how Washington works.

As I began to do the research, review old files and my Washington journals, and begin the writing, research assistants at the University of Georgia Esther Skelley, Jennifer White, and Cynthia McMeekin were enormously helpful. Doris Holden and Kathryn Johnson are not only the world's best computer word processors, they are also indispensable editors, advisers, and cheerer-uppers. My wonderful family—Iêda, Kristy, Howard, Jonathan—shared many of these Washington years, often to the detriment of their own careers, friendships, and school cohorts; none of these Washington adventures would have been possible without them. But, for good or ill, I, not any of those named, am the one responsible for the treatment that follows.

Howard J. Wiarda
Bonita Hills
Athens, Georgia
Spring 2008

Chapter One

Introduction: "The Call"

It was just before Christmas, 1980, a month and a half after the U.S. presidential election in which Ronald Reagan defeated Jimmy Carter. I was in my office at the Center for International Affairs (CFIA); now the Weatherhead Center at Harvard University when the phone rang. The caller asked my name, said "Hold please," and then Jeane Kirkpatrick came on the line. She had just been named a few days earlier by president-elect Reagan as ambassador to the United Nations. "Howard," she said, "I'm going to be moving to New York soon and I want you to come along, with the rank of ambassador in the U.S. UN mission,[1] to deal with the Third World." It was the phone call that would change my life forever.

Until then, I hadn't known Jeane very well. We had met a few times at academic conferences (she was a professor at Georgetown) and Washington policy confabs but these were brief meetings; we had never talked seriously. However, it turned out in that initial conversation that she knew my writings on Latin America and had drawn on them in writing her famous article for *Commentary* magazine on "Dictatorship and Double Standards." That was the article that had attracted Reagan to Jeane and gotten her the appointment as UN ambassador.

To be honest, what really got me the UN job offer was not my academic writings but my Harvard stationery. In 1979 I had been appointed to a year-long stint, renewable for a second year, as a Senior Associate at Harvard University's Center for International Affairs—CFIA. (It had once been abbreviated "CIA" but that confused it with a certain other notorious agency, and during the student protests of the early 1970s it had been changed to CFIA.) The position at Harvard was an adjunct or non-paying one; my regular job was as professor of political science at the University of Massachusetts. The

Harvard appointment entitled me to a shared office, to participate in CFIA activities, and, most important, to use the Center's stationery.

In 1976 I had gotten involved in the national election campaign really for the first time. Although I had always considered myself a Democrat, as a specialist in foreign affairs I had been put off by the simplistic anti-war message of the 1972 McGovern campaign as well as, since I was a professional political scientist, by the sheer incompetence of that campaign. In addition, in 1976, Republican candidate Jerry Ford was from my hometown of Grand Rapids, Michigan. I had written to Ford, to his campaign manager Jim Baker, and to Ford confidants (and from Grand Rapids) Phil Buchen and Bill Seidman offering to assist in the campaign and indicating that in this dangerous Cold War period filled with nuclear threats, rising Soviet power, and instability in much of the Third World, they should emphasize Ford's experience in Washington and international affairs, versus Jimmy's Carter's inexperience and naiveté. But using my U-Mass stationery, all I got back was a form letter saying "Dear Contributor: Thank you for your support."

In 1980 it was different. I was the same person but the institutional name on the letterhead was new. Using my Harvard stationery, this time I got quite a bit of response. It's not, I've learned, that the candidates or their political operatives really want your advice; they already "know" all the answers. It's that they want to have Harvard names and affiliations on their advisory panels. That, presumably, lends prestige and gravitas to their campaigns. So that is how and why I heard from Jeane. I had sent her, as well as the Carter people (we "Harvardites" are not particular about party affiliations; we just assume we should be running the country in every administration) a letter, my CV, and some of my recent writings on foreign affairs. So far as I can tell, the only difference between my unsuccessful efforts in 1976 and the successful one in 1980 was the Harvard affiliation. Now I too carried prestige and gravitas!

The days after Jeane's call were a flurry of activity around our house. Would I quit my tenured U-Mass job? Would we move to New York? Would I give up that valuable Harvard affiliation? Where would we put our kids in school? Where would we live? Jeane must have put my name in the hopper, because soon we heard from colleagues and neighbors that the FBI had been snooping around asking questions about my character and loyalties.

But then a bombshell hit. I received a second call from Jeane. "Howard," she said, "I'm terribly sorry but I have offered more ambassadorships than I have available." She went on to explain that since she knew the other people she'd chosen for her staff (Chuck Lichtenstein, Carl Gershman, Alan Gerson, José Sorzano) better than me, she was forced to drop me from consideration as a member of her immediate UN team. "But," she brightened, "why don't you come to Washington anyway as director of AEI's Latin America Center. And you can help me with my UN responsibilities from there."

And that's how I got to AEI. That's how I became a Washington insider, power monger, and mover 'n' shaker—at least in my own narrow field. The AEI position came to me as a consolation prize for not getting the UN ambassadorship. If truth be told, I had held my nose and voted for Jimmy Carter in 1980, as usual choosing foreign policy experience, however often misguided in Mr. Carter's case, over the inexperienced Reagan. I had no idea what I'd be getting into at AEI or how I might fit in—uncomfortably as it turned out—with all those conservatives and neoconservatives ("neocons") at the Institute. But the opportunity to move to Washington and actually *influence* policy as distinct from just writing about it—every academic's dream—had presented itself, and I quickly jumped at that exciting possibility. When lightning strikes, if you're a policy wonk like me, you've got to be prepared to jump at the chance because, as we know, lightning seldom strikes twice in the same place.

AEI AND THE WORLD OF THE WASHINGTON THINK TANKS

At that time, I didn't know much about AEI. I had been to only one meeting there run by AEI's foreign policy director Robert Pranger, which I found to be boring and unimpressive. I can't even remember the subject matter of the meeting. All I knew was that AEI had a reputation as a conservative and business-minded institution. More than that I didn't know.

AEI was in fact part of a new phenomenon of the 1970s, the rise of the big Washington think tanks. These included the Institute for Policy Studies (IPS) on the far left, the Brookings Institution on the moderate left, the Center for Strategic and International Studies (CSIS) in the middle, AEI on the moderate right, and the Heritage Foundation on the far right. Outside of Washington there were the RAND Corporation and the Hoover Institution, both California-based, and inside Washington there were other, smaller, specialized "tanks." But these were the Big Five.

The rise of the think tanks relates to other, larger changes in American society and politics. Some of them—Brookings, the New York-based Council on Foreign Relations, and the Carnegie Endowment for International Peace—trace their origins back to the early twentieth century and the progressive, good-government movement of that time. The goal, like those of the League of Women Voters that also dates from this time, was to improve government performance, reduce corruption and "bossism," and perfect the practice of American Democracy. Brookings and AEI emerged as rivals in the 1950s and

1960s debating the merits of Keynes versus more traditional market economics, and then clashed again over Lyndon B. Johnson's Great Society programs. Others like the radical IPS and Heritage, of more recent vintage, were a reflection of the greater polarization and ideological conflict of American society of the 1960s and 1970s.

I know all the literature on what think tanks do or are supposed to do. They serve as idea providers in the policy arena, as intermediaries between universities and government, as providers of options to policy makers, as pools of talent to new administrations as well as "resting places" for out-of-office politicians. All these descriptions are accurate; that is what think tanks actually do. More detail is provided in chapter 4.

But I have my own theory about this. As the name suggests, think tanks do the government's thinking for it. This may sound ludicrous to some, because surely with that $3.0 trillion federal budget some thinking must go on in the government. But in fact the government does precious little thinking anymore. The government has no time to think. Even the various policy planning staffs do little actual thinking anymore. For the fact is that if you are a government bureaucrat, your time is so taken up with paperwork, meetings, deadlines, bureaucracy, forms, and reports to fill out that you have no time to think anymore. You just can't do it and certainly not on a sustained basis.

So that is what think tanks do. They provide the background, the history, the context that government officials cannot take the time to do. Think tanks may write legislation, prepare speeches or testimony, and lay out the policy options for decision makers that were once the function of government policy makers. Think tank analysts and position papers may even be telling elected representatives how to vote on various issues. In short, the think tanks have stepped into the vacuum created by the sheer bigness, bureaucracy, and time-consuming procedure of government to provide a useful service. And that is to discuss the ideas and policies and make recommendations on the issues that most government officials and congressman no longer have the time to study in depth. And, let us be clear, these *are* vital, essential services.

AEI

The American Enterprise Institute was founded in 1943 by Lewis H. Brown, the president of the Johns-Manville Corporation. Brown was strongly for free enterprise and against government control of the economy. The founding date of 1943 is important; Brown wanted to ensure that the tight wartime controls that President Franklin Roosevelt had imposed over the economy were discontinued after the war. To that end Brown and AEI urged, lobbied, and cajoled Congress on the merits of free enterprise and the dangers of state control. Hence during this early period AEI was widely viewed as a mouthpiece for Brown and as a business-lobbying group or trade association. It had little if any scholarly credentials.

That changed radically after 1954 when dynamic William J. Baroody took over management of the Institute. Baroody was the son of Lebanese Maronite Christian immigrants and a pillar of the Maronite church; he ran AEI like a Lebanese clan or political party: tightly knit, clan-based, top-down, requiring absolute loyalty, patronage-dominated, fiercely loyal to his friends. Baroody converted AEI from a lobbying group to a real think tank. He recruited such top-notch economists as Milton Friedman and Paul McCracken. His orientation, personally, was conservative, but he was committed to (and elevated into the AEI motto) "the competition of ideas in a free society," recruiting Democrats as well as Republicans into the AEI "family." Baroody was an organizational, political, and fund-raising genius; though lacking an advanced degree, Baroody could more than hold his own with any of the intellectual high-flyers he recruited at AEI.

During the 1960s and into the 1970s, AEI under Baroody's direction emerged as the great conservative counter balance to the Brookings Institution. For at least a thirty-year period the debate between these two institutions and their scholars largely set the parameters of U.S. economic policy. Brookings was liberal, Keynesian, and closely tied to the U.S. Democratic party. Moreover, many of its economists had been in charge of the wartime controls that AEI had earlier railed against. Brookings criticized and opposed Eisenhower's more orthodox economic policy, and was overjoyed when the succeeding John F. Kennedy and Lyndon B. Johnson administrations recruited its leading figures back into government service.

AEI, in contrast, was free-market oriented. Its lodestar, if it had one, was not Keynes but Hayek, the Austrian economist who in his *The Road to Serfdom* warned against statism, socialism, and government interference in the economy. AEI stood for unfettered capitalism; later on in the 1980s it would provide the intellectual basis for Ronald Reagan's campaign for privatization, deregulation, and state downsizing. But still in the 1960s Baroody became a fan of and adviser to conservative ("Mr. Conservative") Arizona Senator Barry Goldwater. He rallied AEI to the support of the 1964 Goldwater campaign. For this overtly politicized role, and technically (everyone else did it!) violating the structures against tax-exempt organizations engaging in political activities, AEI incurred the wrath of Johnson who had the IRS go after AEI. AEI's economists were also in charge when, to their eternal shame and consternation, President Richard Nixon established price controls, declaring, "We are all Keynesians now." That is why the AEI economists were eager to see their newest ideas—privatization, de-regulation, government downsizing—put into effect by the incoming Reagan administration.

Although AEI's focus remained economic policy, by the 1970s Baroody had also recruited some notable political scientists and foreign policy specialists. These included Robert Pranger, who was put in charge of foreign policy, Howard Penniman, and Evron and Jeane Kirkpatrick. They in turn brought in other prominent colleagues and staff: Austin Ranney, Richard Neustadt, Nelson Polsby, Jack Pelteson, Warren Miller. Alone among Washington think tanks, Baroody, because of his own religious background, brought in Catholic theologian Michael Novak to serve as resident philosopher and religion writer. But even with these new hires, the economic team at AEI, now including Gottfried Haberler, Arthur Burns, Herb Stein, Marvin Kosters, and Thomas Johnson, always remained the core group.

In the late 1970s Bill Baroody developed a devastating cancer and passed away in 1980. Hence in 1978 he tapped his son, Bill Jr., to replace him as president. Bill Jr., with a background in public relations, was a wonderful person—after all, he had the good sense to hire me—but he lacked his father's dynamism, energy, administrative skills, and intellectual firepower. Nevertheless, building on the earlier 1970s efforts, the funds kept pouring in and Bill Jr. kept expanding, adding new programs, and hiring new people. It was AEI and its ex-Democrat neocons, after all, which now led the charge against the ineffective Carter Administration. Moreover, upwards of thirty AEI scholars were recruited into the incoming Reagan Administration at high levels—Jeane Kirkpatrick at the UN post, Arthur Burns as ambassador to Germany, Jim Miller as director of the Office of Management and Budget, and many others.

It was precisely at this high point of AEI influence, affluence (a budget of over $10 million), and promise of scaling even higher policy walls that I was recruited.

THE CONTEXT: CARTER OUT, REAGAN IN

AEI was a quite diverse institution when I arrived there in the spring of 1981. Robert Pranger, its foreign policy director, had been a John Anderson supporter in the 1980 election campaign and a member of his foreign policy advisory team; Anderson promised clean, honest, moral government and offered a moderate, sensible, and centrist middle way between Carter and Reagan.

Among Republicans in the Institute, the split was about even between "movement conservatives" who strongly supported Reagan and hoped to be rewarded with posts in the new administration, and more moderate or liberal

Republicans who came out and were often veterans of the Rockefeller-Nixon-Ford-George H. W. Bush wing of the party.

The movement conservatives (it is often hard to tell who really believed the ideology and who just wanted a cushy government job) included Pedro San Juan and Roger Fontaine in the foreign affairs area, economist Jim Miller, theologian Michael Novak, UN Ambassador Kirkpatrick, and foreign policy specialists Mark Falcoff and Joshua Muravchik. The more liberal Republicans with whom I could more freely talk included economists Rudolph Penner and John Makin, journalist Nick Thimmesch, American politics specialist William Schambra, China expert Michael Lampton, and health policy specialist Sean Sullivan.

It may be surprising to some to learn that there were quite a number of prominent Democrats at AEI, including Middle East expert Judith Kipper, journalist Ben Wattenberg, pollster Karlyn Keene-Bauman, American politics specialist Norm Ornstein, pollster William Schneider, census and elections expert Richard Scammon, social policy expert Douglas Besharov, education expert Denis Doyle, political parties specialist Michael Malbin, and, not least, Jeane Kirkpatrick.

Nor were my own politics clearly defined at the time. By family background, sociology, culture, and politics (Grand Rapids!), I should have been a Republican. But by education (University of Michigan), profession (professor), and voting record in 1964 and 1968, I considered myself a liberal Democrat. At the same time, disquieted by the anti-war McGovern campaign, I had voted for Nixon in 1972 and for a hometown boy, Ford, in 1976. But I was certainly not a Reagan or movement conservative and I did not advertise my vote for Carter in 1980 to my AEI colleagues. I felt comfortable with the liberal Republicans at AEI but the "movement" types, the "true believers," left me uncomfortable.

Almost everyone at AEI—Democrats, liberal Republicans, and movement conservatives—were disappointed, disillusioned, and unhappy with Jimmy Carter. His was almost universally considered a failed presidency. But there were degrees of disappointment/unhappiness, and varying reasons for their disillusionment. Some faulted Carter for his excessive moralism, his Sunday School teacher preachiness, and his constant lecturing and hectoring. Others criticized his naïveté or various of his specific policy initiatives. But the simple issue that united all of the diverse scholars at AEI was Carter's foreign policy.

In his famous Notre Dame speech of 1977, shortly after his inauguration, Carter elevated human rights as *the* centerpiece and highest priority in his foreign policy. This focus was very much in keeping with Carter's moralizing character and his background as a Sunday School teacher. It was also in keeping with Carter's belief that foreign policy was just like civil rights policy then stirring the U.S. South. That all that was required was men of good will and pure hearts getting together, seeing the light which Carter himself had defined, and moving forward toward progress and resolution of conflicts.[2] Carter's appointments of such civil rights stalwarts as Andy Young and Patt Darian, and Protestant ministers/missionaries like Brady Tyson, to key foreign policy positions cemented this orientation.

In elevating human rights above other foreign policy values and interests, meanwhile reducing the Defense Department, undermining the CIA, and denigrating traditional national interest and balance of power politics, Carter violated every principle that those of us who study international relations professionally have ever believed in. Most of us are also all in favor of human rights but we do not think it is appropriate for the U.S. to interfere so overtly in the internal affairs of other nations. Moreover, while we favor human rights, we do not think that should be the sole or virtually only foreign policy consideration. The United States has other interests as well as those relating to human rights: economic interests, cultural interests, political interests, diplomatic interests, and military and strategic interests—particular at that time since the Cold War conflict with the Soviet Union was still on and many serious analysts thought that the U.S. was in danger of actually losing the Cold War.

The focus on human rights almost exclusively came at the cost of fundamental U.S. interest in such areas as Asia, the Middle East, Africa, and Latin America. And specifically in such countries as Iran, Nicaragua, Argentina, Brazil, El Salvador. Thus when we criticized our friend and ally, the Shah of Iran, for human rights abuses, it had the effect of undermining his regime and paving the way for the Ayatollah Khomeini and the present Iranian regime, which was not only worse for U.S. interests but also worse for human rights. When the Carter Administration loudly and publicly criticized the Argentine and Brazilian military regimes for human rights abuses, it forced public opinion in these countries to rally around their governments on nationalistic grounds rather than accept the U.S. criticism.

In Nicaragua, by publicly criticizing the abuses of Anastasio Somoza Jr., the U.S. undermined his government and paved the way for the coming to power of the Sandinistas, who were even more inimical to U.S. interests. Similarly in El Salvador: everyone understood the military regime there to be violators of human rights; the issue was, wouldn't a takeover by the Marxist guerrillas be even worse? The issue, in other words, was one of balance and judgment: Carter seemed to go off half-cocked on human rights while ignoring all other legitimate U.S. interests. And from the scholars' at AEI point of view, it was not as though they were opposed to human rights; quite the contrary, almost all of them had been pioneers in civil and human rights. What they objected to was not human rights per se but the overwhelming emphasis in human rights to the complete neglect of all other basic U.S. interests.

Of course since Carter's was a Democrat administration, its criticisms of human rights abuses were directed far more at right-wing regimes than left-wing ones. Iran, Brazil, Argentina, Chile, El Salvador, South Africa, Indonesia, the Philippines came under intense criticism while China, the Soviet Union, Cuba, Angola, Mozambique, Ethiopia, Vietnam received only mild criticism—if at all. Moreover, the public way in which the former countries were denounced indicated that Carter was playing to domestic U.S. constituencies instead of trying to effect change in the countries noted, which, if that was the intent, would mainly call for quiet diplomacy. In many countries, the U.S. criticism had the opposite effect of that intended, forcing public opinion in the countries criticized to come to the defense, nationalistically, of their governments, however abusive, rather than rallying opinion against them.

The policy was extremely controversial within the main foreign affairs agencies as well as outside of them. The State Department, Defense Department, and CIA, in all of which the realist position dominated, were all, in the main, opposed to the policy. For the most part, only Carter's *political appointees* within these agencies approved of the policy. In the State Department, for instance, whenever there was a conflict between the regional bureaus for Africa, Asia, Latin America, etc., where the real country expertise lay, *and* the new human rights office, a special committee headed by Carter appointee (and future secretary of state) Warren Christopher consistently backed the human rights position. And when State Department career officers such as Assistant Secretary of State for Inter-American Affairs Terence Todman, himself black and no stranger to the civil rights struggle, had the courage to criticize the policy, they were immediately fired.

These criticisms added up to a stinging indictment of the Carter Administration. The critics said Carter had alienated such important regional friends and allies as Argentina, Brazil, Chile, Indonesia, the Philippines, South Korea, Taiwan, and South Africa. At the same time we had lost to Marxism-Leninism such key regional countries as Iran, Nicaragua, Ethiopia, Angola, Mozambique, and perhaps El Salvador and others. Meanwhile we were ignoring the immense military build-up and global threat posed by the Soviet Union, which was winning more and more countries (those listed above and others) to its list of allies and supporters.

At home, purges and exposés by the Church Committee and others were destroying the capacity of our own government to respond adequately to the Soviet and communist menace. These criticisms were widespread among the Washington policy elite; then when the American embassy in Tehran was attacked and American diplomats and embassy personnel were captured, humiliated, and tortured—and all this the subject of U.S. television coverage night after night—these issues came home vividly to the American public. In 1980, in large part because of the Iran debacle, Jimmy Carter and his foreign policy were massively repudiated and voted out of office by the electorate.

During this same period a major gravitation to the right had been occurring among American intellectuals and some politicians, who came to be called "neoconservatives" and who now constituted a major, if not *the* major, intellectual current at AEI. Led by such prominent figures as Irving Kristol, Nathan Glazer, Norman Podhoretz, Daniel Patrick Moynihan, Senator Scoop Jackson, Congressman (and Speaker of the House) Jim Wright, Seymour Martin Lipset, Daniel Bell, Samuel Huntington, Jeane Kirkpatrick, Michael Novak, and others, the neocons had been Democrats in the 1960s, supporters of civil rights, the Great Society, and the presidencies of John F. Kennedy and Lyndon B. Johnson. But they, like me, had been soured by the McGovernite-peacenik takeover of the Democratic Party in 1972 and then the triumph of this ideology in the subsequent Carter Administration. They felt the Democrats had abandoned the strong internationalist position of Truman, Kennedy, and Johnson, were ignoring the Soviet build-up and threat, and were (and not just its Jewish members) often insufficiently worried about the Soviet-Arab threat to Israel's existence. All these influences helped push these neocons toward Ronald Reagan, the Republican Party, and AEI.

It should not be thought that the neocons were unanimous or always entirely enthusiastic about these positions and policy reconfigurations. Many of them had long opposed the Republican Party and the policies of Eisenhower and Nixon. Nor were they necessarily strong supporters of Ronald Reagan, whose policies, limitations, and intellectual weaknesses were quite apparent. Even Irving Kristol and Jeane Kirkpatrick (now that she was UN ambassador), who were thought of as the intellectual and policy leaders of the neocons, often expressed (now privately, of course) strong reservations about Reagan, the Republicans, and Reagan Administration policies and personnel. But in politics you have to make choices; and in the context of the early 1980s that meant for the neocons Reagan, the Republicans, and AEI. And if you disagree with some aspects of the policy or program, hold your nose and your tongue and support the main thrusts of the policy.

That is the context in which I joined AEI: traditional Democrats like me thoroughly disillusioned with the Democrat Party and the Carter Administration foreign policy; slowly, often reluctantly, and by no means unanimously gravitating toward Reagan and the Republican Party; often estranged from our own universities whose faculties, strongly shaped by the campus anti-Vietnam War era, were going strongly toward the Left; and attracted to AEI because it promised the opportunity to actually shape policy and not just write about it. And recall that AEI itself, as indicated earlier, was hardly unanimous on these matters, indeed was about evenly split between neocons and more traditional Republicans and moderates. The AEI of the 1980s was not by any means the monolithically conservative institution often portrayed by the press and outside observers; it was in fact a hotbed of intellectual ferment with its scholars representing a vast range of ideas and ideological pluralism across the political spectrum. It was into this hotbed of intellectual ferment and policy dispute that I stepped in early 1981.

NOTES

1. The U.S. has one person designated as ambassador to the UN. But the full U.S. mission to the UN has four or five persons of ambassadorial rank.

2. Actually, Carter's position on civil rights was much more mixed than is presently thought. To achieve the Georgia governorship in 1971, he had run as a racist segregationist candidate. Only later when running for the presidency, out of both moral conviction and opportunistic politics, he changed his views.

Chapter Two

"Mr. Smith Goes to Washington": An Introduction to Washington and AEI

After those initial calls from Jeane Kirkpatrick with the offers, first, to become an ambassador at the UN and then, later, to direct AEI's Latin America program, not much happened for several months. At first I attributed this to incompetence and an inability to get its act together on the part of AEI. Later on, as I learned more about how Washington worked, I came to understand it was the White House personnel process and the long time it took to process and vett new appointments in a new administration that was to blame. I could not be appointed at AEI until my predecessors there actually received their U.S. government appointments and were off the AEI payroll. This vetting process took months, not days or weeks. And since that time (1981) it has only gotten worse: slower, more bureaucratic, intrusive, endless paperwork involving one's financial, political, personal, and security background. So much so that many high-level prospective employees now routinely turn down the opportunity for public government service.

In mid-May I was in Washington on other business for the Department of Education. Along with fellow Latin America scholars Sara Castro Klaren, David Chaplin, John Martz, John Hunter, and Michael Meyer, I had been asked by the Department to evaluate the Latin American studies centers, new and old, originally established by Congress in the National Defense and Foreign Language (NDFL) Act of the 1960s, in the wake of the Cuban Revolution, to help train a new generation of young Latin American scholars. I myself had been a product of that program, being fascinated by Latin America and in 1962 winning one of the first three-year, NDFL scholarships (capped off by a Fulbright-Hays award the third year, to write my dissertation) to complete a Ph.D. in political science/Latin American studies. As expected, the institutions that were the first to be awarded NDFL centers, the universities of

Florida, Wisconsin, Texas, Columbia, Tulane, and UCLA, continued, after twenty years of Department of Education support, to have the strongest programs. By 1981, for example, the University of Texas had over *270* persons on its faculty working on Latin American affairs.

I used this opportunity to go to Washington to reconnoiter with AEI and pay a courtesy call on its current director of Latin American affairs, Pedro San Juan. He was currently waiting for his new appointment as undersecretary-general of the UN to come through; presumably I would take his place at AEI. Pedro was not a scholar and was uncomfortable with scholars and the scholarly world. Only after I got to Washington on a permanent basis did I learn that Pedro had been in charge of Latin American matters for the Reagan transition team and that he had been absolutely heartless in firing or ending the careers of those officials who had served under Carter.

Pedro provided a briefing on AEI's Latin America activities. He said AEI had no separate or institutionalized Latin America center or budget as such; in what should have registered as a red flag but did not at the time, he told me that Latin America was just one of the programs under foreign policy director Robert Pranger and that all expenditures came out of the general fund and had to be approved by Bill Baroody himself. He said there was no other staff besides himself—he was a one-man Latin America program—and that when he needed expertise he called on such scholars as Arthur Burns, the economist, and Austin Ranney, a political scientist, neither of whom had any specialized knowledge about the area. He went on to tell me that AEI's Latin America "program," what there was of one, was concentrated—because "that's where the money is"—on Argentina, Brazil, and Mexico but not on Central America which was then the most controversial issue. Moreover the program was very policy-specific, focused on business, terrorism, and U.S. investment. *All* of these comments should have turned on warning lights in my mind about what would be in store for me at AEI; but I was still naïve in the ways of Washington, mesmerized by the prospect of joining this prestigious think tank, and so eager to play a policy role that, at the time, I didn't think through the implications of what Pedro was telling me. Only later did I understand these implications and how different AEI would be as an institution from my university background.

In June I was again in Washington, this time specifically to be interviewed for the AEI position. From Jeane Kirkpatrick's earlier telephone offer of the AEI Latin America program directorship as a consolation prize, I had thought, again naïvely, that the position was mine for the taking; but in Washington nothing is ever that certain. It turned out there were other candidates being interviewed. I don't know how many other candidates there were but I know there was at least one because I was told that by the search committee.

The search committee consisted of Profs. Howard Penniman, Austin Ranney, and Evron Kirkpatrick, Jeane's husband. Since all of them were political scientists and reasonable, sensible (not ideological or Reaganite) men, I was quite confident about getting the position. In fact I was offered the job during the interview itself. The committee also informed me that the other main candidate was "more junior" and "more ideological." Since all members of the search committee were very close to Jeane, I assume the offer to me was approved by her beforehand. Later I came to understand that Jeane actually preferred the other candidate's writing style and ideological position more than mine but deferred to the search committee on the grounds that I was balanced, level-headed, and a better administrator.

With the job offer now in hand, I was ushered in the next day to see Bill Baroody, AEI's president. He was extremely friendly and cordial and warmly welcomed me to the Institute. I had three issues that I wanted to raise. The first was freedom of expression. I knew AEI to be a conservative think tank but I considered myself a serious scholar who needed to write and say what I thought regardless of ideology or politics. Bill assured me that there was absolute freedom of expression at AEI and that he himself was committed to his father's motto of "the competition of ideas in a free society." Bill went on to say that not only was I free to pursue my own policy and research agenda but that AEI would never tell me what I had to research let alone what conclusions I had to reach. It may be surprising to outsiders to hear this given AEI's posture as a right-of-center think tank (and it is even surprising to me in retrospect), but never once in my eight-year career at the Institute did it ever violate these principles: I was never ever told what I had to research and never ever told what conclusions I needed to reach. Since this is the real world, I must admit that there were some tense moments (to be recounted below) at AEI over policy issues and specifically my writings on them, but there was never any question that I had complete freedom of speech.

The second issue was tenure. There is no tenure or permanence of appointment in the Washington think tanks: issues often come and go quickly, policy-making is often fickle, what is hot one day is cold the next, and the think tanks, unlike universities, need to be able to adjust their policy focus and personnel accordingly. At AEI, whenever anyone raised the tenure issue as I did, he was brought down the hall and introduced to Gottfried Haberler. Gottfried, who had been at the Paris peace talks with John Meynard Keynes in 1918, was already in his late 80s and pushing 90, but still mentally sharp as a tack. He was offered (only half kiddingly) as proof that you could stay at AEI until you were 110 and never have to worry about tenure. Nevertheless I remained sufficiently concerned that rather than resigning my tenured full professorship at U-Mass, I would take a leave of absence instead, enabling me to return if the going got rough at AEI. It was one of the smartest decisions I've ever made.

The third issue was salary and what would go with my position. This was negotiated directly with Baroody. He asked me what my university salary was, and then raised it by 20 percent. He then added another 20 percent to make it an eleven-month contract instead of my nine-month academic contract. He told me that, unlike other think tanks, there were no restrictions at AEI on my earning additional outside income from consulting, writing, and speaking; at the time I didn't realize how lucrative (I doubled my salary the first year) this would become.

AEI also agreed to give me my own secretary, a full-time research assistant, and a second person at the scholar level. My own title was Senior Scholar and Director of AEI's Hemispheric (to include Canada) Studies Program. Fringe benefits included full health care coverage, life insurance, a parking slot under the building, and a contribution of 15 percent of my salary by AEI to a TIAA-CREF retirement fund, without anything being deducted from my own salary. That's the most generous retirement plan I'd ever seen with *full costs* at 15 percent of salary borne by the employer. In addition, I was permitted to keep the full amount (without that being subtracted from my salary) of a Rockefeller grant that I had at the time, to double-dip during July and August when I would have both my U-Mass salary and a special AEI consulting fee as I transitioned into my new position, and to take at least one day per week to travel to Amherst or Harvard—my other positions. I would have unlimited telephone, copying, and travel funds, but it was understood these should not be abused. So long as they were for "business purposes" (everything in Washington is "business," I soon found out), all meals for me and any of my guests in the elegant AEI dining room were *gratis.*

What a package! I'd not known such munificence before. In addition to the exceedingly generous salary, health care, retirement, staff support, meals, services, travel etc., being at AEI soon enabled me to not just double but soon quadruple my income through private consulting, writing, and lecturing. It seems almost a contradiction in terms but over the course of the next few years I became a wealthy academic—"rich as well as famous," as my friends teased! Or, as Washington puts it, I learned how to do well (for myself) by doing good (for AEI and, I hoped, the country).

THE APARTMENT

In July 1981 I was once more in Washington, this time to look for an apartment. Our daughter Kristy was about to enter her senior year in high school.

Iêda and I had a long talk about this: we were in agreement that life for teenagers was difficult enough—grades, looks, friends, cliques, pressures—by now without their parents' activities adding new disruptions to the burden. And Kristy was a great daughter—pretty, athletic, good grades, nice friends, a wonderful person; we wanted to keep her that way. So we decided that the first year, I would go to Washington alone, the family would stay in Amherst so Kristy could finish high school with her class, and I would commute back and forth. This would not be the last time Iêda and I would have a commuter marriage—not easy but still manageable.

The first efforts to find a place to live were discouraging. I wanted to be within walking distance of AEI so I could get to work quickly while also enjoying the urban environment. That meant the Dupont Circle area. The first half-dozen units I looked at were awful: small, roachy, unsafe, expensive, dark, and depressing. I began to have second thoughts: why should I leave my nice, big, beautiful Amherst house with its stream and seven acres for a tiny, depressing efficiency in D.C.? But then around Scott Circle (Massachusetts Avenue and 16th Street, NW) I began to have better luck. I found several places that were acceptable and opted for an apartment at 1500 Massachusetts Avenue, today a bit dreary and in need of renovation but then (twenty-five years ago) quite passable.

It was an efficiency apartment but larger than most. The main room was about 20' x 18'; it quadrupled as my living room, dining area, office, and, with a big foldout couch, bedroom. A quite large kitchenette was at the far end. Behind that was a full and spacious bathroom. A unique feature was a separate storage room, 8' x 10', behind the bath that could have been used as a separate bedroom but which I used to keep my bike, books, and files. The big front window of my apartment looked across 16th Street, at the then headquarters of the National Rifle Association, more recently converted into a luxury hotel. There was a branch of Riggs Bank right around the corner on Fifteenth Street, a CVS only a block and a half away on Fourteenth Street, a Safeway grocery store (we called it the "Social Safeway" since you often saw friends there in the evening) four blocks up 17th, and Dupont Circle's cafes and bookstores only three blocks away. AEI was only two and a half blocks away. The apartment had good curtains but the bright lights from 16th Street shone through anyway making the room quite light even in the middle of the night, and the sirens of the ambulances racing up 16th Street and under Scott Circle rang out in the middle of the night. After living at this address for a year, I found that I could sleep through any combination of light and noise.

I was new to urban living as well as to Washington so this first year was quite an adventure. That neighborhood was a mixed one; I soon learned that Washington neighborhoods and whether they were livable and safe or not varied literally block by block. If I went up Mass. Ave. toward Dupont Circle, it was almost all white and largely safe; if I went down Mass Ave. it turned uncertain very quickly. For exercise, for example, I would run up Mass. Ave at night literally running on the white line in the middle of the road because friends had told me that was safer despite the threat from traffic than running on the sidewalks where you might be held up by robbers. In those years nearby 14th Street and Logan Circle was the strip where the high-heeled, hot-pantsed prostitutes plied their trade; on Sunday mornings when I went to get my *Washington Post* at the CVS I would see them and their pimps in the aisles. Not my cup of tea and I soon stopped going there.

I had our little Volkswagen Squareback along in Washington but the apartment did not have a parking space to go with it. I parked it in the AEI garage (one of the perks!) during the day but had to find a place at night near the apartment. There were plenty of places just north of Mass. Ave. on N or P Streets; but this was a high crime area, not well lit, and often, after a reception, dinner, or evening seminar, I came home late and had to scramble for a spot. As compared with peaceful, bucolic Amherst, in Washington that first year, I quickly learned street smarts, to be acutely aware of my surroundings, and to learn my neighborhood literally block by block.

Since I was in Washington and already on the payroll, I thought I ought to go over to AEI as well. In July (August is even worse) the weather is hot, social and political life slows to a crawl, and few people stick around. Among the scholars only Austin Ranney was there. Austin was one of the country's leading political scientists; up to this point I had known him only through his writings and from a distance when he was president of the political science association. At AEI I found him to be the friendliest (even more than Jeane Kirkpatrick who'd recruited me), most welcoming, and most balanced and level-headed of the scholars. When I needed advice about the internal politics of AEI or the ways of Washington, I went to Austin, whom I thought of as a centrist and serious scholar like me, not an ideologue. Austin was not only open and available but consistently gave me good and sound career advice.

I could not say this about Bill Baroody's chief assistant, Elizabeth Prestridge. Bill was traveling that day, so I had to meet with Liz about office space and the logistics of moving in. She was a severe-looking woman, who wore no makeup (unusual in Washington once you pass the internship stage), always wore the same shiny blue suit, never did up her hair, and talked and acted in aggressive ways. Liz tried to operate in a tough, macho way and was not very helpful because it seems like she had to always "prove" herself and her toughness in any discussion on any issue. I tried to avoid her as much as possible; unfortunately that was not possible because Baroody trusted her with everything and she operated from the position of power of his office.

Toward the end of August we made the big move. I rented a U-Haul and son Howard, then thirteen, helped me load it up and drove down to Washington with me. The load included our large fold-out couch, breakfast table and chairs, recliner chair, end and coffee tables, desk and chairs, several lamps, a couple bookcases, my bike, several boxes of books, a box of dishes, pans, and utensils prepared by Iêda. Plus some frozen dinners also prepared by her to tide us over. That one 5'x 7' U-Haul load, carefully packed, was enough to furnish fully the entire apartment. Since several of the turnpikes between Amherst and Washington do not allow trailers, we had to take the long way around—two extra hours and one hundred extra miles.

Arriving in Washington at 5:00 p.m., it took us two hours to unload the trailer and carry the load up in the freight elevator. How was heroic, carrying all those heavy loads like an adult and holding up his end of that big, steel-lined couch. He then spent three more hours unpacking, helping me put the disassembled furniture back together, and putting up the books and dishes. Poor guy, he was so exhausted by 10:00 p.m. that he developed a splitting headache that carried over into the next day. Then, without complaining and because I felt as a new employee that I ought to spend those days working at AEI, he spent the next three days alone exploring Washington's museums. What a great young man; that was the trouble with this arrangement: we are a very close family, and the hardest part of that commuting year, my journal written at the time makes clear, would be the long, lonely nights away from Iêda, our three children, and our home in Amherst.[1]

FIRST IMPRESSIONS

After three days at AEI, Howard and I decamped for New York and the Annual Meeting of the American Political Science Association, always held on the Labor Day weekend and marking the end of the summer. Meanwhile Iêda came down from Amherst with our other two children and we all met up at the New York Hilton Hotel in central Manhattan. I took the kids and visited the Empire State Building, the New York Stock Exchange, the United Nations, Rockefeller Center, and Central Park. The deteriorated conditions in 1981 in New York (dirty, graffiti everywhere, illegal immigrants, drugs, high crime, run-down buildings) were a shock; even more shocking was what I heard from a Hilton security official with whom I struck up a conversation: that in one day there had been fourteen robberies, not in the streets outside but *inside* the hotel. Fourteen! I was beginning to feel fortunate that my position on Jeane Kirkpatrick's New York-based staff had not worked out.

On Friday evening AEI held its reception at the APSA. All my political science colleagues who also had a connection at AEI were there: Howard Penniman, Jack Peltason, Austin Ranney, Giovani Sartori, Richard Neustadt, Lucian Pye, Warren Miller, Nelson Polsby, and others prominent in the profession. I took an instant dislike to Polsby, who was then editor of the *American Political Science Review* and much more senior than I. I was then editor of *Polity*, the journal of the New England Political Science Association. In an initial editorial in *Polity* I had taken a swipe at the *APSR* for its bad writing, poor style, and efforts in its published articles artificially to imitate the natural sciences, promising that *Polity* would have good writing, a distinctive style, and interesting, readable articles. Now Polsby angrily shot back, seeking to embarrass me in front of the group by pointing out a grammatical error in the inaugural issue of *Polity* I had supervised even while promising good writing. Polsby immediately went up on my radar screen as a person I would shoot down whenever the opportunity presented. Already with this strategy of "Don't get mad, get even," I was becoming a Washington person.

We then adjourned to Jeane Kirkpatrick's apartment in the Waldorf Towers, the official residence of the U.S. UN Ambassador, for a private reception and get-together. This was big-time stuff but both Iêda and I were stunned by how shabby the residence was. Not only was the carpeting frayed and the paint peeling but, with my carpenter's eye, I noticed that the crown moldings didn't match correctly, there was water damage, and the woodwork and some of the furniture were starting to pull apart. It was fun to meet with Jeane at this high level and her chief UN staff: Chuck Lichtenstein, Alan Gerson, Carl Gershman, and José Sorzano. Later Jeane confided in me that she *hated* living in that Waldorf apartment and tried to spend as much time as possibly in her "real house" outside Washington.

We spent the rest of the Labor Day weekend at our house in Amherst. It was nice to get back to everyday, real, "normal" (as compared to Washington and its all-consuming political preoccupations) activities: mowing the lawn, playing with the kids, doing small chores around the house. But duty called: on the day after Labor Day I left very early for the trip back to Washington and now for the real work of my new job at AEI.

I hit the ground running in my first weeks at AEI *and* kept on running, which it turned out endeared me to Bill Baroody and his top staff. Our program immediately established a reputation as among the most active, energetic, and dynamic at AEI, all good traits if you're a Calvinist but not so good from the point of view of some of the less-productive scholars and their less-active programs. I was friendly and tried to be helpful to everyone, but among the scholars the foreign policy director Robert Pranger was immediately the most resentful and hostile. My program was doing far more in terms of projects, publications, and fund-raising than his, and he resented it.

I soon met all the luminaries at AEI:

- Mike Novak was the most friendly and welcoming; he saw me as an ally in his struggle to establish cultural and socio-religious studies at AEI.
- Arthur Burns had just been named ambassador to Germany; when I met him, he nodded without removing the habitual pipe from his mouth and blew smoke my way.
- Herb Stein, once head of Nixon's Council of Economic Advisers, had a reputation as a droll wit, which he was in public; but I don't recall his ever saying a pleasant word to me in all my years at AEI.
- Walter Berns had a rapier-sharp mind but I don't think he had ever gotten over being on the losing side in the great Cornell student revolt of 1969-70.
- Bob Goldwin had a Ph.D. from the University of Chicago and had been President Ford's "intellectual-in-residence"; I don't think he ever understood what a guy with a degree from the University of Florida (me) was doing there.
- Bob Pranger, AEI's foreign policy director, was constantly a pain in the neck; I made him angrier by always going around him directly to Baroody.
- Judith Kipper constantly angered the neocons at AEI by being evenhanded on the Middle East; some said she favored the Arab cause.
- Howard Penniman, a wonderful person and one of my staunchest supporters in the internal policy disputes at AEI; he really believed we could bring democracy to El Salvador. Since this was my field, I tried, futilely, to set him straight; but he proved to be correct: El Salvador, even under a flawed democracy, is better than El Salvador in civil war or under a repressive military.
- Evron Kirkpatrick, husband of Jeane, a gem of a friend, and, like Penniman, one of my strongest supporters; unfortunately he was already with serious health problems.
- Jeane Kirkpatrick—very complex relations. I liked Jeane a lot, she had a very sharp mind, and, after all, she had brought me to Washington. But I disagreed with many of her policy positions, and she almost certainly sensed that. My program at AEI helped her with some policy issues but while she was at the UN I had, surprisingly, very little contact with her. And when we saw each other socially, which was quite often, we talked personalities more than issues. I was and remained closer to her husband, "Kirk," than to Jeane; he was more of an operator, she more ideological. Finally, when AEI later on got in trouble financially, Jeane did little to save my position there.

One of my first tasks at AEI was to hire a secretary. Gabrielle Hills was AEI's director of personnel and arranged the interviews. She found four candidates: a Cuban, a Puerto Rican, an activist, and good typist. I certainly didn't want an *activista* with her own agenda as a secretary, and the Cuban and Puerto Rican both had attitude problems. So I chose Pam Calvert: loyal, faithful, a good typist, and a nice person. As my research assistant I kept on Janine Perfit who had a Masters in Latin American studies from Georgetown and had been Pedro San Juan's RA; she knew the internal workings of AEI and Washington better than I at that stage and was tremendously helpful to me all through my tenure at AEI.

The next step was to choose an associate director for my program. I had in mind former graduate students like Joe Cayer, Al Pinelo, Mike Kryzanek, or Rick Nuccio, whom I knew would be absolutely loyal and whom I could groom in the job; but Kirk suggested Mark Falcoff from the Hoover Institution. It turned out Mark had been a candidate for my position as director; Kirk and the committee had chosen me but they also liked Mark for his sharp wit and writing style. I thought at that stage, not knowing all the givens, I had better go along with Kirk and so offered the job to Mark.

He and I had an uneasy relationship. Mark was a neocon, an excellent writer, a serious scholar, and a razor-sharp mind; but he was an administrative incompetent, lacked political sense, and often did or said things that were quite irresponsible and damaging to our program. You can imagine the further dilemmas: he was closer ideologically to Jeane while I was closer to the more pragmatic Kirk. On the other hand, since I was a centrist and Mark a neocon, he gave me needed protection from sniping on my right flank, enabling me to point to Mark if anyone raised questions about me (they did!) as a *real* conservative even if I was not. Our relations were sometimes tense and testy but we both saw mutual advantage in collaboration: I introduced Mark to the centrist, pragmatic Mel Laird-Jerry Ford-George H. W. Bush wing of the Republican Party while he introduced me to the Irving Kristol-Norman Podhoretz-Les Lenkowski neocon wing.

WASHINGTON LIFE

I quickly plunged into the Washington social life; actually, it would be more accurate to say that it discovered me. Here was one of my first lessons (actually several) in how Washington works.

First of all, much of Washington policy-making takes place at the social level. Most textbooks, usually written by outsiders, tend to focus on the formal institutions of government, and those *are* important. But at least equally important are informal lunches and dinners, sharing a drink with friends and colleagues at the end of the day, attending interest group and embassy receptions, schmoozing, going to the endless forums and seminars that the think tanks put on, attending Redskins' football or Nationals' baseball games, the rare opportunity to go up to Camp David with the president, weekend getaways to the Chesapeake or Eastern Shore. In these informal settings, more of the nation's business gets done than in the formal institutions of government.

In this intensely social atmosphere, AEI had several decided advantages. Along with the Brookings Institution, AEI had a reputation of doing serious, scholarly policy work; its studies were taken seriously. Especially in the new Reagan Administration, everyone knew that AEI was a major player.

But in political Washington it was actually more involved than that. Many people assumed that, as a B-grade movie actor, neither Ronald Reagan nor his administration had any policy ideas of their own. They drew the conclusion, therefore, that it must be AEI that was the source of all the Administration's policy initiatives, even that AEI was "running the government." On Latin America generally, Central America specifically (*the* hot region at the time), and other foreign policy issues, that meant I must be the chief person primarily responsible. The result was that on El Salvador, Guatemala, Nicaragua, Grenada, the Falklands crisis, Panama, anything to do with Latin America, Spain, Portugal, and other hot spots besides, I became the person to see. People beat a path to my doorstep.

All this was flattering but what people believed was not entirely accurate. We were *not* running the government. On the other hand, we *did* sometimes call up the White House, the NSC, or the State Department to recommend such and such party, candidate, or policy. And *sometimes* we were listened to. People had the image of us talking to Ronnie, Nancy (the real power behind the throne), aides Mike Deaver and Ed Meese, or Secretary of State Al Haig on an almost daily basis; but that would be a considerable exaggeration. We did occasionally see socially and talk with these advisers maybe once every couple months but not anywhere as often as the people who courted us thought. On the other hand, since this reputation of talking directly to the president or high administration officials enhanced our own prestige and power, we never said or did anything to disabuse people of the notion that we had more influence than we did.

Also working in my favor was the belief that I was close to Jeane Kirkpatrick. And Jeane was widely believed, correctly, to be influential with Reagan, not just on UN issues but on foreign policy matters generally. Reagan liked Jeane; as the leading intellectual in the Administration, she was able to formulate and articulate the issues and the U.S. policy response better than anyone else. She had Reagan's ear and, it was assumed, I had her ear. Actually, as explained above, I was less close to Jeane than many thought, but again we did nothing to disabuse outsiders of the idea that we had immediate access.

The first person to figure this all out was Ana Colomar O'Brien. Ana was a lobbyist for the powerful, Miami-based Cuban-American National Foundation (CANF), before it established a full-time Washington office. Ana was Cuban-American, loathed Fidel Castro, and was ultra-conservative, far more than I. I believe it was still my first week in Washington that she invited me out to lunch, then dinner, then to her home, more lunches, etc. Since I was the "new boy on the block," the new director of AEI's Latin American program, she and CANF had an interest in knowing which way the Administration's political winds were blowing. She was one of those who shared the view that AEI had a direct pipeline to the White House and therefore they should get to know me better. She was the first of a long line of interest group lobbyists who wined and dined me for insight and access to White House policy-making. I must say it's fun to be wined, dined, and flattered in this way.

But it was not just interest group lobbyists who saw AEI as a channel to power or a means to assess new winds blowing through the Reagan Administration. Foreign embassies, other think tanks, Congress, the media, old friends and colleagues, American diplomatic personnel, and even Latin American presidential candidates all recognized the usefulness, if they wished to have access or to get their views across, of establishing good relations with AEI and specifically my office. This was an extraordinary era in U.S.-Latin American relations when Latin American presidential candidates, if they wished to be successful, needed to be "vetted" politically in Washington before launching their campaigns back in their home countries. As a result, such candidates as Carlos Menem, Salvador Jorge Blanco, Nicolas Barleta, José Napoleon Duarte, Hugo Banzer, and others all came through my office (as well as at the State Department and other agencies) seeking approval *before* going back to their home countries as candidates. All this wining, dining, luncheons, receptions, and dinners were wonderful for me in building political connections, even if a little hard on the belt line, cholesterol, and blood pressure.

Being wined and dined by outside groups was one side of the story; at least equally important was the internal facility, the elegant AEI dining room. It was not particularly fancy, just an interior room with little decoration; but the setting was pleasant, the service superb, the food excellent (a combination of French cuisine and Southern fried) and you could eat all you wanted, and the wine kept flowing. Most important, the AEI dining room like the institution itself was thought to be a place of power and influence. Jeane ate there when she was in town; the AEI economists (often accompanied by members of the Council of Economic Advisers) had their own table; cabinet secretaries came and went; and members of the Securities and Exchange Commission, the Congressional Budget Office, or the Federal Reserve were regular diners. At the AEI dining room to impress your own guest, you could always point to some luminary only a table away and say hello in passing as a measure of your own importance. Plus it was all free, the best free lunch in Washington.

I quickly learned the ropes of the system. My learning curve was accelerated by the fact that my family was still back in Amherst and therefore lunch at AEI became my main meal of the day. For the senior staff, lunch in the AEI dining room was gratis as long as it was for "business purposes." But my "business" *is* politics and in Washington, since politics is virtually the only business, almost everything I did was therefore business related. Hence whenever I had an appointment, was interviewed by a journalist, had business to conduct, or had a political friend or acquaintance over, we would head to the nice AEI dining room where I would sign in and write off the lunch as being for "business purposes."

Two or three times a week I would arrange to meet or invite over for lunch friends and colleagues from Washington policy circles. I started with the people I knew who were working on Latin America: Abe Lowenthal at the Woodrow Wilson Center, Riordan Roett from the School of Advanced International Studies (SAIS), Bill Perry from the Senate Foreign Relations Committee, Constantine Menges from the White House, Georges Fauriol from the Center for Strategic and International Studies (CSIS), Harvey Summ from Georgetown University, Larman Wilson from American University, G. Pope Atkins from the U.S. Naval Academy, Roger Fontaine from the NSC, Scott Palmer of the Foreign Service Institute, Larry Birns of the Council on Hemisphere Affairs (COHA), Bill LeoGrande of American University, Joe Eldridge of the Washington Office on Latin American (WOLA), Margaret Daly Hayes of the Senate staff. All these were friends and colleagues so I could (mostly) unwind and relax with them—even though in political Washington ambition and therefore backstabbing are so intense that you have to watch yourself even when with friends.

But with that AEI dining room and AEI itself as my lure, pretty soon I graduated to higher-level guests. These included assistant secretary of state Tom Enders, assistant secretary Elliott Abrams, NSC adviser Richard Allen, General Vernon Walters, Federal Reserve Chairman Paul Volcker, Secretary of State Al Haig, publisher Frederick Praeger, Amway Corporation President Jay Van Andel, Brazil-Invest CEO Mario Garneiro, Organization of American States Secretary General Alejandro Orfila, various ambassadors, and other high muckdymucks. We even heard of an obscure lieutenant colonel doing big things on

Central America in the White House basement, and so we also invited Ollie North over for lunch. Our first estimates of him written in my journal notes were right on target: in way over his head, doing questionable activities.

And so, in those first few weeks, that is how I got acclimated to Washington: living right downtown, adjusting to an urban environment, scrambling to find my way outside of my familiar academia and in a highly charged political atmosphere. In these endeavors, Kirk Kirkpatrick, Austin Ranney, and Howard Penniman provided good advice and mentoring; Jeane was always more distant.

I had come to Washington as a forty year old, after fifteen years in academia. By then I had published a lot, including two widely read textbooks, and my background at Harvard and MIT (though brief) stood me in good stead whenever I was introduced. Almost every time I went to a reception, cocktail party, or policy forum, some young intern or foreign service officer would come up to me and say, "Oh Professor Wiarda, I'm from such'n'such university and we used your textbook in my course; I'm so happy to meet you." It still amazes me how much access I gained from these encounters; when you write a textbook, you don't think that will also give you entrée at numerous offices in Washington.

There's no doubt AEI and that elegant dining room also played a big role. Because of my institutional position at AEI (remember, in Washington you're important not for who you are but for the position you hold), I was invited out a lot by lobbyists, interest groups, journalists, and others who wanted insight (and assumed I had it) on Reagan Administration policy. During that first year, my recollection is that I cooked only once in my little efficiency apartment. But I also invited large numbers of people to AEI and its dining room as a way of expanding my circle of friends and contacts. Pretty soon I knew on a first-name basis—certainly on Latin America policy but on other policy arenas as well—most of the movers and shakers in Washington.

At the end of my first month in Washington I jotted down some initial impressions:

- people are very nice, polite; even if they disagree, they seldom say so to your face.
- *lots* of activity, action, *movimiento*; I'm busy every minute.
- *everything* is very political and politicized; *everything* is done from political calculation.
- social life is nonstop: lunches, seminars, receptions, dinners, now even breakfast; hard on the liver, beltline, cholesterol.
- very exciting; I'm one of the actors; people actually *read* my writings (unlike in academia where a dean merely weighs your work on a scale) and *listen* to what I have to say.

- the job is going well; Bill Baroody tells me he likes that I "hit the ground running."
- first payday from AEI: more than I've ever made before. Plus lecturing, writing invitations.
- but very lonely. I miss my family. No fun to live alone. That's one reason I fill every minute with activities: to fight the loneliness.
- my generation has now come to power: Abrams, Fontaine, Roett, Lowenthal, Perry, Menges. For the first time I start to think I might want to go into government, instead of just writing about it.

NOTE

1. Our house in Amherst was a beautiful, new, five bedroom (plus library), extended cape with views and acreage that we had designed and built ourselves with the help of a contractor. In 1979-80 I had added a large, three-story barn, built with lumber from our own Berkshire land timber holdings, that I intended to convert into a combined horse stable (lower level), apartment (first floor), and large home office (second floor). The invitation to AEI put an end to these future construction plans, even though the big, empty barn, which was built to look like and be converted to a residence, is still there. However, even this brief description indicates why it would be so hard to leave our Amherst house.

Chapter Three

Into the Swim: A Jaundiced View of the Main Washington Foreign Policy Institutions

One of the nice things that being in Washington and at AEI did for its senior scholars is that it got us into a lot of forums and institutions that as university academics we would not likely otherwise have experienced. Within the first few months of my being at AEI and throughout my years there, I was a regular and frequent visitor at the White House, Congress, State Department, CIA, Department of Defense, and National Security Council. To say nothing of the Brookings Institution, Wilson Center, Carnegie Endowment, Council on Foreign Relations, and other think tanks and policy institutions. We were present in all these agencies not just as tourists or visitors but also as invited speakers, special guests, or conference participants. As such, we got to see and experience quite a bit more than most tourists or one-time visitors do.

This is not to say that I presume to be an expert on the inner workings of State, Defense, or the other agencies. But when you're inside them on a regular basis, as a trained observer you look around to observe and assess the situation, the physical environment, your fellow guests, and your hosts. In my case I often have extensive notes of the programs to which I was invited. Most of these were off-the-record, which means you cannot quote people directly or attribute specific remarks to an individual person. But no one has ever prevented me from taking notes or, in the case of CIA or top-secret DOD meetings, writing up extensive private notes immediately afterwards. And under the off-the-record rules, you are allowed to convey the general sense of the meeting and of the discussion. What follows in this chapter are my impressions of the State and Defense departments, the CIA, the NSC, and the World Bank and Inter-American Development Bank. The Washington think tanks are analyzed in chapter 4; Congress and the White House require separate treatment, and are covered in chapter 10.

STATE DEPARTMENT

The State Department is almost like home territory for me. I've been there many times, I know the institution well, and I feel at home (mostly) with State Department personnel. Among the major Washington foreign policy agencies (State, Defense, CIA), State is the one with which I feel most comfortable.

I started off as a one-time consultant to the State Department in the 1960s when my doctoral dissertation on the Dominican Republic, a country we had just invaded and militarily occupied, was in great demand. In the mid-1970s I was a several-times consultant to the Department on the Portuguese Revolution and its repercussions on Portuguese Africa—Angola, Mozambique, and Guinea-Bissau. During this same time period I won an appointment to the State Department's Scholar-Diplomat Program that brought academic scholars like me to Washington to exchange views with foreign service officers (FSOs), and in 1977 I was the leadoff speaker (on Jimmy Carter's human rights policy) in a new program designed to have outside foreign policy scholars address senior diplomats on issues of major significance.

These experiences whetted my appetite to play a greater foreign policy role and led me to consider (but seldom very seriously) the possibility of going into the Department on a permanent basis. Whenever I had those itchings, however, I quickly thought of the privileged position I already had: a tenured professorship, a light teaching load, lots of free time for research and writing, and the opportunity to influence policy from the outside through my writings, rather than on the inside where one would have to contend with the Department's stultifying bureaucracy, clearance system, and discouraging internal political culture.

It was not until the 1980s and after I'd joined AEI that I started to attend social functions and participate in State Department policy discussions on a regular, sometimes weekly, sometimes monthly basis. I've been all over the building: in the basement cafeteria, the first floor conference and press rooms, the various country desk and regional offices, the fourth floor assistant secretary areas, the seventh floor secretary offices, the Benjamin Franklin reception rooms. Sometimes, unescorted, I've just roamed the hallways and probably gotten into some restricted areas where I ought not to have been. I've been there for briefings, receptions, private meetings, lunches, to give lectures and seminars, to meet one-on-one with country desk officers, and to serve as a consultant. Most of these were for a brief appointment, a morning or afternoon session, an all-day or all-week conference; on one occasion I filled a long-term consultancy that brought me to the Department every day for close to a year. I'm not an "insider" or a career official, but I probably know the Department about as well as any outsider can.

The first thing to say is how badly off, financially and in terms of morale, the Department is, as compared with DOD or CIA. Whereas these other agencies have seen their budgets increase exponentially in recent decades, State's have remained largely flat or only slightly increased. Maintenance has been cut, the building is shabby, carpets are frayed, most offices are windowless; it's a depressing place, physically, to work. Once when I was interviewing a high-level State Department official who was one of the few to have a window, albeit on a grungy inner patio, a big rat scampered across the windowsill.

The poor facilities and working conditions have a corrosive effect on morale. I developed my own gauge for measuring this. Whereas at CIA or Defense Department, if they invite you to an all-day conference, they treat you to lunch; but at State you have to buy your own in the depressing cafeteria downstairs or go across the street to the old National Science Foundation building. Similarly with my "doughnut measure," which acquired a certain fame in Washington: if you consult for DOD they have coffee and doughnuts available; at the CIA you get coffee but no doughnuts (believe it or not, CIA rules, which I tested, prohibit "gifts" to consultants, which has been interpreted to include doughnuts). But at the State Department you get neither coffee nor doughnuts; you're completely on your own.

State Department FSOs are among the most highly intelligent persons in the U.S. government. FSOs are proud of the stringent requirements to join the department; for that reason and because they often come from elite families and colleges, State can be a stuffy, condescending, conceited place. But having a Ph.D. is not highly valued in the foreign service and may work against you career-wise. I have numerous friends at State who have Ph.D.s but whose careers, in part because of that, have not gone very far. That's because the State Department still values generalists over specialists, a throwback to the seat-of-the-pants diplomacy of the past. The FSO, it is argued, has to be flexible, be able to fill any slot, go from job to job and region to region, and not be tied down by any one area or language specialization.

That emphasis seems foolish to me: you want generalists of course, but in this day of incredible global complexity, you also want experts in your foreign service with real specialized knowledge of countries, areas, and languages. Part of our problems in the Middle East and elsewhere is that we have so few area experts with Arabic language skills, and we cannot have a successful diplomacy—look at Iraq—without these. My friends at State tell me this bias is (slowly) changing, and in the Bureau of Intelligence and Research (I 'n' R), there *is* real, scholarly expertise. But for the rest State seems to me old-fashioned, inadequately adopting to new demands (including for expertise and specialized knowledge), and increasingly shunted aside in foreign policy decision-making.

There are other problems with State that, based on my informal observations, are worth mentioning here. One is the problem of time-servers. In my academic fields, people tend to be enthused and energized about the subjects they study, and at State, some people are like that too. But I've discovered too many people who are just putting in their time, filling a slot, with no or little interest in the subject. For them, the State Department is merely a job; they have no particular emotional commitment to the country, area, or issue they work on. Once, when I was teaching at the Foreign Service Institute, the State Department's language and area studies instructional arm, I had one of my students who had skipped all the classes tell me that she was a professional consular officer, didn't care what country she was sent to, and therefore saw no reason to participate in area studies. I suppose at some levels such indifference and lack of involvement can be considered good and professional; but to me, if you have little interest and no enthusiasm for the job or the country you're going to, it's hard to believe you can do it well.

The other big issue is the inability of the State Department to conceptualize. Henry Kissinger, the former secretary of state and my boss on the Kissinger Commission on Central America (see chapter 8), used to complain about this all the time. Most FSOs, historically, have been liberal arts and history graduates, not social scientists. They tend to see each country as unique and all historical events as discrete. Well of course they are, but the social sciences also teach you that there are trends, general patterns, and causative relationships that can be traced and analyzed. For example we know a lot about the trajectories of developing nations, failed states, transitions to democracy, the growth of civil society, nation building, and the like. Had some knowledgeable social scientists (like me!) been in on the discussions that preceded the U.S. invasions of Afghanistan and Iraq, for instance, we would likely have been much more cautious about our ability to nation-build and construct democracy in these two fractured countries.

One other aspect of the State Department during this period commands our attention. And that is the tremendous hatred that FSOs and political appointees have for each other. Because of my AEI position, I knew or was friends with many of the Reaganite conservative ambassadors and other political appointees in the department, even while not sharing their views. The list includes James Theberge, David Jordan, Curt Winsor, Lewis Tambs, and quite a few others, to say nothing of Jeane Kirkpatrick. The professional career officers at State hated these political appointees with a passion, not only on ideological grounds but also because the *políticos* kept the professionals from getting the ambassadorships they thought they deserved. On the other hand, political appointees often despised the careerists for not sufficiently following the election returns and, in some spectacular cases, of undermining

Reagan administration policy. Surely a better balance could be found here: the political appointees need to recognize the professionalism of the career folks, and the FSOs need to acknowledge that they live in a democracy where electoral votes make a difference.

DEPARTMENT OF DEFENSE

In the bureaucratic and institutional turf battles that go on in Washington, D.C., the Defense Department has been the chief beneficiary, in power and influence, of the decline of the State Department. The Pentagon's power, naturally enough, always increases in times of war (the Cold War, now the war on terrorism), but there are other factors operating as well. The question posed here is whether DOD now has *too much* power, whether it has become a government within the government and sometimes operating independently of it, whether Eisenhower's famed warnings against the so-called "military-industrial complex" have finally come true.

Prior to my joining AEI, I had almost no experience with the U.S. military. I was too young (12) for Korea and, in 1965, too old (26) and ineligible (married, a child, and by then a university teacher) for Vietnam. As with the State Department, I did some brief consulting for the Defense Department in the 1960s on the Dominican Republic and in the 1970s on Portugal and Portuguese Africa; but my experience was limited, I do not come from a military family, and I have never served in the U.S. armed forces. My father was a veteran of and Purple Heart winner in World War I, three of my uncles fought in World War II, and my son-in-law was a Marine Corps lieutenant colonel. But that was the extent of it. By family tradition I would be sympathetic to those who served in the military; by educational background, I'm suspicious of military power.

Once I joined AEI, I was over at the Pentagon frequently and lectured at the National War College, Naval Post Graduate School, Army War College, Naval Defense College, Air War College, West Point, U.S. Naval Academy, Air Force Academy, Fort Leavenworth, and the Inter-American Defense College. These encounters helped me understand the so-called military mind and to be more sympathetic to the military institution. Then, from 1991-96, I myself taught at the National War College, an experience that enabled me to visit numerous U.S. military bases, to travel abroad under military auspices, and to teach and therefore absorb the curriculum that senior U.S. officers are taught. I now understand the military culture and institution in ways I never did before.

Let me say at the outset that I have never met in any other institution (including, or maybe I should say especially, in university or academic life) such dedicated, competent, well-trained, gung-ho, bright, disciplined, genuinely nice people as I have in the U.S. military. Especially at the officer corps level, the armed forces tend to be disproportionately Southern and Midwestern, small-town, public school-educated, Christian, Republican, and conservative. The problems are not with the people; rather, the problems are organizational and institutional.

With nearly three million persons (1.4 million in uniform, 800,000 civilians, 700,000 reserves) the Defense Department is one of the world's biggest bureaucracies. Bigness itself is a problem: things get lost, one office or unit can't coordinate with another, no mere secretary of defense, or even the full office of the secretary, can effectively run the place let alone reform it. The Pentagon's five rings and many corridors are a labyrinth of crosscutting lattices that require a bicycle, motor scooter, or Segway to get around. Almost no one understands its full complexity or all that goes on there.

The Pentagon tries to overcome these bureaucratic obstacles by being super efficient. All the parts, including personnel, are supposed to be interchangeable. But that often rules out specialized expertise and tends to reduce policy to (1) what's been done before—i.e., fighting today's battles (Iraq) with the last war's strategy, and (2) the lowest common denominator. The Pentagon has also become highly computerized, but that often rules out nuance and the ability to adapt quickly to new contingencies. For example I was once told by a Defense Department official in an unguarded moment that the Pentagon has contingency plans for invading and occupying every country on the earth. It's probably a good idea to have those plans ready to go, but in the case I know best when DOD had to use these plans, it found the data was out of date, the street plans were wrong, and the wrong airports were listed as suitable, with thick enough cement for big U.S. transport planes. In addition, because this information was computerized and the Pentagon prided itself on its super efficiency, it had troops on the ground and was in effect militarily occupying the country before the slower, more deliberative State Department had decided whether that ought to be U.S. policy.

Rivalries between the services—Army, Navy, Air Force, Marines—are intense and will apparently never be resolved. Despite all the attention recently to "jointness," each service still operates as if it were a separate branch of government. There is tremendous overlap, duplication, and waste in procuring the huge weapons systems that each branch demands. The services are seldom coordinated and do not always get along or even understand each other.

The Pentagon budget, including special supplements for Iraq, is now about $600 billion yearly. By contrast, the State Department budget is only about $30 billion, or one twentieth that of DOD. Almost everyone agrees that this huge imbalance between military and diplomacy skews our foreign policy disproportionately toward the military side. Yet the Pentagon is very good as a political and bureaucratic infighter, is careful to cultivate its position within the Congress, and who would want to go against giving "our boys" (and girls) anything less than what they want to defend the country.

I was appalled by many things I saw and experienced while working in my capacity as consultant and then employee of the Defense Department. First of all, while traveling to U.S. military bases at home and abroad, I was amazed how much they resembled plush country clubs. My recollection of U.S. military bases, from when (one of my earliest memories) my uncle was discharged from the army after World War II, was of Spartan conditions where service to country was the motivation, not plush living conditions. But these bases have multiple golf courses, indoor and outdoor swimming pools, shopping centers, bowling alleys, ritzy officers' clubs, plush housing—in short, they are like a beautiful suburb. I know we have to offer inducements to attract good people to an all-volunteer force, but this is too much; in part at least the sense of sacrifice for the good of the country has been lost.

Second, it bothers me that our regional commanders (North America, Europe, Southcom, Pacific, Central [Middle East], now Africa) have become like ruling viceroys, with vast power, large entourages, and the arrogance that goes with these other things. I have been present when some of the regional commanders swept through my corridors: accompanied by a presidential-level motorcade of cars, with phalanxes of armed bodyguards, lackeys to open doors and hold elevators (and bar others from using them), legions of staff "servants" to cater to their every wish, and a pomposity to match the extravagant displays of power. When they are/travel abroad, the power of these commanders is even more awesome, descending into small countries with an overwhelming presence, overruling local security arrangements and protocols, and of course dwarfing the influence and presence of State Department diplomats. The viceroy image, of overwhelming pomp and power, and even quite blatant colonialism, is the correct one to have.

A third aspect that impressed me, based on my teaching experience at the National War College, is how limited the knowledge base is of the senior officer corps. The military system is that all the parts must be interchangeable: one colonel or general in a post is as good as any other. But, except for lower-ranking FAO (foreign area) officers with limited influence, that leaves out any regional or issue expertise. The result is that officers usually fall back on some disguised prejudice or simplistic principles from their formative years. But that is a terrible way to make policy, whether in Latin America or now in Iraq.

One final aspect that worries me is the growing militarization of U.S. policy. With a budget (including Iraq) of $750 billion, with the Defense Department now reaching into all kinds of areas (drugs, diplomacy, border patrol, domestic intelligence, democracy-building, etc.) it had never been involved in before, the Pentagon not only dwarfs all other agencies but is also expanding its tentacles into areas for which it has little competence, which represents a danger to American liberties. World Wars I and II, the Cold War, and the war on terrorism have gradually expanded military power both in relation to other USG agencies and to civilian society, but now with those vast budgets and military reach we are in danger of the Pentagon acquiring more and more influence in American society.

THE CIA

The third major arm of American foreign policy is the Central Intelligence Agency, now, along with fifteen other intelligence agencies, reorganized under the Director of National Intelligence but still operating largely autonomously. Many Americans, based on seeing too many James Bond movies, have a skewed image of the CIA as doing nefarious things in other peoples' countries (or our own) and practicing dirty tricks at the international level. Actually, the Bond-like Operations branch of the CIA is only one of four branches; my main contacts and experience have always been with the more academic, research-oriented Analytic branch.

My first contact with the CIA goes back to 1962 when I was bored with graduate school and looking for a more policy-oriented career. I took the CIA entrance exam, passed, and was invited to Washington for an interview. In between the exam and the interview I had been awarded a three-year, well-financed NDFL (National Defense Foreign Language) fellowship to finish my Ph.D., so I'd already made up my mind to stay in grad school; but in those days my view was that it's always fun to visit Washington and so I decided to go through with the interview anyway. It was spooky: I was told to be on a certain street corner at a certain hour, I was met by a man in a James Bond-like wrap-around raincoat and pulled-down hat, and we got on an unmarked bus to Langley. At the CIA headquarters there were no pictures on the walls (for fear of "bugs" being planted) and I had to be accompanied at all times, even *into* the bathrooms. Definitely paranoid, I thought.

My first interviewer asked me if I thought of working for the Agency as a way to avoid the draft. Of course I emphatically replied "no" but must admit that the thought (I was then only twenty-two and unmarried) had crossed my mind. A group of us ate lunch in the CIA cafeteria: I, a fraternity boy, immediately noticed that almost everyone there was badly dressed by my standards and spoke with great passion and strange accents; it didn't take me long to figure out that in those days CIA personnel and its targets were mostly focused on Eastern Europe. The *coup d'grace* of my one-day visit came in the afternoon when they gave me the then-standard psychological test: do you love your mother more than your father (or was it the other way around), your sister more than your brother, etc? The test was so transparent (and I'd already decided that I wanted no part of the Agency) that, without reading them, I quickly filled in the middle answer for all the remaining questions. As I turned it in, the examiner told me no one had ever finished the test that fast. I walked out and never heard from them again—until a few years later when the CIA, like the State Department and DOD, wanted to consult with me about the Dominican Republic—or to get a copy of my dissertation. And then again in 1974, 1975, and 1976 but this time focused on the Portuguese Revolution. In both of these cases the CIA stations in-country did a bad job, overestimating the number of communists in the revolution, their influence, and their potential for taking over the country. The U.S. embassies in both these countries, I discovered, were chock full of disguised CIA agents, or had two "political sections" (one was CIA), or had people as high as the deputy chief of mission who was CIA. I was not impressed.

When I went to Washington in 1981, the hot issue was Central America. I was brought out to the Agency on several occasions to meet with officials there who wanted to tap my knowledge. At one point I was asked by these same officials if I wanted to be the National Intelligence Officer (NIO) for Latin America. That is the highest position in the CIA on Latin America. The NIO advises the director, who was then the dynamic and controversial William (Bill) Casey. Casey, like Jeane, had a direct pipeline to Reagan; plus, at that moment the State and Defense Departments were going through upheavals that made them less effective. So that meant the CIA was the most influential of the three; as NIO, in addition, I would have access to reams of classified information that I would never have a chance to see as an academic. I was tempted to accept the offer, but what swayed me against it was the belief that, once I'd worked for the CIA, I would never be able to go back to my academic life. The left-wing climate on many U.S. campuses and the anti-CIA attitude would have ruled out my returning to my professorship. So I turned it down and am not sorry about the decision.

The CIA is plagued by many of the same problems as at State and Defense. It is overly big and bureaucratic, like so many other Washington agencies that began as small and effective and over time grew to be bloated, clumsy, and ineffective. Alongside its dedicated personnel, it also has a lot of time-servers, people who are filling a slot as a country desk officer or analyst but have no real emotional or personal interest in the country or issue for which they have responsibility. My orientation has always been that you look for ways by which the interests of the countries you're interested in (the DR, Brazil, Portugal, others) can be made compatible with U.S. interests so that you produce a win-win situation in which both countries benefit. But at State, DOD, and now CIA, too often I found a much narrower, short-term conception in which *only* U.S. interests count and whatever happens in the long term and to the country affected doesn't matter. What a myopic and damaging view!

At State's I 'n' R and in the regional bureaus, at the Pentagon's various war colleges, and in the CIA's analytic division, I was surprised to find a large number of academics—often failed academics. The CIA's Analytic arm, for example, is filled not with James Bond-like adventurers but with tweedy, pipe-smoking (you can no longer smoke inside the CIA but you could then), sports jackets-and-slacks academic types. Some of these were Ph.D.s who opted immediately after graduate school for a policy role; but a surprisingly large number were people who had tried academia, failed at it, and *then* gone into public service. Most often they were poor teachers or else they couldn't write and publish, and so they didn't get tenure.

But if they were failures in academia, why should we have confidence that they would succeed in the at least equally demanding career as a policy analyst? The answer is, we should not. But the State Department, DOD, and CIA needed these people to do the serious and specialized research that everyone knew was necessary in our more complicated world. My experience in these agencies was, however, that if a person was a poor communicator as a teacher, he was also a poor communicator in the government. And if he couldn't write sufficiently well to get tenure as an academic, his writing and analytic skills were unlikely to get better by going into government service. I have come across a lot of good people in government who are dedicated, thoughtful, and good analysts; but I have also come across a lot of duds about whom you wonder how and why they got where they are.

THE NSC

The National Security Council (NSC) is one of the few places in the U.S. government where academic/think tank guys like me can hope to influence policy at the highest level.[1] It is a small agency with only about seventy-five professional staff. It is located in the White House Executive Office Building (EOB) or in the new EOB across the street on Pennsylvania Avenue and 17th Street. The NSC is the president's *personal staff* on foreign policy; if you're one of the only two or three people there who deal with Latin America, Asia, the Middle East, Europe, Africa, etc., you may have as much power and influence as the entire State Department, DOD, or CIA. The NSC is probably the highest position in the USG to which an academic type like me can aspire.

The trouble is, the NSC under Reagan was full of incompetents, from the top down, and was probably the worst functioning NSC since the agency's creation in 1947. Reagan's first NSC advisor was Richard Allen, a smart, experienced, and ultra-conservative analyst who lacked a Ph.D. but nevertheless liked it when others called him "Doctor Allen" and didn't correct them when they did. But that is anathema to real Ph.D.s like me who worked hard for their *earned* degrees and resent it when others claim the same credential. I liked Dick even while finding him arrogant and conceited; his big mistake was in being arrogant to Nancy Reagan, and he was soon dismissed after only one year in the position.

The next national security adviser was a Reagan buddy from California, Judge William Clark, who in his congressional confirmation hearing demonstrated a remarkable lack of knowledge of geography, international politics, and the countries with which he would have to deal. Judge Clark politicized the NSC even more than had Dick Allen, but at least Allen was smart. To everyone's relief, Clark went back to California after only a year and a half in the position.

Clark was succeeded by Robert ("Bud") McFarlane, October 1983–December 1985—a military colonel who had little experience in foreign policy. By this time people were fed up with a politicized and incompetent foreign policy; McFarlane was thought of as a competent officer who knew how to answer the phones, didn't talk back, and could manage an efficient office. With a military guy in charge, the NSC operated like a staff agency so that others (Jeane, Secretary of State George Shultz), presumably, would make policy. But McFarlane was the one who carried the infamous key inside the cake to Iran and embroiled the Administration in the Iran-Contra scandal, which almost resulted in Reagan's impeachment.

Disgraced, McFarlane attempted suicide and became a sad figure at Washington gatherings. He was succeeded by Admiral John Poindexter, McFarlane's deputy, who lasted less than a year. Poindexter had a Ph.D. but in physics, lacked knowledge about international affairs, and was accused of lying to Congress. Hence only when Frank Carlucci, a consummate Washington insider and former ambassador to Portugal (and former college roommate of Donald Rumsfeld), took over the NSC in 1987, and then Colin Powell assumed the post in 1987–89, did we begin to see order and coherence restored to the NSC. With the exception of Carlucci and Powell, none of Reagan's National Security Advisers could be considered impressive or heavy hitters in the tradition of Henry Kissinger and Zbigniew Brzezinski.

At the staff level the situation was just as bad as at the top, maybe worse. Recall, this is an agency that has lots of Ph.D.s and historically has had as staff some of the smartest people on foreign policy in America. Roger

Fontaine was the first NSC adviser on Latin America: Roger was a serious scholar; unfortunately he had gotten the job by eschewing his academic qualifications and turning into a conservative ideologue. In addition, in office Roger proved to be not very articulate as a spokesman (part of the job) for administration policy, substituting one-word responses for clear and convincing explanations.

Constantine Menges, Roger's successor beginning in 1983, was perhaps the most difficult: a very intelligent man, well-educated, with a Ph.D., and articulate, but so right-wing as to make people wonder. Constantine (known around Washington as "Constant Menace") treated me well, invited me to lunch at the White House Mess, and respected my scholarship. But he was such an ideologue that it drove moderates like me, to say nothing of the Democrats in Congress, to frustration. Constantine saw "communist plots" under every innocent event; even fifteen years after the Cold War ended Constantine was still crying, "the commies are coming, the commies are coming."

Given what we said before about the historic high prestige of the NSC and the opportunities for academics there, I have to confess that the thought crossed my mind that maybe I should serve on the staff. I certainly could do better, at least in my own mind, than the dummies and incompetents that I'd seen appointed. But I was happy with my AEI position and—probably a mistake—I never approached Jeane with the idea of serving. Nor did she ask me. In retrospect, I think that was perhaps my best opportunity to serve in government at the highest level and might have led to even higher things. However I never pursued it seriously, and the opportunity slipped by. Meanwhile I was already beginning to plan on returning to my regular academic position.

A key turning point for me was when Jeane arranged to have her assistant, Jackie Tillman, appointed to the NSC as Constantine's assistant. Jackie was even more of a conservative ideologue than was Constantine, but at least "Constant Menace" was knowledgeable and articulate. I'm not sure if Jackie even had a college education; before coming to Washington she had directed a day-care center in Hartford. I have sat in on White House meetings when Jackie was doing the briefing: she was not very articulate, got her facts wrong, and was so far right it even drove the Reaganites crazy. For me, Jackie's appointment to the NSC was the last straw: if this was what working at the NSC was like, I wanted no part of it. Shortly thereafter, we did go back to Amherst for a two-year stint, and then with Clark, McFarlane, and Poindexter heading it, whatever desire I might have had to serve on the NSC was lost.

I don't think we ever had such an incompetent NSC as we did under Reagan. From top to bottom the agency was full of incompetents, ideologues, and know-nothings. What a shame, because this agency in the past was one of the bright spots of Washington policy-making: heavy hitters at the top and extremely well-trained people at staff levels. I'm sorry that for me it couldn't work out.

THE ECONOMIC AGENCIES

My first, quasi-permanent experiences in Washington were in the 1980s when the Cold War was still raging. I was at AEI from 1981–1988, which covered virtually the entire two terms of Ronald Reagan and was just before the tearing down of the Berlin Wall, the liberation of Eastern Europe, and the collapse of the Soviet Union in the 1989–1991 time period. So it is not surprising that as a foreign policy analyst most of my contacts and consultations were in the main foreign policy agencies described above: State, DOD, and CIA.

Looking back on my Washington experiences, I don't think I ever once visited or was invited to the main economic departments or agencies: Treasury, Commerce, the Office of the Trade Representative. This is a curious omission in many ways. For one thing, Treasury and Commerce, among others, had already created international divisions which were growing rapidly as the U.S. economy was becoming more international; I was already in the 1980s telling my students and interns they should apply for jobs there because they would have a better chance for a good career and promotions than in the more staid and stagnant State Department. For another, we all understood even in that earlier period the growing impact of international trade, foreign investment, and international capital on foreign affairs.

But it really took until the end of the Cold War, and the Clinton Administration, 1992–2000, for economic issues to rise to the top of the foreign policy agenda. The Cold War's end meant we could concentrate on trade, money, investment, and commerce, as compared with the diplomatic and strategic issues of the past, for the first time in a long time. In addition, rising globalization meant that all economies were becoming interdependent—"globalized"—really for the first time. It was during the Clinton presidency that the main economic agencies—Treasury, Commerce, OTR—began to supplant the State Department as our main foreign policy agencies. And when State itself began to concentrate more on economic and commercial issues.

But there was another force operating back in the 1980s that kept foreign policy analysts like me away from economic issues. And that involved a certain division of labor. On the one hand, political scientists like me felt a certain reluctance to get involved in disputes over economic policy, which was not our forte. On the other, my economist friends at AEI and in the government's economic agencies made it clear that they didn't want political scientists meddling in their turf. A good example of this was the "great" Third

World debt crisis of the 1980s. The issue was always approached as an economic issue, and AEI's economists took steps to make sure it stayed that way. But once a country is at the point where it cannot pay and is considering default, then it becomes a political issue: who *will* pay (guess!) if not the debtor nation? Yet not once did I or other AEI political scientists get called to the Treasury Dept. to advise on Third World debt issues.

While my contacts with these public economic departments were almost nil, I did have some contacts with the big international development banks. But even these were often strange, awkward, and even downright embarrassing. At the Export-Import Bank, for example, I met with a group of economists, arranged by my AEI colleague Marvin Kosters. In our discussion, I indicated that the Bank would have to adjust its strategies to fit the distinct statist-corporatist-mercantilist economies of Latin America and other developing countries. The bankers were astounded that I would think they should take cultural, social, and political factors into account when making loans and fashioning development projects. For them, the economic models they used were timeless and universal, applicable in all times and places. I thought their position was naïve and downright stupid. *Of course* you cannot defy the laws of economics, but equally obvious, you must adjust these "laws" to the countries or culture areas in which you're working. By now at least two Nobel winners in economics, Douglass North and Robert W. Fogel, have gotten the prize for making this point.

My next experience with international bankers was at the Inter-American Development Bank (IDB). I was hired by the IDB with a whopping honorarium to write a report on Latin America's future development. Of course when you write that kind of broad report, you have to take Latin America's social and political conditions into account. Since I was urged to do so, I also included a chapter based on my interviewing of the Bank's own officials and field officers that was quite critical of the bank itself and its operations. Both of these elicited strong objections from the Bank. They said—a ridiculous argument—I should not talk about what they called "extraneous" social and political factors in development, and they were even more worried that my chapter critical of the Bank would be used against it in upcoming budget discussions with the Congress. So we reached a compromise: the social and political material would stay in the book but the chapter critical of the Bank would be delayed until the congressional hearings were over and then published separately.

My experiences at the World Bank were even more revealing of how economists thought in those days—and maybe still do! I had been invited to the Bank to give a lecture on Third World debt issues. They apparently liked what I had to say because shortly thereafter I was invited back to the Bank for a job interview. But in the course of the interview the Bank found out that I was a political scientist (how could they not have known?), not an economist. The interview ended abruptly right there: the Bank said, "We cannot, and are prohibited by our charter, from taking political considerations into account when making our loans."

Well, first of all, that's not true; the World Bank almost always takes political considerations, even if disguised or subconscious, into account when making loans. Second, the Bank confused political science with partisanship. Of course I would not be partisan or "political" in the job but I would take such political factors as good governance or corruption or transparency into account in making loans—a point now universally recognized as valid even within the Bank. Third, just as the Bank belatedly discovered its loans had an impact on indigenous peoples and therefore hired a handful of anthropologists for its staff, so too it has of late discovered "governance" factors. Indeed those have now become dominant in World Bank loan considerations, and so the Bank has also recently hired a handful of political scientists. But twenty years ago when I was considered for a Bank position, such "political" concerns were anathema.

* * * * *

Visiting, walking the corridors of, and consulting for all these Washington agencies gave me insights into their internal practices and ways of operating that I'd never had before. It is one thing as an academic to read about and study how the State Department, Defense Department, CIA, NSC, etc. function. But it is quite another matter to be *inside* these agencies, working for them, and interacting with their personnel on a daily, weekly, or monthly basis. That gives you insider knowledge, teaches you about the political culture and standard operating procedures (SOPs) within each of these agencies, and enables you to experience first-hand the bureaucratic rivalries ("bureaucratic politics") *between* these oft-competing agencies. For all this I have AEI to thank: AEI's reputation, connections, and cachet enabled me to get access to these agencies, and without AEI I would have never had the opportunity to work there and see them from the inside.

In the next chapter we follow up on these themes by focusing on the world of the Washington think tanks. At one level, this chapter is a serious analysis of the roles, ideologies, and functions of the main Washington think tanks, but at another it is an insider account of what it's like to work in one of these "tanks." We return to many of these same themes in chapter 10, where we provide another view from the inside of both the Congress and the White House.

NOTE

1. We need to clear up any possible confusion about the name. Technically the NSC consists of only the president, vice president, secretary of state, secretary of defense, and others whom the president may designate (possibly the UN ambassador, CIA director or Homeland Security secretary, National Intelligence director). But in practice the NSC refers to this small group *plus* the staff mentioned earlier. The NSC director is referred to as the National Security Adviser (NSA), not to be confused with the National Security Administration (also NSA), which manages spy satellites and electronic eavesdropping.

Chapter Four

Think Tanks and Foreign Policy

I had come to Washington in 1981 to join one of the country's leading think tanks. But at the time I didn't know very much about these think tanks and how they operated. I knew they were prestigious and influenced policy, but beyond that I had little idea how they influenced policy and how they functioned. Joining AEI soon gave me an eye-opener on Washington politics that I'd never had before.

Think tanks are major new actors on the foreign policy scene. The phenomenon of the think tanks and their role in international affairs is a new one, of the last thirty years, and the role they play and the influence they exercise on policy are not well understood by the public. I would argue the think tanks on many issues are as influential as political parties, interest groups, and other major institutions. The think tanks have taken their place as among the most important actors in Washington policy-making. Plus they are fun, fascinating places to work.

WHAT ARE THINK TANKS?

It took me only a few days, at most a few weeks, to get used to and feel comfortable in the think tank world. After all, it was my generation that was now running the world; I had friends and colleagues in all areas of government and in every one of the think tanks. Despite the frequent policy differences, there was tremendous cross-fertilization among the think tank scholars, journalists, and government officials who attend the seminars, policy forums, and conferences the "tanks" put on.

Think tanks are unlike other institutions with which we are more familiar. They are centers of research, debate, and learning; but, unlike universities, they have no students (except interns), do not offer courses, and do not try to cover all subject areas. Instead they concentrate on key public policy issues.

Nor are think tanks like foundations eager to give money away; rather they seek to raise funds for their various projects. They do not offer fellowship grants; instead they bring in scholars to strengthen policy research topics already decided upon, or to examine new policy issues that the think tanks have deemed important.

Think tanks are not corporations, nor are they profit-making. While they have a product (research, ideas, published studies) that they try to sell, the goal is policy influence, not profit. Nor are think tanks like interest groups whose sole purpose is lobbying; think tanks *do* seek to influence policy outcomes but they do so by shaping the policy debate, not by arm twisting or donating to election campaigns. Some of the more ideological think tanks do cross the line into lobbying and partisan activity, but that is a violation of their tax-exempt status and can land them in trouble with the IRS.

Think tanks may therefore be defined as research organizations that have as their primary purpose research on and dissemination of their views on *public policy issues*. The most influential think tanks are located in Washington, D.C., where they can most effectively influence policy outcomes. There are no departments of chemistry or biology here as in a university; rather, think tanks focus chiefly on economic, social, and policy issues, including foreign as well as domestic issues. They seek not just to do abstract or "pure" research on these issues, however, but to influence the policy debate about these issues toward the think tank's point of view and to put forth solutions to public policy problems.

Think tank scholars *think*, write, publish, appear on television, give congressional testimony, attend White House briefings, and advise the State, Defense, and other departments as *advocates* of their positions. The think tanks, often more than Congress, parties, interest groups, or the White House, set the policy agenda and define the issues. They do the government's thinking for it, hence the term "think tanks." It may sound ludicrous but the fact is these days neither presidents, Congress, nor the big government departments have the time, resources, or personnel to do much thinking. They are too busy with meetings, paperwork, deadlines, bureaucratic requirements, and everyday administrative matters. So the think tanks do their thinking for them.

The tanks have the ideas and expertise, the specialized knowledge, and the long-range vision that government officials lack or have no time for. Think tanks do the necessary background work and research, explore the policy options, and make the reasoned recommendations that big government rarely can do on its own. Think tanks also seek to put their ideas into an attractive form that is translatable into specific policy proposals and appeal to the public as well as policy makers.

The journalists, scholars, and former (and often future) government officials who work at the think tanks are usually experts in specific policy issues: housing, health care, education, the economy, welfare, or foreign policy. They seek to influence policy through their own research findings or by holding conferences where they tap the country's best minds on the subject. The think tanks are often able to cut through a divisive issue like social security or immigration reform in ways that a public institution like Congress or the bureaucracy cannot.

Think tanks often serve as integrating agencies, able to pull together diverse influences and present a coherent policy proposal. They can be nonpartisan as well as partisan. They are also part of a larger process just getting underway in the early 1980s, the privatization of American policy-making. Think tanks often do the government's policy work for it; in this respect, they fill a large void. In my years at AEI I have written speeches for current and former presidents and other high officials, prepared policy option papers for the State and Defense departments and the CIA, advised secretaries of state and the National Security Council on policy matters, appeared on television talk shows numerous times to influence public opinion about an issue, and lobbied strenuously for my preferred policy outcomes.

There are risks and dangers in the privatization of policy as well as advantages. The advantages include real expertise being brought to hear on public policy issues; the danger is that there is no accountability or oversight of these activities, especially as the think tanks perform public policy roles. Moreover, with the proliferation of think tanks in recent years and their range all across the political spectrum, the think tanks have become as partisan and divisive as other institutions. I learned in my Washington years that the think tanks often both reflect and add to the partisan divides and hence the increased fragmentation, politicization, and paralysis of the American political system as a whole. But it sure was a wonderful ride and learning experience while it lasted.

WHY THINK TANKS HAVE SO MUCH INFLUENCE— AND ACADEMIC SCHOLARS DO NOT

During my years in academia, 1965–1981, I had discovered that many of my colleagues were frustrated policy makers. At U-Mass and other academic institutions the frustration was high because while the faculty had considerable knowledge and expertise, no one in government ever called on them for advice. Here they were with specialized information on obscure countries, regions, and issue areas, but no one ever tapped them for advice. To many of my colleagues, this was extremely frustrating. I, too, had sought at times to play a greater policy role but I never felt as frustrated as my colleagues since I went to Washington often and, on my main issues—the Dominican Revolution of the 1960s, the Portuguese revolution of the 1970s, Latin American politics in general, U.S. foreign aid and development assistance—I had frequently been consulted by U.S. government agencies.[1]

After I'd moved to AEI, I continued to be fascinated by the issue of academic influence (or the lack thereof) on policy. First, quite a number of my former colleagues, while critical of my joining a conservative think tank like AEI, were nonetheless green with envy that I had this plush Washington think tank job with direct influence into the channels of power. Second, I discovered that even among colleagues in the Washington, D.C., universities—American, George Washington, Georgetown, University of Maryland—even though they were close to the corridors of influence, they too were frustrated because they were seldom called on for policy advice. Third, as I spent more time in Washington, I learned that there were often good reasons why the expertise of university-based academics was not often sought out on major policy issues. And, in contrast, how and why the advice of major think tank scholars *was* influential.

First, academic writing is often too abstract and theoretical for policy makers to deal with. Policy makers need sound, concrete advice on how to respond to immediate events; they do not have the time or the patience to put up with abstract academic arguments.

Second, most academic writing is concerned with developing models and fashioning general laws of behavior, but policy has to deal with the immediate, the particular, the real. Policy makers cannot be bothered with grand debates over dependency theory, corporatism, or capitalism versus socialism; they need answers on how to vote or how to proceed *today, now.*

Third, most academics are on the left or far-left politically, way outside the mainstream of U.S. public opinion. But most politicians and policy makers, if they wish to be reelected and/or keep their jobs, must operate close to the center. When I went to Washington in 1981, the gap between a conservative administration (Reagan's) and a professoriate radicalized by Vietnam was as wide or wider than it's ever been.

Fourth, most academics do not understand the bureaucratic politics of Washington policy-making. These big bureaucracies are severely constrained in their freedom of action or ability to pursue new and innovative solutions; academics from the outside do not comprehend the severe organizational and institutional limits under which government officials operate. Much of policy is decided as a response to these bureaucratic rules as well as institutional turf battles and not in accord with the best or most desirable policy option.

Fifth, similarly with politics: most would-be academic policy advisors parachute briefly into Washington from the outside; they are often unfamiliar with the everyday political ups and downs, who's in and who's out, the rise and fall of rival political factions. Hence their advice is often not politically attuned to what's possible, what's feasible, what can *realistically* be done.

In all these areas the Washington think tanks have the advantage over outside academics, which helps explain why the former are influential and the latter are not. First, think tank writing, which because of my journalism background I was quickly able to master, has to be clear, direct, and concrete—although I would sometimes "sneak in" a theoretical aside which I thought it important for policy makers to know. Second, I dealt in specific policy recommendations, although here too I would often furtively include some more general propositions. Third, I stuck close to the center politically: on Central America, for instance, I embraced neither the White House position ("the commies are coming, the commies are coming") nor that of the opposition ("it's all due to poverty"). That centrist posture would later enable me to be part of the solution, in the form of the Kissinger Commission for Central America (see chapter 8). Finally, by reading *The Washington Post* (especially its style and gossip sections) and by attending endless lunches, receptions, and dinners, I made sure I was well tuned to the political and bureaucratic currents and nuances of Washington.

I quickly learned some other things about Washington policy-making that stood me in good stead as I ventured more and more into the policy arena. First, it's not possible for an individual scholar like me to "take on" the Defense Department or reverse the course of the Reagan Administration. But if you're knowledgeable about the internal infighting or the bureaucratic rivalries that exist in any administration, you can feed advice, information, and arguments to one faction in these internal struggles and then see the possibility that your preferred solution will win out in the end. And that is what gives you policy influence. I had done that before on issues relating to the Dominican intervention of 1965, foreign aid issues, the Portuguese revolution of 1974; now I would practice the same strategy on Central America and other Latin American issues.

Second, I learned quickly how to mobilize allies and build political support for my preferred policy options. For example, many journalists were traveling to Central America during this period but they lacked serious academic background on the area. So I spent endless hours briefing journalists, talking to them by phone, filling them in; as a result, when their stories appeared, I was frequently quoted or else my analyses found their way into their writing. I also organized a number of major conferences at AEI, on human rights policy, Brazil, Argentina and the Falklands, Central America, Spain and Portugal, and investment in Latin America, which brought some of the country's leading scholars as well as policy makers to AEI. Third, I brought in speakers who, because of their high profile—Elliott Abrams, General Vernon Walters, Assistant Secretary of State Thomas Enders, Assistant Secretary of State Tony Motley—attracted large audiences and considerable publicity.

Fourth, I accepted many lecture invitations, not only because they enhanced my income but also because they got my message out to a wide audience. Fifth, I wrote a lot—op eds, papers, book chapters, articles; these as well as the edited volumes we published at AEI—on human rights, Central America, American foreign policy, U.S.-Brazil relations, trade—served both to spread our name and to envelop others—contributors, collaborators, audience participants—in our expanding web of allies and supporters.[2]

All these activities enlarged our range of friends and contacts and gave the policy positions papers coming out of AEI's Center for Hemispheric Studies a large and receptive audience including key policy makers. As a key player in the policy debates of the time told me, "Howard, if a World Bank official, a deputy assistant secretary, or an NSC advisor has your book or article open and in front of him as he's writing his own memo to the secretary, the director, or the president, that's when you have influence."

I have long viewed the Washington think tanks as providing the essential link between the world of academic scholarship and the world of policy-making. Recall that before going to AEI, I had had a sixteen-year career as an academic scholar, had already published extensively, and was already quite well known in my field. Because of these connections, I could elicit the support of academic colleagues, pull them in to give academic gravitas and a heavyweight roster of speakers to our conferences, and have my invitations to them to collaborate on my various projects responded to favorably.[3] For our various forums and seminars we were able to pull in some of the best scholars in the country, and these in turn drew to our meetings large crowds of journalists, congressional staff, and executive branch personnel.

Think tanks also serve a transmission belt function. They link academic research to policy. Their role is as both an original source of research and policy ideas through their own resident scholars, *and* as an agency that can draw upon the research of university-based scholars, translate it into terms and language Washington understands, and pass it on to policy makers. Think tanks are thus both originators of knowledge relevant to policy, and brokers of ideas or knowledge from other sources. The think tanks perform liaison functions.

They sift and filter academic ideas searching out those that are useful and can "fly" in a policy sense.

Think tank scholars help make their own and others' academic research realistic and down-to-earth. They learn to write in a style that is direct, eschews theory and jargon, and appeals to congressmen and policy makers. I locate that style as somewhere between academic prose and journalism—"high journalism." But in addition to their writing style think tank scholars must be politically savvy, plugged in, and understand the bureaucratic and political pressures. They have to know how, where, and when to feed their ideas into the process, which ideas will work and which won't. In these ways the think tanks help define the options, provide them with arguments and justification, and steer policy in their preferred directions. Think tanks can thus define the outlines of the debate, educate the public and Congress, show what will work, and demonstrate how to get from here to there. This is "political" work, not always in accord with the supposed "purity" of academic research, but practical and with a far greater effect on policy.

FROM OLD TO NEW ELITES ON FOREIGN POLICY

For a long time, through the 1950s, discussions about American foreign policy were largely confined to a small elite centered in New York and Washington and organized mainly in the Council on Foreign Relations (CFR). The Council, based in New York, had been formed after World War I to help lobby for the Fourteen Points of Woodrow Wilson's Versailles peace treaty; even though Wilson failed to secure Senate ratification of his treaty, the Council continued as a meeting place and forum to hear reports on distant places and issues. At a time before globalization and modern jet travel, and when the country was still mainly isolationist, the Council was a center of internationalist thinking. Its membership consisted of wealthy New Yorkers, chiefly bankers, businessmen, diplomats, lawyers, and financiers who had an interest in international affairs. It put on programs, invited outside speakers to talk about their travels, and published the journal *Foreign Affairs*.

Membership in the Council was by election only; it remained a small, select, and highly prestigious group. To join, you needed to be nominated and voted on; only a small percentage of those nominated were elected to membership. During the 1940s and 1950s much of the nation's foreign policy leadership came from this select group: Dean Acheson, John Foster Dulles, Douglas Dillon, Nelson and David Rockefeller, Averill Harriman, John Cabot Lodge, Christian Herter, Allen Dulles, John McCloy. Although there were partisan differences, most Council members thought of themselves as moderates and centrists, nonpartisan. They were the backbone of the consensual, bipartisan ("partisanship ends at the water's edge") American foreign policy that prevailed up until the Vietnam War. Truth in packaging demands that the author of this book indicate he has been a CFR member since 1983.

During the 1960s and 1970s criticisms of the Council became widespread. The well-known economist John Kenneth Galbraith denounced it as "irrelevant" and resigned. It was said to be too WASPish, too old-fashioned, and with too few women, minority, and younger members. As a New York-based organization, it was denounced by conservatives as part of the "Eastern liberal establishment." As a bulwark of post-World War II foreign policy, it was held responsible for the assumptions that produced Vietnam.

In the 1980s and continuing to today, the Council sought to refurbish its image. It recruited new members among women, minorities, and younger persons. It opened a branch in Washington and developed a National Program for other major cities. It hired new personnel and developed its own research program. In short, the Council refashioned itself as a still New York-based think tank with a Washington branch. But by then, it had already been overtaken and largely bypassed by the Washington-based think tanks.

This transition marked a major turning point in how American foreign policy is formulated and carried out. The Council on Foreign Relations had lost its monopoly. The center of foreign policy influence had shifted from New York to Washington, from the CFR to the Washington think tanks, with a major impact on foreign policy. Let us sum up these important changes as follows:

1. Power in foreign policy has shifted from New York to Washington.
2. It has shifted from the Council on Foreign Relations to the Washington think tanks.
3. It has shifted from the Wall Street bankers, lawyers, and financiers to the public policy specialists in the think tanks.
4. Foreign policy has become more democratized.
5. It is now in the hands of younger, less establishment figures.
6. It has become more partisan and ideological, reflecting the political positions of the several think tanks.
7. It has become less middle-of-the-road, less consensual, less bipartisan.
8. It has also become more divisive, more fragmented, and less continuous from administration to administration.

Hence while the think tanks now have more foreign policy expertise, they have also become polarizing agencies. Indeed all the problems of American foreign policy—lack of consensus, partisanship, division, fragmentation—

can be found in the Washington think tanks. Are the think tanks mainly a reflection of the deep divisions that exist in American politics generally, or are they also responsible for those divisions? Or maybe both.

THE WORLD OF THINK TANKS

Think tanks come in a variety of forms: big or small, university-connected or independent, single-issue or general, Washington-based or not, government dependent or not. Earlier in my career I had spent a year writing a book on the Dominican revolution and the U.S. intervention of 1965 at the comparatively small Mershon Center for National Security Affairs at Ohio State University; from my Harvard years I was acquainted with the Cambridge-based Institute for Foreign Policy Analysis, and later in my career (and the subject of a future volume) I spent a year at the similarly small ($1–2 million budget) Foreign Policy Research Institute (FPRI) in Philadelphia.

"Tanks" that are dependent mainly on the government, chiefly the Defense Department, for contracts and support include the RAND Corporation, the Center for Naval Analysis (CNA), the BDM Corporation, and CACI. Another category is big, influential tanks that are outside of Washington (the Hoover Institution, the Hudson Institute); recently those two have opened Washington offices. Then, there are the smaller, specialized institutes; in my area these include the Council on Hemispheric Affairs (COHA), a one-man, far-left operation headed by Larry Birns, and the Washington Office on Latin America (WOLA), another far-left organization supported by the Methodist Church but run by its radical, clerical members who were far removed politically from the church's voting membership.

Our main concern here, however, is with what we called "the Big Five," the five main, general, Washington-based think tanks: the far-left Institute for Policy Studies (IPS), the moderately left Brookings Institution, the centrist Center for Strategic and International Studies (CSIS—my future home), conservative AEI, and the far-right Heritage Foundation.

IPS represents the hard left in American politics. Founded by radical critics Markus Raskin and Richard Barnett, it was long funded by the Rubin family of Fabergé cosmetics fame. It took up strong positions against the Vietnam War, called for the overthrow of capitalism, called the U.S. "the most evil society in history," and advocated the reconstruction of society on socialist lines. IPS, to my knowledge, had never seen a U.S. strategic or foreign policy that it could support. Except for an occasional debate with one of its activists (Barnett or Robert Borosage), I had little contact with IPS during my years in Washington; it was too far out of the mainstream of American politics.

As compared with the other major Washington think tanks, IPS had a very small ($2 million) budget; eventually it faded from view.

Brookings, on the moderate left, was a very different story. For one thing, Brookings had a large budget (approaching $20 million) and a big endowment, which meant Brookings scholars and administrators, unlike AEI's later on, didn't have to scramble for money all the time and had a nice cushion in hard times. Second, Brookings' work was mainstream and its scholarship serious (*too* serious, some said, with its 600 page tomes that no one read); it focused mainly, from a Keynesian perspective, on economic policy and supplied much of the background studies and personnel for Democrat administrations. Brookings had influence that IPS lacked.

But in my years in Washington Brookings was very weak on foreign policy. Its director of foreign policy studies, John Steinbrenner, was not a very productive scholar or a dynamic force, nor with a couple exceptions (Bill Quant on the Middle East) did Brookings recruit leading scholars to flesh out its foreign policy team. It never developed the area studies expertise that AEI had nor did it cover the full range of foreign policy issues. Its staff remained small and concentrated on Europe, NATO, and the Middle East.

As a moderate, my relations with Brookings were always good, and I went over there on numerous occasions to participate with their scholars in panels and debates; at one point I even explored with Brookings the possibility of joining their staff. But Brookings scholars did the same with AEI, which shows that despite the ideological posturing the two institutions were not all that far apart. For example Kennedy economic counselor (and a Brookings scholar) Charles Schultz was frequently in the AEI dining room, and Jimmy Carter stalwart Robert Pastor, who was then at Brookings, applied to my program at AEI for a position.

Our closest relations were with the centrist Center for Strategic and International Studies (CSIS). Not just physically (CSIS was only three blocks from AEI, Brookings four) but intellectually and in terms of exchanges as well. CSIS had been founded, after all, by former AEI scholars David Abshire and Richard Allen with the strong assistance of Admiral (and former Joint Chiefs of Staff head) Arleigh Burke; it liked to call itself an "action tank" rather than a "think tank." It was in the realist, centrist-Republican school of foreign policy as exemplified by Henry Kissinger, James Schlesinger, and now Anthony Cordesman.

I was personally very close to the Latin American scholars at CSIS: Bill Perry, Georges Fauriol, Delal Baer, and, in an earlier incarnation, Roger Fontaine. I had always thought of Roger as a serious scholar and a centrist but to get a job in the Reagan Administration he had shifted radically to the right. Roger eventually paid the price: after serving on the Reagan NSC staff for a short while he was unable to find a suitable position in either the academic or think tank worlds. Our relations with others at CSIS were always extremely close and cordial; we participated in each other's programs, exchanged ideas in each other's dining rooms, and invited each other to contribute (with honoraria!) to our respective books and anthologies. I'm sure this closeness explains why when I eventually left AEI, CSIS was my first choice as an alternative think tank "home."

As a centrist and realist I was closest to CSIS, but my AEI colleague Mark Falcoff was closer ideologically to the hard-right Heritage Foundation. Heritage had been founded in the early 1970s by conservatives Ed Feulner and Paul Weyrich; it was unabashedly supportive of the Barry Goldwater-Jesse Helms-Ronald Reagan wing of the Republican Party. Heritage was the think tank of "movement" conservatives; its funds came from Joseph Coors and the far right wing. Instead of serious scholars, it hired mostly young graduate students (cheap labor) to do mainly superficial, "quickie" analyses based on newspaper clippings files. Those of us at the mainstream think tanks AEI, Brookings, and CSIS didn't think much of Heritage's research products. On the other hand, we had to admit their undoubted success in money-raising, mobilizing conservatives, and slapping their "instant analyses" down on congressmen's desks on an overnight basis. Over the course of the 1980s, as we shall see, Heritage managed to outflank and surpass AEI on both the fund-raising and the political influence fronts.

There's a neat symmetry here: IPS and Heritage on the far-left and far-right respectively, Brookings and AEI on the center-left and center-right respectively, and CSIS in the middle. As a practical matter that meant that CSIS had influence in all administrations whether Democrat or Republican, AEI had influence in right and center-right administrations, Brookings in left and center-left administrations, Heritage only in conservative administrations (Reagan, Bush II), and IPS only in liberal-Democrat administrations (Carter, Clinton).

But this neat pattern, which largely held during the 1970s and 1980s, eventually gave way. IPS faded as the Soviet Union collapsed and the socialist option looked threadbare. Heritage gained in strength, surpassing AEI for a time; Brookings hired a Republican president and cozied up to conservatives and the business community; and AEI suffered a major financial *cum* administrative shakeup in the late 1980s. Only CSIS under Abshire stayed relatively constant, but with new president John Hamre it partially abandoned its centrist-realist position and hired a corps of liberal internationalists from the Clinton Administration. Meanwhile the CATO Institute developed over time as a serious libertarian think tank, the Center for American Progress under John Podesta supplanted Brookings on the liberal left, AEI recovered its élan and its financial health, and a *host* of new, specialized think tanks rose up to challenge the biggies.

HOW THINK TANKS EXERCISE INFLUENCE

How do think tanks go about influencing policy? The question is harder than it seems because it's often difficult to measure influence. Moreover influence is often subtle, quiet, cumulative, unseen: a spoken word, a telephone conversation, a seminar presentation that touches someone, a discussion among friends and colleagues based on mutual trust. It's hard to measure this precisely or empirically. One good measure is to compare what comes out of the political system in the way of policy versus what went in, from think tanks and others, in the way of recommendations. Another, my favorite already mentioned, is when a lower-ranking official uses your book or paper as background when he's preparing his own memo for the decision maker. But even then, you may not know definitely if it's your recommendation that triumphed. Influence is often murky, hard to untangle, sometimes indirect or second-hand. Here at least are the strategies that AEI employed:

1. Breakfasts, lunches, dinners, seminars. Virtually every day AEI and the other tanks have programs on one theme or another—often several per day. To these meetings are invited congressmen and their aides, White House and State Department officials, journalists, other think tank scholars, interest group representatives, and opinion leaders in general. There may be an AEI scholar presenting or a distinguished guest often from abroad: president, prime minister, defense minister, foreign minister, etc. I often was amazed and even in awe at the top-level officials we were able to draw. The food, snacks, meals, etc. are always good and the setting pleasant. There events served to publicize our activities, introduce us to ever widening circles of the Washington policy community, and give our writings and ideas legitimacy and standing in that community.
2. Television and media. During the 1980s I was frequently on television on the major news shows. A small part of this was my own expertise; a larger part came from the fact that AEI had its own television/media office, headed by former producer Heather David. Heather had numerous friends in the industry and was adept at getting us on the news and talk shows; AEI also produced its own programs for PBS and C-Span. Aiding our frequent media appearances was the fact that ABC's Washington news bureau was right across the back alley from our offices and CBS was only three blocks down the street. We could thus be at their studios on a mo-

ment's notice, a decided advantage in time, logistics, and expenses over scholars with equal expertise but farther removed from the major studios.

3. Public appearances. In my heyday at AEI, I was giving two or three (or more) public presentations per week, to trade associations, government agencies, university audiences, World Affairs Councils, and at other think tanks. Some of these were freebies that one did for the good of the cause, but most involved honoraria ranging from quite modest to quite munificent. Within the think tank world, if one was invited to be a presenter or contribute to an anthology at another think tank, the expectation was that you would soon reciprocate the favor, to everyone's advantage. All these public appearances not only padded my bank account but led to my views and recommendations becoming well known in Washington policy circles.
4. The presumption of expertise. When you're at the big Washington think tanks—AEI, Brookings, CSIS—it's simply assumed that you have expertise and are at the top of your field. The Washington think tanks are like Harvard in this respect: just being there, able to use the official stationery, and having your name associated with the institution means you are the best. Or at least the presumption is that you're the best. And that presumption translates into influence.
5. Access to policy makers. Because of all the forums, seminars, dinners, etc. noted above, think tank scholars have access to policy makers in ways that academic scholars do not. During the 1980s when Central America was a hot issue, I was at the White House at least once a week, the State Department and Congress once a month, and the CIA and Defense Department once every couple months. Over time you become well known in these agencies, you're on a first-name basis with people there, and policy influence often becomes a simple matter of picking up the phone or having lunch. Since most bureaucrats lack specialized knowledge, my experience is that they usually welcome input from informed sources.
6. Congressional testimony. I often knew personally the congressmen and staffers on the foreign affairs, defense, and intelligence committees and subcommittees; hence when an issue came up on Latin America or foreign aid, I was often called on to testify. Such calls are usually more institutional than personal: since I was at AEI, I would get called on, often to balance someone from Brookings or WOLA. But I was a centrist, a maverick, and did not echo the Reagan Administration line. I remember the congressmen before whom I was testifying often looking at me quizzically because they were actually hearing something new or unexpected. Over the course of the 1980s as Congress became more and more divided and its hearing a partisan circus, I made the decision not to testify any more.

7. Advisory Panels and Boards. Think tanks have high-level boards and advisory groups for all their programs. These consist of outside persons usually prominent in business, banking, and law. In this way think tanks can list prestigious and wealthy persons on their letterheads and annual reports, which in turn gives them cachet and fund-raising possibilities. Wealthy board members donate and help raise funds for the think tank; they in turn get a break from their business activities and a chance to participate in Washington policy-making. In my years at AEI I got to hobnob socially with the likes of David Rockefeller (Chase Bank), Walter Wriston (Bank of America), Rupert Murdoch (publishing), Richard Madden (Potlatch Corporation), Joseph Coors (beer), and many others.
8. Personal contacts. Over the course of my first couple years in Washington, the staff and I developed a large rolodex of personal contacts, and we continued to add to it. These included not just other scholars but journalists, government officials, business acquaintances, congressmen and their staffs, labor officials, foundation heads, representatives of foreign governments, and so on. The list of contacts was far larger and broader than I'd ever had as an academic; periodically we would use our interns to update the list. The list was eventually computerized and used for fund-raising, invitations, the sending of publications, etc. Each individual program had its own list while AEI maintained a master list; the system became so sophisticated that we could cull and target even more refined sublists for mailings, fund-raising, and invitations.
9. Revolving doors. The think tanks are prime recruiting grounds for new government talent. Here you have very knowledgeable people who also understand Washington politics and bureaucracy. They do not have to undertake on-the-job training. Many long-time think tankers have gone in and out of government several times in a revolving-door fashion that brings them into high policy positions, then back to the think tank again if their party loses the next election, then often back into government at a higher level, and so on. It's a heady experience and a chance to put your ideas into practice. Both the government and the think tanks are enriched by these "in'n'outers": the government gets new and fresh ideas while think tanks benefit from the real-life policy experience of their colleagues who serve in official capacities. During my time there, some thirty AEI scholars went into government service, including most prominently Jeane Kirkpatrick (UN), Richard Cheney (Defense), Rudy Penner (CBO), Arthur Burns (ambassador), Jim Miller (Council of Economic Advisors), Fred Iklé (Defense), Max Kampelman (human rights).
10. Studies and Publications. AEI scholars, with no teaching and few administrative responsibilities, are able to produce a prodigious amount

of policy writing. Op-eds, papers, articles, monographs, books; some of the scholars even had their own monthly or quarterly newsletters which they mailed to supporters and government officials. Herb Stein the economist (father of comedian Ben Stein) had the best of these: wry, amusing, well-written and well-argued, deft at arguing his policy positions.

11. Aiding all this scholarly productivity was the fact that AEI had its own highly professional editorial and publications office, which turned out all those written products mentioned earlier, its sophisticated mailing lists to make sure these products got to the right hands, and its own public relations office to get their op-eds published and ensure publicity for AEI scholars and their writings. As a former academic scholar, I had never before had the advantage of an entire production staff like this to get out and publicize my writings; with this kind of support, one could be enormously productive. In those first years at AEI I published far more than I had ever done previously; moreover, the AEI PR staff made sure it got into the right hands, the same targeted audiences we used for invitations and fund-raising. AEI could make sure your work was actually *read* and that it got into the hands of key policy makers who made decisions. In Washington, that's how you have influence.

QUESTION MARKS?

Think tanks are really nice places to work. As a scholar, they're ideal: no students, no committees, little bureaucracy, plus you have influence. Salaries are high; there's unlimited postage, telephone, copying, computers. You have your own research assistants, secretaries, library, travel funds, support staff. You can supplement your salary by outside engagements; many of the larger tanks have their own dining facilities. The work and the surroundings are very pleasant.

But there *are* some drawbacks. Young scholars ought to be aware of these before they abandon their academic goals and rush pell-mell into the think tank/policy world.

1. There is no permanence or tenure in the think tank world. And Washington policy-making is very fickle, flitting from one issue to the next. As long as your issue (Central America in the 1980s, Russia in the early 1990s, Iraq and the Middle East today) is hot, your job is also safe; but if the administration in power or the policy focus changes, your job can quickly be in jeopardy.

2. Fund-raising. When I was at AEI initially, the think tank was so wealthy that I didn't need to do fund-raising. Later, as AEI faced a financial crisis, the scholars were obliged to do fund-raising, and that is now the norm at all the think tanks. You may have to raise funds for your own salary and projects; fund-raising may take 30-40 percent of your time, and you have to decide if that's worth it. I found fund-raising to be a skill that you learn and master like any other and I enjoyed doing it for maybe 5–10 percent of my time, but not everyone will be successful at it and some scholars find it demeaning to go out and ask for money.
3. Policy research. If you opt for the policy world, you need to be prepared to do policy-oriented research. And that is very different from academic research: the writing style is different (direct, clear, no jargon), the organization is different (shorter, briefer), the audience is different (generalists, not specialists), and the approach is different (policy recommendations, what to do *now*, no theoretical or ideological harangues). If you're prepared to adapt in this way, you may belong in the think tank world; if you continue to write as if you want to get published in the *American Political Science Review*, you probably don't belong in Washington policy-making.
4. Ideological conformity. This is a delicate issue. But the fact is that most of the big and not-so-big think tanks are identified with clear ideological positions: AEI with Republicans, Brookings with Democrats, etc. But suppose you're a Democrat and you happen to be at AEI (we had quite a few of those), a Republican at Brookings, or like me, someone who's not very partisan or ideological. Or suppose you're liberal on some issues but conservative on others. But the media and everyone will *assume* that if you're at AEI or Brookings, you *must* be in accord with their presumed image of those institutions.

   From personal experience I can tell you that being an outsider politically in these institutions can be a lonely and difficult position. Outsiders, your own colleagues, and perhaps your own institution may expect you to take a certain position on the issues; but if you don't there can be not just raised eyebrows but also political fights. At AEI I got into conflicts with Mike Novak over statism versus free markets, with Ben Wattenberg over population policy, and with the powerful contingent of superstar economists over the universality of their models, especially in Third World contexts. All of these resulted in bruising battles, put my job in jeopardy, and left me with the choice of keeping quiet or continuing the battle against more powerful and influential people than I. Tough choice.
5. Contract research. Since the big think tanks are engaged in a constant struggle for funds, the issue of contract research (research paid for by the government or other contracting agencies) constantly came up. But of

course if you accept contract research, then the assumption is strong that the contracting agency (usually the Defense Department or CIA) will influence the research and even the conclusions reached. So most of the think tanks seek to limit contract research to from 5 to 15 percent of their budgets. However, since that's where the big money is, the temptation to fudge the rules and accept more is always present.

6. Bias. The bigger think tanks *all* get most of their money from big business and business foundations. But not from labor, farmers, or—obviously—poor people. Doesn't that inevitably bias the research? Of course it does. I don't recall *ever* seeing a think tank study, from *any* of the bigger institutions that was critical of business, business lobbies, or the American economic model. Some subjects, therefore, especially critical ones, because of the constant money needs of the think tanks, are simply untouched, unstudied, off-limits.

CONCLUSION

Let us go back to the propositions with which we began. In the broad sweep of history, power in foreign policy-making has shifted from New York to Washington, from the old Council on Foreign Relations to the Washington think tanks, from Wall Street bankers, lawyers, and generalists to think tank scholars with specific and specialized knowledge, from centrists to more partisan and ideological analysts. Since the think tanks where power has shifted range all up and down the political spectrum, the changes outlined above have added to the division and fragmentation of our foreign policy.

The Washington think tanks are both a reflection and the instruments of this more partisan and ideological trend. They mirror the cultural and ideological divisions that already exist. The older unity and consensus in foreign policy have broken down in favor of a more politicized, fragmented, and often polarized debate. Our disagreements about foreign policy reflect the more contentious and divided country we have become; the think tanks and their talking heads reflect as well as reinforce these currents of fragmentation and division.

Think tanks have assumed a far larger role than previously in our policy debates. They are new actors on the stage, influential in providing ideas and justifications for decisions often made elsewhere, but in agencies and offices where what the leading think tanks recommend on the issues matters a great deal. The think tanks feed options, information, policy positions, and, not least, their own people into governmental decision-making. They alter perspectives, affect policy decisions, and sometimes exercise direct influence over policy. They help define the boundaries of the policy debate, offer agendas and options, catalyze and popularize new ideas, help bridge the gaps between agencies and between the academic and policy worlds, provide advice to policy makers, and serve to educate and inform Congress, the media, policy makers, and the general public. From my perch at AEI I concluded that think tanks are now among the most important actors in Washington, right up there with major interest groups, political parties, and lobbying organizations.

NOTES

1. When I went to Harvard in 1979–81, I discovered a somewhat different issue. There, the faculty simply assumes it should be running U.S. foreign policy and, ultimately, the world. At Harvard the presidential candidates come calling, looking for *you* and to put you on their foreign policy advisory panels, for the sake of having a Harvard name on their roster, instead of you looking for them. For an amusing, tongue-in-cheek account of my own experiences in this environment during the 1980 election campaign see Howard J. Wiarda, *Universities, Think Tanks and War Colleges* (Princeton, N.J.: X Libris, 1999).

2. Up to this point my publication record, although already quite extensive, had been close to the typical academic pace: several papers and scholarly articles per year, a smattering of op-eds and shorter pieces, and a book every few years. But at AEI, with no teaching and few administrative responsibilities, my own superb research and typing staff, wonderful financial and administrative support, and an in-house editorial, conference, television, and publications staff, my productivity expanded exponentially: several volumes (almost all edited anthologies) *per year*, various papers and articles (often reprinted several times), numerous invited book chapters and briefer contributions, several op eds. Since little of this was peer-reviewed (the academic standard), some of my university-based colleagues wondered at this explosion of productivity; for my part, I was very happy to be able to get my writings out to a wider audience without all the hassles and long delays of the academic writing marketplace.

3. Some former academic colleagues on ideological or partisan grounds were reluctant to collaborate with AEI with its conservative orientation, but my experience was that an invitation to come to Washington for an AEI conference coupled with a handsome honorarium in *all cases* overcame this occasional reluctance.

Chapter Five

Latin America on the Agenda: Foreign Policy in a Peripheral Area

I had been brought to Washington as an expert on Latin America, specifically Central America. In the 1980s Central America was a hot issue; that had been the basis of Jeane Kirkpatrick's invitation to me to join her staff, and that was the position I had at AEI as director of the Center for Hemispheric Studies.

But if truth be told, after a decade of living in and writing about Europe, I was more interested in that area than I was in Latin America. And coming off two years at Harvard's Center for International Affairs, where I'd retooled as a foreign policy analyst, I was more interested in general foreign policy issues than I was in the narrower problems of Central America per se. We had earlier noted that Jeane's invitation and the AEI position brought me back, intellectually, to Latin American affairs after some ten years of focus on other issues. But even now my emphasis was quite different than it had been earlier. In earlier years I had been involved in Latin America for its own sake; now I had a broader perspective and was mainly interested in two things: the place of Latin America in the larger pattern of global interdependence and development, as well as the position of Latin America in the overall foreign policy of the United States.

Within weeks of going to D.C. and joining AEI, I was enmeshed in these larger issues. I was already thinking of a book—maybe two—on the subject. The first and somewhat narrower focus was on the place of Latin America in U.S. foreign policy-making. The second would be on how U.S. foreign policy worked (or failed to work) in general—i.e. the domestic basis of U.S. foreign policy. My journal notes show that within a few days of going to Washington, I was recording not just the adventures of my suddenly strenuous social life but also jotting down thoughts about Latin America and where it fit, or didn't fit, in U.S. foreign policy, *and* how American foreign policy worked in general: the partisanship, the conflict, the gridlock, the posturing and logrolling.

Hence this chapter focuses on Latin American issues and, specifically, the usually condescending, patronizing way we have always viewed and treated the area. Chapter 6, a preview of the book I would later write on American foreign policy, treats of domestic foreign policy, and the *process* of how foreign policy works. Both these chapters reflect a growing cynicism, bred by my semi-insider AEI foreign policy vantage point, about American foreign policy, how it works, and whether "the system" as we know it is worth saving and can at this date be salvaged.

AROUND WASHINGTON

Within a few weeks of my joining AEI, I was already starting to feel like a Washington insider. I led a strenuous social life, received more and more invitations, and was soon visiting on a regular basis institutions and groups that I'd mainly only read about before. Pretty soon I was feeling and operating like a Washington person, at home and comfortable in virtually any social or political environment and an almost daily (or nightly) denizen of the Washington social *cum* policy circuit.

What follows is a series of vignettes all derived from my early Washington experiences and recorded at the time in my journal. It should be said that this is only a small sampling; there are in my journals literally *thousands* of adventures, experiences, and misadventures from which to choose. They chronicle my growing understanding of Washington policy-making, my impressions of the people I met and the institutions visited. They also serve as a preclude to the more systematic foreign policy conclusions found later in this and the following chapter.

- October 26, 1981, at the State Department for a discussion of the Reagan Defense Department buildup. Featured speakers are former Secretary of Defense Melvin Laird and current undersecretary Fred Iklé, a strategic policy intellectual. Iklé talks of the need for the Navy to buy spare parts; Laird, a politician, says the Navy wants more *ships* and calculates that it can fill in the parts later. Iklé comes off as a Reagan-era "Dr. Strangelove"; Laird, the old pol, runs rings around him politically and intellectually. My conclusion: give me a savvy pol in policy-making over an intellectual anytime.
- That same day, at another State Department briefing by Latin America Assistant Secretary Thomas Enders. Enders is impressive, provides a *tour d'horizon* of Latin America. We tried, he says, to work with the new Nicaraguan San-

dinista government; they rejected us and now force must be used. In El Salvador we must resist a guerilla takeover. Cuba is seen as an economic failure but extraordinarily successful in maintaining political coherence. Argentina was viewed as open to investment but having a "Mussolini type" (corporatist) political system. We support Mexico's clientelistic one-party system because it is stable and allows for upward mobility. Overall, there is a wide perception in the government that South America is more important to us now than in the past but Central America will be the center of our attention and may drag the entire region down.

- October 27, 1981. Dinner at the Madison Hotel with business leaders in Washington for their annual briefings on U.S. policy. The dinner is superb, one of the most pleasant evenings ever. I'm impressed with how well informed these business leaders are and their grasp of global issues. Often they're better informed than the U.S. government officials briefing them. They have access to all top-level U.S. officials.
- October 31, 1981. Out to Arleigh House in rural Virginia for a policy meeting on Venezuela. I drive out with Jeane in her government-issue limousine, decide it's nice to have a car and driver like this. The countryside out here is beautiful. The meeting is very high-level: former Kennedy aide Ted Sorenson, Amb. Pete Vaky, Amb. Sally Shelton, Amb. Bill Leurs, Woodrow Wilson Center Latin America director Abe Lowenthal, high-powered lawyer (and former assistant secretary) William Rogers, Luigi Einaudi from the State Department, Amb. James Theberge, Secretary Enders, Venezuelan *político* (and future president) Rafael Caldera. It's clear the U.S. is backing the Christian democrats in Venezuela and elsewhere; gone is the support for the democratic-left Acción Democrática. Jeane tells me she's already fed up with her UN job; she's a contemplative person and may not be cut out for diplomatic/political work. On the other hand she's also thinking of running for office—and is being urged to do so by many admirers—but is not yet certain where or when, possibly for the Senate from Maryland (her present residence) or Oklahoma (her home state).
- November 10, 1981. I'm invited to the Carnegie Endowment for dinner and a discussion of statehood for Puerto Rico. Among the guests were Riordan Roett of the Johns Hopkins School of Advanced International Studies (SAIS), ex-Carter NSC adviser on Latin America Bob Pastor, Amb. Vaky, Margaret Daly Hayes of the Senate Foreign Relations Committee, Peter Bell from the Inter-American Foundation, Amb. Ben Stephansky, Ted Van Dyke from the Democratic National Committee, Jorge Heine of the Wilson Center, and State Department spokesman John Trattner. By this time, after only two months in Washington, I think I've met all the movers and shakers in Latin America policy. It's not a large group, seventy or so.

- November 17, 1981. I'm being considered for a professorship in the Georgetown Government Department. I've also been approached to head Georgetown's moribund Latin American studies program. But when I meet with President/Father Healy, the first thing he tells me is that I will need to fund-raise my own salary. No thanks!!! Why should I leave AEI or my tenured professorship at U-Mass for that kind of uncertainty? And why, if I can raise that kind of money, should I give it to Georgetown? Much of Washington operates this way: there's *less* than meets the eye.
- December 2, 1981. I'm invited to the Heritage Foundation for the first time for a program on Latin America. These are the real ideological "movement" conservatives with whom I'm not acquainted; I have to whisper to my research assistant Janine Perfit to identify most of them: Lyn Bouchey who has his own conservative think tank, right-wing defense intellectual Cleto De Giovanni, fellow right-winger Constantine Menges from the CIA, Cuban community lobbyist Ana Colomar O'Brien, Amb. Lewis Tambs who authored the right-wing "Santa Fe Report," my old friend Roger Fontaine now at the NSC, AEI colleague Mark Falcoff. All these people are *way* more conservative than I am but they're a power in the Reagan Administration and I need to be careful around them with what I say.
- December 1981. AEI's Public Policy Week. Very impressive. A solid week of seminars and panels on all the hot-button issues. Very high level, involving congressmen and cabinet officers as well as AEI scholars. We put on a program on Central America; Senator Nancy Landon Kassebaum, who becomes a good friend, is the commentator. The last night of Public Policy week is a black tie dinner. I haven't worn my tux since my college fraternity days. We AEI scholars, irreverently, call it "prom night." President Reagan is the after-dinner speaker, showing off our ability to draw big names and attracting the cream of Washington society. Reagan is impressive and delivers a superb speech; he's a pro at this. First time I've met him and seen him up close: very pleasant, cordial, sharp (contrary to the popular image), and seemingly younger than he is.
- February 12, 1982. I'm invited to an all-day conference at the State Department on Nicaragua. All the academics present—Bill LeoGrande, Joseph Thome, Meg Crahan, John Nichols, Jack Child, Richard Millett—are still hopeful about pluralism and democracy in Nicaragua; newly-appointed U.S. ambassador to Nicaragua Tony Quainton and I are more skeptical. Arch-conservatives Otto Reich and Constantine Menges are also in the room; they're convinced Nicaragua is already "lost" to communism. Wanting not to stray too far from my academic colleagues but ever-mindful of my position at the conservative AEI, I balance between the two positions. At the meeting Brian Latell asks me to be a consultant to the CIA.

- That same day I write, "What fun to be in Washington! Something new and exciting everyday. A conference that's stimulating, a fancy dinner, lunches with interesting people, new offers, lectureships, consultantships. U-Mass will be very dull by comparison."
- A little later I write, "I love everything about Washington that the rest of America hates: the politics, the hypocrisy, the grandstanding, the lying, the backslapping, the nasty partisanship, the sleazy deals. I think I've given up on policy outcomes but the process is endlessly fascinating. It's all grist for the book I want to write."
- February 12, 1982. Our Tinker Foundation Grant came through! Between that, Smith Richardson, Brazilinvest, Mellon, and the Argentines, we've raised almost half a million dollars in my first six months here. That ought to make my job secure at AEI!
- February 18, 1982. Invitations to go to Brussels, Madrid, Germany, Rio, and Buenos Aires. Can I do this all? And finish building my barn in Amherst at the same time?
- February 19, 1982. Alaskan Indians are brought to Washington by some lobby group. The hostess scrambles to find reindeer meat for them. But the Indians, while saying it was delicious, indicate it's not reindeer meat. Turns out to be horse meat which the hostess served when the reindeer meat failed to arrive on time. Isn't Washington fun?
- February 22, 1982. Quite a week! Lunch with Mexico lobbyist John Haas. The next day an interview on Central America with Jerome Demereaux of *L'Express*. After that Jackie Tillman, Jeane Kirkpatrick's aide, brings a group of Nicaraguan, anti-Sadinista Mequito Indians to AEI. I serve as host. It's a disaster! Jackie is a former secretary and not well educated or up on the issues; the Mequitos have never done a press conference before. There's mass confusion, everyone speaks at once, the point the Mequitos want to make is completely and hopelessly lost.
- February 24, 1982. Salvador Jorge Blanco, president of the Dominican Republic, at AEI. I serve as host. President Jorge from the left-of-center Dominican Revolutionary Party; other than the fact I'm a friend of the party, his aides wonder what they're doing at conservative AEI. His speech is a rousing defense of democracy. But his definition of democracy includes economic democracy, not exactly what the AEI economists want to hear. Ringers from IPS (the radical think tank) and WOLA (missionary leftists) crash the presentation. For the first time, Baroody vetoes my plan to publish the speech and discussion.
- Later that day, a conference at the State Department on the new Caribbean Basin Initiative (CBI). No coffee or doughnuts—State is cheapo! CIA and DOD do better at their conferences. "Caribbean Basin" is a new term; no

one's ever heard of it before. Came about because congressional Republicans wanted aid to Central America on anti-communism grounds while congressional Black Caucus favored aid to the Caribbean. The result was the CBI: both groups got what they wanted even though logically, ethnically, politically, or economically it made no sense to tie these two areas together.

- Week of March 2-6. Lunch with Steven Vetter of Inter-American Foundation; Larman Wilson of American University and Sam Mujal-Leon of Georgetown; and former French foreign minister Michel Jobert. I'm invited to join the Inter-American Foundation board and was offered an adjunct teaching position at Georgetown.
- March 3, 1982. Invited to a reception for El Salvadoran rebel and so-called "social democrat" Guillermo Ungo. Hosted by Reverend Joe Eldridge, the director of the Washington Office on Latin America, a left-wing lobbying group with Methodist Church affiliation. I'm *by far* the most conservative person in the room. Mostly the attendees are idealistic young college kids (unpaid interns) and a few "old lefties"—Ben Stephansky, Larry Birns, Mark Schneider. Only wine and cheese are served, more like a college reception than at AEI's fancy lunch digs. I'm no longer at home with these left-wing types.
- March 4, 1982. Lunch with Jaime Wheelock, one of the leaders of the Sandinistas. Not an ideologue, you can still talk with him. Bianca Jagger also there: almost emaciated, not pretty; what's attractive about her? The same day I go to the swearing-in for ultra-conservative James Theberge in the State Department's Ben Franklin room on the top floor. Great views, great food, a long ways from WOLA both politically and in the culinary sense. All the conservatives are here: Reich, Menges, Tambs, Bouchet, Fontaine. I don't much like either the left wing or the right wing nuts but as long as they feed me before I go home at night it's OK.
- Spring 1982. I run into a former student from U-Mass, a graduate of our Hotel and Restaurant Management School, currently working the front desk at one of Washington's prestige hotels. He tells me Chris Dodd is dating Bianca Jagger who stays there; she keeps him waiting and pacing in the lobby. No one keeps a U.S senator waiting! It's revealed that Bianca is an agent of the Sandinista government, while Chris is chair of the Senate Foreign Relations Committee's subcommittee on inter-American affairs holding hearings on Nicaragua—no conflict of interest here? Later I learn from Chris's brother Tom, with whom I co-teach a course on Central America at the Foreign Service Institute, that the Dodds had to call a family pow-wow where they forced Chris to give up Bianca for the sake of his career. Isn't Washington gossip wonderful?

- March 1982. Lunch with AEI President Bill Baroody and David Dana and Mario Garneiro of Brazilinvest, one of our BIG sponsors. Mario the CEO, very handsome in a Latin, Rudolph Valentino sort of way; Baroody's secretary swoons. They want us to put on a big, prestigious conference with the money they give us, using the gorgeous OAS building as a venue. They couldn't care less about the topics covered (my strengths), just so we get big, cabinet-level names as speakers. AEI, in contrast, wants to keep the money for other purposes and spend as little as possible on the conference. What an eye-opener this is for me on conference planning and money-raising. Brazilinvest gave us endless grief in setting up the conference; it's enormously time-consuming but eventually we bring it off—thank goodness for the AEI staff. Garneiro is later indicted in Brazil for tax evasion.
- March 5, 1982. I attend a session on U.S foreign policy at the Latin American Studies Association. That's a very left-wing group; to these people, centrists and moderates like Abe Lowenthal and me are viewed as far-right wing—"Reaganites." LASA is more sympathetic to the U.S.'s enemies than to the U.S.; when Sandinista Jaime Wheelock walks into the plenary session he gets a standing ovation. Abe and I try over the years, in vain as it turns out, to educate LASA in how to draft a resolution or write a position paper so that it actually has a positive effect on policy and is not simply dismissed as laughable.
- March 10, 1982. I meet with Evron Kirkpatrick (Jeane's husband) who tells me how policy on Latin America is made. First, it's all made in the White House. Second, it's made by a small coterie that includes Jeane, General Vernon Walters (a legendary figure who speaks seventeen languages and served with Brazilian forces in Europe in World War II), and General (ret.) Gordon Sumner who formed part of the ultra-conservative Group of Santa Fe. Third, they are the *only* persons whom Reagan listens to on Latin America. Fourth, the rest of the White House staff (Fontaine, Menges, Elliot Abrams, Col. Ollie North) are only implementers of the policy. Fifth, the State Department, National Security Administration, and Department of Defense are largely cut out; only the CIA director William Casey among the foreign policy agencies has direct access to Reagan.
- April 20, 1982. I'm off to Harvard (remember, it was the use of my Harvard stationary a year earlier that had been responsible for my getting the offer to go to Washington) to give a lecture on how Latin America policy gets made in the Reagan Administration. It's a homecoming of sorts; I had been at Harvard in 1979-81. It's a large crowd at the Center for International Affairs, and all my friends are there for the lecture: Jorge Domínguez, Larry Harrison, Joe Nye, James Cheek, Sam Huntington, Pedro Pick, Sally Shelton. The lecture goes well; it was in preparing for this lecture that I first formulated

both the thoughts on Latin America policy-making that follow in this chapter, and the comments on U.S foreign policy-making in general in the next chapter, which also formed the basis for my foreign policy textbook.

LATIN AMERICA'S PLACE IN U.S. POLICY

It's always nice as a scholar to study a place or issues that you think to be important. When I first started studying Latin America in the late-1950s, early 1960s—the Cuban Revolution, the Bay of Pigs, the Alliance for Progress, the Dominican Revolution, and U.S intervention—I thought Latin America was important, or was becoming more so. Furthermore, I had the naïve, graduate student belief that my writing about it—specifically in my case about the Dominican Revolution and U.S. military intervention, about which I'd written my doctoral dissertation and first books—would help make it important. That policy makers and the public would read my books and learn from them. How young and naïve I was in those days!

I'd already come to understand even in my academic career that was not how things worked. But when I went to Washington in 1981 and observed and participated in policy-making from the inside, whatever idealism I had about educating this country on Latin America quickly disappeared. My experience in Washington led me to be deeply cynical about the policy process. Perhaps at AEI I saw and experienced too much. I suppose, deep down, I still harbor a streak of that youthful idealism, but by now it's worn pretty thin. In fact the more I learned about Washington and the political process, the more cynical I became. At this stage in fact I've pretty much given up on expecting good, enlightened foreign policy out of Washington, from either party or any administration. I've largely abandoned my earlier quest for good government and good government policy; I've given up on the *ends* of policy but I still find the *process* of policy-making endlessly fascinating and amusing. Isn't that a sad commentary on the American political system!

What follows in this chapter, as presented preliminarily at the Harvard seminar, is an analysis of Latin America's place in U.S. foreign policy. I can't document all of this; the present account is based on the conclusions I reached as I roamed around Washington, went to all those receptions and dinner parties, spent time in all the foreign policy agencies, began to peel away the layers, and learned how the system operates behind the scenes and below the surface. This chapter provides in numbered form some of the conclusions I reached about Latin America; chapter 6 presents my conclusions about American foreign policy in general.

1. Latin America is seen as a peripheral area. From a U.S. national security point of view, Latin America ranks way behind Russia (formerly the Soviet Union), Western Europe (our NATO allies), East Asia, and the Middle East. Even when the Cold War came to Latin America in the form of the Cuban Revolution, the rise of Marxist guerrilla movements in the area, and the crisis in Central America, U.S. policy was still to treat it as peripheral to the main arena which was the conflict with the Soviet Union mainly in Germany and Central Europe. Hence the doctrine that applied to Latin America was "economy of force": keep it pacified but do not waste very many resources on it that would be better spent on the main action.

   The U.S. was interested in keeping Latin America as "our backyard," "our sphere of influence." Some 170 years after the Monroe Doctrine, it was viewed as a "special preserve" of the U.S., despite various academic writings that pronounced the Monroe Doctrine "dead." Latin America was seen as a rich source of raw materials for U.S. industry and as a ready market for U.S. manufactured goods; other nations (the Soviet Union was only the most recent of these) were warned to keep hands off "our" preserve. We would pacify, stabilize, and police the area; no one else should interfere. And when the crisis of the moment—now Central America—had disappeared, economy-of-force dictated that we would quickly turn our attention and resources elsewhere.
2. Latin America occupies a low priority in our foreign policy considerations. It ranks behind not only Russia, Europe, Japan, and the Middle East, but now also behind China and probably India, despite our being far more interdependent with Latin America on a host of issues—oil, natural gas, tourism, drugs, water supplies, investment, immigration—than any of these other areas. In the world's rating scheme of countries and continents, Latin America simply doesn't count for very much; we therefore assume we can take it for granted.
3. Latin America is viewed as a secondary or derivative area. This point is related to the previous two and reflects the area's low priority and lack of strategic importance. By secondary or derivative we mean that, given Latin America's low rating, it only achieves importance when it becomes a part of some bigger, larger issue. For example, the Cold War. In this sense Latin America becomes important not for its own sake or in its own right, but only when it is sucked up in some larger crisis like the Cold War. However even then it is viewed as a secondary front with the real battlefield terrain located elsewhere—i.e., along the Iron Curtain. Unfortunately for Latin America, in the current war on terrorism, given the absence of any serious terrorist threat stemming from the area, it is not even viewed

as a secondary or derivative area. Hence it receives almost no attention whatsoever. "Benign Neglect."

4. There are many prejudices about Latin America and Latin Americans, almost all of them negative. Latin Americans are often seen as volatile, unstable, disorganized, unable to govern themselves. U.S attitudes tend to be condescending and patronizing: Latin Americans are viewed like little children who must be educated in the ways of democracy and capitalism. As President Woodrow Wilson once said, before sending the Marines to Latin America once again, "We must teach them to elect good men."

   Latin America is seen as still primitive and uncivilized. Americans are perplexed as to why Latin America cannot achieve democracy and economic growth, as we did. Latin Americans are seen as frivolous, unstable, untrustworthy. They take too many *siestas*, they look "swarthy" and greasy, you would not want your daughter to marry one. They are Latin and Catholic, triggering an entire register of prejudices that hold sway in the "Anglo-Protestant" (Sam Huntington's phrase) United States. And because there are large numbers of Indians, blacks, mulattoes, and mestizos in Latin American society (we seldom see educated, sophisticated Latin Americans in the United States; because of immigration, we mainly see lower class—and darker—Latinos), there is racial prejudice—"greasers" is only one of the terms used—as well.

   These prejudices are extended to those who study the area as well. In one infamous declaration, Latin America was said to be "a second-rate area for second-rate minds." First-rate minds would presumably study Europe, Asia, or perhaps Russia, not Latin America. Some of this changed post-Castro during the course of the 1960s—but the earlier prejudices remained strong. In my own experience in Washington in the 1980s and 1990s, I frequently found the old prejudices alive and well in such Washington institutions as the State Department, Defense Department, White House, Council on Foreign Relations, and others. The question frequently asked me was, "Why would *you* (obviously a first-rate as distinct from second-rate mind!) study Latin America?"

5. The United States' primary interest in Latin America is stability. Stability is the *leit motif* of U.S. policy going back to the nineteenth century, seen as the best way of preserving U.S. interests in the area. Moreover, the underlying interest of stability is continuous, regardless of political party or administration. We may disagree over the means to achieve that goal but rarely over the policy itself. U.S. interest in stability helps explain our longtime support of authoritarian regimes in Latin America; our interest in economic development through the Alliance for Progress in the 1960s,

seen as creating a middle class that would be a bedrock of stability; and our emphasis on human rights, democracy, and civil society today, now viewed as the best way to achieve long-term stability as compared with the dictators we supported in the past. Stability, peace, pacification, the absence of threats to U.S. interests—these are the foundations of U.S. policy in Latin America, best achieved through the stabilization of the region. Note that this emphasis on stability also corresponds nicely with other features of U.S. policy toward the area: economy of force, the low priority afforded the region, our prejudices toward it, and so on.

6. Specialization in Latin America hurts your career. For several years I taught part-time at the Foreign Service Institute, the State Department's teaching arm. FSI provided training in language and area studies for the Defense Department, CIA, USIA, DEA, FBI, and other U.S. government personnel, as well as foreign service officers. On numerous occasions the students in these classes, all professional personnel and often mid-career, told me that their careers (promotions, salary, advancement) had been hurt by the fact that they had specialized in Latin America. If Latin America is indeed viewed as a "second-rate area for second-rate minds," one can see how being associated with that area, let alone specializing in it, could be damaging to your career.

   By about 1984-85, however, Central America was being considered a dangerous and a priority area. Word went out from the White House and the Secretary of State's office to funnel our best young FSOs into Central America. My students at FSI told me that for the first time their careers were not being hurt—and maybe advanced—by being assigned to Latin America. But that attitude ended as quickly as it had begun: as the Central American countries by the end of the 1980s achieved a modicum of peace and stability and through a peace process resolved their internal squabbles (and when Daniel Ortega and the Sandinistas were voted out of power in Nicaragua in 1990), Central America again was relegated to the back burner of U.S. foreign policy. And along with that, the prospect of being rewarded in your foreign service career by specializing in Latin America also evaporated.

7. Americans are uninterested in Latin America, except now as they perceive we have lost control of our borders and are being flooded with immigrants. But even with the immigration issue red hot, Americans are not interested in its causes or in understanding Latin America; all they want to do is build a fence and put up barriers to keep the illegals out.

   Americans have long harbored strong prejudices about Latin America—or plain indifference toward it. We view America as a successful society—economically, politically, and in other ways—but we see Latin America as unsuccessful. Latin America ranks low on our thermometer scale; and if it is so unstable, underdeveloped, and backward, what could we possibly learn from studying it? We don't mind sending it some aid to keep it pacified but we do not want to take it seriously. Former *New York Times* foreign affairs columnist James "Scotty" Reston summed it up neatly over forty years ago when he wrote, "The United States will do anything for Latin America except read about it."

8. Not only is the public uninterested but so are government officials. It is rare to have anyone at assistant secretary, undersecretary, or cabinet rank who is really interested in Latin America. The only one at high levels I can think of with an interest in the area in the last forty years is Jeane Kirkpatrick. More than that, she had Reagan's ear, and he was interested in Latin America. With my close connections to Jeane while she was UN ambassador, I learned how she went about influencing the president, other cabinet members, and the rest of the government. In contrast, when you have no one at high levels carrying water for Latin America, policy flounders, there is no coordination, and there is no one to champion the area before Congress or the media. President George W. Bush began with an interest in Latin America but largely abandoned that focus after 9/11.

At lower levels in the bureaucracy the situation is not much better. I found a handful of officials at CIA, the State Department, and at Defense who knew, had real expertise in, and served as advocates for the area. Often they were former academics who either failed to get tenure or preferred the policy world to the academic one. They told me of their battles against hostility or indifference within their own agencies. Alternatively what one often finds in these agencies at the country-desk or even office head levels are time-servers. These are people who have been assigned ("tasked" is the usual term) by their chiefs to deal with Latin American issues. They have no expertise in Latin America, no real interest in it, and with no need in their view to speak for the area. They are merely serving time, filling a post that needed filling, and hoping to move on soon to a better positions, one that better advances their careers. This is not the way to run a serious policy.

Secretary of State George Shultz told me once that he had to *fight* to keep the Middle East from consuming 100 percent of his time. So for him, Latin America was kind of a luxury, a way of avoiding the all-consuming issues of the Middle East. But not a good way to budget your time or decide policy priorities. His comment also tells you a lot about the relatively little attention, except sporadically, devoted to Latin America especially at high levels.

9. Latin America is viewed as comic opera. It is not taken seriously as a player on the world stage. It cannot govern itself or get its act together. None of its members are part of the G-8 or the Security Council. Neither Wall Street, nor investors, nor financial markets consider it a serious actor in global economics. Not one of its countries is in the top lists of economic achievers. In the *opera buffet* category, Latin America is popularly seen as only one step above Africa.

   Attitudes toward Latin America are shaped by *New Yorker* cartoons or old movies full of unacceptable stereotypes: comical, mustachioed men-on-horseback charging in and out of the presidential palace; peasants in big sombreros taking siestas under the banana trees; Carmen Miranda types dancing gaily with pineapples on their heads; John Wayne or Butch Cassidy and Sundance shooting hapless Indians; Woody Allen's *Bananas*, Charro babbling insanely in the TV ads for Geico, or Carlos and Gabriele in *Desperate Housewives* confirming every stereotype about Hispanics. Although we're too polite to use these terms publicly, most Americans still think of Latin America as consisting of irresponsible, unstable "banana republics."

10. A final point to make is that often Latin America does its best to conform to its own stereotypes. When there are coups in Bolivia, Ecuador, or Paraguay, the entire area is made to look like a bunch of banana republics. When Venezuelan President Hugo Chávez foams at the mouth and says and does irresponsible things, it makes it look like Latin America is still back in the era of nineteenth century *caudillo* (man-on-horseback) politics. Or when Bolivian President Evo Morales, who has perhaps less international experience then any other national leader in the world, tells us he wants to bring his country back to 1491 and reconstitute it on the basis of some pre-Columbian, fifteenth century, indigenous model, it makes Latin America look not only silly but disconnected from the modern, Western world.

    I saw this bias against Latin America numerous times in my Washington experience. No one takes the Organization of American States seriously as an international peacekeeping organization; as President Lyndon Johnson once famously said, "the OAS couldn't pour piss out of a boot." At the World Bank and International Monetary Fund, the economists look down on the companion Inter-American Development Bank as staffed with "third-rate economists and political hacks." When I went over to the Defense Department, I found that officials there thought of the Inter-American Defense Board and the Inter-American Defense College (located at Fort McNair) as a joke, and that a Latin America specialization as a military Foreign Affairs Officer (FAO) or assignment to

> SOUTHCOM (the Southern Command, then located in Panama) as a definite career-ender. Latin American countries, peoples, and institutions simply carry no credibility in Washington.

All these features make the carrying out of a long-term, credible, mature policy toward Latin America in Washington difficult at best, and perhaps impossible. Instead of decent policy you encounter prejudice, indifference, hostility, insuperable stereotypes. Worst of all is the sense that Latin America is unimportant, that it counts for little, that what happens there—except for some occasional dramatic events that often call forth U.S. military intervention—doesn't matter very much.

Such prejudices and stereotypes are all-pervasive. They detract from and get in the way of having good policy. In my years in Washington I found myself constantly running up against these barriers. Everyone knew, on a bipartisan basis, what a good policy on Central America, for example, ought to be: some foreign aid, lots of investment, some military pressure, lots of diplomacy, decent, middle-of-the-road governments, getting both the right wing and the left wing under control—but it was these prejudices, stereotypes, indifference, etc. (to say nothing of a lot of partisanship) that kept getting in the way. Time after time I had to butt my head against these walls to get anything done in a policy sense.

Eventually I tired of the battle. I got sick of butting my head up against those walls. At first I abandoned the naïve notion that by my writings I could not only influence policy but also educate the public and policy makers on Latin America. I discovered that the policy makers already knew what they wanted to do; all they wanted from me were rationalizations for what they'd already decided, not dissenting views or a one-man educational campaign. Over time I concluded that the stereotypes and prejudices about Latin America were too strong to be overcome.

Moreover, I concluded, sadly, that they would *never* be overcome, certainly not in my lifetime. And when you reach that conclusion, sad though it is, it's time to abandon the battle. Un-American though that is, that's the conclusion I reached: I gave up on ever seeing good policy on Latin America, and other regions as well, coming out of the U.S. government. And when you reach that conclusion, it's time to abandon the effort. You need to find a new area, a new issue, or a new job. And that's eventually what we did: abandoned Washington for a time, thoroughly disillusioned with policy outcomes or the ends of policy, but still finding the policy process itself endlessly fascinating.

Quite a number of my contemporaries, attracted like me to Latin American studies in the 1960s because it seemed an exciting area that might actually go somewhere, have similarly given up. Not just on U.S. policy, however, which forever seems hopeless, but also on Latin America itself. Chávez, Morales, the reversion to the past, and the abandonment of the Washington consensus—democracy, free trade, open markets—mean Latin America is going backward rather than forward. My colleague Riordan Roett, a Latin Americanist from the same era as I, has said that if he knew then what he knows now, he never would have become a Latin America scholar. I haven't quite reached that stage. But I'm very close to it. Which explains why in recent years I've spent more time in Europe and Asia than in Latin America. It's a sad story, but mainly it's sad for Latin America itself.

Chapter Six

Power and Policy-Making in Washington, D.C.: How Foreign Policy Gets Made

My journal notes indicate that within two months of coming to Washington in September 1981, I was already starting to formulate some general ideas and theories about how American foreign policy works.[1] These were not just random jottings and impressions—although my journals also have plenty of those—but more general and systematic propositions about the American foreign policy political process and how it works or, more often than is known, fails to work. These ideas and my notes about them ran contrary to much of my academic training in international relations and foreign policy; for me, now observing the process up close and firsthand, this was a real eye-opener. Welcome to Washington!

I had begun carrying a notebook regularly and regularly writing in it during my trip to Israel and Southern Europe (Greece, Italy, Spain, Portugal) in 1977. But at that time I still only used it to record foreign travel experiences. Then in 1979–1981 when I went to Harvard's Center for International Affairs (CFIA), I became so fascinated by what I was seeing and hearing that I began keeping a daily journal. Right from the beginning, therefore, when I went to Washington and AEI in 1981, I knew I was going to keep a detailed journal of those events as well. For at this stage I was at the center of the action on Latin America and other issues, and at a level that not very many academics attain. I saw and heard so much, and it was so interesting, that I felt I had to capture it all on paper.[2]

At first I had thought of my journal entries as a commentary only on Latin America policy-making, my specialty at AEI and the reason I was hired. But after my two years of retooling at Harvard as an international relations/foreign policy generalist, I quickly realized that what I was writing about the highly politicized and often misguided U.S. policy in Latin America was true in other areas as well and carried broader implications. The result was that while I continued to focus on Latin America and more specifically Central America in my everyday think tank work, I was already thinking of a larger project on U.S. foreign policy in general. Hence my writings at AEI in the early-to-mid-1980s were mostly on Latin America. But when I spent a nice year at George Washington University in 1987–88 teaching as a visiting professor of foreign policy, I used that opportunity to think generally about the growing problems of American foreign policy. The result was a two-volume set of books, the one focused on the *processes* of foreign policy-making and how it works, and the other, an edited volume on the main *issues* in U.S. foreign policy.

Because it focused so heavily on the domestic *politics* of foreign policy, the first book was criticized by some scholars as relying too little on what was happening "out there" in the world and too much on the domestic side. But that is what my insider Washington experience has taught me: it's *all* domestic politics. In the first edition of the book, written when Reagan was still president but published during Bush I, I said that 80 percent of American foreign policy was domestic politics driven. Then when Clinton was president and the second edition of the book came out,[3] I raised it to 90 percent!

FIRST IMPRESSIONS

I had been invited to Washington to direct AEI's Center for Hemispheric Studies; Latin America was my "job." My background and experience to that point had also been mainly focused on Latin America, although by this time I also knew a lot about Europe and the Middle East and I had just spent two intensive years at Harvard's Center for International Affairs under the tutelage of such foreign policy generalists and superstars as Samuel Huntington, John Montgomery, Joseph Nye, and Stanley Hoffmann. When I first went to Washington and started keeping a journal, my thought was that I would use that experience to write a book on American foreign policy toward Latin America. Hence my early journal entries from which this chapter derives focused mainly on Latin America. But over time I went beyond the Latin America focus and began to formulate broader ideas about American foreign policy in general.

By November 1981, I'd already been wined, dined, and immersed in the Washington social scene, mostly the foreign policy community. Here are some of the ideas I jotted down at the time, still concentrating on Latin America but already seeing the broader implications of what I wrote:

1. Latin America and other developing areas don't count for much in the Washington policy community. Even with the Central America crisis, it's

a low-priority area. Latin America is looked down on as backward and unable to govern itself. Not taken seriously. Africa even worse. Peripheral to U.S. key interests. A secondary area in the Cold War and viewed as a derivative region and through Cold War lenses: if and when the Cold War comes to Latin America (Cuba, Dominican Republic, Chile in earlier years; now El Salvador, Guatemala, Nicaragua), we pay it attention; absent the Cold War (or now terrorism—also absent), we ignore it and practice "benign neglect."

2. The Washington foreign policy-making community is quite small and close-knit (everyone knows everyone else and their background and expertise), numbering only in the hundreds and centered in the Washington meetings of the Council on Foreign Relations. Within these ranks are various subgroups: specialists in defense policy, arms control, or human rights policy, for instance; or with area specializations such as Asia, Europe, Africa, the Middle East, or Latin America. The community consists mainly of lawyers, government officials, congressmen and their staffs, some military officers, a few journalists, think tank personnel, a handful of academics; as described in chapter 4, they all go to each other's receptions. This "community" serves as the primary recruiting grounds for high-level foreign policy positions, with many of its members going in and out of government on several occasions.
3. Policy on almost all key issues is mainly made in the White House; the United States really *is* a presidential system. Congress plays a dissenting role but seldom leads on policy, mostly deferring to the president. But if policy is made in the White House, that's (1) where there's the *least* amount of expertise on the issue, and (2) where, because of electoral calculations, the issues are most politicized.
4. I was surprised to find how weak the State Department, which is supposed to be the lead agency, is on foreign policy. In addition to the fact it (mostly) follows the president's lead, State Department policy makers are often shunted aside in favor of powerful interest groups, the Pentagon, the CIA, the Treasury Department, and other agencies.
5. Arriving in Washington as a newcomer, I was a little surprised at the power of organized business. I'm here talking about trade associations, the Chamber of Commerce, the National Association of Manufacturers, business lobbies, individual CEOs and their reps, sugar industry reps, agri-industrial concerns, banks, other big business groups. Not only can these business groups far outgun organized labor but they also can outgun (more knowledge, more lawyers, more expertise, more money, more lobbying power, more White House connections) the State Department and most other federal agencies. The business of America really *is* business!

6. A variety of other groups also play into the political process: ethnic lobbies, universities and "old school ties," religious groups, single-cause groups (human rights, the environment, nuclear disarmament), local, regional, and state interests, etc.

   In my days at AEI, the group that bothered the neocons there most was WOLA, the Washington Office on Latin America. WOLA had little money, no Wall Street connections, no high-powered lobbyists, and no mass base. But it did have a strategic location across from Congress on Capitol Hill, an office in a complex owned by the Methodist Church there (even though WOLA was way to the left of most Methodists), and, most importantly, a group of current or former nuns, priests, and ministers who were adept at getting their pro-human rights and anti-Reagan Administration message across.

   These were persons who would never be caught dead on the streets in their nuns' habits or clerical collars, but when they testified before Congress *always* wore clerical garb and testified in the hushed tones of the confessional. And if you're a congressman with a religious constituency, who better to have before your committee than someone with the authority, sincerity, and wholesomeness of the clergy or the convent. I always got along well with these folks (former minister Joe Eldridge, former nun Heather Foote) and even invited them to AEI programs, but their presence at the Institute and, even more, their influence on the Democrat members of Congress, drove my Reaganite colleagues crazy.

7. One of the most interesting conclusions after my first four weeks in Washington, which sounds even more obvious now, is how scattered and fragmented power and policy-making in the United States are. Is power located in the White House, the Congress, the cabinet, Jeane's UN office, business and lobbying groups, think tanks like CSIS and AEI, or maybe all of these combined? Or, more likely, separately. And on each issue the lineup of forces would be different: AEI vs. WOLA on one issue, labor vs. business on others, State Department vs. Congress, White House vs. Congress, or different combinations or permutations depending on the politics and interests involved.

   Above all, I learned that power in Washington was not monolithic. It was diffused, constantly shifting, always being renegotiated. On some crucial strategic issues (in my time, the Cold War, Soviet relations, even Grenada; nowadays it would be the war on terrorism), the president could operate almost autonomously, above and beyond the usual Washington pluralism and jockeying for power; but on other issues including Central America, everything was up for grabs and everyone had their hands in the policy pie. And then all the incredible diversity and pluralism of the American political system would manifest itself.

8. Coming from outside of Washington, it was a little bit surprising to me how powerful the media had become. I had known this intellectually but now I was seeing it up close. At AEI we not only had our own television producer and programs (mainly C-SPAN) but there was also a concerted campaign to influence and get our ideas into the main network media. Some of my colleagues spent *hours* on the phone with reporters. AEI had, through its publications office, all kinds of connections through which our op-eds got published, all our events (seminars, guest speakers, book launches) were heavily covered by the media, and all of us scholars appeared on the evening news and talk shows regularly. I regularly briefed and was interviewed by reporters on Central America. It was obvious to us all that the media, especially television, was enormously influential, including on foreign policy.

   But most of the reporters I talked to, while often bright, were woefully ill-informed on foreign affairs issues, and particularly on Central America and other regional areas. Or else, like some of the *Washington Post* whose one-sided reporting almost single-handedly brought the Nicaraguan *Sadinistas* to power, they were so biased as to violate all my cannons of evenhandedness and professional responsibility. Almost all the journalists I knew were politically on the left and anti-Reagan; these impressions were confirmed by my colleague Robert Lichter whose careful research on "The Media Elite"[4] revealed that in the elite media in the United States, Democrats outnumber Republicans by ratios of ten or more to one.

   I would have media people call up and want to spend *hours* on the phone gathering background information; unlike my colleague Norm Ornstein who *would* spend hours on the phone with reporters, I didn't have the patience or time for this. My attitude on first coming to Washington was, if you're that ignorant on the issues you're covering, you should not be covering those issues—or else you should take my class.[5] But given the media's disproportionate influence, that is clearly the wrong attitude to have; in Washington you have to live with, cultivate, and suck up to the media whether you wish to or not.

9. The other institution whose influence I had underestimated is Congress. Most of us policy wonks tend to be dismissive of Congress especially on foreign policy and to concentrate our energies and influence on the executive branch (White House, NSC, State Department, Defense Department) where most decisions are made. The executive leads, the old saw goes, while the Congress reacts.

   In addition, with elections every two years, Congress is the most political and partisan branch of government. Aside from the foreign affairs, armed services, and intelligence committee members, most congressmen have little knowledge of or interest in international affairs—unless an issue like Vietnam, Central America, or now Iraq begins to affect their reelection possibilities. If the truth be known, most of us in the think tanks and on the executive side tend to see the Congress as "clowns," constantly interfering in our "rational" policy formulation on the basis of a profound lack of knowledge, narrow partisan interests, and short-term and parochial constituency interests and reelection calculations.

In my first few years in Washington, I testified before the Congress on three different occasions. All my worst fears were realized: the congressmen were poorly informed, the hearings were entirely partisan, witnesses (me) were expected to reinforce the political positions the congressmen had already reached, there was little room for nuance or a centrist, evenhanded approach. I came away so thoroughly disillusioned by the entire process, which on some occasions resembled a circus, that I vowed never to testify before Congress again.

At the same time, with all its limitations, Congress was tremendously powerful: it would (and did!) block Reagan Administration appointments, hold up funding (for the *Contras* or for aid to El Salvador), invoke the War Powers Act, hold embarrassing hearings on human rights progress (or the lack thereof) in El Salvador, and stymie Administration policy on dozens of fronts. Depending on your point of view, you could say either that Congress was able often to frustrate administration policy or that it brought a bad policy back to the political center. Whatever one's view on this issue, the *facts* are that Congress played a much bigger role in policy than I had previously thought, and its views need to be calculated into the equation whenever foreign policy is made.

10. My final early observation, according to my notes of November 1981, on Washington policy-making was this: with all this pluralism, diversity, and give-and-take, I'm not sure exactly where power in Washington lies. But I am sure it is *here*, in Washington. Only rarely can you influence it from the outside. Without knowing the actors personally and not being cognizant of the everyday shifts in power, politics, and personality, you cannot (here I'm thinking mostly of academics) hope to put your stamp on the policy process. Washington *is* the center, the hub of the wheel, where the action is. If you're seriously interested in influencing policy, you'd better be *in* Washington: full-time, year-round, all the time, for a considerable period. All of this was good advice for would-be policy wonks; discerning readers will know it was mainly aimed at myself and the big question I was then weighing: whether to stay at AEI and in the Washington policy world or go back to Amherst and the academic world. We stayed.

DEEPER ANALYSIS

The above represents some of my early impressions of Washington policy-making and how it works, written within three months or so of my arrival there. But as I stayed longer, I began to have a better and deeper understanding of the process in all its complexity. Over time and in my journal entries, I tried to capture these complexities; a couple years later, I wrote about all this in a textbook published first by Little Brown and in a second edition by Harper Collins. What follows are some of the insights that went into these books.

Bureaucratic Politics

The term "bureaucratic politics" refers to the fact that not just rival interest groups, president and Congress, or business and labor have competing interests that they wish to advance, but so do the big Washington bureaucracies: State and Defense, CIA and FBI. These agencies compete for budgets, personnel, and influence. At least three areas are involved.

The first is turf. All these agencies compete for money, influence, and power. They resent it when other agencies intrude on their turf. For example, the Defense Department now does foreign policy analysis that used to be the province of the State Department, the FBI does foreign intelligence that once was the preserve of the CIA, and the newly created Homeland Security Department seems to be poaching on nearly everyone's turf. All these rivalries create jealousies, bickering, and struggles for turf. I once had a high State Department official tell me that the real struggles in the world were not over the Cold War or the war on terrorism but between the State and Defense departments.

A second component, more complicated, is institutional. The fact is that State and Defense, CIA and FBI, Treasury and the Office of the Trade Representative (OTR) often have overlapping responsibilities. They both are assigned the same tasks and responsibilities. And, usually, legitimately so. So of course they bump up against each other, become rivals, defend their turf against others' incursions.

The third component is behavioral and cultural. Each of these agencies has its own culture, its own way of behaving and facing problems, its own Standard Operating Procedures (SOPs). For example, the Justice Department consists mostly of lawyers, so it approaches issues in an adversarial, legalistic way, while the State Department tends to pursue political compromise. The Defense Department is two-thirds military personnel (often southern, conservative, more religious) while State and CIA are usually better-educated and East Coast; they think differently! The same with Treasury and State: the former houses mainly economists while State has mostly historians, political scientists, and international affairs graduates. In all these agencies, I quickly discovered, the style of dress is different, the educational background is different, culture and behavior are different.[6] No wonder we have bureaucratic turf battles; no wonder American policy often goes several ways at once. And all of this is now made even more complicated by the creation of the Department of Homeland Security, the office of the so-called National Intelligence Czar, and greatly expanded Transportation Security Administration (TSA).

The Self-Aggrandizement Model

In the foreign policy/international relations literature, there are several models of decision-making. First is the "rational actor" model, the idea that policy makers are presented with policy options papers where all the consequences of the several options are spelled out, the decision maker weighs them carefully and "rationally," and makes his choices based solely on considerations of the national interest. The second is the bureaucratic politics model presented above, that the several Washington policy-making agencies have different, overlapping, but all quite legitimate tasks and responsibilities, and that these institutional factors affect both their behavior and the fact that they sometimes have turf battles and step on each other's toes. The third model, called organizational, relates to the internal culture, sociology, and behavior of these different agencies: State, CIA, Defense, Treasury, FBI, Justice, etc. All have different kinds of personnel; they think differently, and they therefore react and behave differently.

To these formulations I now added some models of my own. The first of these I called the "Self-Aggrandizement Model." The more I got to know quite a few congressmen, government officials, White House personnel, etc. on a close and personal basis, the more I became convinced that they were mainly in it *for themselves*. Just like the rest of us! They were looking out for Numero Uno: themselves. The language they used in their campaigns or job applications was always that of self-sacrifice and serving the public interest, since that is what got them elected or chosen. But I came to see this cynically as smokescreen for self-interest. For the fact is, Washington and its suburbs are wonderful places to live and work, the pay is excellent, the perks are grand, everyone seeks to do your bidding, you have power and prestige, lobbyists wine and dine you and throw money and trips your way, there are thousands of young and beautiful interns ("political groupies") who worship the ground on which you walk, and everyone pays you deference. You can't get any of that back in Peoria!

The attractiveness of a high Washington position, in Congress, the executive branch, or the think tanks, is best evidenced by the fact that no one ever leaves there. Even defeated politicians never leave D.C.; they stay on as lobbyists or ambassadors. So when you hear a congressman badmouthing the pay, saying he could do much better in the private sector, and threatening to step down, don't believe a word of it! They *love* it here and will *never* go back. Washington is the most powerful city in the most powerful country in the *world*. Who would want to give that up? No one! So keep in mind the "Wiarda model" of self-interest and self-aggrandizement: congressmen and others are mainly in it *for themselves*. Serving the public interest is often a by-product of serving the private interest of oneself. At best what we can hope for is that the public interest also gets served while the private interest is being pursued. Or as Washington likes to say, "you can do well [for yourself] while also doing good."

Partisanship above All Else

I first went to Washington armed with the political science literature, as well as my own notions, that party politics was in decline and partisanship was dead or dying. Worldwide, in Japan, Western Europe, and the U.S., voting turnout, party activism, and party politics were in retreat. When you ask people nowadays where their primary loyalties lie, it is to family, community, clan, neighborhood, country, ethnicity, or identity, not to party. The days when the party or the local machine did you favors, got you a job, bailed your kid out of jail, and, not incidentally, told you how to vote are pretty much gone.

But not so in Washington, D.C. Washington runs on partisanship. It is the *capital* of partisanship. Everything in Washington is based on partisanship. Jobs, positions, appointments, congressional testimony, think tank appointments, friends, colleagues, even "watering holes" and the parties you attend—all are decided on the basis of having the correct party loyalties.

I have to confess that I find most of the partisanship not just excessive but downright silly. Only lawyers (Congress is 70 percent lawyers) with their backgrounds in advocacy and taking up polarized positions could have produced a system like this. The issues become polarized, politicians are required to exaggerate and grandstand on behalf of the extremes, and moderate, centrist, workable, middle-of-the-road positions are squeezed out. In this atmosphere nothing gets done because the congressmen are too busy playing politics with the issues; compromise becomes next to impossible. Partisanship rules all.

As an academic, I am used to exploring all sides of a complex issue and then reaching a reasoned decision. I do not want to be pigeonholed in one category or another or with one party or the other. Arriving in Washington,

I was always uncomfortable with the partisan nature of the Central America and other debates. Over time I was able to overcome those barriers and now, if called upon, can deliver a rousing stump speech (on either side of the issue!) with the best of them. But I still don't like the partisan style and believe today's excessive partisanship is ruining the country and spoiling our ability to make decisions on major issues, not just foreign policy issues like Iraq but also health care, education, immigration reform, and social security.

It's all Domestic Politics

During most of the Cold War, we managed for the most part to keep domestic politics out of foreign policy considerations. Under the threat of 30,000 Soviet nuclear weapons ready to rain down upon us, the world was considered to be too dangerous a place to interject domestic politics, partisanship, and logrolling into considerations of international affairs. To quote the classic comment of my former senator from Michigan, Arthur Van Den Berg, "politics stops at the water's edge."

Most scholars of foreign policy and international relations understand that politics plays a role in foreign policy decisions; we also understand, intellectually, the case made by Graham Allison several decades ago that there are organizational and bureaucratic factors that play into decision-making as well as rational-actor choices. But deep in our hearts most scholars still believe in and prefer the rational-actor model. Why? First, the rational-actor model is neater, easier, and more amenable to logical calculation (if you choose this option, that follows; if another option, something else happens). Second, in the absence of knowing all the political, organizational, and bureaucratic factors that play on decisions, scholars are more comfortable with the rational actor model because that is the field they know cold.

I shared that view when I first went to Washington. I knew the other explanations intellectually but I still preferred to think decisions ought to be made according to the rational-actor system, by the listing of a variety of foreign policy options and then the careful weighing of the pros and cons of each one. Imagine my surprise then when, upon going to Washington, I discovered it was *all* domestic politics. My former colleague at U-Mass, David Mayhew, now at Yale, demonstrated empirically that when you hold all other factors constant—religion, gender, party, region of the country, rural or urban, etc.—the one factor that explained congressional voting behavior better than any other was: the desire to be reelected.[7] My own experience on Central America and other issues confirmed this finding: it was *all* about partisanship, no one was interested in the nuances of Central America, the *only* interest congressmen had in the issue was to gain partisan advantage from it. White House political operatives thought the same way.

When in the late 1980s I wrote my book about American foreign policy, I estimated that 80 percent of our foreign policy was driven by domestic political considerations, and only about 20 percent by what was happening "out there" in the real world. Then, when the consummate politician Bill Clinton was occupying the presidency and the second edition of the book came out, I raised it to 90 percent. With George W. Bush and Karl Rove in charge of foreign policy, I would raise it again, to 95 percent. Partisanship governs everything, to the detriment of good foreign policy *and* to the consternation of the public which clearly wants nonpartisan problem-solving in both foreign and domestic policy.

Bureaucratic Politics Revisited

Most of us are familiar with Graham Allison's contribution to our understanding of foreign policy decision-making.[8] He demonstrated through study of the 1962 Cuban missile crisis that decisions were made not just on the basis of the rational-actor model. Instead, turf battles between agencies were involved, the agencies had different internal political cultures, their standard operating procedures (SOPs) were different, and they had (State vs. Defense, for example) distinct responsibilities, which caused them to respond in different ways.

My own contribution to the bureaucratic politics literature was to expand on the Allison analysis. For by the late-1980s when I was writing my book, globalization was already occurring and "everything"—trade, business, industry—had become international. That brought such hitherto primarily domestic agencies as the Commerce Department, Agriculture Department, and Environmental Protection Agency into the foreign policy mix, and added new actors to the bureaucratic politics rough and tumble. Then, after the Cold War ended and American policy in the 1990s concentrated much more on international *economic* policy, the Treasury Department, the Office of the Trade Representative, and other primarily economic agencies got into the act. As immigration also swelled in the 1990s, the Justice Department (Immigration and Naturalization Service) got involved. In other words, as U.S. foreign policy priorities shifted and as trade and international economic relations after the Cold War replaced diplomatic and security relations for a time, all the agencies responsible for these new programs joined State, DOD, and CIA as major foreign policy actors.[9]

More recently, with the war on terrorism, the web of agencies involved in the bureaucratic politics of foreign policy making has both shifted and expanded. Now, in addition to the agencies already mentioned, the FBI,

Energy Department, Transportation Department, and of course the Department of Homeland Security have all assumed new or greater importance. And again, these agencies compete for turf, budgets, and influence with the older foreign policy agencies. The rise of these new agencies not only makes foreign policy more complicated, but it also adds to the stalemate, gridlock, and paralysis within the U.S. government. Despite repeated efforts to get all these agencies to cooperate and work together, the 9/11 Commission revealed that U.S. policy is as uncoordinated, as disorganized, and as divided as ever. Bureaucratic politics is not just a continuing problem; it is getting worse.

The Complexity of It All

Maybe I was naïve to begin with but before going to Washington I had a fairly simple idea of foreign policy. The President and his NSC led; Congress checked and balanced; State, Defense and CIA were the major actors, and some interest groups (big business, big labor) were involved; think tankers and academics offered advice. That was pretty much it.

But once in Washington, it took me only a few weeks to figure out the incredible complexity of the system. Among my early realizations:

1. There are *thousands* of interest groups involved, not just two or three. Maybe upwards of 40,000.
2. On each issue the lineup and coalitions of interests shifted: the groups that were interested in Latin America policy were not the same as those involved in Middle East policy.
3. How personalistic it all was: everyone on a particular issue knew everyone else on a personal basis.
4. There were layers upon layers of complexity. How, where, and when to plug into the system? It was an art form that took years and years to master. I doubt if anyone really understands it all.

CONCLUSION

Within two months of my going to Washington, I had already learned that foreign policy was not carried out the way I had been taught in the academic literature, and I was already beginning to formulate some more general ideas about the foreign policy process. Mainly I learned how intensely political and politicized it all was; careful and "rational" calculations had little to do with how the issues were seen. Instead, everything had to do with denouncing the administration (Reagan's) in power and seeking partisan advantage for the Democrats. Of course the political operatives in the White House did exactly the same thing: seeking to discredit the opposition Democrats and enhance the Republican position. It was all a big game; the trouble was, there were lots of victims (in Central America) of these games.

Over the years I spent in Washington, I became more knowledgeable about and understanding of how the "game" worked. I advanced my knowledge. Over time, as I contemplated a textbook on these themes, I began to formulate some more general and theoretical propositions about American foreign policy. My contributions included an elaboration of the bureaucratic politico model, an emphasis on the complexity and constantly shifting actors in the process, the overwhelming influence of domestic political considerations in foreign policy, and the addition of *two* new "models" of my own: what I came to call the "self-aggrandizement" model (looking out for Number One—oneself) and the "political process" (election and reelection calculations) model. Eventually I turned my notes and jottings on all these ideas and experiences into two major books on U.S. foreign policy.

I also began to turn cynical in the process. Maybe I had seen and experienced too much. But it sure was a fun ride. While expanding my knowledge on foreign policy, however, we also had to turn our attention to internal developments at AEI.

NOTES

1. Howard J. Wiarda, *Foreign Policy without Illusion* (Glenview, IL: Scott, Foresman / Little Brown, 1990); Wiarda (ed.), *On the Agenda: Current Issues and Conflicts in U.S. Foreign Policy* (Glenview, IL: Scott, Foresman / Little Brown, 1990).

2. As indicated in chapter 4, I was invited to White House briefings, mainly on Central America, about once a week. At first my reaction at these briefings, which were often ludicrous and full of misstatements, was to cover my eyes with my hands in a gesture of disbelief, whispering to myself, "I don't believe what I'm hearing, I don't believe what I'm hearing." But I quickly overcame that reaction and started writing furiously, trying to jot down everything. The result is that my notes contain the unvarnished comments of such Reagan luminaries as Ed Meese, Jeane Kirkpatrick, Constantine Menges, Fred Iklé, Ollie North, and even President Reagan himself in an off-the-record forum in which my notes may be the only records of these meetings.

3. Howard J. Wiarda, *American Foreign Policy: Actors and Processes* (New York: Harper Collins, 1996).

4. Robert Lichter et al., *The Media Elite* (Bethseda, MD: Adler and Adler, 1986).

5. In the interest of truth in packaging, I have to confess that as an undergraduate at the University of Michigan I once flirted with the idea of becoming a journalism

major. But then a dean, James Robertson, who more than once gave me life-altering good advice, said, "Howard, instead of journalism you should major in something substantive (history, political science) because you can always pick up journalism on the side by writing it or working for *The Michigan Daily*—sound advice that I took to heart.

6. The author's comments in these regards are informed by the fact that he has worked for both the State and Defense departments, was a consultant for the CIA, and has visited or lectured at the other agencies listed. What a *world* of difference there is between what we'll call the internal "political culture" of all these agencies.

7. David Mayhew, *Congress: The Electoral Connection* (New Haven, CT: Yale University Press, 1974).

8. Graham Allison, *Essence of Decision* (Boston, MA: Little Brown, 1971).

9. I used to tell my students interested in foreign policy careers, don't apply just to the State Department or CIA. In addition, apply to the international divisions of Commerce, Treasury, EPA, etc. In short, go where the money is, to those agencies whose budgets were increasing, who were hiring, and who offered better opportunities for rapid career advancement.

Chapter Seven

The Democracy Initiative in American Foreign Policy

Like the seasons, foreign policy issues and the panaceas set forth to solve them tend in Washington to come and go very rapidly. One day (or week) it's Lebanon, the next North Korea, then Iraq, Iran, Afghanistan, Israel, South Africa, terrorism, Cuba. Foreign policy follows the headlines and the television news; Washington's attention span is usually very short-lived. I quickly learned that long-range planning in Washington is an oxymoron; what Washington politicians mean by "long-range planning" is until the next election, when everything changes again.

The solutions we offer have a similarly short life expectancy. One day it's agrarian reform as the key to solving the problems of the Third World, next it's community development, then, in rapid succession, family planning, basic human needs, human rights, privatization and state downsizing, sustainable development, transparency, foreign direct investment, governance, the millennium challenge account.

Among the most recent of these cure-alls is democratization. Actually, the United States has long waxed hot and cold on democracy programs, supporting them at some times, ignoring them at others. Democracy nowadays is seen as the solution for all the world's problems, good not only for the countries that undergo a transition to it but also a magic formula for U.S. foreign policy. The promotion of democracy not only makes us feel good in a moral and ethical sense but it also solves, we believe, the problems of instability, failed states, and terrorism in other countries. An added bonus is that standing for democracy gets the Congress, the media, the public, both parties, and even our erstwhile allies to support the policy.

There is nothing intrinsically wrong with any of these programs; I could be persuaded, in the right circumstances, to support any or even all of them.

Who, after all, could be opposed to democracy and human rights? The problem is not with these programs per se; rather, the problems lie in our inconsistency in supporting them, the boom 'n' bust nature of our commitments, the fickleness and partisanship of the policy process, American ethnocentrism (viewing other countries through the rose-colored glasses of our own experience), our missionary zeal in proselytizing for them, and perhaps above all the naïve, simplistic American view that U.S.-style democracy, human rights, *et al.* are the right formula for all peoples at all times. Such a view is based on faith, not reality; yet the attractiveness for both moral and political reasons of the democracy agenda is such that no American administration can resist its siren call.

The United States cannot simply export its institutions to other countries where the history, culture, and sociopolitical traditions and structures are entirely different. It cannot and will not work. Not only will it not work but also it often produces the result to boot of destroying the basis for stability and functionality of the traditional institutions in the country affected. That leaves the country in the worst of all possible worlds: neither the stability of a consolidated democracy, nor the stability of a traditional regime, but with all the possibilities for fragmentation and breakdown of a country in the "gray area" of confusion and transition. Read Iraq or Afghanistan.

How did we get in such a mess? This chapter endeavors to explain.

ORIGINS AND BACKGROUND

The United States has, in a sense, always had a pro-democracy foreign policy. We perceive ourselves to be "the exceptional nation," a "beacon on a hill," the "first universal nation," whose revolution in 1776 inspired a global desire for freedom and democracy. The founding fathers certainly believed that American values were applicable everywhere, and when we took Texas and the Southwest from Mexico in the 1830s–40s, or Cuba and the Philippines from Spain in 1898, we believed we were doing so to bring justice and enlightenment to these benighted lands. The pro-democracy, self-determination, Wilsonian tradition in foreign policy is now nearly a hundred years old, carried on in Jimmy Carter's campaign for human rights, Ronald Reagan's democracy initiative, and the Bush I, Clinton, and Bush II administrations. The defense of democracy, however unevenly applied at times, is not something new in American foreign policy.

More immediately, a number of other factors came together in the late-1970s and early-1980s to help make the climate propitious for Reagan's democracy initiative, the subject of this chapter. For example, at AEI, a number of those members of the Coalition for a Democratic Majority (CDM-longtime-

Democrats who believed in a strong defense and foreign policy, a number of whom would soon become leading neocons)—Jeane Kirkpatrick, Jim Wright, Ben Wattenberg, Austin Ranney, myself—argued that we should take the offensive against the Soviet Union by emphasizing freedom and democracy, and not just MADD (Mutually Assured Destruction) or containment. Second, the AFL-CIO was already pushing a pro-democracy foreign policy agenda. Third, after Jimmy Carter's human rights campaigns, there were quite a number of activists and groups in Washington that advocated a pro-democracy campaign, in contrast to the earlier "realist" Kissinger foreign policy.

When I arrived at AEI in the late spring of 1981, the debate was already under way and heated. I have to confess I'm generally closer to the Kissinger realist than to the McGovern-Carter idealist school; I get uncomfortable when the U.S. goes off on an unrealistic missionary crusade to change the world. And one of my first publications at AEI was an edited volume criticizing Carter's human rights policy.[1] But I learned quickly that in the United States of America one cannot follow a completely realist foreign policy. In this country you cannot ignore the plight of blacks under apartheid in South Africa, of Jews and Baptists in the Soviet Union who want to emigrate (addressed through the Jackson-Vanick amendment, one of the first pieces of U.S. legislation with an explicitly human rights purpose), or of nuns and peasants in El Salvador who are raped, brutalized, and murdered by an oppressive military regime. In *America* at least, you need to find a way to combine realist policies with high moral purpose. Incidentally, when I worked for him on the Kissinger Commission on Central America (see next chapter), this is one of the things we had to convince Henry of: even if you're a realist, you had to see human rights in Central America as part of a realist position; human rights could not simply be ignored.

My conversion in this regard was parallel to that going on within the Reagan Administration. Almost everyone at AEI and in the Reagan Administration had been against Carter's human rights policy because it was un-evenhanded and ignored the Soviet Union, undermined authoritarian regimes that were anti-communist and friendly to us (the Shah, Somoza), and led to regimes (Khomeini and the Islamic fundamentalists, the Sandinistas) that were even worse from both a democracy and a U.S. policy point of view. Recall that Ernest Lefevre, Reagan's first nominee for the position of assistant secretary of state for human rights, while not *at* AEI, was a friend of and worked closely *with* AEI, promised if confirmed to abolish the position for which he was being considered. Lefevre had to withdraw his name from consideration; that defeat also marked the beginning of the Administration's (and AEI's) turnabout on the issue.[2] As Jeane K. said to me about this time, "What are we as a nation if we don't stand for democracy and human rights?"

The immediate impetus for a new foreign policy emphasis stressing democracy came over El Salvador. That poor, deeply divided country had recently been torn by revolution, repression, and civil war. The main contending forces appeared to be the Marxist guerrillas and a brutal, repressive military; the country had polarized, and the political center was all but squeezed out of existence. But neither of the main actors were satisfactory to the U.S.; at the height of the Cold War we could not allow Marxist-Leninist guerrillas to take power, while the rape and killing of the nuns and the killing of priests and peasants made it impossible domestically to support the military. What to do? Democracy was the answer.

At AEI the chief democracy advocate was Howard Penniman, backed strongly by Mike Novak, Ben Wattenberg, Austin Ranney, and Jeane and Evron (Kirk) Kirkpatrick, the Pennimans' best friends. Howard was not only a scholar of democracy, an expert on electoral processes, and editor of the well-known "Democracy at the Polls" book series, he was also a democracy enthusiast. He, Kirk, and Austin could talk for hours about the most arcane aspects of elections anywhere in the world.

Though he didn't know much about Latin America, Howard was a strong advocate of democracy in El Salvador. He took this stand first and foremost because he believed steadfastly in it. But he also believed that democratic elections would allow the center to reemerge, would isolate the extremes, would produce a reformist but middle-of-the-road government, and would thus help reduce the tension, the polarization, and the violence. And that is precisely what Penniman did over the next three years, producing first local, then parliamentary or constituent assembly, and finally presidential elections that in 1985 brought Christian-Democrat reformer José Napoleon Duarte to power. Penniman deserves credit as a heroic figure; he more than anyone saved our policy chestnuts in El Salvador.

As the resident expert on Latin America and director of AEI's Hemispheric Studies Program, I was deeply involved in all these activities. But I was a skeptic: I didn't believe the United States could engineer democracy in El Salvador. Or that El Salvador was prepared for or wanted democracy all that much. I recall numerous meetings at AEI and several heated and semi-heated exchanges with Penniman, Novak, and Wattenberg—to the extent that I was eventually shut out of some of the planning meetings and not brought along on some of the election observation trips. I thought I knew El Salvador: its violence, its rigid two-class and caste system, its underdevelopment, and its political culture of elitism and authoritarianism. I was not favorable to the military regime but I didn't think democracy would take root there; I favored something akin to the Mexican civilian-controlled, one-party, corporatist system. That I thought had a chance; U.S.-style democracy did not.

In March 1982, Penniman reported on his first trip to El Salvador on behalf of the democracy/elections agenda. By this time the war in El Salvador was becoming a major domestic issue; the room was full of reporters. I served as host, introduced Penniman, and let him hold forth. It was interesting that he spoke on the narrowest and most technical of issues—arcane things like the mechanics of voter registration, the type of ballots to be used, the issuance of voter identifications cards. Meanwhile I was interested more in the grand, cosmic issues: does El Salvador really want elections, does it want democracy, what are the purposes of elections in this context, can its social structure and political culture be supportive of democracy, what if democracy produces the wrong outcome? But I kept these concerns to myself; in retrospect, it's likely Penniman was correct to speak only on the technical issues and leave these other, grand philosophical issues, which are probably unanswerable, unaddressed.

But I do need to reproduce some of my journal notes from this event (Vol. III, pp. 49–50) because they shed light on future, even more intense debates over this issue. On March 31, the day of Penniman's press conference, I wrote:

> One of these days I ought to drop my bombshell: not only is Latin America not democratic but it may not want to be! This town [Washington] isn't ready for that yet. It's amazing to me how *everyone* accepts the legitimacy of democracy and assumes that everyone wants to be just like we are. The notion needs to be challenged but in Washington that would go over like a lead balloon.[3]

That same spring of 1982, I became aware that Jeane, Kirk, Penniman, Novak, Wattenberg, and probably others were working on President Reagan to get him to launch a major, global democracy initiative. The first El Salvador election had gone so well and shown such promise of producing a democratic center that the "democracy true believers," as I came to call them, wanted to expand it to other difficult countries: Guatemala, Poland and Eastern Europe, even the Soviet Union. It helped their cause that the oppositionist Solidarity Movement in Poland was gaining strength at this time and that the Polish pope, John XXIII, was involved. The impetus also came from Congressional Democrats, mostly those in the Coalition for a Democratic Majority, including Speaker of the House Jim Wright and Senators Sam Nunn and Scoop Jackson. Reagan was attracted by the idea that a democracy initiative would give added legitimacy to his administration and that it could garner bipartisan support.

We also discovered that, independently from AEI, other prominent groups and individuals were working on a democracy initiative. Many of these were then brought in to the Kirkpatrick-Penniman-AEI-CDM group. These included Congressman Dante Fascell of Florida; the AFL-CIO's President Lane Kirkland; Bill Brock, who was then chairman of the Republican National

Committee; and Charles Manatt, the former chairman of the Democratic National Committee. These were the big guns; at lower levels the activists with whom we were involved included Eugenia Kemble of the Free Trade Union Institute; Keith Scheutte, then an aide to Secretary of State Al Haig; political scientist George Agree; historian Allen Weinstein; Chamber of Commerce official Mike Samuels; Fascell aide Spencer Oliver; and CIA official Constantine Menges. These were, it hardly needs saying, the advocates of a center-right democracy initiative; out there on the left, veterans of the Carter Administration and the anti-war lefties from the Vietnam era were formulating their own version, heavily laden with peacenik, anti-war, anti-Reagan rhetoric, of a democracy initiative.

While there was diverse support for the democracy initiative throughout the government and among private groups, the key was to get Reagan to sign on and lead it. Here Jeane Kirkpatrick played the key role. In the spring of 1982 she met with and pulled together the leading actors mentioned above. She also met with the Reagan staff, the so-called "troika" consisting of Michael Deaver, Ed Meese, and James Baker. In pushing this agenda she had to overcome the opposition of Al Haig, Henry Kissinger, and the "realists" (me included). She then met with the president; remember, she was one of the few people Reagan listened to on foreign affairs. Out of these meetings a plan and a presidential speech began to emerge.

The speech was delivered as an address to the British Parliament (the "mother of all parliaments"; what better place for a speech on democracy) on June 8, 1982. It was a stirring speech, among the most important of the Reagan presidency. Prime Minister Margaret Thatcher was in attendance and had welcomed Reagan to London, even though she had told us privately that she was not in favor of a democracy crusade that overthrew existing governments. However she did see its usefulness in the Cold War as a way of putting added pressure on the Soviet Union.

Reagan said:

> The objective I propose is quite simple to state: to foster the infrastructure of democracy, the system of a free press, unions, political parties, universities, which allows a free people to choose their own way to develop their own culture and to reconcile their own differences though peaceful means.

He went on:

> This is not cultural imperialism; it is providing the means for genuine self-determination and protection for diversity. Democracy already flourishes in countries with very different cultures and historical experiences. It would be cultural condescension, or worse, to say that any people prefer dictatorship to democ-

> racy. Who would voluntarily choose not to have the right to vote, decide to purchase government propaganda handouts instead of independent newspapers, prefer government to worker-controlled unions, opt for land to be owned by the state instead of those who till it, want government repression instead of religious liberty, a single party instead of free choice, a rigid cultural orthodoxy instead of democratic tolerance and diversity?[4]

Reagan then announced that a "bipartisan foundation" was being established to study "how the United States can best contribute as a nation to the global campaign for democracy now gathering force." He said further that he intended to use the "recommendations of a panel of political leaders" that he had appointed "in the common task of strengthening democracy throughout the world." You can probably guess that the "bipartisan foundation" and the "panel of political leaders" consisted of all the people (and AEI members or friends) previously mentioned: Fascell, Kirkland, Brock, Manatt, Jeane, Scheutte, Agree, Weinstein, etc. Agree, a political scientist, whose career had been mainly that of a political operative, was named to head the new "foundation."

A few weeks after Reagan's path-breaking speech, on July 22, 1982, we all met with Agree over lunch at AEI. The lunch was organized by AEI political parties specialist Michael Malbin and included all the colleagues who were players in this campaign: Novak, Penniman, Kirk, Wattenberg, constitutional law specialist Walter Berns, Bob Goldwin, myself. Agree's job was to drum up support for the proposal not just at AEI but among other think tanks, foundations, and interest groups. What he had to say was very disturbing to me; among the persons gathered, I'm sure I was the one most skeptical of the entire proposal.

Agree talked initially of the goals of the program: democracy, elections, free societies. Nothing new here. But then he went on to speak of the program's politics. Because of the need for bipartisan support, both political parties had to be involved. They would both create new international branches designed to promote democracy abroad, rather like the German political party "foundations" devoted to international affairs. However there was no appreciation of the fact that German political parties are very different from American parties and that they have long played a far more extensive international role. Involvement of the two main U.S. parties also meant the program would be politicized in unacceptable ways. In any case, this is how the National Democratic Institute (NDI) and the International Republican Institute (IRI) were constituted.

Next Agree told us that it was necessary, again for political purposes, that both the AFL-CIO and the Chamber of Commerce be involved. For the Chamber, this was a new and unprecedented venture; the Chamber's interest in this program was not so much democracy per se but in helping to improve the climate for business and U.S. investment abroad. The AFL-CIO was a different story; it had long been enlisted in efforts during the Cold War (still on at this time) to assist anti-communist trade unions abroad. Unfortunately when it was revealed the funds for that program came almost exclusively from the CIA, the program was discredited and came crashing down. The AFL-CIO therefore saw this proposal as a way to refill its coffers and stimulate its activities using overt, congressionally mandated funds instead of covert. For the democracy program advocates, however, the support of the Chamber and the AFL-CIO, as well as the political parties, was necessary to get the proposal through Congress.

A third problem I saw in Agree's comments was that it was exclusively a U.S. formulation. No effort had been made to that point to solicit the views of foreign interests, not foreign governments or political parties or democracy advocates. No one had asked any Third World countries if they really wanted democracy, how strongly they wanted it, whether other interests (stability, development, social and political peace and order) were involved, whether they wanted it in precisely U.S. form, or if they wanted the U.S. parties, the AFL-CIO, and the U.S. Chamber of Commerce involved in their internal affairs. It was immediately obvious to me (and I later wrote about that)[5] that the democracy initiative would, for good or ill, be a close reflection of the U.S. political system; whether that was appropriate or functional in other countries was another matter.

One final point deserves raising. It was plain to me in that gathering that the democracy project was ultimately aimed at the Soviet Union. It was a Cold War policy. Poland and its communist oppositionist Solidarity Movement were already in the headlines; Mike Novak told us he was in touch with the Vatican to coordinate policy between Washington and the Holy See. But the neocons had a bigger project in mind: they wanted to undermine not only Marxist-Leninist regimes in Eastern Europe but also the Soviet Union. They believed that pushing for democracy there could undermine communism and end the Cold War. They now had an unexpected ally in President Reagan. In this they were correct: the democracy initiative *did* help undermine communist regimes in Eastern Europe and added one more pressure point on top of many others to the Soviets' problems. The problem would come twenty years later when they tried to carry this same formula—a romantic view of democracy coupled with American military might—over to Iraq and Afghanistan.

Agree quickly responded to my comments. He said the U.S. political parties had to be involved because otherwise the program would not get through Congress; their newly envisioned international institutes had to be part of the package because certain key congressmen viewed these not just as agencies of democracy but as expanding their patronage opportunities. As to the AFL-CIO and Chamber of Commerce, he said their involvement was also necessary to get congressional support and to drum up a domestic lobbying campaign. So, interestingly, the structure of the new international democracy project was in large part about domestic politics. As for the idea of other countries possibly having their own route to democracy, Agree responded that he was convinced that in two hundred years *all* countries would be democratic. He might be right but how could you ever prove otherwise? And two *hundred* years? That's a long time for a sustained U.S. policy in Iraq or Afghanistan.

To most of the others around the table, mostly trained as American politics specialists, the issues I raised were quickly dismissed. Perhaps as a foretaste of what the neocons believed about and pushed for in Iraq, those gathered at AEI simply assumed that, if given a choice, all peoples would opt for democracy. And that American power should be applied to achieve it. Moreover, it was a democracy that necessarily would closely resemble the U.S., or how they imagined a generally idealized American democracy to be. Bob Goldwin, Mike Novak, Walter Berns, and others in the room simply assumed the model would be U.S. democracy. No other model was conceivable. They were dismissive of my more relativistic concerns. Fortunately I had another important, overlapping meeting (on Argentina's invasion of the Falklands) across town that afternoon and had to leave the AEI gathering early, before the exchange became even more heated.

In the fall of 1982 the Agency for International Development (AID) put up $400,000 in seed money to fund the Democracy Program. It also had the endorsement of the Reagan Administration. On its initial board sat most of the initial founders: Agree, Brock, Fascell, Kirkland, and Samuels. Weinstein was named Program director, though he was passed over for the presidency when it was converted into the National Endowment for Democracy. Agree also left the Program over the course of the next year when he saw the direction it was going: less ideological and more pragmatic. Nevertheless all these persons did yeoman service in lobbying Congress, think tanks, the White House, and AFL-CIO and the Chamber of Commerce to support the program.

The biggest, splashiest event in this campaign was a joint AEI-White House conference on democratic elections held on November 4–5, 1982, also sponsored by AID. Penniman, Kirk, Jeane—all the AEI team—were the chief organizers. At my suggestion they invited my old graduate student mentor Harry Kantor, a strong advocate for Latin American democracy from the University of Florida, and Luis Alberto Monge, president of Costa Rica, to be the keynote speaker. Most of the conference sessions were held at AEI or the nearby Mayflower Hotel; as often in Washington, these panels were a mixed bag, meant more to rally political support and give all the stakeholders a chance to state their positions than to provide enlightenment on complex issues. Intellectually they were not up to the level of the American Political Science Association or the International Studies Association. The hard bargaining over the shape and future direction of the Democracy Program went on behind closed doors.

The high point of the conference was a lunch at the White House hosted by President Reagan. This was my first White House lunch, a chance to rub shoulders with the high and mighty. First there was a reception in the West Room attended by a bevy of White House military aides and a military orchestra playing chamber music. Then a receiving line to greet Presidents Monge and Reagan—I still have a picture on my wall from this event, of Reagan; Monge; Selwa Roosevelt, the White House protocol chief; and me.

This was the first time I'd greeted Reagan up close and face-to-face. He looked very young and in good shape for his 71 years. The midterm elections had occurred only two days earlier, on November 2, in which the Republicans had suffered a stinging defeat; that plus his age had already gotten people speculating, including me as a political scientist, that Reagan probably wouldn't run again in 1984. But seeing him in person, so young-looking, so animated, and obviously (or else he's a very good actor) so enjoying the job, I now thought it likely he *would* run again.

We moved on to lunch in the East Room. Monge spoke eloquently about democracy and the dangers of dictatorships on both the left and the right, but in this room he was obviously speaking to the choir. The table service in the White House was about at the level of a good hotel—good but nothing special. Unfortunately the chicken served was not quite done all the way through; there's nothing worse than uncooked chicken. And I saw no sign of Nancy Reagan's new, very expensive, and, for that reason, very controversial china, a hot topic at that time. But I shouldn't complain; after all, I don't get invited to the White House for lunch with the president every day.

At Washington events like this you meet a much greater variety of people than you do at an academic conference or a professional association meeting. Most of those invited were there to help drum up support for the Democracy Program, including labor leaders, journalists, Chamber of Commerce representatives, congressmen, and the political party officials who were expecting to head the new Republican and Democrat international affairs branches. I met for the first time Ergun Obuzden, a Turkish political scientist with whom I was cooperating on a transitions-to-democracy project, and Arendt Lipjardt, a Dutch political scientist well known for his writings on democracy and consociationalism. Also incongruously present (but then this is Washington and that's how things work) were two Nigerian tribal chiefs dressed in native costumes who were reported to have expressed support for democracy.

A short while later another, closely related, AEI-hosted conference was held, this one on constitution writing. It was intended as a way to assist countries in transition to democracy with the writing of new, democratic constitutions. The main AEI participants in this conference were Bob Goldwin, Walter Berns, Bill Schambra, and Art Kaufman, all of AEI's Constitutionalism project and all neocons; but Penniman, Austin Ranney, and I as a comparative politics specialist were also involved. The conference brought together leading constitutional lawyers from around the world, mainly persons who had a hand recently in the writing of new democratic constitutions such as the Spanish constitution of 1979. As with our White House conference, this one was very high-level and lavishly funded; part of the program was booked into the U.S. Supreme Court building with some of the justices ("The Supremes," we called them, after a music group of my era) in attendance.

The problems with the constitution-writing conference were, in my view, parallel to those accompanying the White House democracy-and-elections conference. Under first Penniman's and now Goldwin's direction, the panels all focused on smaller, technical issues: whether to have a parliamentary or a presidential system, federalism versus unitarism, economic and social versus more narrowly defined political rights. But that assumed that all countries, cultures, and people wanted to rewrite their constitutions in this way, wanted democracy, or wanted it in accord with the U.S. model. The approach—constitution writing—was also excessively legalistic and formalistic, an approach that political science had largely abandoned thirty years earlier.[6]

The conference's underlying assumptions were also questionable. They assumed that if you changed institutions—the constitution—political values, behavior, and the political culture would somehow change correspondingly, which is probably the reverse of how things actually work: first change the political culture, especially in developing or non-Western nations, and then the institutions can be changed quickly. Spain, one of the countries of main focus at the conference, is a prime example: first the country's economy, society, and entire political culture had changed drastically in the 1960s and 1970s, so when the institutions also needed to change in the late-1970s after Franco's death, it was fairly easy to do that because public opinion and the basic substructure of society and values had already been transformed. That would not be the case in many other nations embarking on a post-authoritarianism transition.

Finally, the conference begged the questions of whether constitutional democracy was the best form of government for all peoples at all times. And whether they might not prefer order and tranquility to change and upheaval. Or a regime true to their own culture and realities (think, currently, of Putin's Russia) instead of one imported from the outside. Or one that preserved the traditional and homegrown institutions instead of eliminating them. Or a strong state able to deliver real goods and services instead of a checked-and-balanced (à la Madison) government unable to deliver. There are many bigger questions here and issues that the conference—and the entire democracy project—failed to address, because to do so would open a whole Pandora's box of problems that the conference, its sponsors, and the main actors involved preferred not to address.

Both these conferences attracted widespread publicity, including for AEI. Both were specifically mentioned, in anticipation, by President Reagan in his British Parliament speech launching the project. And both helped start a flurry of activity as both the U.S. government bureaucracy and a number of foreign governments geared up for the democracy campaign. But as the AEI and White House publicity machines roared into action, more and more critics simultaneously came out of the woodwork. The criticisms included that we were wasting our money on a global democracy campaign, that the policy was too idealistic and "Wilsonian," that it would alienate and possibly undermine friendly but non-democratic regimes,[7] that we should spend our money on armaments to deter the Soviet Union and not unrealistic wil-o-the-wisps like democracy promotion.

In April 1983, the Democracy Program issued an interim report urging the establishment of an institution to promote democracy abroad. By the fall, the White House was ready to introduce its legislation. Despite being denounced in some quarters by some congressmen as a "boondaggle," the legislation passed easily. Who could be against democracy, after all? Democrats liked its democracy provisions, and Republicans were content that it would be anti-communist and remain in Reaganite and conservative hands. Of course the administration had to engage in the usual congressional logrolling to get the legislation passed—that's what the inclusion of the AFL-CIO, Chamber of Commerce, and the two party (NDI and IRI) institutes was all about.

The National Endowment for Democracy (NED) was now a going concern but the process had produced its casualities. George Agree, who had been one of the principal forces behind the democracy initiative and had come to AEI to sell it to our scholars, now dropped out of the program. It is unclear whether he was pushed out or dropped out voluntarily because of opposition to the form that NED took—typically in Washington, it was probably a combination of both. Similarly with Allen Weinstein: although he had been project director of NED's predecessor, the Democracy Program, he was passed over for the presidency of NED when it was created. So he took his bat and ball and went home in a huff—specifically, to Santa Barbara California, where he took the old and moribund, 1950s-era Center for Democratic Institutions and recreated it as the Center for Democracy, running several conferences in which I was invited to participate. It's always nice to get out to Santa Barbara and on one visit I even went up to visit the Reagan ranch in the hills above the city. Weinstein eventually returned to Washington and was named to the position of National Archivist by President George W. Bush.

Meanwhile, back in Washington, Lane Kirkland protégé and Jeane Kirkpatrick aide Carl Gershman was named president of the newly created NED, a position he still holds today. Carl had come up through the labor movement, the Coalition for a Democratic Majority, and Jeane's UN staff; he was a neocon but, among these, an open-minded and quite centrist one. He was a Democrat but, as a neocon, acceptable in Republican circles as well, and thus able to survive in that job for twenty-five years under four different administrations.

As it was created, the NED retained that cumbersome, unwieldy, dysfunctional, but very political structure that we have noted before: the two political party institutes, the AFL-CIO, and the Chamber of Commerce. They were supposed to work in harmony but of course they were soon going in completely separate directions, with separate agendas, and funding their own clientelistic subgroups instead of working jointly for democracy. NED was set up as a private agency (this to avoid the charge leveled against earlier democracy agencies that they were CIA fronts) but its funding came exclusively from Congress, it was responsible and had to answer to Congress, and de facto it functioned as an arm of the U.S. government. Because of its board's makeup (Rep. Fascell, Kirkland, Wright, as well as Reaganites) it enjoyed bipartisan support, but quite a number of congressmen persisted in viewing it as a waste—or even worse. However when the Soviet Union collapsed and the Iron Curtain across Eastern Europe and the Berlin Wall fell in 1989–1991, NED was widely acclaimed to be among the agencies responsible for winning the Cold War. Thereafter its budget increased exponentially and its critics in Congress and elsewhere were forced to keep quiet.

The initial budget allocation for NED was only $18 million. Not much could be accomplished with that small amount. Moreover, Congress had placed prohibitions during the first four years on any of the money being directed to the party institutes, and only small grants were given to the Chamber's Center for International Private Enterprise (CIPE) and the AFL-CIO's Free Trade Union Institute, which had been established by their parent organizations to administer the program.

Compared to these meager amounts and commitments, NED's mandate was huge: no less than the democratization of the globe. That included aid to both anti-authoritarian and anti-communist groups. It also included technical assistance to help new democracies run elections, develop free markets, build political parties, aid civil society, and fashion pluralism. It goes without saying that all the groups assisted were supposed to be pro-American and anti-communist.

Today the requirement would be pro-American and anti-Islamic fundamentalist. You can see the basis for problems here: if we say we favor civil society and pluralism, then we may at some time have to accept civil society groups whose agendas we may not favor, such as socialist trade unions, the Muslim Brotherhood, or even Hamas or Hezbollah.

In the first couple of years of the program, NED committed some horrendous gaffes that came within a whisker, in Congress's eyes, of leading to its abolition. A program to aid the opposition in Korea brought protests from the U.S. embassy in Seoul that it was undermining the government. Assistance to the Nicaraguan opposition was funneled to the Contras in violation of Congress's prohibitions against Contra aid. NED provided funds to the Catholic parties in Northern Ireland (including the IRA) but failed to provide any to Protestant groups—so much for evenhandedness. In Panama, aid went to the campaign of Nicolás Ardito Barleta, who was widely thought to be a front for the military; in Bolivia, NED funds assisted the campaign of General Hugo Banzer, a former dictator and human rights abuser. But, modest though it was, most of NED's funds were spent in appropriate and useful ways.

In the spring of 1983, just as all these NED programs were first getting off the ground, the United States Information Agency (USIA) sponsored a high-level conference on NED and Project Democracy. The speakers were Allen Weinstein as host, Scott Thomson from Tufts University, Lucian Pye from MIT, Samuel Huntington from Harvard, Robert Wesson from The Hoover Institution, William Zartman from Johns Hopkins, and yours truly. Huntington was then in his hopeful, optimistic, "third wave of democracy" phase and before his pessimistic "clash of civilizations"; he believed that democracy was universal, that the U.S. could successfully export it, and that NED was a great idea. Zartman and I, more grounded in fieldwork than the conceptually inclined Huntington, were very skeptical. Thomson, Pye, and Wesson staked out middle positions.

After the initial flurry of activity of a year earlier when the Democracy Project was first initiated, I had not followed closely the legislative process by which it became a law. The USIA conference was thus one of the first unveilings of NED's legislation and its plans. I was all in favor of democracy but very skeptical of the U.S. government's ability to do it right. So while in my presentation I threw cold water on NED's organization into the two-party institutes plus the AFL-CIO and the Chamber of Commerce and on the patronizing, quasi-missionary campaign to bring democracy to "our little brown and black brothers" (the term is used purposely to indicate the condescending attitudes toward the Third World involved), I nevertheless applauded the final legislation. It provided for what I thought was an appropriately small staff and budget, it shied away from some of the earlier grandiose plans to "remake the world," and it had removed much of the earlier ethnocentrism that had suggested all other countries must follow the U.S. democratic model. In this form, I suggested, NED could do only limited harm and might even do some good.

Shortly thereafter I weighed in with a longer and more detailed critique that got my concerns out into the public domain in a more organized and thoughtful way. Entitled "Is Democracy Exportable?" (of course not, if that is the way the question is posed), the paper caused a major stir in Washington and especially in the AEI-neocon community. The paper was presented first at AEI, then at the Woodrow Wilson International Center for Scholars, next at professional meetings, and then was published and republished in occasional paper, article, and book chapter form.[8] Of all my writings, this, along with some of the earlier "corporatism" and "ethnocentrism" writings, had the most widespread impact, and particularly so in the Washington policy community.

In the paper I argued that the democracy agenda was part of a Cold War strategy, that it was highly partisan, and that the motives behind it were not always the stated ones. I argued that the program was still ethnocentric, that we could not expect to implant the American institutions of democracy in countries where the history, culture, and sociology were quite different from our own, that we should avoid large-scale missionary campaigns and concentrate on small, above all realistic projects.

I warned about the limits of our power to effect change (think, Iraq), about excessive intervention in the internal affairs of other nations, and about the nationalistic resentments this would engender. I suggested (which some readers would consider almost anti-American) that other countries might not want democracy and capitalism as much as we wanted it for them, or in precisely our institutional form. I also warned against sharks and opportunists in both the U.S. and abroad who would take advantage of the program, persons who would manipulate it for partisan advantage, and corrupt officials who would take the money but do precious little democratization. There were other criticisms; it was quite a broadside! People who had spent extensive time abroad generally supported my position; idealists who had never lived in the Third World were the most critical.

Eventually the debate died down. Given the strong critique I'd made, people are often surprised that, in the end, I too favored the NED and the democracy program. I was glad when NED—and democracy—succeeded. But NED still makes mistakes and the issues I'd raised early on—issues of ethnocentrism, of America seeking to remake other countries in our own image, of excessive missionary campaigns, of partisanship and manipulation, of running roughshod over other people's cultures and institutions—are still often with us. I'm glad the United States *stands for* democracy in the world but I get a little worried when we start ramming it down other people's throats.

NOTES

1. Howard J. Wiarda (ed.), *Human Rights and U.S. Human Rights Policy* (Washington, D.C.: AEI, 1982).
2. Tamar Jacoby, "The Reagan Turnaround on Human Rights," *Foreign Affairs* (Summer 1986): 1066–86.
3. This is a period when I was writing particularly about ethnocentrism; see my *Ethnocentrism in Foreign Policy: Can We Understand the Third World?* (Washington, D.C.: AEI, 1985). This collection of essays got me in deep trouble with my AEI colleagues.
4. I'd like to think that some of the sensitivity Reagan shows here to cultural differences reflected the points I'd made in some of the Democracy Initiative's planning meetings, but probably that's exaggerating my own importance.
5. Howard J. Wiarda, *The Democratic Revolution in Latin America* (New York: Holmes and Meier, 1990). This book contains a longer, more detailed, and more academic review of U.S. human rights and democracy policy.
6. I have in mind the works of Carl Friedrich, Herman Finer, and Karl Loewenstein, all constitutional lawyers by training but out of touch with contemporary political science writings.
7. Adam Garfinkle and Daniel Pipes (eds.), *Friendly Tyrants* (New York: St. Martin's Press, 1991).
8. Howard J. Wiarda, "Can Democracy Be Exported?" (Washington, D.C.: Woodrow Wilson International Center for Scholars, 1984); reprinted in Kevin Middlebrook and Carlos Rico (eds.), *The United States and Latin America* (Pittsburgh: University of Pittsburgh Press, 1985), and in *Revista de Ciencia Politica* (No. 1, 1985.)

Chapter Eight

The Kissinger Commission on Central America

During the course of its two full terms, the Reagan Administration was bedeviled by events in Central America. Central America poisoned the political atmosphere probably more than any other issue of the Reagan presidency. It spoiled Reagan's relations with Congress, the media, the professional bureaucracy, a good part of the electorate, church and religious groups, and numerous allies. Only when then Secretary of State James Baker stepped in, like a shrewd bridge player, to finesse the issue and get it out of our consciousness (and off our television screens!), and then finally when Sandinista Daniel Ortega was defeated in the 1990 Nicaraguan presidential election, did Central America disappear as a troublesome, divisive issue.

The crisis in Central America involved three different countries: El Salvador, Guatemala, and Nicaragua. Costa Rica was safely democratic and relatively prosperous, while Honduras was more traditional and more-or-less peaceful; neither was torn by the kind of conflicts ripping apart the other three. Of course each of the three crisis countries was *sui generis* and their problems and issues were different, but there were some remarkably common patterns and parallel trajectories involved.

In El Salvador a more-or-less centrist military regime had been replaced in 1972 by a more repressive military that cancelled the country's recent elections, snubbed out the few remaining democratic institutions, and instituted a rein of terror against reformist groups that polarized the country and led to guerrilla revolution and civil war.

In Guatemala a similarly moderate and democratic government, attacked by both extreme left and extreme right, was overthrown in the early 1970s, and the subsequent military regimes turned to brutality and repression, and likewise triggered polarization, a widespread guerrilla movement, and civil war. In Nicaragua the conditions were only slightly different. There, the authoritarian but quite pragmatic regime of Anastasio Somoza sought to perpetuate the family dynasty by passing power on to his sons. But the second son, Anastasio Jr., lacked his father's political skills, turned to repression, and thus triggered the 1970s civil war that led to the triumph of the Sandinistas in 1979.

Note the pattern here. A moderate and centrist regime, civilian or military, is replaced by a more extreme and repressive regime. The repression polarizes the country, destroys the middle, and leads to widespread violence, human rights abuses, a guerrilla uprising, and civil war.

The United States is then faced with some terrible foreign policy dilemmas. It cannot support the Marxist guerrillas because the Cold War is still on and that would concede another country to the Soviet Union. But it cannot support a repressive military regime that rapes and murders nuns, peasants, and the moderate opposition because that is untenable in domestic U.S. politics, to say nothing of among our allies. What then to do?

One answer is the Democracy Program, as described in the previous chapter. Another option is to create a special presidential commission to study the problem and offer solutions that, hopefully, the president, his opposition in Congress, and the general public can accept and implement. With the debate over Central America waxing hot and heavy in the early 1980s, that is the strategy to which President Reagan turned.

Presidential commissions can serve a president in several ways. They can be used to stall for time if the president is under pressure to "do something" but he's not yet ready to make a decision. Or, where the facts of an issue are unclear, a presidential commission can be used to do fact-finding. Or suppose, as in the then recently completed Greenspan Commission on social security, everyone agrees on what reforms are necessary but it is politically unpalatable for politicians from either party to say so publicly. Then a presidential commission can make the case but, by doing so, deflect political blame away from the politicians. All these purposes were on display in the case of the Kissinger Commission.

EARLY STIRRINGS

The immediate precipitating factor in the process of setting up a presidential commission on Central America was Ambassador Jeane Kirkpatrick's fact-finding trip to the area in February 1983. Although Jeane was billed as a Latin America expert and was the chief spokesperson on Latin America in the administration, she had never been to Central America before. She was appalled by what she saw and heard there, both by the violence and poverty she saw on the one hand, and by the weakness of the governments, the growth of the guerrilla forces, and the growing inability to cope with the insurgency on the other. When she got back from the area, she immediately met with Reagan and reported on her trip. Since Jeane was one of only a handful of people that Reagan listened to and trusted on foreign policy, her message had a galvanizing impact.

Soon after Jeane's meeting with the president, an ad hoc Central America working group was set up in the State Department.[1] It drew representatives from all the main foreign policy agencies—State, DOD, CIA, NSC—and was organized as a mid-level interagency body. It met regularly in the State Department's seventh-floor operations center, which is reserved for crisis situations. It was superseded in this space by a new interagency group formed to deal with the horrific bombing of the U.S. Marine Corps barracks in Lebanon in October 1983. Functionally, it was also superseded by the Kissinger Commission during this same time period: summer/fall 1983.

I first received an inkling of what was afoot when I got a call from Jeane on July 22, 1983. She had already informally told me her impressions from her Central America trip earlier that year; now she told me of the plans for the Commission. In the course of the conversation she told me that she was nominating me for membership on the Commission. But then her husband Kirk met with me a couple days later to tell me Central America was so dangerous and so crucial that the administration had decided to constitute the Commission at a higher level. However if I was willing, I would serve as a chief staff person and consultant to the Commission. This was not the first time I'd been offered a position by Jeane only to have it pulled back and a consolation prize offered instead. Oh well, that's how Washington works.

A short time later, in early August 1983, I received a call from Ambassador Harry Shlaudeman at the State Department formalizing Kirk's offer. I'd known Harry since the Dominican Republic revolution and U.S. intervention of 1964–65. He was one of the Department's shrewdest and most slippery[2] officials; he along with high-powered Washington attorney Bill Rogers, both of whom had worked closely with Henry Kissinger when he was secretary of state, had now been recruited to work with him on the Central America commission.

Shlaudeman asked me if I would agree to be the "lead consultant" to the Commission. That was a curious title; no one then or since has been able to tell me what exactly it means. He and Rogers both knew my writings on Latin America; besides, I'm sure Jeane and Kirk had put in the good word on my behalf. He said that I would be responsible for lining up a "balanced slate" of witnesses for the Commission. I would also be responsible for distilling their testimonies, incorporating my own views, and doing preliminary drafts of position papers for the Commission that would later be converted into chapters for the Commission's report.

The work would begin in late August and might last several months, I would be part-time but very handsomely paid as a State Department consultant, and I would work closely with the commissioners, witnesses, and the State Department staff team then bring recruited. My closest contacts and best friends on the staff, in addition to the higher-ranking Rogers and Shlaudeman, were Ray Walser, a young foreign service officer with a Ph.D. in history from the University of North Carolina; Winston Lord, who would go on to be ambassador to China and then the president of the Council on Foreign Relations; and Josh Bolten, a young State Department lawyer who would later rise to be George W. Bush's chief of staff.

Shlaudeman went on to list the topics (later reduced in number) for which I would be responsible for securing witnesses and writing preliminary reports: the social and economic development of Central America, political development and democratic prospects, human rights, military and insurgency issues, external and internal influences on the region, strategic concerns, and U.S. policy. Well, I guess that pretty much covers all the issues, which helps explain why my drafts constituted about half the final report. Shlaudeman instructed that I should provide a broad overview, tell how Central America would evolve over the next five years (what constitutes "long range planning" in the State Department—exactly the length of Reagan's remaining tenure in office), and lay out the various policy options along with my own recommendations. I was to collect all the relevant literature, provide my own synthesis, and also relate my recommendations to Project Democracy—just then getting started. Whew! A huge task. But also very exciting, to be in on policy this way. My experience on the Kissinger Commission proved to be one of the most exciting periods of my life.

On August 22, exactly a month after Jeane's initial call, I met with Henry Kissinger, the Commission's chairman, himself. I had met him once before briefly, at Harvard's Center for International Affairs; by now he was a larger-than-life figure. I found Kissinger to be the most difficult and demanding boss I'd ever worked with, who insisted on absolute loyalty and unlimited hours from his staff. He treated the staff, even high-powered lieutenants such as Shlaudeman, Rogers, and Lord, like errand boys, or maybe graduate students: do this, do that, get the phone, make copies, write a memo. He made it plain he did not like to be interrupted or for others to finish his unfinished sentences. He said he'd not been impressed so far by the scholars he'd read on Central America.

He told me he was reading a lot on Central America and asked me what he should read. Naturally I handed him a sheaf of mainly my own writings. He told me he anticipated the work of the Commission would be 90 percent political and only 10 percent substantive. He told me I should feel free to say whatever I wished in my draft reports "because Bill Rogers will write the final report anyway"—how's that for an ego deflator? In advance of the Commission having heard from the substantive witnesses yet, he told me that our job would be to write a centrist report and then "sell it" to a very conservative administration. The biggest task, he said, was to build a consensus among the commissioners since "I already know what we want to say." There we have it: the famous Kissinger arrogance, certainty, and confidence in his own intellectual superiority all on display at the same time.

Kissinger went on to tell me the commissioners, the staff (myself included!), and the witnesses were to be chosen for political reasons: to guarantee the *appearance* of partisan balance and to satisfy domestic constituencies. I was chosen as lead consultant because my appointment killed two birds with one stone: I was known as a centrist but I was affiliated with AEI. My AEI colleague Mark Falcoff had meanwhile also been selected to participate because he would provide a link to the neocon Right, for whom Henry had no use at all and who had already denounced the Commission and was planning to issue its own report. All during this discussion Kissinger was animated, vigorous, and extremely cordial to me, even while joking around a lot on these political themes. I was a little surprised how brutally frank (and realistic!) he was on the politics and political issues involved, and immediately took a strong liking to a fellow smart-alecky and ironic academic who had managed to succeed at the highest levels of the policy world.

Later, in the hall, Shlaudeman told me that the once disgraced (because of Vietnam, wiretaps, Nixon, Watergate, and détente) Kissinger also had his private agenda: he would write a report designed to please all parties and all factions, and thus make himself available for a comeback as secretary of state if George Shultz left early or perhaps under future president George H.W. Bush. In short, for Kissinger, the Commission that came to carry his name was an exercise in rehabilitation. But if Kissinger was indeed thinking in these terms, he had underestimated how much he was still disliked and distrusted in conservative (including at AEI) Republican circles and how inflammable—to the point of ruling him out of consideration—the mere mention of his name was.

ORGANIZATION

The executive order, number 12433, for the creation of the Commission had been issued by President Reagan on July 19, 1983. But at this early stage, the plans for the Commission and even its composition were still a work-in-progress. It was to consist of no more than twelve members with no more than seven from the same party. Its function, as stated in the executive order, was to study U.S. interests in Central America and the threats posed to them. The Commission was to respond to the challenges and provide advice on building a U.S. consensus for policy in the region. It was to report to the president by December 1, 1983, later amended to February 1, 1984. Members served without compensation but staff and consultants could be paid.

Members of the Commission were former Secretary of State Henry Kissinger; former New Jersey Senator Nicholas Brady; San Antonio Mayor Henry Cisneros, former Texas Governor William Clements, Jr.; Yale economist Carlos Díaz-Alejandro; San Mateo businessman Wilson Johnson; AFL-CIO President Lane Kirkland; Washington political scientist Richard Scammon; Boston University President John Silber; former Supreme Court Justice Potter Stewart; former Democratic National Committee Chairman Robert Strauss; and William Walsh of Project Hope. Although the Commission was supposedly bipartisan in accord with the executive order creating it, in fact the Commission was the creation of a conservative Republican administration and the Democrats chosen to serve tended to come, with two or three exceptions, from the southern, conservative wing of the party.

The chair was of course Henry Kissinger (the name "The President's National Bipartisan Commission on Central America" was quickly shortened to "Kissinger Commission"); the executive director, who had recruited me, was Ambassador Harry Shlaudeman. Tom Korologos from the State Department handled congressional relations, while Herbert Hetu was director of public affairs. Joshua Bolten served as the executive assistant and the person with whom on a daily basis I had most contact; Ray Walser, a historian by training, was the research officer. There were five military aides.

A stroke of genius, now common on all presidential commissions, was to name eight congressmen as "counselors" to the commission. Four were Democrats, four Republicans; four were from the Senate, four from the House. That way, when the Commission recommended legislative action in its report, it already had a core group of bipartisan supporters in the Congress. The counselors were Senators Henry Jackson, Lloyd Bentsen, Bob Mathias, and Pete Dominici, and Congressmen Mike Barnes, Jack Kemp, William Broomfield, and Jim Wright. Jeane Kirkpatrick was also named a non-congressional counselor to the Commission. As with the Commission itself, the tilt of the counselors was Republican and *conservative* Democrat.

Next came the "lead consultants." That was my position title. When I was first asked to serve in this capacity, I was led to understand that I would be one of only two lead consultants, and that we in turn would select the witnesses to appear before the Commission. But it turned out that there were to be two lead consultants for *each major subject area* that the Commission wished to cover. Moreover, for each subject area, there had to be one Republican lead consultant and one Democrat lead consultant. Thus Amb. Bill Luers and Carl Gershman (from Jeane's UN staff and the future president of the National Endowment for Democracy) were the lead consultants on U.S. interests, Alan Stoga and Sidney Weintraub on economic development, William Doherty (AFL-CIO) and Ed Marasciulo (Pan American Development Foundation) on social development, Margaret Daly Hayes (Senate Foreign Relations Committee) and Greg Treverton on security issues (ultra-conservative General Gordon Sumner also got thrown onto this list), and Mark Falcoff (AEI, my assistant) and Bob Hunter (CSIS) on diplomatic options. Although all the lead consultants were technically equal, some were more equal than others: *de facto*, Bill Luers, Pete Vaky, and I, perhaps because our subject areas were the most sensitive or maybe because we were seen as centrist figures, were at the Commission on an almost daily basis and had a strong hand in writing the final report.

While the lead consultants were supposed to choose the witnesses, in fact it was more complicated and political than that. Quite a few of the witnesses—including former presidents Nixon, Ford, and Carter—were chosen on political as well as courtesy grounds. Pete Vaky and I were careful in selecting witnesses that were serious, balanced, and levelheaded, and we received plaudits from the commissioners for our choices. But, in the ways of Washington, new and unexpected witnesses, who had political influence or represented an important interest group, were often added to our and the other lists. Some of these witnesses represented what I (and most of the commissioners) viewed as quite nutty positions but we had to listen to them anyway for political reasons. I was later reassured by Kissinger that all this was just window-dressing; we *had* to listen to these folks but in the end we would write the report that *we* (Kissinger, Shlaudeman, Bill Rogers, Vaky, me, the staff) wanted to write.

The initial hearings had been held on August 10–11. First the Commission heard from Reagan National Security Adviser William Clark, Assistant Secretary for Inter-American Affairs Tony Motley, Undersecretary of Defense Fred Iklé, and AID administrator Peter McPherson. Next on August 31–September 1 came former secretaries of state Cyrus Vance, Alexander Haig, Dean Rusk, and William P. Rogers; ambassadors and former assistant secretaries Thomas Mann and Sol Linowitz; and former presidents Carter and Ford. On September 7–8 there was a large panel of a dozen witnesses on social development; September 21–22 was devoted to security issues; and on September 28–30 came my panel, led off by former president Nixon (more on this below) on political development. On October 7 there was more testimony on economics and on October 21–22 the final scheduled session was held on U.S. interests. Each of these panels had a dozen or more witnesses, and even after the formal panels ended more witnesses, often self-selected, continued to be called on into November and early December. By these latter dates the Commission was already writing its report.

The Commission met initially with President Reagan on August 11 at the White House to receive his charge to the Commission. It then met with him on October 21 to deliver an interim report and on January 11—after a long weekend of work by Kissinger, Shlaudeman, the commissioners, the counselors, and even me to convince Jeane and the White House to accept the report—to receive the final, printed report. The Commission also met several times with Secretary of State Shultz, who had by now replaced Haig.

GETTING STARTED

For me, although the Commission had already held some preliminary meetings, the work of the Commission started a few days after I had met with Kissinger. My journal shows that my first full day on the job was August 27. I went over to the Commission's State Department office, checked in, did some paperwork so I could get paid ("first things first"), and started organizing the work. Our offices were in the suite usually used by the transition teams between administrations; we didn't have a lot of space and the room dividers did not afford a lot of privacy. As I walked in I heard Kissinger berating his secretary to the extent that she was crying. Today we would call it harassment. Embarrassed and not knowing what to do, I retreated to the hallway so at least I didn't have to listen or hear the sobs. Shlaudeman told me cheerfully and from long experience with Henry that it happened all the time, with *all* of his staff, that I shouldn't take it personally. I now have to amend my earlier statement: working for Kissinger was probably the most intellectually exciting but also personally difficult and trying time of my life.

What I found at the office was a very sloppy operation in terms of which topics we were supposed to cover, how the witnesses were to be chosen, who would be selected to write the position papers, how these are balanced, etc. Perhaps I should have gone back to Kissinger's comment in that first interview that he already knew what we wanted to say; the witnesses, therefore, were mainly shadow play, on the way to arriving at Kissinger's own consensus. But I did find out that the other commissioners as well as the congressional "counselors" wanted a "Republican" and a "Democrat" perspective on all the issues. This was a wake-up call for me in Washington partisanship; as a scholar and centrist, my orientation was to get a single, well-informed but *nonpartisan* witness, not an extreme ideologue, for each of the main topics. The result was, we had to search to find a right-wing and then a left-wing scholar or policy official on each subject. In this process, as on the television talk shows, the centrist position often gets overwhelmed and submerged by the extremes and "nuts" on both sides. But that was also so Henry and the Commission could look like the only centrist and sensible people around.

The process was entirely political. For example, I brought in Dr. Margaret Hayes, a sensible centrist who worked for Senator Richard Lugar on the Foreign Relations Committee, to testify on U.S. security interests; but the Republican right wing distrusted her and insisted that I bring in General Gordan Sumner, whom I thought of as a real ideologue, to counter Margaret. On political issues, liberal-Democrat Congressman Mike Barnes (chair of the House Subcommittee on Inter-American Affairs) insisted we bring in far-left scholar and Cuba sympathizer William LeoGrande, while the conservatives insisted we hear from Bruce McComb of the conservative Freedom House, whom I regarded (with good reason—more on this below) as flaky. The liberals wanted to bring in Ambassador Viron ("Pete") Vaky to counter my influence from the "obviously" right-wing AEI, but Jeane Kirkpatrick, who oversaw these entire proceedings, sought to veto him on the grounds that as assistant secretary during the Carter presidency the mild-mannered Vaky had "lost" Nicaragua to Marxism.

I now went into the office on a just about everyday basis. I usually did my AEI work in the morning (including starting to write my own position papers for the Commission) and went over to our State Department offices in the afternoon. I continued to be amazed at how ad hoc, disorganized, and downright sloppy the policy process was. Yes, I was told, there are *always* political, personal, and partisan ingredients that get into the process, to say nothing of accidents and screw-ups. In the Commission's case, dates got changed, programs and witnesses changed, and there was much disorganization. As usual, the State Department didn't quite know what it wanted but it did know what it *didn't* want and quickly vetoed some of the consultants' early position papers. The Department provided us no guidance, no direction, no instructions. It sought to schedule and reschedule almost at will the witnesses I'd lined up, depending on Henry's and the other commissioners' travel schedules. Some of this chaos and disorganization leaked out to the press and the impression grew that the Commission didn't know what it was doing. But if that was so, how could it expect to enlighten the public and policy makers?

To be fair, the Commission was under tremendous political pressure and in the glare of public and often highly partisan spotlights. Lots of people are calling me and the commissioners wanting to testify. Some of these I regard as "crazies." But we get calls from the White House, Jeane, congressmen, politicians, think tanks wanting their favorites to be on the witness list. We resist some of these but have to bow to others. It's all very political. No wonder ad hoc-ism prevails.

The internal dynamics among the commissioners are interesting. Some of their discussions are behind closed doors but others I sit in on. I'm even getting to know some of the more active members and am soon on a first-name basis with Henry Cisneros, Dick Scammon (from AEI), Bob Strauss, Carlos Díaz-Alejandro (whom I knew previously from academic connections), John Silber, and Bill Walsh. Already the committee is dividing into its stronger and weaker members: those above plus Lane Kirkland, Potter Stewart, and Nick Brady on the strong side, while Bill Clements and Wilson Johnson were the weak reeds, either indifferent to the work or else too busy with other (Texas) obligations. The lightweights were soon shunted aside and the heavyweights dominated the discussions.

The Commission was supposed to be bipartisan but some members were more partisan than others; in addition, the personal relations among the members were sometimes testy. Kissinger and Strauss used to joke a lot but there was often a sharp edge to their kidding. One time when Henry came into the office, Bob was sitting in the chairman's chair holding forth. Henry walked over and said, "I always knew you wanted my chair, Strauss." Bob replied, "The way you're running this commission, no one would want your chair." Good-natured fun at one level, but obvious rivalry at another. Neither of these two were exactly shrinking violets.

Of the commissioners, only Díaz-Alejandro knew anything more than superficially about Latin America. He was a professional economist, one of whose fields was Latin America, but he was new to Washington politics. The commissioners relied on him for his area and technical expertise but not for any policy recommendations. When the decisions on the final commission report were made, Díaz-Alejandro was not one of the heavyweights.

In the first couple of weeks of committee meetings, we continued to have disputes over the slate of witnesses to be brought in. I wanted to bring in people with real Central America expertise—Roland Ebel, Richard Millett, Ronald McDonald, Thomas Anderson, Tom Karnes, Gary Wynia, Edward Williams. But some of the right-wing commissioners, believing that the "commies" were behind all the troubles in Central America, wanted to bring in Soviet foreign policy experts. Moreover, they saw no need to have experts in *both* Central America and the Soviet Union; the latter they saw as sufficient. We ended up bringing in two specialists in Soviet third world policy; almost all the other witnesses were Central America regional experts.

Several commissioners believed initially that the crisis in Central America was "just another" superpower conflict that could be negotiated between the U.S. and the U.S.S.R. In this calculation, Central America was unimportant and irrelevant. It was merely a puppet in the larger, global Cold War struggle; Central America in itself was a pawn. This was another instance of the points made in chapter 5 that Latin America is unimportant, that it is irrelevant to the big issues in the world, that it is purely derivative in the great Cold War chess game.

That view was particularly widespread among the military aides that Kissinger brought into the staff. Henry had a certain view of military men: that they were good staff aides, carried our orders well, didn't talk back, were good at answering the phone and running an office. So in whatever government position he'd held, he'd always surrounded himself with young military aides. The Central America Commission was no exception. I don't think these men had any policy influence on the report we eventually wrote but they did serve to reinforce the views of some of the Commission members.

Of all the commissioners, the most ideological was Mayor Henry Cisneros of San Antonio. Cisneros was then being touted as a Democrat comer and a possible vice presidential candidate. He came to the Commission with his own agenda and deeply held ideological beliefs. As witnesses he wanted to bring in people who were sympathetic to the Salvadoran guerrillas and the Sandinistas in Nicaragua: such left-wing academics as Tommie Sue Montgomery, John Booth, and Thomas Walker. Cisneros let it be known—before he actually knew anything or went into the field—that he himself was sympathetic to the left-wing cause. My reading of Cisneros was that, like many Carterites, he naively saw the guerrilla struggles in Central America as akin to the civil rights struggle—in his case on behalf of Hispanics—in the U.S. That is, of poor and oppressed peoples battling against a brutal and oppressive establishment, with all truth and justice on one side. In this Manichean view there was little room for subtlety or shadings, let alone the suggestion that such outside powers as the Cubans, Soviets, Czechs, East Germans, and Bulgarians *were* involved in Central America. Cisneros's visit to Nicaragua a few weeks later would cure him of most of these illusions.

Of course the problems in Central America were at their base social and economic: poverty, a rigid class-caste system, lack of jobs and opportunity, power and wealth held by a few while the mass of the population was largely excluded. But we on the Commission, or in the U.S., cannot solve those fundamental problems in a few days, years, or even decades. Moreover, when the issue comes to full-scale civil war as in El Salvador and Nicaragua, a little rice and beans food aid will be not sufficient to solve the problem. In addition, while some of those fighting on the guerrilla side were well-meaning idealists, social democrats, and liberation theology Catholics, there is no doubt that the main guerrilla groups in El Salvador and Guatemala, and the Sandinista government in Nicaragua, were under the control of Marxists and even Marxist-Leninist elements. Finally and in addition, there was no doubt by now that Central America was not just and no longer a local or a Central American affair; instead the guns for the guerrillas, the training, the R and R, the political advice, etc. were all coming from actors (Cubans, Soviets, etc.) outside the area. All this made Central America considerably more complicated than Cisneros and many like-minded persons thought.

Among the commissioners and senior staff, I was probably among those closest politically to Kissinger himself. Trained in international relations, I identified more with the realist than the idealist position; people who hold romantic, delusional, and peace-at-any-price positions make me nervous. I hadn't known Kissinger well before this, but he knew some of my writings and relied on me for knowledge and information on Latin America. Every evening I would put a pile of readings on Kissinger's desk; when he came in the morning it was clear he had not only read but also absorbed it all. It was fun to watch the wheels in Kissinger's mind work; he was undoubtedly one of the most brilliant persons I'd ever met.

Part of my role, as I at least defined it, was to convince him that democracy and human rights in Central America mattered. As a realist thinker, and one who a decade earlier as secretary of state had opposed the first human rights legislation, Henry was not inclined to see democracy and human rights as important; but he grasped immediately that democracy and human rights had to be in Central America part of a realist solution. I'm proud that I, along with Bill Rogers and Harry Shlaudeman, helped educate Henry Kissinger on the importance of democracy and human rights issues.

It was amusing to see how Kissinger treated the materials we gave him. While we piled the readings on him, he forbade us to share the same materials with the other commissioners. That way, when the commissioners all appeared before the cameras on the evening news broadcasts, Henry would be the only one well informed and thus the only one to be quoted on the news. Only after the evening news broadcasts were we permitted to distribute the same materials to the other commissioners.

GETTING SERIOUS

On September 15, about three weeks after the Commission had commenced its serious work, I had lunch with Jeane Kirkpatrick, at her invitation. She was just back from her August vacation in the south of France; a few years earlier she and Kirk had purchased a house in Le Beau, Provence, to which I would also be invited in future years. She said that while in France, Henry had been calling her "every day" to talk about the Commission and its work. She voiced suspicions of Congressman Mike Barnes (D-MD) who talked to her "out of both sides of his mouth," and told me she had vetoed Woodrow Wilson Center's Latin America director Abe Lowenthal as a witness. Other than these moves, she said she had not been following the work of the Commission very closely and asked me what I thought of the proceedings so far.

I told her my view that the Commission was disorganized and unsure of its direction, that it was bowing to too many political pressures ("every wind that blows"), and that the Commission was having a hard time finding knowledgeable moderate and conservative witnesses to offset the many liberal and radical spokesmen. Jeane responded that she would call Henry the next day and get these problems straightened away. I then told her that Americas Watch, the self-appointed human rights overseer, had been so aggressive and persistent in bugging Henry that he had agreed to let them testify as well. At this news Jeane exploded. She told me that Americas Watch and particularly its director, Aryeh Neier, were so arrogant and ugly that they had been banned from her New York UN office. "I can't stand those people," she said.

When I got to the office the following Monday, Henry was fuming. As only Henry could fume. Jeane had called him over the weekend. He wanted to know what I'd said that got her so angry. I replied that I had given Jeane a report on the Commisson, including who had been invited to appear at witnesses on the several panels, and said I was sorry if this caused him any problems. He said grumpily that he was too old to have problems and didn't worry about it a bit. Hah! It was fascinating for me to think of Jeane chewing out Henry; I'm sure that didn't happen to him very often. But in the present circumstances Jeane outranked him and he had no choice but to listen. Plus Jeane has access to Reagan; the last thing Henry needed if he still had ambitions for another prestigious appointment was to get on the wrong side of the president.

Another result of this exchange was that Henry, now knowing that I had a direct pipeline to Jeane (she had earlier asked me to be her eyes and ears on the Commission), treated me with greater deference and circumspection than he had before. In fact I noticed the other commissioners and staff now went out of their way to solicit my views; after this minor blowup with Henry the number of phone calls asking my advice suddenly *quadrupled*.

Meanwhile I hear that the strategic policy panel is to be a circus. We had managed to have Iklé testify earlier so that the paired witnesses now consisted of the serious, balanced Gregory Treverton (Harvard Ph.D. and former Church Committee intelligence staff member) on the Democrat side and equally serious and level-headed Margaret Hayes on the Republican. But I now learn that Jiri Valenta, a former Czech student leader in the 1968 uprising who spoke no Spanish and had never been to Central America, had been put on the witness list, as had General Gordon Sumner, co-author of the far-right-wing Report of Santa Fe; Colonel Sam Dickinson, another right-wing military guy who was a favorite of Ollie North and the White House; and even an anonymous representative of the Veterans of Foreign Wars (VFW)! As a serious scholar I was appalled at some of these selections; on the other hand I remembered Henry's earlier injunctions to me that the witnesses were mainly window dressing and to keep domestic groups happy, and that "we" (Henry, me, Shlaudeman, Rogers) would end up writing the report we wanted regardless of what the witnesses said. As a newcomer to the nation's capital, this experience is sure teaching me a lot about Washington policy-making.

Even in a relatively small operation like the Kissinger Commission, or maybe especially there because it's an appointed presidential commission and the lines of authority are unclear, there's tremendous confusion and uncertainty. I dealt on a daily basis with then low-level State Department staffers like Ray Walser and Josh Bolten; I was constantly amazed that the staff didn't know what it wanted or which direction it was supposed to go. It was so confused and uncertain that they were sometimes calling witnesses without having the slightest idea who they were or what they would testify about. Among the commissioners I had especially good relations with Cisneros, Díaz-Alejandro, Kissinger, Silber, and Walsh; they looked to me to provide careful and balanced views.

And then there were Rogers and Shlaudeman, the "old hands." They were both clever, subtle operators with the advantage of having long worked for Kissinger and intent on keeping the Commission under control so they could basically write the final report. I had good relations with both of them because I knew Central America well and also had the conceptual knowledge about the area and on development themes that they could use in their report. Finally there was Henry himself; I got along surprisingly well with him and we remain good friends, but there were tensions, we disagreed on quite a few issues, and there was always a certain strain to our relations because he *way* outranked me in accomplishment and status and therefore I should defer to him. On the other hand I knew things that he didn't know about Central America, plus there was the Jeane connection.

In the office I had long talks with Pete Vaky, who had become, over Jeane's objections, my counterpart in our relations with the Commission and who was a wonderful source of lore and information on policy-making. Pete and I disagreed on almost nothing, so that when I eventually wrote my position paper for the Commission,[3] it was accepted as a consensus document which, with some new additions, served as a basis for the Commission's final report. Pete told me, contrary to my expectations, that when he was assistant secretary for inter-American affairs, very little of this domestic pushing and hauling took place. Interest group lobbying, he said, took place in the Congress but not the State Department. There, a "rational actor model" (see Graham Allison) prevailed: we decided on policy and then implemented it without a lot of outside interference. But that was then (the late 1960s, before the politicization of foreign policy caused by the Vietnam War), and this is now. In Pete's time the State Department could carry out policy largely insulated from domestic political pressures; by the 1980s foreign policy had become as much politicized as domestic policy was.

By late August the Commission had settled down somewhat, gotten into a routine, and was scheduling more and more witnesses. For reasons that I never understood and were above my pay grade, the first witness called on my panel was former President Richard Nixon. Nixon was a shrewd practitioner of foreign policy but he knew little about Central America. I assume he was called because of his longtime ties to Kissinger, or because this was part of Nixon's ongoing efforts to rehabilitate himself after Watergate, or maybe as a way to keep his hand in on policy-making. Or perhaps because some of the conservative commissioners wanted his views on Soviet machinations in Latin America. Actually, the other former presidents, Ford and Carter, had already testified, so as a courtesy Nixon had to be invited too. I caught a glimpse of Nixon as he passed in the hall, but I did not get to hear his testimony because Kissinger had decreed that staff was to be excluded from that hearing.

Nixon was the leadoff witness that day but other witnesses had been scheduled to appear immediately after him. However, Nixon arrived a half hour late; and when he was finished Henry decided he wanted to go to lunch. On his way out he instructed Shlaudeman to handle all the negative fallout this would cause. Among other things, that left the other witnesses cooling their heels; some of them were angry. When I remarked to State Department staffer Josh Bolten about how inept, *ad hoc*, and shoddy-appearing this all looked, his response was that I shouldn't complain because the immediate staff was treated even shabbier. Not only was the staff also excluded from Nixon's testimony but they had not yet even been given a full witness list, which continued to change on an hourly basis.

Let me provide a little flavor of the difficulties we had with witnesses. The one who gave us the hardest time was conservative Bruce McComb of Freedom House. McComb was an ideologue, personally difficult to get along with, and not my favorite fellow; but he represents important conservative constituencies and he's personally close to some of Jeane's staff at the UN. On September 27, just before he was scheduled to testify, McComb called me early in the morning at my home. He complained of the "circus atmosphere" at the Commission that had by now scheduled and rescheduled his testimony several times, much to his annoyance and inconvenience. And despite the earlier agreed-upon format, he was now refusing to testify alongside the more liberal William LeoGrande; McComb wanted his own private session. I tried to reason with him since I was the one responsible for securing witnesses but to no avail: McComb withdrew from his promise to testify.

Two minutes later Josh Bolten called, very distraught. Since McComb was close to Jeane, I assume he had called her office, who had then called the Commission. Not wanting to antagonize Jeane, Bolten was wringing his hands; what have we done, he asks. I respond that I'm now having trouble with all my witnesses who are busy and important persons and resent having their time wasted by the constant scheduling and rescheduling of their testimony. Bolten is torn: he works for the Commission but he also has an interest in an orderly and successful witness process. He asks me to call McComb again.

When I call him again, McComb is still mad and resentful. He says his time is valuable and that it should not be wasted or he "victimized" by Kissinger's lunch schedule. I tell him the scheduling process *is* inexcusable but that he should swallow his pride, think of the larger purposes of the Commission, and agree to reschedule his testimony for the sake of getting his "important message" (what lies you have to tell in Washington!) across. He says he'll consider it.

A few minutes later Harry Shlaudeman from the higher staff levels of the Commission calls. "What's the problem?" he asks. So I explain the whole situation all over again. Harry's response is that McComb should be happy he's been asked to testify. He says further and a bit mysteriously that McComb's problems are nothing compared to those of the staff. Since I know him better and can keep him calm, we agree that we will wait a couple hours and then I will call McComb again. Maybe he will have cooled off by then. Shlaudeman thanks me for my help.

Two minutes later Shlaudeman calls again. While we were talking earlier, McComb had left a message at his office. So Harry will call him back immediately rather than waiting for our planned two-hour cooling-off period. We both assume from the message left that McComb has changed his mind and is now willing to testify. But no, all he wants to do is bawl Harry out some more. Harry has to take it; as a career diplomat he's used to both the chaos and confusion of policy-making and to being reamed out by others.

I try again that afternoon. McComb is still angry. Worse than that, he's paranoid. He's afraid that his interlocutor on the panel, Bill LeoGrande, will either best him in the debate or else leak his testimony around Washington as a way of ruining McComb's chances for a position on the Organization of American States (OAS) Human Rights Commission. So *that* is what this to-do is all about! I tell McComb that's preposterous, no dark conspiracies are involved, all we're interested in is his testimony, and that will be confidential.

He calms down a little but still is undecided. I report this all back to Bolten and Shlaudeman.

A few minutes later Bolten calls back. McComb has agreed to testify. But only after Henry K called him personally. Before doing that, Bolten reports, Henry gave the staff a tongue lashing that hadn't been heard in the State Department since Kissinger himself left the seventh floor. My reading was that Henry was reading the political tea leaves and assiduously protecting his right-wing, Reaganite flanks. He wanted to stay on the good side of Jeane and the neocons. So he was willing to personally call McComb to get him to testify. But the condition was, McComb would testify by himself, without LeoGrande in the room. My conclusion: paranoia runs high in Washington, D.C.

All this is pretty small-time stuff. And petty. But it illustrates how the U.S. government works—or maybe doesn't work. You get so caught up in the endless meetings, the pettiness, the telephone calls, the messages back and forth, the personal and bureaucratic one-upsmanship, in this case the insecurities, that the substance of policy is often forgotten or relegated to the back burners. Even in my own journal, I find I have several pages devoted to these endless negotiations with McComb but not one word, after all that coming and going, of what he actually said in his testimony. Whatever he said, in any case, had absolutely no impact on the report we were already planning to write. But by being so difficult, it probably ruined forever whatever career he might have had in mind in Washington. Not long afterwards, McComb disappeared from the national political scene seldom to be heard from again.

For those of us who have to work with him on an everyday basis, it's sometimes hard to tell who's worse on a personal level: McComb or Kissinger. Kissinger is imperious, conceited, condescending, arrogant. He treats people like dirt—not me, fortunately. Poor Josh Bolten as a hard-working but junior staffer is just about beside himself with fear; he seems ready to have a nervous breakdown. Henry treats everyone with disdain, demeans his staff as well as fellow commissioners, and rules by verbally terrorizing underlings. Pete Vaky is so incensed by Kissinger's haughty treatment of witnesses and their time that he wants to forget the whole enterprise. Kissinger, he says, rules by intimidation.

Kissinger cannot and will not delegate any authority to those below him. He does not trust their knowledge or judgment compared to his. I was partially exempt from this because I have a Ph.D. and had specialized knowledge on Central America and development themes that Kissinger needed to tap. Moreover he wants to hog all the glory for himself by monopolizing the information flow, press briefings, and television appearances. He was both arrogant and insecure at the same time—probably the two traits go together.

Everything done by the staff was done to flatter Henry, make him look good, and serve his private political ambitions. My colleagues with greater experience in Washington told me he's the worst manager they've ever seen, worse than anything on Capitol Hill or in the State Department: no delegation of responsibility, intellectual brow-beating, self-aggrandizement. I found it to be one of the most trying but also fascinating periods of my life. For others on the staff, such as Peter Rodman and Alan Stoga, Kissinger made it ultimately rewarding, though often painful, through offers of cushy positions with his private consulting firm, Kissinger Associates.

I found the staff to be very good and hard working. But they were all scared stiff of Super K, as he came to be called. Nor could they do anything without his prior approval. And since Henry was only there half the time, little got done. What was done, furthermore, was mainly to flatter his ego. Fortunately I was not a career foreign service officer, not a part of this large bureaucracy, and not constrained by the same red tape or fear of job insecurity as my colleagues.

Finally the time comes, September 28–30, for all the witnesses I'd lined up to testify. Margaret Hayes and Greg Treverton on U.S. strategic interests were both good: careful, balanced, non-partisan. Roland Ebel from Tulane was too abstract and theoretical; he presented good background information on the politics of the Central American city-states but was weak on policy recommendations. Tom Farer was good on human rights issues and so was Allen Weinstein on the need for democracy. Elliot Abrams was similarly good as were Orville Shell and (surprisingly) Aryeh Neier and the Americas Watch team. But Bruce McComb, after all his huffing and puffing, proved to be a weak witness with little to say, while Bill LeoGrande's testimony, according to two of the commissioners, "blamed the United States for everything" and was "indistinguishable from that of the Nicaraguan (Sandinista) ambassador."

My friend Ronald McDonald from Syracuse proved to be equally inept: he argued that since the Salvador military was certain to lose, we should therefore start aiding the guerrillas—a position that as Kissinger pointed out could never be sold either to Congress or the Reagan White House.[4] John Booth, appearing on Commissioner Cisneros's behalf, was similarly unrealistic, staking out a pro-Sandinista position that was untenable in the present circumstances. Quite a number of these witnesses reinforced my growing sense that ivory tower academics have little of use to offer policy makers.

That left as the final witnesses Pete Vaky and myself, and we complemented each other very nicely. Pete, a levelheaded career FSO, former ambassador, and former assistant secretary of state for inter-American Affairs, presented a careful, thoughtful, balanced diplomatic perspective. Nuts and bolts: what to do, how to do it, new initiatives. My own presentation reflecting my academic background was more abstract and theoretical: how to achieve democracy and human rights in Central America on their as well as our terms, the crying need for socioeconomic development, the need to support political development and civil society, the required balance between military and diplomatic pressure on the one hand and the willingness to negotiate with guerrillas as well as Sandinistas on the other.

Bob Strauss was so happy with this round of witnesses and the fact they were balanced, non-ideological, and (generally) non-partisan that he was almost literally jumping out of his skin. He particularly singled out Vaky and myself for praise and told Kissinger and the other commissioners that he wanted us to write the report. But Kissinger had his own righthand man, Bill Rogers, whom he wanted to write the initial draft. Rogers, a tough, shrewd, and very pleasant Washington insider in his own right, caught the drift of things and hurried over to ask Vaky and me if he could use our papers in writing his own report. And that's how you have influence in Washington: if a desk officer, staffer, or assistant secretary has *your* book or paper open and in front of him when he's writing his own memo to the secretary, then your views are going right to the top. In this case, my papers prepared for the Commission served as the foundation for three of the chapters in the final report. That made it all—even having to deal with Bruce McComb—worthwhile.

These three days of hearings were the most continuous contact I'd had with the commissioners. Since all of them were part-time and serving on a voluntary basis, I didn't see most of them very often; my relations were mainly with Kissinger and his State Department career staff. But the witnesses on democracy and political development were my "show" and over that period I worked closely with all the commissioners. I was tremendously impressed with their intelligence, toughness, and political smarts. All of these men I found to be very clever, able, experienced, shrewd but also good-humored. Men like Kissinger, Strauss, Silber, Kirkland, Scammon, Stewart, and Walsh didn't get to their level by being dolts or wallflowers. Wow, these guys are really good. I'd take them over most of my academic colleagues any day.

Bob Strauss in particular, whom my original journal notes written at the time describe as the "Bette Midler of politics." Strauss was cute, clever, a bit vulgar, murderously tough when he wanted to be, and *very* effective. He was almost a match for Henry himself, who is extremely clever. Both men use others and their staffs outrageously. Both told sharp-edged jokes, often with a personal hook to them, and then looked around to check who was laughing. Both were domineering—but perhaps born of some deep-felt insecurity. Both were Washington insiders and operators in the best sense.

At one point in his testimony, Elliot Abrams was arguing in favor of democracy and elections. He said, "We can't tell a country or people when they should have democracy or what year—1976 for example—is the right year for elections." Whereupon Strauss, a Democrat, retorted to general laughter that "Nineteen seventy-six [Jimmy Carter] was a hell of a lot better year than 1980 [Reagan]." Or, when McComb was testifying, Strauss ambled over to me and whispered, "In academic terms, this would be called *bull shit*."

Kissinger, too, was very clever politically and bureaucratically. In a private meeting he told me he liked my paper because it included just the kind of positive, optimistic, forward-looking ideas you want to get in a presidential report: progress on democracy, human rights, development, and security. And all of these at once. He went on to offer me some lessons in foreign policy. "When you're on the seventh floor of this building [the State Department]," he said, "you face 150 problems each day, five of which are serious." He continued, "With that many problems, even dealing with big ones subtly and with sophistication in all cases is all but impossible. But you can't delegate, either," he said, "because the State Department is hopeless." This was an oft-repeated Kissinger lament; as secretary of state he used to complain constantly over the Department's inability to conceptualize, to see patterns, the big picture, the whole chessboard. "So you do what I do here," he said, "you assemble a small staff that you can trust, work them to death, watch them closely, and you can have good policy." But of course that only works when you have a serious, knowledgeable international relations specialist like Kissinger as secretary.

Back in the hearings, Kissinger makes a nasty crack about the State Department. "If Freedom House can draft three documents on peace processes in a matter of days, why can't the State Department do the same?" Then he turns to Ambassador Bill Luers, a career officer who's been working with the Commission as a lead consultant and asked if he, Kissinger, is making the staff paranoid. Luers responds, "It's Harry [Shlaudeman] that I'm worried about." And in fact Shlaudeman had been looking even grayer, more rumpled, and down-and-out than usual lately. So Henry turns to him, slaps him on the knee, and says, "Everyone knows that Harry is in charge here"—and then does one of his looks around the room to see who's laughing. Only me, who alone among the staff doesn't depend on Kissinger or the State Department for my job and career. What's funny about this exchange is: (1) the staff *really is* paranoid, (2) they're mainly afraid of Henry himself, and (3) everyone knows that it's really Henry who's in charge, not Shlaudeman. In short, when Kissinger is around, the tension level goes way up and so does the paranoia, and the room is alive with electricity as multiple agendas at multiple levels are acted out.

BUILDING CONSENSUS

In all this to and fro and trading of insults, an amazing thing begins to happen: a consensus begins to build among the commissioners and between them and the senior staff and lead consultants. First, the commissioners have already concluded that a multi-pronged approach—democracy, human rights, development, military reform, diplomacy, U.S. pressure, security—is necessary both for their report and for policy success. Second, the Commission is surprised that quite a number of the paired witnesses—Hayes and Treverton, Weintraub and Stoga, Falcoff and Bob Hunter, Vaky and myself—were so close together in our analyses and recommendations. With the debate in Congress, the press, and on television so polarized, the commissioners expected our testimonies to be far apart as well. When they were not, the commissioners were pleasantly surprised and began to see the framework of a potential bi-partisan (as the president's charge to the Commission had demanded) report.

What really cemented the emerging consensus, however, was the trip the commissioners took to Central America in early October 1983. For up to this point the Commission was still quite divided along partisan and ideological lines. Right wingers like Silber and Walsh were inclined, for example, to give the Salvadoran colonels the benefit of the doubt and to rationalize the many human rights abuses there as the inevitable outcome of civil war and a counter-guerrilla strategy. In a parallel fashion, the left wingers like Cisneros and Strauss were inclined to excuse the excesses of the Sandinistas as the inevitable result of naïve, inexperienced "robin hoods" in power for the first time and not quite knowing what to do with it.

But in their visit to El Salvador, even the right-wingers were so appalled after their meeting with Roberto D'Aubuisson and the armed forces chiefs over their cavalier dismissal of human rights, their disdain for democratic processes, and their near-fascist ideology that they came away saying they could not support this regime and reforms were necessary. Much of the same thing happened in Nicaragua but on the opposite side of the political spectrum. There, President Daniel Ortega kept the commissioners waiting, was scornful and disdainful of them when he did see them, and used the opportunity to denounce all things American. How stupid can you be! You do not keep Bob Strauss, John Silber, or Justice Potter Stewart waiting like this, you are not dismissive or treat them with condescension, and you do not denounce the United States. After this meeting even Cisneros and Strauss came away convinced either that the Sandinistas had to go or that the United States needed to keep the pressure (including support of the Contras) on them.

The next stop was Costa Rica and President Luis Alberto Monge, whom I'd known from earlier democracy conferences. The message there even from liberals and social democrats like Monge was that the vast Sandinista arms buildup, from the USSR and other communist countries, had the potential to inflame and destabilize the entire area. The message from all the Central American presidents (often different from what they said in public) was that the Sandinistas had to *go*. Not a negotiated settlement but their actual removal from power! Wow! That's a strong message and it had a powerful impact on the commissioners, Democrats as well as Republicans.

The Commission also went to Honduras and Panama. Although they are not considered part of Central America, Mexico and Venezuela were included in the trip since these countries had vital interests in its outcome and/or were members of the Contadora group seeking to achieve peace in the area. This fact-finding trip was from October 9 to October 16—seven days. By my calculation, with seven countries visited, that works out to one day per country. Not enough time, exactly, to acquire area expertise. But at least enough time, for busy men, to get some strong impressions.

In the next few days there was a flurry of meetings. I met privately with John Silber who had a few choice words for commissioners Cisneros and Strauss for going public on television with the Commission's trip findings, but was nevertheless coming around to support the emerging consensus position. At the State Department I had a meeting with Shlaudeman, who had just received a presidential commendation and $10,000 for meritorious service, to go over some revisions to the chapters I was writing. Dr. Bill Walsh called up to tell me more stories of how Kissinger was making the other commissioners' lives miserable, how he insisted on being the only face in front of the television cameras, how he vindictively changed meeting times to inconvenience other members of the Commission. There was a consensus emerging but it was a difficult process made more so by political and personal relations.

What Walsh mainly wanted to talk about, however, was political strategy. He said that Cisneros, Diaz-Alejandro, and Strauss were still pushing to include language in the report that was strongly critical of Reagan Administration policy. But that would not do. This was, after all, a presidential commission appointed by Reagan himself. To criticize the administration and president who had empowered the Commission was a non-starter. For if the White House refused to accept and support the recommendations of the Commission, its report would go nowhere. Walsh himself, Kissinger, I, and everyone else recognized the Administration's false starts and misdiagnoses in Central America, but to dwell on those in the report would turn it into a political document, campaign fodder in the 1984 election campaign, and the administration could not permit that. So Bill, Henry, and others were already meeting with Jim Baker and Ed Meese at the White House, and they wanted me to work on Jeane Kirkpatrick and make sure she was on board. Because after her initial flurry of interest, Jeane had not taken a strong interest in the day-to-day work of the Commission.

What a wonderful lesson in politics this was for me! As an academic, I'm a follower of the adage that you "speak truth to power." My natural inclination would have been to praise the Administration when it got things right and lambast it (as often in Central America) when it got it wrong. But serving on a presidential commission, you couldn't do that. You might speak the truth to power but if that led the administration to repudiate your report, it would do no good at all. So you learn to go along in order to get along, pull your punches in order to produce a document the administration can live with, compromise in order to write a consensus report, and reserve your critical judgments for the sake of getting at least some of what you want. From the Kissinger Commission experience I sure learned a lot about policy-making.

While all this politicking was still going on, we were also busily writing the report. Ray Walser, a historian by training and a part of the State Department staff, was doing the historical section. I was writing the sections, based on the earlier papers I'd submitted, on democracy, human rights, and development. Bill Rogers and Shlaudeman were doing the diplomacy and security sections. Meanwhile the commissioners themselves were dividing into subgroups, going over our drafts, and writing some sections themselves. As the report began to come together, master presidential speechwriter Ray Price was brought in to clarify and sharpen the language. With Price's help, the report that emerged was well argued and beautifully written.

SELLING THE REPORT

Politics in Washington is never ending; the "permanent campaign" began long before Bill Clinton and James Carville invented that term. By the end of November-early-December we pretty much had the report written. In academia, once you have that final draft written, that's pretty much the end of the matter; off it goes to the publisher. But in political life, the writing part is easy; it's the "selling" of your report to a skeptical Congress, White House, media, and public that's difficult.

The report came out on January 10, 1984,[5] timed to get maximum attention just as people were getting back from Christmas holidays and New Year's. It was published simultaneously in both English and Spanish, the first time that had ever been done with the report of a presidential commission.[6] Henry

Kissinger wrote a brief foreword; the report was dedicated to the late Sen. "Scoop" Jackson whose idea the report had been and who had served as one of its counselors, but who had died before its completion. It contained eight chapters largely following the structure of the witness panels we had organized. There was a brief introduction, then an overview chapter, next a chapter on the current crisis, then chapters on economic, political, social, and security issues, a chapter on peace processes, and a brief conclusion. It is not our purpose to go through the substance of the report here except to say that it came out strongly for democracy, human rights, social and economic development, and peace and security. The report was definitely the centrist, bipartisan document that we had all along wanted to produce. All twelve commissioners signed on to it.

In the week before the report's release there was a flurry of activity. We sought both to garner a favorable press and to swat down any negative comments already circulating about the report. I had a good friend at the *Washington Post*, Joanne Omang, to whom I provided background and several newsy tidbits of information. Although the report itself was closely guarded, commissioners and staffers alike—myself included—were leaking like mad to ensure a positive reception.

The biggest target of the pre-publication campaign, however, was the White House. The White House had earlier heard rumors, including from conservative members of the Commission, that the report was too liberal, too much a Democrat report, too critical of the Administration. In fact it was a centrist, middle-of-the-road report and was not critical of the Administration. But the White House was nevertheless suspicious. In the White House, Ed Meese (later attorney-general) was to be the first reader of the report. Kissinger (who was not himself above suspicion in the Reagan Administration) as well as Silber, Walsh, and Stewart went to work on Meese as well as Baker and Deaver, the White House "troika." Rogers and Shlaudeman worked on their colleagues in the State Department as well as the NSC. I was asked to call Jeane and to get her on board, in the hope that she and Meese combined could convince Reagan.

The problem was the one Bill Walsh had warned us about earlier. This was a *White House* and a *presidential* commission. If our report was repudiated or even unenthusiastically received by Reagan and his advisers, it was the kiss of death for our recommendations. Kissinger later told me that he and the key staff—Rogers, Shlaudeman—spent the entire weekend prior to the report's publication on the phone with the White House, explaining, informing, persuading. Meese came around, he convinced the other members of the troika, they in turn persuaded Reagan. After all this, the White House still had reservations but it kept these to itself; Reagan and the Administration came out solidly behind the report. Reagan enthusiastically presented it to the public, Congress, and the media.

THE AFTERMATH

The Kissinger Report was not an unqualified success—but then, few things in Washington politics are. Bill LeoGrande, one of our more left-wing witnesses whose views were not incorporated in the final report, wrote a bitter and biting review that mainly revealed his own complexes. Congressman Mike Barnes, before whose subcommittee on inter-American affairs I had testified several times but who knew next to nothing about Central America (Mike was actually *my* congressman, from D.C.'s Maryland suburbs), made some statements indicating he didn't think the report would change the debate very much on Capitol Hill. The pro-Sandinista, pro-FMLN (the Salvadoran guerrillas) crowd in WOLA and the Latin American Studies Association (LASA) were critical, as were the right-wingers associated with the Group of Santa Fe. But if we lopped off the two extremes and were able to win over and form a consensus around the broad middle, which was Kissinger's, Rogers', Shlaudeman's, and my aim from the beginning, then the report had achieved its goal.

The report helped move the Reagan Administration back toward the center and the mainstreams of American foreign policy. By standing strongly for democracy and human rights in El Salvador and for diplomatic openings as well as military pressure in Nicaragua, it isolated the extremes and moved toward a consensus on Central America.

The report had other advantages:

- it defused foreign criticism
- it defused media criticism
- it defused the criticisms of religious and other human rights groups
- it gave clear direction to the foreign affairs agencies and the bureaucracy—State, Defense, CIA, etc.
- with all this, it got Central America off the front pages and off our nightly television screens so it could be dealt with unemotionally and professionally by our diplomats.

When I first went to Washington and AEI in 1981, it became immediately clear, to me and eventually to others, that I was not part of "the movement." That is, of the ideological conservatives at AEI or the Heritage Foundation. As a professor of political science and international relations, I'm not very comfortable with any such ideological movement, and I was equally opposed to what I saw, since the 1960s, Vietnam, Nixon, and Carter, as the growing polarization of the country. I'm a centrist and a consensus builder, not a polarizer. And that's how I saw my task at AEI, of which the Kissinger Commission was one very important part: on the area I knew best—Latin America—to pull Reagan Administration policy back to the center, to the mainstreams. Working with Kissinger, Strauss, Rogers, Shlaudeman, etc. who shared this goal, that's exactly what we did. For the Kissinger Commission report was just that: a centrist document meant to rebuild the consensus on foreign policy that had been missing on this issue for too long.

Once the report was written, published, and that frantic weekend over that we had spent lobbying Jeane and the White House, the commissioners largely went their separate ways and my role (and consultantship) wound down and came to an end. Now began the more overtly political, legislative, and administrative part of the process. I recall meeting with Senator Jeff Bingaman (D-NM) and Congressmen Jim Wright, Jack Kemp, and William Broomfield about the report, and with Amb. Jim Michel and Deputy Assistant Secretary of State Richard Holwill, who were placed in charge of shepherding the Commission-proposed legislation through Congress.

On February 22, a little over a month after the report came out, I testified in support of its recommendations before the House Foreign Affairs Subcommittee on Inter-American Affairs—Reps. Barnes, Lagomarsino, Hyde, Bereuter, Kostmayer, Gejdenson, Weiss, and Reid. Henry Hyde, knowing my affiliation, expected me to echo the AEI-Kirkpatrick line, while the Democrats on the Committee I could sense were prepared to be hostile. But mine was again a balanced, centrist, and informative testimony that surprised both groups: I could see the eyes of the congressmen light up. We actually had a good discussion, something that is extremely rare in Washington policy-making. But after that, although I stayed attuned, we let the professionals in legislative relations take over the negotiations and logrolling to get our program through Congress. The legislation that emerged was very close to what the Commission had recommended.

It took awhile for the report to sink in, and for the legislation, known as the (Henry "Scoop") "Jackson Plan for Democracy, Development, and Peace in Central America," to be enacted and implemented. The debate on particular issues also dragged on. But the main controversies had been defused and, with the elections in El Salvador and the larger democratization program now under way, Central America died down as an immensely partisan and polarizing issue. Then, when Jim Baker, who among the troika of high White House officials had been most supportive of the report, became secretary of state in the later George H.W. Bush Administration, he moved quickly to resolve the still-remaining issues of El Salvador and Nicaragua. We on the Commission not only cheered Baker's moves but also saw his diplomatic work as the culmination of the work the Commission had begun a few years earlier.

NOTES

1. Cynthia Aronson, *Crossroads: Congress, the Reagan Administration, and Central America* (New York: Random House/Pantheon, 1989).

2. Shlaudeman had been up to his neck in the early 1970s in the U.S. efforts to unseat President Salvador Allende of Chile in 1973. Although both of them "shaded the truth" in their testimony under oath to the Congress about this affair, CIA director Richard Helms was convicted of perjury for his statements while Shlaudeman, more skillful with words, got only a mild reprimand.

3. The Commission Papers were published as *Appendix to the Report of the National Bipartisan Commission on Central America* (Washington, D.C.: Government Printing Office, 1984).

4. Such a strategy of talking to and buying off the guerrillas was followed by James Baker, when he ultimately moved to resolve the Central America crisis in the late-1980s.

5. The report was published by the Government Printing Office; a commercial edition was published by MacMillan (New York, 1984) as *The Report of the President's National Bipartisan Commission on Central America*.

6. But the Spanish edition had to be published by commissioner John Silber's Boston University because the State Department ran out of money.

Chapter Nine

Am I Entitled to Be Called "Honorable"? Serving the White House at Home and Abroad

When you're in Washington at one of the big think tanks, you have more opportunities than you do as an academic scholar. You get more phone calls, receive more invitations, have more opportunities to speak and write, and earn more in royalties and honoraria. It's a nice feeling to be so popular, and your ego and sense of self-importance tend to inflate as well. If your guys happen to be in power, as with Reagan and his relations with AEI, you may even receive calls and invitations from the highest levels of the U.S. government, the White House and the Oval Office.

That is what happened to me in the mid-1980s, not only the invitation to serve with the Kissinger Commission but other opportunities as well. These include (1) AEI and White House efforts to create a conservative international to match the left-wing one; (2) various lecturing opportunities abroad where I spoke semi-officially on behalf of U.S. policy; (3) the Presidential Task Force on Project Economic Justice of which I was a member (not just a "lead consultant"); and (4) a White House appointment as the U.S. representative to the Institute for Latin American Integration (INTAL) in Buenos Aires. Each of these assignments or appointments involved some wonderful opportunities, got me into some situations that I would never otherwise have seen, and added further to my storehouse of stories and lore. But the question lingers: do these appointments, some of which came at the presidential level, enable me to be called "Honorable"?[1] On that question alone hangs another interesting tale.

A CONSERVATIVE INTERNATIONAL?

In late 1983, early 1984—about the same time the Kissinger Commission was completing its work—the idea began to percolate in the White House and at

AEI that there ought to be a conservative "international" as a counterpart to the Socialist International (SI). The idea came from Jeane and the neocons; they convinced AEI President Bill Baroody that AEI ought to be the center and intellectual font for this new undertaking. Reagan and the White House were equally enthusiastic.

It was not just the SI that was to be the foil in this project. Rather, we had all (myself included) come to realize that, growing out of the Vietnam era protests, the 1972 McGovern campaign, and Jimmy Carter's presidency, the Left (think tanks, academia, foundations, the media, interest groups) was much larger and better organized than was the Right. Remember, this was before Rush Limbaugh, talk radio, FOX News, and the ascendancy and even dominance of the conservative think tanks and agenda by the end of Reagan's second term. In 1983–1984 we on the center-right still ran up against the fact that the media, publishing, universities and university audiences, etc. were *overwhelmingly* on the Left or liberal side. Frankly, we got tired of the fact that when we wrote, lectured, or appeared on television, our message was consistently outvoted, drowned out, or even silenced by the Left (see chapter 11). That was the motivation behind AEI's subsequent efforts to fashion its own *internationale* in opposition to the dominant left-wing one.

At AEI we had several meetings on this theme in early 1984. Jeane and the neocons were all in favor of forming a better-organized conservative movement at home and abroad and waxed eloquent about the various times they were purposely misquoted, shouted down, booed, ignored, passed over for opportunities, and so on. Bill Baroody, initially skeptical, was won over by the assurance that funds from the major conservative foundations—Scaife, Bradley, Olin, Smith Richardson—could be secured to carry out the program.

Given the immense differences between U.S.-style think tanks, political parties, foundations, and interest groups, *and* those in other countries, I was skeptical that we could succeed in constructing this conservative international. And in finding like-minded scholars, business associations, foundations, and the like abroad. Not only were these very different countries but the relations of these groups to the state or government—less independent, less privately funded, less autonomous—were also very different than in the U.S.

Nevertheless the funds materialized, and who am I to pass up a free trip abroad? Given my background, and the fact that I was en route there anyway for conference and research purposes, I was asked to explore the possibilities in Spain, Portugal, and Latin America. I also did some limited sounding out of the prospects in Paris.[2] Other of AEI's scholars went to Margaret Thatcher's England and to West Germany where they met with private business groups as well as, respectively, groups and think tanks associated with the Conservative and Christian Democratic parties.

Even before embarking on the first of several trips to those parts of the world for which I was responsible, it seemed to me that the prospects of finding AEI counterpart organizations in England and Germany were much better than those in Iberia or Latin America. Among other reasons, "my" areas had no tradition at that time (early 1980s) of independent think tanks (or even any other kind), most of the few that did exist were dependent on the state for financing and support, and they had no tradition of independent research. All these countries still had weak civil societies and a small private sector, had in most cases just emerged from years of authoritarianism, and were still poor countries that could not afford, or even contemplate, philanthropy or independent think tanks that were not in the pay of and beholden to some party, faction, individual, or government.

My first trip abroad on behalf of the conservative international project was to Spain and Portugal in the summer of 1984. First, Lisbon. Actually, I was in Portugal mainly to update research I had earlier done on the Portuguese revolution of 1974 and to begin another research project for which we had recently received a large grant from the Tinker Foundation on Iberian-Latin American relations. Portugal in 1984 was still very shaky politically with a weak and unstable coalition government; economically, the country was just beginning to recover from the devastation caused by the 1974 revolution, but it had not yet experienced the spurt of growth brought on by the election of a stable government in 1985 and its joining the European Economic Community (EEC, the predecessor of the European Union, EU) in 1986.

The still uncertain political situation in 1984 and poor economic conditions affected my research and political agenda in major ways. First, Portugal was still so preoccupied by its volatile internal politics that it had almost no active foreign policy and certainly not in Latin America, not even in Brazil, a former Portuguese colony. Second, in 1984 Portugal was still very weakly institutionalized and lacking an organized civil society; it had none of the think tanks, foundations, business groups, or party branches with an international orientation with whom we hoped to establish contact. After the revolution, private business and business groups were still reviled in Portugal, and the foundations that existed (Gulbenkian, Oriente) were playing it very cautious politically and shied away from any formal ties with outside groups, especially if they were American and conservative.

The next step was Madrid. Spain was in much better shape than Portugal. It had not had a revolution after Franco's death in 1975, its political system was stable, and its economy was booming. Hence I found Spain with an energetic foreign policy including in Latin America where it hoped to broaden and strengthen its ties.

I had very little success in finding AEI counterparts, however, with whom we might establish mutually beneficial ties. The problems encountered were immediate and obvious: few think tanks in Spain, almost all of them non-autonomous creatures of the state or the political parties, under-funded and under-institutionalized, and almost all of the conservative ones associated with Francoism, Fascism, monarchism, or extreme nationalism—none of which I thought AEI ought to partner with.

First I met with Antonio Sánchez-Gijon at his Instituto de Cuestiones Internacionales. This was probably the closest thing in Spain at that time to a U.S.-style think tank, but it had been close to the former government, it was distrusted by the now-governing Socialists, its government funds were being cut off, and it received only a small amount of assistance from the U.S., which made it even more distrusted by the Socialists. When I visited its headquarters I found no staff, no library, no facilities, and only Sánchez-Gijon fuctioning as a one-man operation. Not a good match for AEI with its (then) 150-person staff and $15 million budget.

Next I met with Tom Haigh and Tom Entwistle of the Institute for International Studies in Madrid. They treated me to the best salmon dinner I've ever had, at the Balzac Restaurant (behind the Prado) with its—unusual then in Spain—all-female wait staff. They were conservative enough for AEI's taste but not really a think tank; instead, they made money as an exchange program sending Spanish kids to the U.S. and teaching American exchange students in Spain. Again, not what we were looking for.

In rapid succession I visited the Jean March Foundation, the Ortega y Gassett Foundation, and the newly renamed Instituto de Cooperaación Iberoamericana (the former Institute of Hispanic Culture). In one form or another, all were dependencies of the state—not AEI's cup of tea; nor were any of them really comparable in their functions and purposes to AEI, CSIS, Brookings, or the big U.S. think tanks. I knew that going in; my visit to Spain reinforced what I already knew. Nor had the Elcano Institute, which *is* comparable to a U.S. think tank and with whom CSIS later worked out an exchange, been organized as yet. For the purposes of AEI's plan to form a conservative international, the visit to Spain paid few dividends.

The next year, 1985, we were back in Spain and Portugal again, this time en route to Paris for a meeting of the International Political Science Association (IPSA), a professional association. The purposes for this trip were the same as for the previous one: (1) to stay current and update our materials on Spain and Portugal for the edited book we were doing on Iberian-Latin American relations and now a second planned book on comparative Spanish and Portuguese politics, and (2) follow up on the conservative international project.

It was an exciting time to be in Portugal. We had timed our arrival to correspond with the Portuguese parliamentary elections, and I wanted to be an electoral observer. The elections were peaceful and orderly, the center-right Social Democratic Party came within a whisper of achieving an absolute majority (and *did* achieve that unprecedented feat in the 1987 election), and stable, effective Anibal Cavaco e Silva was elected prime minister and served for the next ten years. Portugal had finally settled down politically and, with its entry into the EEC in 1986 and as a bonanza of European subsidies began to pour in, its economy took off as well. All this was wonderful for my books but on this trip I have to say I had no more luck finding AEI-counterparts than I had the year before.

Spain was also doing well under the Socialist government of Felipe González. I visited friends, did some interviewing, went over to the American Embassy where I had a fascinating lunch in the residence with Ambassador Tom Enders (he of Central America policy, which is mainly what we talked about), and visited ministries and favorite book stores to collect materials for my writing.

Though I had many doubts about the project, I tried to pay more than lip service to the AEI goal of building a conservative international. One of my stops was at the conservative Canovas del Castillo Foundation where the officials I interviewed were amazed at the size, budget, and range of activities of AEI, compared to their small operation. Small size was one problem; another difficulty with this proposed alliance was that Canovas del Castillo was purely a partisan organization, close to the right-wing Alianza Popular (AP), and not really an all-purpose, research think tank like AEI.

I tried a new tack on this trip, concentrating on the Spanish business community rather than trying to find a (nonexistent) matching research institution. Here I had good contacts in the Círculo de Empresarios (the Businessmen's Circle, an old corporatist term, left over from the Franco era): Secretary General Carlos Cortés Beltran, Vice Secretary General Lucila Gómez-Baeza, and economic adviser José Manuel Solé Mariño. The Cículos had 142 members, all CEOs of major Spanish firms. But it had only fifteen employees including secretaries and errand boys; its activities were limited to doing specialized studies and market surveys of interest only to its members. It was a business association, not a think tank, but we did negotiate a limited agreement of cooperation.

Through the good offices of former Spanish Ambassador Beladieux whom I'd first met in Washington, I was invited to the annual convention of the European Medium and Small Business Union, then meeting in Madrid. That was fascinating: the Germans dominated the proceedings as expected, the Scandinavians assumed a superior, patronizing attitude toward Spain, and the French seemed to apologize for being in business at all. I was the lone American in attendance, not even a representative from the embassy—shameful. The thrust of the conference was to lament that small and medium-sized businesses were ignored by governments, the media, the state, and international finance, all of whom seemed to concentrate on larger firms. As an honored foreign guest, I was introduced to all the Business Union's officials and especially to the Spanish branch headed by González Noriega.

One of the high points of this visit was the sumptuous lunch Amb. Beladieux invited me to later in the week at the ritzy José Luís, Madrid's finest restaurant. Present were the Ambassador, González Noriega from the business association, and Senator Carlos Robles. All present were staunch, conservative AP supporters; all were eager to reach out to AEI and sign an agreement of cooperation. Now we were finally getting somewhere with the conservative international idea; this high-level delegation spoke not just for themselves but also for their party, their professional association, and, since all boards of directors in Spain are interlocking, some of the other foundations and associations with whom I had spoken earlier.

The trouble was, these guys wanted *AEI* ("all Americans are rich") to help finance *their* activities, when in fact part of Bill Baroody's plan in supporting the conservative international was to get foreign businessmen (AEI was already by 1985 beginning to feel a financial pinch) to support *our* activities. We did actually reach an agreement with these groups to share information, exchange publications, and more-or-less periodically pay each other a visit, so I guess I did my part in Spain for the cause of a conservative international. So far as I know, these relations and exchanges never developed much further than those indicated, but perhaps, given our countries' differences, that's all that could be expected.

From Madrid we flew on to Paris for the IPSA meeting. Frankly, in Paris the last thing we wanted to do was to be cooped up in a boring professional meeting, so I limited myself to presenting my paper and going to several of the receptions that IPSA and its friends and sponsors put on. One of these was at the American College of Paris, another at the Sorbonne, and the third hosted by Jacques Chirac, then mayor of Paris, was at the Hotel d'Ville, the city hall. I took time out for interviews at the American Embassy, the Inter-American Development Bank Paris office, and the French Conseil d'Etat (Council of State). We had lunches with the publisher Fred Praeger and his new wife, with IDB official Georges Landau and his new wife, and at the American Embassy. This was all sandwiched in between visits to Notre Dame, the Louvre, and the new Pompidou Museum.

Later in the week, as part of our conservative international project, I met with Chirac and a group of his advisers. Already at that stage the American

Embassy had him pegged as a future leader and an alternative to Socialist President Francois Mitterrand. Chirac listened politely and promised to study the AEI proposal, but it was plain to me that he, as a Gaullist, had no intention of associating his party with AEI or following the neocon agenda. Later, on Iraq, the by then Prime Minister Chirac let his disagreement with U.S. policy and leadership show in spades.

I also met with leaders of the French business community. It was a frosty meeting; unlike their counterparts in Spain, the French business leaders saw no advantage in associating with AEI. They were very nationalistic and even protectionist; if they were to establish close ties with anyone, it would be with the EC, not the Americans. Or even an American think tank. They were much more domestically than internationally oriented, not at all ideological, and saw no need whatsoever for an association of conservative organizations. Some of the neocons at AEI had contacts in French extreme nationalist, anti-immigration, and even monarchist groups but I decided these would not be good partners for AEI and stayed away.

Upon my return to Washington I wrote Baroody a long memo on the conservative international project. I told him of the lack of organizations in Portugal, the relative successes in Spain, and the attitudes of the French. Overall, I said: (1) there are few think tanks or research organizations in Europe comparable to those in the U.S.; (2) very few of them are conservative or center-right; (3) most are creatures of the state or political parties, not independent; (4) most are too small or too specialized to be equivalent AEI partners; and (5) many house some pretty unsavory characters: anti-immigrant nationalists, fascists, and monarchists with whom AEI ought not to ally. Since Baroody was always sensitive to AEI's associations (for example, he would not accept CIA money for our projects), I think my memo was the kiss of death for the idea of AEI officially organizing a conservative international, although some AEI scholars individually (and the Institute itself eventually under a reorganized AEI) continued to follow up.

Sandwiched in with these two trips to Europe in 1984 and 1985 was a trip to Central America in January 1985. The Central America excursion was part of the new democracy initiative described earlier and was designed to educate and convince Central American political and intellectual leaders about the National Endowment for Democracy and the Plan for Democracy, Development, and Peace growing out of the Kissinger Commission. We met in San José, Costa Rica.

I have described this meeting and our visit to Costa Rica at length in another place;[3] here let me just talk about the plans for the conservative international and where—if at all—Central America fit into that scheme.

We stayed and had our conference in the plush Cariari Hotel on the outskirts of San José. At the meeting were forty guests, half from the U.S., half from Central and South America. The meeting was billed as a "high-level" conference of representatives from think tanks, research institutes, universities, and foundations. Among the speakers were Mike Novak and I from AEI, Peter Bauer from London, Charles King of the Liberty Fund, Roger Fontaine from the NSC, Chilean intellectual Oscar Mertz, university professor Enrique Baloyra, and other scholars and university administrators from Central America. It turns out, when I met with U.S. Embassy officials later, that there are so few think tanks, research centers, and foundations in Central America that to fill the roster for the conference they brought in random university administrators and ministry of education officials—not quite what we had in mind.

The person who really set my teeth on edge was Francisco Ayau of Guatemala. At that time he not only had his own university (Ayau University) but the only institution that could pass as a think tank in all of Central America. Ayau was also a major businessman and a large landowner; all his efforts, it seemed to me, even his university and think tank, were dedicated to enriching Ayau himself.

In what he paraded as a great show of academic freedom, Ayau told us that when Guatemala's Catholic bishops came out to his university to tell him to stop teaching market economics, he turned them down flat. This part of Ayau's agenda I could support. But then he went on to say that all the violence in Central America stemmed from "communist influences," as if the army, police, and right-wing death squads were not at least equally responsible. He says his latifundia (large estate), which he inherited, is "honestly earned"; the peasants don't need or want land, he announces, except for the "communist mobilizers" egging them on. He says the Church (he's a member of its Opus Dei, far-right wing) is "going communist" and that liberation theology is a "communist ideology." Ayau defends Guatemalan President Efraín Ríos Montt's "self-defense forces" (really vigilantes) and is an admirer and financial backer of this human-rights-abusing man-on-horseback. On top of this abhorrent ideology, which seemed to me to be close to fascism, Ayau is also an arrogant and unfriendly person, not someone you'd like to have a beer with.

It's worth noting here that a few months later when AEI, Bill Baroody, the Kirkpatricks (Jeanne and Evron), and the neocons were again discussing the right-of-center political party and think tank international, Ayau was one of the persons whom they suggested I include. I declined, arguing that this was just the kind of person AEI should *not* be associated with and that it would harm the project and AEI if he were brought in. That argument convinced Baroody who, fortunately for me, did not force the issue.

The idea and plan for a conservative international faded away for a time at AEI, but it remained alive in the minds of some of the more ideological neocons. I lost interest in the project because in the countries and areas I covered we could not find comparable institutions with which we could work, but I know the other AEI scholars and Reagan Administration officials continued to pursue the agenda, particularly in Margaret Thatcher's Great Britain and Helmut Kohl's Germany where the climate and institutional networks were more propitious. Then, when Bill Clinton took over the White House in 1993, I found it amusing that presidential speechwriter Sidney Blumenthal sought to do again exactly what we at AEI had done earlier—to create an international "third way," except that this time it was on the left instead of the right. I wished him well, even while noting that he made many of the same mistakes and with many of the same unintended consequences that we on the center-right had faced a decade earlier.

ESOPS AND PROJECT ECONOMIC JUSTICE

ESOPs are Employee Stock Ownership Plans. ESOPs provide a means by which employees can buy out and become owners of their own companies. Usually ESOPs are organized by employees whose companies are on the edge of bankruptcy; ESOPs are a method by which employees can save their companies and thus save their jobs. Among the most prominent ESOPs at that time were Avis Car Rental and Trans-World Airlines. ESOPs have been referred to as a form of workers' capitalism.

Ronald Reagan was a believer in ESOPs. He had at some point become convinced of their usefulness. Knowing Mr. Reagan's working-class roots, his role as a labor leader in Hollywood, and his ideological commitment to free markets and capitalism, it is easy to see why ESOPs would be attractive to him. ESOPs involved capitalism, ownership, and entrepreneurship. ESOPs were presented to Reagan as an alternative to socialism and statism. They involved not only workers' control but also worker ownership. All these features appealed to Reagan.

ESOPs had gone through their political "baptism by fire" in Washington in the 1960s and 1970s—before my time there. Their chief advocate was Louis Kelso, a lawyer and flamboyant spokesman for what he called "people's capitalism." Kelso argued that ESOPs, by which employees acquired a majority of the stock in their own companies, were a means of "democratizing capitalism." By giving workers a stake in the company's success, Kelso argued, ESOPs boosted morale, increased productivity, and helped save the capitalist system.

The program was controversial when first proposed among both employers and labor unions. But Kelso gave it a populist appeal and acquired the support of Louisiana's populist senator Russell Long. Long introduced legislation that gave companies, most of which were on the verge of bankruptcy, hefty tax breaks if they converted to ESOPs. By the late 1980s, some 9,800 companies, employing some ten million workers, one fourth of the U.S. labor force, were enrolled in an ESOP plan. Of these companies, 1,500 involved workers owning a majority of the stock.[4] The motto could be, in a takeoff on Avis' famous slogan "We Try Harder," "Owners Try Harder."

The connection that brought me into the ESOPs fold was Central America. I didn't know much about ESOPs at first but was willing to be open-minded. However Reagan, an ESOPs true believer from the days he traveled the country for General Electric, became convinced that ESOPs were good not just for the United States but for Central America as well. By spreading ownership of firms and plantations in Central America, Reagan was convinced, he could improve the lot of the people, expand capitalist ownership, and defeat communism. All in one fell swoop! To that end he established a White House Task Force on Project Economic Justice. This time, instead of being a staffer and consultant as I'd been on the Kissinger Commission, I was appointed a member of the Task Force. It was my first White House appointment. Does that enable me to be called "Honorable"?

The chief driving force on the Task Force was Norman Kurland. Norman was a Washington lawyer, a disciple of Kelso and therefore a true believer in ESOPs, and an ardent admirer of Reagan. Kurland's law practice was built mainly on ESOP projects; he also had his own center, the Center for Economic and Social Justice (CESJ), mainly for his ESOP activities. He believes—contrary to my understanding, but for now I hold my tongue—that the ESOPs idea has universal applicability, that it is relevant to all countries.

At one point Norman confided in me how he got the Task Force created and funded by Congress. First he convinced his rabbi of the merits of ESOPs. The rabbi, Herzel Kranz, who became a Task Force consultant, spoke to Congressmen Mike Barnes (Norman's as well as my congressman) and Philip Crane, both of whom supported the idea and agreed it should be nonpartisan. Norman and Rabbi Kranz then spoke to Senators Richard Lugar and Chris Dodd who also agreed to sponsor the legislation. When populist Senator Long agreed to push it through the Senate it quickly passed. Republicans backed it because it favored capitalism, Democrats because it favored workers. Hey, this is Political Science 101.

While Kurland was the driving force, the chair of the Task Force was William Middendorf. Bill Middendorf was a wealthy Baltimore banker, a strong Reagan supporter, a big donor to the Republican Party, and, in turn, ambassador to the EEC, the OAS, and the Netherlands. He was also a strong ideologue, with syntax worse than Eisenhower's, and so extreme and outrageous in his way of expressing himself that it was worse than—pick your least favorite ideologue from the Reagan or Bush II periods

(Constantine "Constant Menace" Menges, Ollie North, Donald Rumsfeld, Dick Cheney, "W" himself)—anyone you can think of. I used to laugh (silently of course) at Middendorf's goofy statements but he thought I was the cat's meow; at one point he asked me to serve as his chief foreign policy adviser.

In addition to Kurland and Middendorf, other members of the Task Force were:

- Walter Bish, president of the Independent Steelworkers Union in Weirton, W.V.; the Weirton plant was an early ESOP.
- John Carbaugh, lawyer, former chief of staff to Senator Jesse Helms on the Foreign Relations Committee, tough, sometimes nasty.
- Robert Crane, president of Native American International
- Richard Derham, assistant administrator for AID.
- William Doherty, executive director of the American Institute for Free Labor Development (AIFLD) and a shrewd Washington insider.
- Steve Hanke, ultra-conservative economist from Johns Hopkins.
- John McClaughry, president of the Institute for Liberty and Community in Concord, VT.
- Paul McCracken, one of my professors at Michigan and future, acting president of AEI.
- Keith Miceli, director of Latin American affairs at the Chamber of Commerce.
- Michael Novak, my colleague at AEI.
- Malott Nyhart, vice president of the Nyhart Company of Indianapolis.
- Carlos M. Perez, president of Banana Services, Inc., representative of the Cuban exile community.
- Norman Weintraub, chief economist and director of the International Brotherhood of Teamsters.
- Me.

Well, there you have it: a quite prestigious group, fairly high level (but not as high level as the Kissinger Commission), and quite conservative. And very political: not just conservative but carefully selected for political purposes in terms of its labor, business, and academic members. Bruce Mazzie, another Washington lawyer and Kurland associate at CESJ, was chosen as Task Force executive director. And, like the earlier Kissinger Commission, the Task Force had four "counselors" that I know of: Joe Recinos, a businessman with reactionary Central American ties; Rabbi Kranz (Kurland's rabbi); William Shirra, and Colonel Vincent McGrath, a military officer with close Reagan Administration connections.

The Task Force was far less institutionalized than had been the Kissinger Commission. It had only a small budget, was unable to bring in outside witnesses, and used private bank office space provided by Middendorf. Nor did the Task Force attract much controversy or publicity (the same thing) as did the Kissinger Commission.

The Task Force was sworn in by President Reagan on March 3, 1986. Reagan was his usual jovial self, throwing out a few one-liners, smiling broadly, shaking everyone's hand, and also providing a serious charge to the Task Force members. At this same meeting we received from the president our formal letters of appointment. Does that qualify us to be called "Honorable"?

As a "Washington person" by now, I have to confess that I was not so much interested in the day-to-day work of the Task Force (I'm not opposed but ESOPs are not my thing) as in the glory of a presidential appointment and being associated with a prestigious group. So I didn't attend all its meetings or throw myself into the work as I had with the Kissinger Commission. The meetings I did attend were often entertaining and sometimes enlightening; but since I had no expertise on ESOPs, the parts of the report that I worked on dealt with Central America and the dynamics of state-directed economies.

At one of our early meetings,[5] conservative economist Steve Hanke told us that at Johns Hopkins the radicals in his department regularly stole his mail—"anything that looked important." So he had everything sent to his home. Middendorf, as chair, immediately jumped on this as an opportunity to lambaste all those "nutty professors" out there in academia. But then he caught himself: "Except Howard, of course."

The next issue was serious—and even more contentious. One of our members, John McClaughry, had somehow gotten hold of a letter sent to AID by executive director and Kurland associate Bruce Mazzie using Task Force stationery and requesting $8 million for Kurland's Center, which also happened to be located in his private law office. Moreover the letter called for the administration of the Task Force's activities, including its funds, to be implemented through the CESJ. This had been done without any authorization of the Task Force or its chair, and was obviously a ploy to use the *public* Task Force as a means to enrich Kurland's *private* Center. McClaughry was very angry and, as a lawyer himself, gave both Mazzie and Kurland a trial-like grilling and dressing-down. Kurland's defense was that his Center was impoverished, short of staff, and needed the money; he also turned on his associate Mazzie saying that he had sent the letter on his own. But it is hard to imagine Kurland would not know about a letter requesting $8 million going out over his name and on his stationery.

Middendorf, to his credit, saw right away that the letter should not have been sent nor Task Force stationery used without the members agreeing. So he instructed Rabbi Kranz and McClaughry to draft a new letter taking back the first letter until the Task Force could agree. To compensate, Middendorf put a hefty sum of *his own* money into the Task Force's account to pay for operating expenses. It must be nice to be a wealthy banker.

The next question taken up was the audience for our report, some paragraphs of which were already circulating in draft form. The first paragraph, written by Kurland and his rabbi, began to talk about genocide and the Holocaust, obviously a searing experience but perhaps not entirely appropriate for a report on Central America. One of our members noted that the first reader of the report in the White House would be Ed Meese, which sounded eerily familiar from my Kissinger Commission experience. But based on that same experience I suggested we aim for a wider audience: the White House, yes, but also the public, the media, the policy community, and, hey, how about Central America too, the ostensible subject of our own labors. That view won the day.

At this time Treasury Secretary James Baker was spending much of his time dealing with the issue of Third World debt, and there was considerable sentiment that our ESOPs recommendations ought to be tied into the Baker Plan. But others on the Task Force argued that the Baker Plan was merely a smokescreen, a shell game, aimed at disguising from the American public that we, the U.S. taxpayers, would ultimately be forced to pay for Third World debt. Some pronounced the Plan dead. In the end we decided to relate our recommendations for private investment in Central America and for employee ownership to the Baker Plan like, as one of our members put it, "an ornament on a Christmas tree," but not to become so tied in with it that if it failed, we failed too.

McClaughry next argued that it would be absolutely necessary to have a person in the White House to champion our report, as Jeane Kirkpatrick had done for Central America issues earlier (she had recently resigned her UN post) in the Reagan Administration. The name of my friend and former think tank colleague Bill Perry, now serving on the National Security Council, was one name set forward. Other suggestions included AID director Peter McPherson, who liked ESOPs because they complemented his foreign assistance programs, and United States Information Agency (USIA) official (and former think tank colleague—from the Foreign Policy Research Institute—FPRI—in Philadelphia) Richard Bissell. The argument that won the day was that we would use all our "horses," not just one.

In all these deliberations the split between the more ideological "true believers"—especially Kurland, Mazzie, Hanke, and the chair, Middendorf—and the pragmatists like McClaughry and myself was evident. Some others—Micheli of the Chamber and Derham of AID—were there because of their institutional positions, and they too were pragmatists. I was not sure about Crane, Bish, or Nyhart—either why they were there or whom they represented. Meanwhile, as the meetings dragged on, Novak, McCracken, and Carbaugh showed up less and less.

One of my activities for the Task Force was to keep other interested groups informed of our activities and recommendations and to negotiate over the differences. Among others, I met with Bill Doherty, the legendary head of the AFL-CIO's American Institute for Free Labor Development (AIFLD). Bill was stocky and red-faced—a good Santa Claus at Christmas time—but, as an old labor leader, tough as nails in negotiations and very well informed on Central America for which his group received substantial U.S. government money.

Bill had written a long letter to the Task Force and was known to be a critic. In the letter he indicated support for ESOPs in general but warned against thinking of them as substitutes for labor unions. He cautioned that ESOPs should not be viewed as a panacea or cure-all for Central America, that ESOPs do not necessarily lead to workers' control, that ESOPs may not help produce democracy. His letter warned against using government subsidies to fund ESOPs and that employee ownership programs in Central America would not solve the problems of poverty, class strife, instability, or Marxist activity. Contrary to the advice we were getting from our Central American members, ESOPs should not be thought of as replacing unions or union activity. He concluded that ESOPs would not guarantee political freedoms or human rights, nor were they necessary for securing democracy.

Rather a broadside. Essentially his arguments repeated those of earlier decades that had been applied against Kelso and ESOP advocates. All along, organized labor had been, if not opposed, then highly skeptical of ESOPs. For, by providing for employee ownership, ESOPs *did* in fact undermine the need for labor unions. Doherty's letter also foresaw the possibilities for ESOPs to be used for leveraged buyouts, to the detriment of employees. But in the end, after all these criticisms, and undoubtedly seeing the handwriting on the wall—i.e., that the Reagan Administration approved the plan—AIFLD came around to supporting the program. Probably, it hoped to subvert or coopt it later on, but at least for now we had gotten the support, or at least neutrality, of perhaps the key interest group involved in the process. Part of the deal involved the late appointment of Doherty himself as a member of the Task Force.[6]

By mid-summer 1986, the Task Force was well along in its proceedings and moving ahead on its agenda. First, we had decided to give our report a broader appeal by aiming it at the media, business, labor, religious groups, Congress, the foreign affairs bureaucracy, as well as the White House and

NSC. Second, our emphasis was not just on ESOPs but also on larger issues of democracy, human rights, economic development, freedom and justice. Third, we argued that, as with the Kissinger Commission, there would be both a report and a supplemental volume of collected reports, witness statements, and papers prepared for the Task Force. Since all of these plans were in accord with my own thinking, I felt comfortable drafting some pages for the report on economic development, its relations to democracy, and the need for a comprehensive, multi-dimensional approach.

There were still controversies. Hanke became a pain in the neck for repeatedly trying to inject his far-right views into the language of the report. Carbaugh continued in his confrontational ways, while the reactionary Latins on the Task Force always seemed amazed that some of us saw it as serving public rather than private self-interests. Several members, especially McClaughry, remained suspicious of Kurland and Mazzie, cross-examining them on more than one occasion to make sure the funds were not just going to their own private center. Meanwhile, Middendorf, who must be smarter than he sometimes seems, continued to use the Task Force as a forum to air his own, often outlandish and even comical views, denouncing agrarian reform in Latin America as "communistic," denouncing President José Napoleon Duarte in El Salvador as a "front man for the guerrillas," and even reaching back to the Alliance for Progress of John F. Kennedy as producing "statism and socialism."

With some of these wild-eyed ideas and wild men on the Task Force, and with the private agendas of some of the members competing with its publicly stated one, it is a wonder that (1) the Task Force was able to produce a more-or-less centrist and consensual report, and (2) it was, if I may say so myself, a quite good report. It came out of course for ESOPs but in a measured as distinct from true-believer way. It did not present ESOPs as a new panacea but embedded these recommendations in a larger plan encompassing democracy, development, and private investment. Not only could I live with that kind of report but also I was proud of it and of my role in helping to draft it.

President Reagan was kind enough to host us a second time at the White House to receive our report. Reagan was, as always when I saw him, gracious, amiable, and warmly welcoming. Our chairman, Middendorf, managed to squeeze in some of his usually outlandish comments on the world even while presenting the report, but Reagan, a consummate actor, remained unflappable. It was a nice, pleasant meeting but our report, much narrower in scope and not as timely or controversial as the Kissinger Commission Report, received far less attention from the media. It had some, very modest impact on Central America, legitimizing the ESOPs idea in the area while otherwise, in its more general recommendations, supporting the same policy principles as the Kissinger Commission. And don't forget, my appointment to the Task Force may also enable me to be called "Honorable."

ON THE LECTURE CIRCUIT IN EUROPE AND LATIN AMERICA

In the first year of my residency at AEI, I somehow got on the White House invitation list. I don't recall if it was at my initiative or hers, but I'm sure Jeane Kirkpatrick had something to do with it. Soon I was going down to the White House or the Executive Office Building next door on a weekly basis, sometimes more. This was heady stuff: the "little boy" from Grand Rapids, Michigan, walking the corridors of power in *the* absolute center of power and responsibility in the American system: the White House.

On different occasions, I was invited to lunches in the White House mess, receptions on the back lawn, presidential statements proclaimed in the rose garden, presidential lunches and conferences, our Task Force initial and final meetings, and sometimes even high-level policy discussions. But what I want to report on here (and from another perspective in the next chapter) are the weekly meetings and briefings put on by the recently created White House Office of Public Liaison.

Faith Whittlesley, a Reagan stalwart and energetic campaign worker, ran the Office of Public Liaison during this period. Once a week she would summon us to the EOB for a briefing on Reagan Administration policy. Almost all the participants (I might have been the sole exception) were true believers, "Movement" conservatives from the Heritage Foundation, AEI, the Chamber of Commerce, the Hill, interest groups, etc. The aim was to bring together policy influentials, brief us at the highest levels on Administration initiatives, and have us carry the Administration's message back to our groups and agencies for broader dissemination. On successive weeks we were briefed by Secretary of State Al Haig, Defense secretary Cap Weinberger, NSC officials Constantine Menges and Oliver North, President Reagan, Margaret Thatcher, CIA director Bill Casey, to say nothing of numerous lower officials from inside the Administration.

At first, when the likes of Ollie North or some of the more ideological and "Movement" lesser lights were spouting their ideas, I would put my hands over my eyes in mock exasperation and whisper (to myself), "I don't believe what I'm hearing, I don't believe what I'm hearing." But, as an inveterate note-taker, I quickly realized that, in this setting, the White House, I was an eyewitness to history. So I uncovered my eyes and started writing it all down. I may have been the only person in the room who took extensive notes during these briefings.

Although I'm not by any means a "Movement" conservative, just being in the room, and my AEI affiliation, must have given me credibility with the Office of Public Liaison. The White House also knew that I was the director of AEI's Hemispheric Affairs Center. Those were apparently credentials enough; after attending several of these meetings I was approached by the Office of Public Liaison to see if I would be willing to go abroad and lecture to foreign audiences on American policy in Central America. All expenses would be paid and there would be a modest ($200 per day, if I recall, the same rate as Fulbright lectures) honorarium. U.S. embassies abroad through their cultural affairs officers would coordinate my visits. Do these White House assignments entitle me to be called "Honorable"?

So off I went over the next couple years to Mexico City; San José, Costa Rica; Lisbon; Madrid; Paris; Cologne; Amsterdam; and Vienna. All to lecture on Central America policy. Most of these were quick trips, in-and-out, one-day. Sometimes I'd make a one-stop single trip to an individual country, sometimes two destinations would be included in one trip. In none of these did I stay long enough to get more than a superficial impression (or to write about in my journals or subsequently), but on a couple of occasions I stayed on for a few days beyond my lecture either to attend a conference or do my own research. While these brief individual visits were seldom newsworthy, the collective experience is worth talking about.

First of all, the audiences were almost uniformly hostile. Mexican and European audiences were strongly opposed to the U.S. Central America policy. They saw it as the U.S. "shark" beating up on the Central America "sardines." Moreover they viewed the U.S. as backing the corrupt oligarchy and the repressive army, as against peasants, workers, and "the masses" as represented by the Marxist guerrillas. It was little "David" or a group of Davids, against the brutal "Giant," the United States. It was similar to the European attitude today toward U.S. policy in Iraq. Sometimes when I'd walk onto the stage or up to the lectern, I'd be greeted by boos and catcalls. On some occasions I noticed that the first ten or fifteen rows were filled to a person with people wearing the scarf of the FMLN (the Salvadoran guerrillas) or the red armband of the Nicaraguan Sandinistas. Not exactly friendly audiences.

The audiences were usually large. Central America was the new Vietnam, a cause for which to rally. The topic drew large, vociferous audiences. Most of these were university students but there were professional diplomats, journalists, the interested public, as well as Trotskyites, Marxists, Anarchists, and street people of various sorts. In Cologne, I recall, not only did the audience jam-pack the room, but there were people in the window wells and spilling out into the grassy courtyard below. In Amsterdam the buzz in the auditorium was that, while my name was recognized as an obviously Dutch (Fresian) name, I was speaking on behalf of an "obviously" incompetent, wrong-headed, *American* government. In Mexico City I'm sure the audience was 100% Marxist and anti-American; in San José people were more moderate and civilized.

What an adventure! In my university teaching career, I was not used to dealing with such hostile audiences. But now, between these foreign junkets and the lecturing I was doing at U.S. universities (as told in the next chapter), I got used to it fast, and also what to do about it. Here are my tricks of the trade. First I would tell some insider Ronald Reagan stories, all of them funny and mildly critical, usually focused on his limits as a president, which immediately disarmed my audience, made them think I was on their side, and dissolved the tension in the room.

Second, I would focus in the body of my speech on the *processes* of U.S. foreign policy-making rather than the policies per se. That's my field after all; I have written textbooks on this subject, and have real foreign policy expertise on how the American system works. I found that most Europeans were fascinated by this because they didn't understand the U.S. system well, how it worked, and how it was so different from their own parliamentary systems. By the time I got into such subjects as the National Security Council, interest group politics, bureaucratic politics (rivalries between agencies), Congress and partisanship, the role of public opinion, etc., I found my audiences were not only fascinated by the subject but had mainly forgotten what they were hostile about.

Only then would I launch into an explanation of Central America. Since I knew the area well, I could present it coolly and factually. I was clearly not a shill for U.S. government policy but I was not an unabashed critic either; I tried to be fair to both sides, meanwhile setting forth my own centrist positions. I would explain the complex overlap of domestic and international forces in Central America, the history of the area and why these countries were being torn apart, as well as U.S. policy and interests in the area: that the U.S. wanted a peaceful, stable, democratic, and developed Central America; that we sympathized with Central American aspirations but that the Cubans, Soviets, and others were stirring the pot; that we wanted human rights and economic growth but that one had to deal realistically with the *fact* of civil war and Marxist-Leninist guerrillas; that we had no interest in occupying Central America permanently but wanted to get out as soon as possible. Please note that much the same language and arguments were incorporated in the Kissinger Commission Report; a good part of that was *my* language. After almost every one of the presentations, I would have people come up to me and say this was the first time they had ever heard U.S. policy in Central America presented in a balanced and logical way. Normally, all they received were cartoon presentations, hyperbole, and biased opinion.

But then the White House would undo all my good work. No sooner would I leave the country where I'd just lectured than one of those know-nothings from the White House Office of Public Liaison would come through with the simplistic message, "the commies are coming, the commies are coming." I could have wrung their necks. For *everyone* in Europe and Latin America knew it was not that simple. All except the Reagan White House apparently. But that's why we had written the Kissinger Report.

INTAL

In 1984–1985, fresh from the Kissinger Commission Report, I was asked to undertake a special mission to Latin America for the Inter-American Development Bank (IDB).[7] The Bank is a regional development bank, comparable to the World Bank but of less prestige and stature, focused on Latin America.

The Bank wanted me to undertake a survey of Latin America, its problems and potential, and write a report both on this theme and on Bank operations in the region. We agreed that, since the Kissinger Commission had just finished its report on Central America, I would focus on the big, important countries that were not then receiving so much attention: Mexico, Peru, Argentina, and Brazil. The Bank paid me an exceedingly generous honorarium, arranged for first class air tickets, booked me into the best of hotels, and assisted with customs, immigration, and transportation at every stop.

I was under no illusion as to what all this largesse and VIP treatment were all about. I was told as much by Marion Czarnecki, the Bank's executive director. During this period our AEI economists and the Reagan Administration had been severely critical of the Bank's failure to support the free-market, laissez-faire, state-downsizing, privatization policies of the Administration. The charge was true: the Bank was full of ex-cabinet ministers and economists from Latin America who supported the statist approach. Since I was known as a moderate on these issues, by hiring me and paying me handsomely the IDB hoped to curry favor with AEI and the Administration while simultaneously producing a report that was less strident and more centrist on the issues.

One other aspect of this assignment was interesting, and particularly important for this chapter. Along with preparing the report, Czarnecki and Bank President Enrique Iglesias asked me if I would serve as the *official* U.S. representative to INTAL, the Institute for Latin American Integration. In this capacity I would succeed Ambassador Viron ("Pete") Vaky, one of the State Department's most respected Latin America diplomats. INTAL, located in Buenos Aires, was a Bank subsidiary dedicated to promoting Latin American integration efforts. I would serve on its advisory board, on the editorial board of its journal *Integración*, and travel to Buenos Aires once every other year to attend board meetings and give lectures. Since I was already headed to BA as part of my round-the-continent tour, I would time the trip to correspond to the INTAL board meeting. This appointment had to be formally authorized by the White House; once again I need to ask, does this appointment entitle me to be called "Honorable"?

It was a very interesting and exciting trip. In every city where I stopped—Mexico City, Lima, BA, and Rio de Janeiro—thanks to Bank, U.S. Embassy, and my own contacts, I saw people at the very highest levels: cabinet officers, U.S. ambassadors and embassy officials, IDB country directors, and even two Latin American presidents, Alan García and Raúl Alfonsín. I had wonderful access and collected reams of information useful to my report. Most interesting—and surprising—was the degree to which Bank officials in the field opened up to me, were very critical of their own institution, and simply "unloaded" on the IDB's inefficiencies and shortcomings.

I put all of this in my report. I also wrote a chapter, based on my interviews, severely critical of the Bank itself. When I submitted the manuscript, Czarnecki and the Bank loved the report but not, naturally enough, the chapter about the IDB's own inadequacies. They went so far as to ask me to remove the offending chapter. Why, they reasoned, give the Bank's enemies even more ammunition, especially in a report funded by the IDB? But this was a form of censorship and was equally unacceptable. We settled on a compromise: my report would be published in book form but without the "evil" chapter. That would be published, we argued, after the book and separate from it, in article form. Meantime the "missing chapter" ("*capítulo perdido*") circulated widely in Washington, including in the Bank, in typescript form.

I went to Mexico City first, then Peru, a brief stopover in Chile, and then over the Andes to Buenos Aires. In BA I had two main activities: to do the research for my IDB report and, now, fulfill my obligations to INTAL. At the IDB office in BA, I met with its director Marcelo Ribeiro. He is a Brazilian in an overwhelmingly Argentine office—not good for good relations. He was wonderful, not only informing about the bloated, inefficient, patronage-dominated IDB office in which he himself worked but also telling me how difficult it was to be a Brazilian working among Argentines.

That afternoon[8] was the first in a series of meetings of the INTAL executive committee—my other reason for being in BA. Its offices occupied two floors of a plush, as usual, downtown office building *overlooking* the Casa Rosada. I made a point of getting there early so I could talk to the secretaries—always the best way to get the lowdown on an organization. They told me that INTAL had about twenty regular employees but that there were an additional sixty persons on the payroll. What do these others do, I asked; no one had any idea nor did they ever see them. In addition, INTAL had an unknown number of consultants who regularly received stipends but whose work or responsibilities were similarly unknown. Already INTAL was starting to sound like a patronage-dominated and not very efficient organization.

The director-general of INTAL was Juan Mario Vacchino, an Argentine (all these international agencies—IDB, OAS, INTAL, etc. seemed to be dominated by Argentines, with *just enough* Brazilians and others to avoid a revolt). Vacchino initiated the discussion by telling us he was under "tremendous pressure" (from the U.S. presumably) to change INTAL's focus to emphasize private sector development. But he disagreed with that emphasis arguing that the private sector in Latin America was not very viable, it was equated with the robber barons, there was no tradition of private enterprise, the "invisible hand" didn't work and in any case leads to abuse, open markets and capitalism had bad reputations, and that state direction was needed to give cohesion to the economy. I actually agreed with much of that analysis but as the "official U.S. representative" to the board I felt that I ought to say something in favor of a "balanced" (public and private) economy.

Felix Peña, ex-director of INTAL and now the IDB's director on integration efforts (and another Argentine), chimed in that while the Bank had a statist orientation, that was because its charter and organization *obliged* it to deal with *governments* and *state agencies*, not the private sector. How interesting this discussion was turning out to be! Deregulation and privatization, he said, had not yet arrived to the Bank *or* the Latin American governments. Yet it was under enormous pressure from the U.S. Congress (from whence its funds came) to reform its assistance programs to emphasize private sector development. The Bank was becoming the favorite "whipping boy" (it had no constituency) in the U.S. for Latin America's mounting economic problems.

During the next three days the INTAL executive committee talked nonstop of the Bank, integration efforts, and Latin America's mounting debt and economic difficulties. The mood was pessimistic as Latin America's debt continued to mount. Felix Peña, an ultra-smooth ex-diplomat, led the discussion, as usual among Latin Americans blaming the area's economic difficulties on "external forces" (meaning the U.S.). I chimed in arguing that the problems were mainly internal—social, political, and cultural—and that Latin America should stop blaming the outside world and start solving its own problems. Roderick Rainford, the CARICOM (Caribbean Common Market) representative and the odd man out among the Spanish speakers, talked of the new pragmatism in the Caribbean. Other speakers included the "father" of Latin American integration efforts, Felipe Herrera of Chile, Argentine Dante Caputo, Gustavo Magariños, José Maria Aragão, Carlos Quijano, Gustavo Lagos, and Julio Rodríguez.

At INTAL headquarters and in the evening we were wined and dined extravagantly. Full-course steak dinners with lots of wonderful Argentine wine (from Mendoza) were served *twice* per day—no meatless days in Argentina for us! Argentine president Raúl Alfonsín came, with no security, to one of our meetings to give a presentation and mingle with the delegates for a time. So did famed economist Raúl Prebisch, founder of the Economic Commission for Latin America (ECLA), now 82, still sharp as a tack, along with whatever wife (people had lost track of the number) he was up to by now. We also ate brunch at Clark's, the famed British watering hole and a center of the still sizable Anglo-Argentine community, and were guests of honor at a late-night tango show.

I had listened carefully to all the polite speeches and deliberations, none of which seemed to focus on the key problems, and I indicated to Peña and Vacchino that I wanted the opportunity to address the group. After some stalling and consternation (because they knew I would be a bomb thrower), my presentation was scheduled for the next day. The subject was the future of INTAL. I talked (I thought quite diplomatically) about the death of the older mercantilist or Import Substitution Industrialization (ISI) model, the twin problems of corruption and bureaucracy, the debt issue and the requirement that it be faced realistically, the need for privatization and for aid to the private sector, the manifold problems of state enterprises, and the relation of democracy to integration. I thought these were quite mild suggestions compared to what my AEI colleagues were saying, but *not so* in Latin American elite circles, and both Peña and Vacchino saw fit to attack all my premises. It was actually quite a memorable exchange and impressed on me just how powerful and difficult to change the statist tradition in Latin America was. I am not by any means a rabid free marketer; my association with INTAL and all the Latin American economists, diplomats, and ex-cabinet members who make up its council taught me to be skeptical of the possibilities for success in Latin America of a policy like the Washington Consensus that demanded a reduction of state size and relied so heavily on the private sector.

It was a fascinating visit, especially the INTAL parts. My notes on our three days of discussion there run to over one hundred pages; unfortunately I lack the space to recount all the give and take of this and subsequent INTAL meetings that I attended. But the experience was invaluable to me. In the U.S. the free market-private sector message is like a mantra, the official orthodoxy, and virtually the only position ever heard. But within INTAL's circles and among all these high-powered Latin Americans of cabinet rank, my position was the minority (and only) one. Their view was (and is) decidedly statist; they don't believe the private sector emphasis will ever work in Latin America, and they are determined at all costs to protect their perks, positions, and extensive, multiple entitlements, *all* of which flow from the state. I am not an apostle of statism but I am equally skeptical of the free market model working there. But if neither model works, Latin America is condemned to perpetual stagnation, which has in fact often been the case.

In the summer of 1987 and then again in 1989, I was back in Buenos Aires, still in my capacity as the *official* U.S. representative to INTAL. On all three of these trips, in addition to my AEI salary, I collected an honorarium for being a member of the board, more honoraria for giving lectures in BA, and a per diem that far exceeded my actual hotel and meal (themselves quite luxurious) expenses. Wow, I decided, the life of these international banker types is not only plush but also remunerative. Not long after I decided to apply for a position at the World Bank.

In each of these trips I met with U.S. embassy officials, the ambassador, DCM, Argentine journalists, and friends from the Argentine academic community.[9] But my primary responsibility was INTAL and the INTAL board meeting. I went over to the INTAL's offices prior to the meeting, had a delicious lunch—more superb Argentine beef and wine—talked to the secretaries (the source of much information), and met preliminarily with INTAL officials to see what was new and exciting.

The most informative of these was assistant director Endes Bezerra Galvão, the lone Brazilian at INTAL (it's supposed to be a hemisphere-wide organization but its employees are actually 95 percent Argentine), who somehow knew I was married to a Brazilian and therefore welcomed me to the "family." Surprisingly frank, Galvão told me INTAL was basically a patronage organization whose employees consisted mainly of the wives, ex-wives, girlfriends, nephews, nieces, and friends of legendary ex-ECLA (Economic Commission for Latin America) director Raúl Prebisch. He called it an "Argentine mafia" and told how he as a Brazilian and the few employees from other countries were made to feel unwelcome.

He explained how formal, stiff, and hierarchical Argentine society is as compared to relaxed, informal Brazil. He said the political culture in Argentina was not very democratic, that the Argentines were constantly seeking individual or personal advantage but could not work together as a nation. He told me that integration (what INTAL had been established to promote) in the Central America Common Market was working quite well but that in the Andean Pact and MERCOSUR it was not. In Brazil, only Rio Grande der Sul, Brazil's southern-most state, was interested in integration with Argentina because it had markets here; the rest of Brazil was skeptical of integration, especially with the Argentines whom they hated because of their racism and haughty airs.

My lecture that afternoon on the politics of Third World debt went very well. About one hundred people were in attendance at INTAL's "Prebisch

Auditorium"; Eliana Prebisch (referred to irreverently as the "merry widow"—she was *decades* younger than her recently deceased former husband and did not waste any time after his death resuming her strenuous social life) presided. The speech was covered by the press and television; old friends like sociologist José Miguens, historian Roberto Cortes Conde, political scientist Torcuato de Tella, plus people from the U.S. Embassy attended. The Q and A was lively but deferential; in this audience no one used the opportunity to harangue the U.S. or me. Afterwards I mused to myself that all this deference, respect, and the invitation itself to INTAL come to me because of my AEI connection and that when we went back to Amherst and teaching, I would receive far fewer invitations.

I had another free day in Argentina, with time to roam around and collect my thoughts:

- Argentina had made a genuine transition to democracy; it was freer and more open than on previous visits.
- Yet it was one of the most hierarchical and status-conscious countries I'd ever been in with an exaggerated sense of place, pride, and its own grandiose position. Could these traits be reconciled with democracy?
- Raúl Alfonsín, the elected president, had begun well and with a good international reputation; now he was behaving like any other patronage politician.
- The Argentine economy was not doing well. Rich country, poor performance—that was the Argentine paradox. Foreign debt and paper money were used to finance the Argentine's lavish lifestyle. Trouble lay ahead.
- Everyone was scrambling to be put on the public payroll—artists, moviemakers, writers, the Church. I sensed corporatism—even corporatism run amuck—was still functioning much as before in Argentina.
- Crime, corruption, violence were all on the rise again, after declining during Argentina's early, euphoric, democratic years. It was about Argentina that Kalman Silvert was thinking when he wrote his classic "Conflict Society."
- I sensed little commitment to the public interest or public weal in Argentina. Instead it's everyone for himself.
- In 1920 Argentina was one of the richest countries in the world; now it had fallen to Third World levels. Another cause of the Argentine psychoses.
- Lots of complexes here. Argentina acts like it's rich and First World, but it's not. Buenos Aires pretends to be another Paris, but it's not. Argentina is defensive, often feels rejected, is full of complexes, feels inferior, lashes out. No wonder there are so many psychiatrists here.

The INTAL board meetings were more peaceful, less rancorous than on my first visit. Latin America was slowly adjusting to the message of democracy, free trade, and open markets that over the course of the next decade would come to be called "the Washington Consensus." INTAL was also adjusting to me and me to them; gone were the tensions and histrionics of our earlier meetings. I wouldn't say that consensus reigned but we were edging toward a middle position.

Before leaving BA, I had a final meeting and reception with the INTAL staff and its director, just returned from Mexico, Juan Mario Vacchino. Vacchino had been my *bete noire* on the earlier visit. I expressed some guarded optimism about the future of Latin American integration but emphasized it had to be practical, realistic. To this message there was almost no response from the staff or director. Frankly, I'd gotten the impression that even the INTAL staff had little enthusiasm for their project, integration. Rather, these were time-servers, patronage appointees, friends of those in charge. They were there mainly to socialize and collect their checks; I detected little hard work going on here or even *espirit d'corps*. Rather this was a technical, professional as well as political organization; there was no sense of cause or calling. Not my kind of organization, even while it treated me extremely well and we seemed to be agreeing more and more. I knew INTAL's charter was up for renewal this December; would it survive? This is a bureaucratic organization so I knew it would, regardless of shortcomings, but I myself had doubts whether it should.

INTAL did survive and I managed to get one more trip (and honorarium!) out of this arrangement. It was a worthwhile connection for me: I learned a lot over the course of these visits about the IDB, INTAL, and Argentina. Most of what I learned was not very flattering. Perhaps the hard-nosed AEI economists had been right all along: the IDB was corrupt, patronage-dominated, and not very effective as an international lending bank; maybe it should in fact be abolished. But then we'd only have to create something similar to replace it.

Mine had been a political appointment as the U.S. representative on the INTAL board, I'd assumed, to curry favor with AEI and the Reagan Administration. I had succeeded Pete Vaky, a Carter appointee, on the board. Therefore I assumed, when Bill Clinton was elected in 1992, that I would in turn be replaced by a new appointee.

Imagine my surprise, then, when I was not—or at least not that I know of. Although I no longer received the handsome honoraria that went with the appointment or the first-class, all-expenses-paid trips to Buenos Aires, I continued to be listed as an INTAL board member as well as on the editorial board of *Integración*. This condition continued for many more years. So far as I know, I have never received notification that my appointment as the U.S. rep to INTAL has been terminated nor, despite numerous inquiries in Washington, have I discovered when or if I acquired a successor. Either the Clinton Administration, and now that of George W. Bush, never got around to appointing anyone to this position (perhaps it was too low in the appointments "Blue Book" to be noticed), or else no one in subsequent administrations or their friends or donors ever put in a claim for the position. So far as I know, I may still be the U.S. rep to INTAL. If that is so, I would be the longest serving incumbent *ever* in that position.

* * * * *

I can lay claim to five possibilities for having the adjective "Honorable" attached to my name. Some of these claims are very thin, some may be serious. But, hey, in Washington, anything that you can do to put an "Honorable" before your name is worth arguing and fighting for. Washington is a highly status-conscious town; any claim to being "Honorable" gives you a stature that few people have.

The first claim is because of my service as lead consultant to the Kissinger Commission. But that was a staff job, I was not a member of the Commission itself, and I did not receive a presidential appointment. Close but no cigar.

My second claim comes from my efforts over a several-year period to establish a conservative international. But that was mainly an AEI and neocon operation; although it did have the White House's encouragement and blessing, that was unofficial and there was no presidential appointment involved.

The third claim comes from my appointment to the White House Task Force on Project Economic Justice. This is a *serious* claim: it was a presidential appointment, we were commissioned and our report was received in the White House, and my name is in the Federal Registry as having an official, presidential appointment. Sounds like a persuasive case to me.

My fourth claim stems from the lecturing I did in Europe and Latin America for the White House Office of Public Liaison. But this was a consultancy position; I don't think it had any official status, and there was no *presidential* appointment involved—although I could claim to be operating as an agent of the presidency.

Finally, there is INTAL. I doubt very much if my appointment as the U.S. rep to INTAL attracted Ronald Reagan's attention. Or that of any of his close advisors. Nevertheless it was an *official* appointment, it was a *presidential* appointment, and I was the representative of the United States government.

So there! I don't know if I'm entitled to be called "Honorable" or not. Obviously I prefer to be so designated! And, in my own eyes, I'm certainly "honorable." My friends of course treat this as a joke—or an ego statement. I'm not too serious about it myself. But until I learn otherwise, I'm going to continue using the "Honorable" designation. Put it in my C.V.!

NOTES

1. I ask this question at least half in jest; the "honorable" issue is here used as a literary device to tie some diverse themes and stories together.

2. For more details on these individualized trips, see Howard J. Wiarda, *Adventures in Research* (Lincoln, NE: iUniverse, 2006), vol. IV, chapters 8, 12, 13.

3. *Adventures in Research*, vol. IV, chapter 1.

4. One consequence of the tax breaks given ESOPs is that they encouraged leveraged buyouts. Investors who launch a takeover can reduce their borrowing costs if they set aside part of the stock for employees. At the same time, companies seeking to ward off buyouts could use an ESOP to place its shares in friendly hands, its employees'. Kelso, in addition to championing ESOPs, used the strategy above to take over other companies and became a billionaire in the process.

5. Based on my journal entries, XVIII, pp. 83, 87, 157; XIX, pp. 121-30.

6. Doherty was appointed in April 1986; the rest of us had been appointed the previous December.

7. The report was published as Howard J. Wiarda, *Latin America at the Crossroads* (Boulder, CO: Westview, 1985).

8. The analysis here is taken from *Adventures in Research*, chapter 14.

9. *Adventures in Research*, vol. IV, chapter 6 for more details.

Chapter Ten

Congress, the President, and Foreign Policy Decision-Making: Conflict and Confrontation

If your work is in the executive branch of the American political system—the White House, the NSC, the State Department, Defense, CIA, other foreign policy-making agencies—you tend to despise the legislative side. It is on the executive side where policy plans are formulated, options weighed, priorities established, and carefully laid-out possibilities considered. The executive branch tends to think it is the repository of knowledge, rationality, and good sense. Here is where what in foreign policy analysis we call the "rational actor model" purportedly resides: well-drawn position papers, all options carefully and fairly presented, and the president decides "rationally" among the alternatives. It is a comforting image—and even true up to a point. The big think tanks, including AEI, and certainly on foreign policy, operate mainly in this executive branch milieu.

All this stands in marked contrast to the other end of Pennsylvania Avenue. The Congress is seen by those who inhabit the executive branch as parochial, uninformed, and driven entirely by partisanship. Whereas the executive side does "rational" policy analysis, Congress responds only to partisan and constituency demands, and we *know* how uniformed the American public is. There is a wealth of political science literature that demonstrates that if you hold all other variables constant—party, gender, region, rural-urban, rational decision-making—the one that explains congressional voting the best is: the self-interested desire to be reelected. Not the national interest or foreign policy rationality but simply the parochial wish to perpetuate oneself in office. The executive branch, in short, is the repository, hopefully, of foreign policy knowledge, good sense, and rationality, while all the Congress does is play politics, usually destructively, with the issues. And the staff is there, mainly or even exclusively, to make their congressman look good.

In my dealings with the Congress, I noticed one other thing, especially among the younger members. Almost all of them are handsome, appropriately graying at the temples, meant to look good on television—what in my old fraternity days we used to call "good face men." We see the same type in many of the television anchors, network as well as local; think Tom Brokaw, the late Peter Jennings, Dan Rather, and now Brian Williams or, on the feminine side, Katie Couric. That is, they may be eminently presentable and nice appearing on television but they usually have limited knowledge and often weak analytic skills. One gets the sense sometimes that they were elected for their looks or hair and not much else. I have met, testified before, or sat next to at dinner parties numerous congressmen, and I can testify that few of them know much more than superficially about foreign policy. Moreover they often don't know enough even to ask the right questions. And yet these are the people who presume to lead us.

My views on this subject are obviously shaped by my experience on the executive side. That is where we think tankers tend to operate. We would, as chapter 4 illustrates, channel our reports and policy briefs mainly to the executive branch. Of course, with a Republican president, Reagan, in office, we had a sympathetic ear in the White House; perhaps I'd feel differently about it if I'd come to Washington under Jimmy Carter or Bill Clinton with the executive branch under Democrat control. But it's more than that: in the American system the president is the commander-in-chief, the national leader, and the main voice on American foreign policy. Regardless of partisanship, therefore, it's to the executive branch (maybe the State Department, DOD, or CIA if the other party controls the White House) that you go if you want to guide, initiate, and formulate foreign policy, whereas the Congress is looked to only to frustrate executive leadership.

THE CONGRESS

When I first went to Washington in 1981, I was thrown into, because of my AEI position, a lot of social situations to which as a "mere" academic I would never have been invited. These included foreign embassy receptions, lunches and dinners with lobbyists of all sorts, State Department and White House receptions, Georgetown (and elsewhere) dinner parties, seminars and lunches at AEI or the other think tanks, and at least once-a-month dinner-*cum*-policy discussions at the chief "watering holes" for foreign policy wonks like me: the Council on Foreign Relations, the Carnegie Endowment, or the Woodrow Wilson International Center for Scholars. I wouldn't say we were on the "A" list of desirable social invitees but, depending on the host and the circumstances, maybe on the "B," "C," and "D" lists.

I went to a lot of these social gatherings especially that first year in Washington when my family wasn't with me, in part for the foreign policy discussions, in part also because that way I wouldn't have to cook at night when I got home. This strenuous social life put me in contact almost daily with numerous diplomats, journalists, government officials, fellow think-tankers, and congressmen and their staffs. When you share a lunch, a dinner table, a drink and conversation with someone, you learn to size them up fast, discern whether they know anything or not, and tell where they're coming from in a policy sense. It's also a quite heady experience to mingle as an equal with all these high policy types whom before you've only seen on TV.

One of my first tasks at AEI was to organize a conference, the commitment to which I'd inherited from my erstwhile predecessor Pedro San Juan, in collaboration with BrazilInvest, a Brazilian company headed by Hollywood handsome Mario Garneiro. The arranging of this conference is a long story in itself; suffice it to say that Garneiro was very difficult to deal with, tried to take advantage of AEI, and was later convicted of tax evasion in Brazil.

Garneiro wanted only a high-level conference: Vice President George H.W. Bush, Senator Charles Percy, Republican National Chairman Bill Brock, Senator William Roth. Roth was then chair of the Senate Finance Committee; dealing with his office taught me a lot about how Washington works. When I'd first contacted him, Roth wanted (remember this is twenty-five years ago) $1,000 for a fifteen-minute appearance; in the interim between our first and second talks the Senate had changed the upper limits on congressional income and Roth now wanted $2,000. I was told by his office that if he was already "over his income limit" for this year, I could pay him next year. If both years were already over the limit, I would be obliged to give to one of his campaign funds or to a charity (quote, unquote) of his choice and in his district. From this I learned quickly how money-grubbing congressmen and their staffs are.

Meanwhile, on the Washington social circuit at the Carnegie Endowment, the Wilson Center, the School of Advanced International Studies (SAIS) of Johns Hopkins University, my own and other think tanks, and various embassy and Capitol Hill receptions, I was thrown in contact with a wide variety of Washington congressmen. The list included Dave McCurdy, Marty Meehan, Chuck Robb, Wyche Fowler, John Warner, Chris Dodd, Edward Markey, Birch and Evan Bayh, Dan Quayle, John Kerry, and quite a few others. Note that my list is bipartisan, Republicans and Democrats. I was always impressed by how well coiffed, how expensively dressed and tailored (compared with my suits from Jos. A. Banks), and how presentable before the cameras these men were. But at the same time how poorly informed they were on foreign policy issues and Latin America, the region I knew and loved.

Do I expect too much? After all, congressmen are not, nor are they expected to be, experts on any particular country or region. Their job is to be politicians, to be able to translate their constituents' wishes and the interests of the country into national policy, and to synthesize a lot of information from diverse sources into briefer statements and policies that make sense politically. But far too often in my view, these statements come out as superficial, simplistic, at the sound bite or bumper sticker level, and with the design in mind not of solving the problem at hand or making sensible policy but of garnering headlines and advancing the reelection possibilities of the congressperson and his party. Moreover since most congresspersons are lawyers and have little experience with foreign languages or cultures, their recommendations are almost always ethnocentric, reflecting the *American way* of doing things (the only one they know) and not necessarily what works best in the country that is the subject of our policy.

All this posturing, theatrics, and superficiality came out most clearly in the times I testified before Congress. At first I thought it was an honor to be asked to testify before Congress; but after several times doing so I came to view it as biased, serving purely partisan purposes, and a waste of time. The congressmen did not want to hear my ideas; they already had reached their own biased and partisan conclusions and were only looking for arguments to support their already established views. Eventually I decided not to testify anymore.

My first hint of what I was in store for came when I was asked to testify before the House Committee on Foreign Affairs, Subcommittee on Inter-American Affairs, headed by Michael Barnes. Mike was actually *my* new congressmen from the Washington suburbs in Montgomery County. I, newly transplanted from Massachusetts, had actually met Mike the first weekend my family moved to Montgomery County and we attended the annual Labor Day Parade in Kensington, Maryland. He rode in the parade; I knew Mike was very liberal but poorly informed on foreign policy. He once told me that he knew "nothing" about Central America and only headed the subcommittee because no one else wanted it.

Nor was the actual call to testify very reassuring. It came from Rob Kurz, the chief staff guy on the committee for the Republicans. Rob was very cynical: he told me that by testifying, scholars *think* they have an influence over policy. But mainly, he said, it gives Capitol Hill's many interns a chance to write their term papers. "Don't expect many congressmen to show up," he said, "they already know the answers."

My testimony took place on July 20, 1982, in the Rayburn Office Building. The stated subject was U.S. policy in Latin America after the Falklands/Malvinas war, but the real topic was Central America. I prepared a fifteen-page paper which I thought was fair and balanced. The room was packed (Rob

Kurz had been right—mostly interns, a few journalists) but the only congressman present was chairman Barnes and, eventually, Robert Lagomarsino on the Republican side. The other witnesses were Bob Leiken then of the Brookings Institution and Mario del Carril, an Argentine journalist.

Barnes as a lawyer and experienced chair handled the meeting well. He offered a brief introduction—entirely written by staff. His questions were so simplistic—"Why can't the other countries be more like Costa Rica?"—and eventually I told him so. To my surprise, he was not insulted by the comment nor did he take it personally because the questions, too, had all been written by staff. Twice during our testimony the bells rang summoning the members to vote while we witnesses twiddled our thumbs. The poor turnout of congressmen illustrated my earlier points: the U.S. was not much interested in Latin America; to them it was a secondary area, and the congressmen were interested in other issues where there were more headlines and television coverage.

The second time I testified, on February 2, 1983, it was before the Senate Foreign Relations Committee. This time I was asked to testify on the progress of human rights in El Salvador, because the Congress in its wisdom had by now passed legislation that mandated there had to be progress on human rights before any more aid could be given to El Salvador. This requirement gave rise to an elaborate dance between Congress and the Reagan Administration. Every year someone from the Administration (or me, in this case) had to go before the Congress and proclaim there was "progress" on human rights in El Salvador. In fact everyone knew, both congressmen and Administration officials, that there was precious little "progress," nor was there likely to be much as long as the country was engulfed in civil war. That was the nature of the "beast."

So I went up and lied before Congress (but not under oath!) just like numerous other Administration officials had done. Why do this? First, I objected to the entire certification process, arguing that it unduly (and probably unconstitutionally) and too rigidly tied the executive branch's hands (precisely what the Democrat-controlled Congress intended when it passed the legislation) on a foreign policy issue of great complexity and sensitivity. Second, I believed the government in El Salvador had made progress in the last year (even though the human rights situation remained terrible) and deserved to be rewarded for that, while also believing it would be a bad mistake to cut off all aid at this particularly sensitive moment.

So on the basis of these justifications I went up to the Hill and lied; the funny thing was, all the senators present (Dodd et al.) knew it was a lie but they didn't really want to cut off aid either and didn't challenge me. That's because the Administration had recently made it clear that if the Congress cut off aid and the Marxist guerrillas then took over El Salvador, the White House would not be above pointing at Congress and in the next election fingering specific congressmen as the ones who "lost" El Salvador to communism. That threat was sufficient to keep Congress from pressing too hard on the human rights certification issue.

The third time I testified before Congress, again before the House Subcommittee on Inter-American Affairs, came in 1984. Once again the topic was Central America but this time most of the committee was present and there were real fireworks. Mike Barnes asked a question that I thought was really stupid and insulting, so I told him he and the Democrats ought to be more careful with their statements and votes because otherwise the White House would target them in the next election as sympathetic more to the guerrillas than to U.S. policy in El Salvador. Barnes took umbrage at this and told me in open session that I should stick to my testimony and leave the politics to the politicians. Nasty stuff.

The way things work in such hearings is that there are usually three witnesses. If Democrats control the House (as then they did), two of the witnesses are Democrats and one, as a sop to the minority party, a Republican. That of course biases the hearings in advance—precisely what the majority wants. In this hearing I was chosen, as a fellow at AEI, to represent the Republican side. But I'm a serious scholar, not an ideologue, and not much of a Republican, let alone a Reagan Administration apologist. In my testimony I didn't exactly tow the party line. During my testimony I remember Congressman Henry Hyde (R-IL) looking at me curiously with his eyebrows raised and quizzing me closely afterwards like the prosecutor he once was. Similarly Robert "Bomber Bob" Dornan (R-CA) gave me some dirty looks and went ballistic afterwards.

By this time I was fed up and had determined not to testify before Congress again. For one thing, these were not serious hearings: the testimony was biased and most congressmen had long ago made up their minds. For a second, the hearings had turned into a circus of partisanship; I wanted no part of this comic opera. And third, I was attacked personally at these hearings and, entirely inappropriately, had my credentials as a scholar questioned. Sorry; no one does that to me. To hell with them! I never again testified before Congress. And I'm sure my treatment as a witness has a lot to do with how I have treated Congress in my books and the almost entirely negative image I have of the institution still today. Judging from the polls, in which Congress ranks even lower in popularity than President Bush, the public agrees with me.

THE WHITE HOUSE

I'd been in or at the White House several times in 1982, once for a joint AEI-White House conference on democratic elections, another for lunch in the

White House mess (not as nice at the AEI dining room though *maybe* more prestigious) with Constantine Menges, another time in May to welcome visiting Brazilian president João Figueiredo. Figueiredo was Brazil's last military president before the return to democratic rule; recognizing Brazil's rising importance, the White House went all out with a full reception, state dinner, and twenty-one-gun salute. Reagan was there, and Nancy, the first time I'd seen her up close. She had a reputation as aloof and a bit of a dragon lady but Jeane Kirkpatrick told me she was always friendly and gracious to her. It was so hot that day that the military honor guard and members of the band were fainting on the White House lawn. I decided that one of these stilted, formal, protocol ceremonies was enough for me.

My journal notes are not specific enough, and my memory is even faultier, but some time in 1982–1983 I started going down to the White House regularly (conveniently, it was only five blocks from AEI) for the weekly meetings held by the White House Office of Public Liaison. I don't know if it was my AEI affiliation, my relations with Jeane, or my presence on some social guest lists; all I know is that one day I received a White House invitation to attend a briefing on U.S. foreign policy. The White House's goal was to reach out to its friends and supporters, especially those in leadership positions, and brief them on administration goals and policies. The ultimate goal was to have these leaders go back to the groups ("civil society") they represented and rally public and congressional support for the Administration's policies. The Reagan White House innovated in many of these outreach-oriented, public diplomacy, secure-the-base, your-own-(partisan) civil-society-groups activities. Now these kinds of activities are the norm in all administrations.

The first director of the Reagan White House Office of Public Liaison was Elizabeth Dole. Libby was the wife of senator and 1996 presidential candidate Bob Dole; appointed in 1981, she served until 1983 when she went on to be president of the Red Cross, chair of the Republican National Committee, and eventually senator from North Carolina. The next director, with whom I had most contact, was Faith Whittlesley, 1983–1985. Faith was a nice lady but very conservative, not too shrewd politically especially on foreign affairs, but a big donor to Reagan's election campaigns—which ultimately earned her an appointment as ambassador to Switzerland. The third director at least in my time of intensive dealing with the White House was Robert Reilly. Bob was a foreign policy professional (United States Information Agency—USIA) who at least knew something about foreign affairs, but in the Reagan White House you had to echo the political "party line" and Bob soon learned the advantages of doing that. He later became director of the Voice of America and then senior adviser to the Iraqi Ministry of Information during Operation Iraqi Freedom.

One of the first times I went down to one of these meetings was on June 29, 1983. Faith Whittlesley presided; Morton Blackwell was her assistant. It was held in the Executive Office Building next to the White House. Faith told us that her Office of Public Liaison aimed to resurrect the Reagan conservative coalition that had atrophied since the last election. Our meeting (one of several run by her office) was aimed at rallying a bipartisan coalition for the president's Central America policy. I noticed my Cuban lobbyist friend Ana Colomar O'Brian in the audience and sat with her. Ana in turn pointed out who was who in the audience: mostly PR types, very shallow, lacking more than rudimentary knowledge about the area, people whose expertise (which is also how they thought) could be summed up in a bumper sticker or 30 second sound bite.

After these preliminaries Faith introduced Jackie Tillman, Jeane Kirkpatrick's highly ideological former secretary, recently appointed to the NSC, by saying that she was another stalwart of the Reagan revolution but—common in these circles, I found—with no mention of what skills or talents besides loyalty to Jeane had gotten her this position. Jackie said some rah-rah cheerleading things and then introduced Nicaraguan ex-Sandinista Miguel Bolaños. Bolaños claimed to be a former Sandinista intelligence official and then proceeded to read an anti-Sandinista statement that had clearly been prepared by the White House. It was heavy on alleged Sandinista murders, kidnapping, and corruption, but short on analysis or verifiable evidence. The meeting turned into a fiasco as it became obvious Bolaños could not read, in either English or Spanish, and so Jackie had to read it for him. Bolaños was not a credible witness; after a series of gaffes like these I had to wonder how and where Jackie turned up so many losers like this. Is anyone surprised that at these meetings I was continuously putting my hands over my eyes in disbelief?

A week later I was down at the White House again. This time, in Faith's absence (we're already on first-name terms), Morton Blackwell presides. He introduces Amy Morris, who's in charge of "dirty tricks." She's there to report on efforts to have a pro-Administration rally to counter the anti-Reagan Central America policy protest of the previous weekend. Amy reported: the pro-Administration rally started a day before the "anti" one so the "pro" one got more publicity. She got pro-Administration, ex-Black Panther Eldridge Cleaver on national television; she used veterans and "captive nations" exiles to offset the left's appeal; she secured five pictures in the *Washington Post* for her rally versus one or two for the opposition; she sent pro-Administration demonstrators with large signs into the anti-Administration rally to disrupt it; she took pictures of the left demonstrators with their pro-Soviet flags and files to turn over to the FBI; and she set up a media event that got lots of coverage of captive nations with pictures and memorabilia. I sat back in wonder as Amy ran through her list: and I had naively thought dirty tricks died with Nixon!

The meeting takes on qualities of a political rally. An unknown announcer says four students from El Salvador are coming next week on a speaking tour of New England; are there volunteers to find them housing? Another big media event is scheduled for next week on the fourth anniversary of the Nicaraguan Revolution; the White House is writing op-eds for twelve willing congressmen—and you thought those congressmen wrote their own op-eds? Ralph Reed, then looking even younger than he looks now and at that time president of College Republicans, tells us August 13–23 is the anniversary of the fall of the Berlin Wall; College Republicans will be building their own wall on the Mall and then knocking it down with sledgehammers—another major media event.

Roger Fontaine of the NSC comes in to tell us that six weeks ago it looked like the "communist" guerrillas might win in El Salvador; now things were looking better. He tells us that Administration officials are being asked to testify before Congress on human rights progress in El Salvador when in fact there is no human rights progress in El Salvador. On another front, he warns that a military victory by the Contras in Nicaragua was unlikely but the U.S. wanted to keep up the military pressure to give us an enhanced bargaining position. He tells us that the Soviet Union will do anything short of nuclear war with the U.S. to support its ally in Nicaragua.

Richard Wirthlin, Reagan's pollster (Reagan was the first president to have a pollster full-time on the White House staff; since then, every president has had one), comes in to report on how badly the public is informed on foreign policy. Only one third of the electorate knows where El Salvador is, less than one in ten knows which side we're on there, about the same number had heard something about a major policy speech Reagan had delivered on the subject only two days before. The public was very fearful of "another Vietnam" and didn't like the U.S. associating with regimes that rape and murder nuns. Wirthlin informed this group of Reagan "true believers" that it had a lot of work to do to better inform Americans of what was at stake in Central America.

On July 13 I'm again in the White House for a briefing by Jeane K. on efforts to spread democracy abroad. I've heard all of this before and, as chapter 7 indicates, was involved in the early meetings that led to Project Democracy and the National Endowment for Democracy. As I'm listening to Jeane, I'm writing down my own doubts about the project: whether we will take it too literally and seriously, whether we will allow room for forms of democracy other than our own, whether we know what we're doing when we impose our democracy in other peoples' countries.

But Jeane's speech is only part of the program. Faith Whittlesley announces that next week we will discuss anti-Semitism under the Sandinistas in Nicaragua, an obvious ploy to get Jewish support for Reagan's Central

America policy. But I was about to debate Nicaragua's Jewish ambassador to the U.S., Carlos Timmerman, who clearly was *pro*-Sandinista. Then, ultra-conservative ambassador to the OAS Bill Middendorf came in to harangue us in his usual inarticulate way about the looming "commie danger." Right-wing think tanker Lyn Bouchey spoke of the plans to turn Nicaragua's National Day on July 19 into an anti-Sandinista rally. And Richard McCormick of the State Department, one of the few conservatives in the Department, told us that Secretary George Shultz was convening a special group to deal with Central America issues.

Most of these White House presentations are done by PR and media types. My notes written at the time show rising disgust with this aspect of the policy. After the July 13 meeting I wrote:

> All these PR/media types! So shallow. If they were more concerned with substance we'd all be better off. But then I guess that's their job. It's all hype and cheerleading; they're more concerned with getting their message on TV than with the quality of the message. No wonder we're in such bad shape. Increasingly I fear it's the PR types who actually *define* the policy rather than the policy determined first and then the PR designed around the policy.

As if in response to my comments, the next meeting on July 28 is much more substantive. Faith Whittlesley does an introduction. First she reintroduces herself: she always says she's speaking on behalf on the president and how grateful she is for our being here. Next she talks about El Salvador, saying it is 100 years behind the U.S., that it had never had democracy in 700 (??) years, and that we apply too high a standard there. She then goes on to talk about President Reagan as "the last conservative president we will ever have" and "the last one who will lead rather than follow public opinion."

She then introduces three congressmen who speak about Central America. Republican Mark Siljander warns that we must pay attention to Central America because otherwise it will cost U.S. jobs, oil and trade will be cut off (??), terrorism will spread, and the USSR will be right at our border. He says we can't rely on the liberal U.S. media to get this message to the American people so our group must do it.

Congressman Vin Weber of Minnesota, and much more reasonable, then says that the real battle over Central America is being waged not there but in Washington, D.C. And, he claims, we are losing that battle. The American people have little interest in Central America; we can't convince the Congress to vote for the president's policies if their constituents have no interest. The opposition, he says, is well organized and articulate; the message it conveys is that Nicaragua is just wonderful, a group of Robin Hoods, while El Salvador is terrible. If Congress is to be persuaded, it must feel the heat. That is our job!

Next assistant secretary for Inter-American Affairs Tony Motley comes in to tell us the plan for El Salvador. Motley was ex-Air Force and a "businessman" of uncertain means. I had never thought he knew much about Latin America but he had a tough-guy image and Reagan liked him. He indicated a four-part policy for Central America consisting of economic development, democratization, security, and dialogue and negotiations. Precisely the formula we called for in the Kissinger Commission Report.

At the one August meeting of our group before everyone went on vacation, we returned to the PR campaign of earlier meetings. Our leader Faith, we're told, is in briefing the president to get more favorable publicity for our group. The issues here are media coverage, your picture in the papers, time on the evening news. It's all packaging and no substance. As one of Faith's deputies tells us, "Any of you who can write, send it to us and we'll try to get a congressman to sign off on it." Ugh! He also warns us that "speaking before a disagreeable audience these days is like going into an ambush!" My conclusion: there's lots of superficiality as well as paranoia in the White House.

By October 1983 we're back to the regular weekly meetings begun early that summer. At the October 26 meeting the speaker is the legendary Irving Brown of the AFL-CIO, the man responsible for CIA dirty tricks in Greece, France, and Italy after World War II to keep their trade unions from falling into communist hands. Brown has wonderful stories to tell of those days; presumably that European experience will now be applied to Central America. The message is unobjectionable: oppose the extremes of communism and fascism so the center can survive. The question is whether any of this applies to the rural, peasant-based, non-unionized, still quasi-feudal societies of Central America.

Following Brown, Roger Fontaine of the NSC comes in to brief us on the Grenada invasion of earlier that month. This involved a lightning U.S. military intervention in a small Caribbean island to oust a government that had recently come under the control of Marxist, communist, and radical Black power elements. He reports gleefully (1) the U.S. government kept a secret (plans for the intervention) for a change; (2) the intervention was carried out successfully; (3) there were more Cubans on the island than our intelligence had indicated; (4) we got the Eastern Caribbean states to OK the intervention; (5) the Soviet Union and other communist countries were involved in the earlier regime; (6) fortunately there were lots of grateful Americans on the island whom we could rescue (the stated reason for the intervention); and (7) we're already in the process of organizing a provisional government and future elections. All good news; if only Iraq were as easy as a tiny Caribbean island whose chief (and only) export was nutmeg.

On October 31, only five days later, I was back in the White House (the Indian Treaty Room of the Executive Office Building) for a reception for Norman Bailey who was leaving the NSC. Reagan adviser Ed Meese, NSA Bud McFarlane, Agriculture Secretary Block, and other high administration mucky-mucks were present. Of course the food was wonderful but the most interesting part was the gossip. The room was rife with it. Why was Norman leaving (was he too close to recently ousted NSA Dick Allen, did he not get the Treasury job he wanted, was his job too low profile for him); who would replace him; how did other NSC staffers Roger Fontaine and Constantine Menges get along; would Jeane Kirkpatrick impose her staff choices on the dysfunctional NSC? This was a very high-level gathering but even at this level the conversation was all at the personal and gossip levels; there was nothing of substance.

On November 3 the public liaison group gathers again. It's the largest meeting ever with over two hundred "groups" represented. As an individual scholar, I'm not a member of any group as far as I know but they count me as "representing" AEI. That's OK with me as long as I keep getting invited to what are turning out to be very revealing (and not by any means always in a positive way, as indicated here) series of meetings.

Today we're briefed on the amount of tonnage that is transported through the Caribbean, as an indication of our security stakes in the region. The Heritage Foundation announces it is organizing a trip by conservatives to Granada to offset the recent trips there by Speaker Tip O'Neill and Rep. Mike Barnes. Amy Morris updates us on plans for the November 12 counter-demonstration entitled "Requiem for the Brezhnev Doctrine," on Soviet expansion into Third World areas. Jim Michel, deputy assistant secretary of state, gives us a detailed briefing on the Granada operation. Contrary to my emerging foreign policy models (see chapter 6), Granada was not a "bureaucratic model" operation with all its politics and log-rolling; instead this was a top-down operation run secretly out of the White House with no congressional, interest group, or bureaucratic rivalries.

Joke of the day: the "saving" of the 1,000 U.S. medical students from Granada may have come at the cost of 100,000 lives lost, in terms of the patients the graduates of this fourth-rate, "diploma mill" medical school will work on! Who says conservatives have no sense of humor! Sick (literally) humor besides.

At the November 16 meeting Faith Whittlesley tells us that Central America is not our "backyard" but our "front garden." She then reads a list of all the local, county, and state agencies ("local foreign policy") condemning U.S.

policy in Central America, while in only one state was there a resolution in favor of U.S. policy. She reports that all the polls showing negative public opinion on Central America policy were "B.G."—before Granada. After Granada, she says, "we" (the White House) expect to "go on the offensive." That means a new PR campaign. To me this is all theater; the trouble is, in Washington the theater has become the substance and vice versa.

Next we hear from Lt. Col. Oliver North, the "obscure" Marine lieutenant colonel working on Central America in the White House basement whom I recently had to lunch at AEI. North reports approvingly on the growing fissure between the Catholic Church and the Sandinista government in Nicaragua, a feud that we were helping to stoke. He said "our" situation throughout Central America was precarious, laying the basis for the justification of the covert, Iran-Contra arms deal that would get Reagan in so much trouble and almost impeached. He sought to peddle the argument that the U.S. was only interested in democracy in Granada and Central America when everyone knew that stakes were really strategic: preventing any further Cuban and Soviet incursions into the area. North's presentation confirmed my earlier, face-to-face impressions of him as glib, very political, but lacking depth and substance. After all, he was only a lieutenant colonel, yet here he was essentially running U.S. Central America (and other) policy out of his basement White House office.

Later at that same briefing we heard from Nicaraguan Eden Pastora, the famed Contra leader nicknamed "Comandante Zero." His presence (like that of Jackie Tillman's Mesquito Indians) illustrated the problem of bringing in foreign leaders who don't speak English very well and don't understand the U.S. system. Pastora, though small (or maybe because of being small), came in with a swagger and full of exaggerated *machismo*. He had been a Sandinista rebel leader but became disillusioned with the communists' presence in the revolution (or was it because he did not get a high-level job in the revolutionary government?) and went over to the other side. He was a swashbuckling leader, good at self-dramatization, but unable to work with other Contra leaders. I thought of him as rather like Jonas Savimbi in Angola: charismatic but unable to subordinate his individual self-importance for the common good, and fighting as a guerrilla in the "bush" for so long that it had become a permanent occupation.

At the November 30 (my birthday) White House briefing the rumors are confirmed that Roger Fontaine is out and Constantine ("Constant Menace") Menges was now the chief NSC person on Latin America. Constantine was much smoother and more articulate than Roger but so conservative as to see "communists" under every bush. Even I, though at AEI, was suspect in Constantine's eyes. He continued to fulminate against the "communist threat" even after the Berlin Wall fell, Eastern Europe was liberated, and the Soviet Union had disintegrated.

At today's meeting a group of Honduran peasants are brought to the White House and paraded before us. We are told that Cuba is trying to take over Honduras too. Poor people: they speak no English, have never been outside of Honduras or on an airplane before, and appear in the White House briefing room in their *sombreros* and work clothes. We're given a glimpse of these Rousseauian "noble savages" as though their lifestyle is what we're fighting for in Central America. Whose crazy idea is this?

Next comes Arnaud de Borchgrave, the conservative (one of a handful) newspaper reporter and editor—the *Washington Times*, *Newsweek*. He's covered sixteen wars, had seven tours in Vietnam, and interviewed more heads of state than any other journalist. De Borchgrave, who's also the author of such spy novels as *The Spike*, is an expert on Soviet intelligence, the KGB, and disinformation techniques. He's good on Soviet activities but has no firsthand knowledge of Central America. Arnaud knows a lot but is treated as a pariah and outcast by the rest of the far more liberal journalistic community. I find his message not very helpful in understanding Central America.

The December 12 meeting features an appearance by Jerry Falwell, the rising star of the "Moral Majority" whose votes the White House is trying to cultivate. He is introduced briefly and then leaves, thankfully without lecturing us on Central America. Elliott Abrams is next up speaking on human rights in Central America, arguing unsurprisingly that conditions are worse than thought in Nicaragua and better than thought in El Salvador. Elliott is quick and sharp, a fierce debater, but exceedingly weak on his knowledge of Latin America. His fervor for the cause would later land him a conviction for lying to Congress about the Iran-Contra caper; when he then staged a comeback as an NSC official in the Bush II Administration, he was one of a handful of neocons who orchestrated and continued to argue for the Administration's justifications for the Iraq disaster.

This same week I had lunch with Christine Lund of the Office of Management and Budget (OMB). Christine was an Aaron Wildawsky student from Berkeley in political economy. She had done a study for OMB of the capacity of Central America to absorb all the aid and largesse the U.S. was now showering upon it. She had found its absorptive capacity to be low, a conclusion the White House didn't like and therefore it had shelved her study.

Christine told me, without any urging on my part and completely independently of my own conclusions, that she didn't think much of very many of the White House staff, particularly those on the NSC. She said both Ollie North and NSA director Bud McFarlane were "disasters." She said they lacked the knowledge and background to deal with foreign policy issues competently.

They were, she said, good administrators and paper shufflers but not idea men. In fact, they had been chosen for precisely that reason because Reagan, Jeane, and the White House were disappointed with the NSC and wanted to run their own foreign policy without the staff getting in the way and having their own agenda. Christine found especially the military veterans on the NSC to be good staff persons, polite, deferential, and good at carrying out orders, but lacking a developed sense of history and with only a weak understanding of the rest of the world. Those were, after six months of attending the weekly White House briefings, my own sentiments exactly; how nice it is to find someone who agrees with you completely.

The first White House meeting of the new year was held on January 4. General John W. Vessey, chairman of the Joint Chiefs, gave a leadoff presentation on how El Salvador was part of a larger, global, Soviet subversion campaign. Bill Middendorf (OAS ambassador) whispers to me that the Latin American countries privately support our invasion of Grenada even while denouncing it publicly. Constantine Menges, coming from a meeting with Jeane and Southcom General Paul F. Gorman, reports that there is bad news from El Salvador: this is the season when the guerrillas begin their surge. Ana Colomar O'Brien, the Cuban exile lobbyist, asks if there is any *evidence* El Salvador's ARENA party and its leader, Roberto D'Aubisson, are involved with the death squads, or are these allegations only for domestic political purposes. From the tone of her question it is clear that Ana and the Cubans she represents favor D'Aubisson.

On January 11 the AFL-CIO leads the program. Bill Doherty, a rotund, red-faced Irishman with vast experience in Latin America, is the main speaker. Bill heads up the AFL-CIO's international division, succeeding Irving Brown, the American Institute for Free Labor Development (AIFLD), a division long plagued by its connections with and funding from the CIA. Bill is a trade unionist who came up from the ranks, not an academic, think tank, or policy wonk. He views the world differently from the rest of us. Bill is a labor guy, working class, a spiritual socialist but also strongly anti-communist. It is the latter trait that endears him to the Reagan Administration but the former that keeps him suspicious and at a certain distance.

Bill is a tough guy, very clever, who wraps you in a large bear hug but is simultaneously suspicious of your motives and political position. The Reagan Administration treated him respectfully and with kid gloves because it wanted AFL-CIO support for its policies in El Salvador, Nicaragua, and Granada. Bill and I got along well—at first—because I know a lot about trade unionism in Latin America. But then he discovered, or perhaps someone gave to him (the ways of Washington), an article I'd written years before accusing AIFLD of dividing, undermining, and essentially ruining the trade union movement in Latin America. It was a long argument, essentially saying that AIFLD had taken a labor model that had been successful in Europe after World War II and applied it unthinkingly to Latin America where the conditions were entirely different. That was the end of our friendship; worse, Doherty got revenge by vetoing my candidacy for the presidency of the Inter-American Foundation on whose board he sat.

At the January 25 meeting Senator Jeremiah Denton (R-AL), just back from a weekend fact-finding trip to Central America, was the principal speaker. More and more senators and congressmen were flying off for such weekend fact-finders; apparently a weekend was all you needed to qualify as an expert on the region. But since congressional weekends were long (Thursday—Tuesday), you could actually do a lot in a few days; plus, warm Central America or the Caribbean was not a bad place to be in a Washington January. So the drill was, you would fly to El Salvador on Thursday afternoon, be briefed and entertained by the embassy staff, have a late dinner with the president, fly over to Nicaragua (a half-hour flight) on Friday, spend Saturday and Sunday on the beaches in lovely (and peaceful) Costa Rica, be briefed and entertained by Southcom on Monday, and get back to Washington in time for your first vote on Tuesday afternoon. Not a bad life.

I didn't think much of Senator Denton; he's not too sharp. In the midst of his presentation he completely lost his train of thought; it must have been written by his staff because he then had no thoughts of his own to fall back on. He told us he saw the same patterns of violence and upheaval in Lebanon, El Salvador, and Detroit. Detroit? No one quite dared ask what he meant by that. Denton was followed by another touring group of Nicaraguan Indians arranged by Jackie Tillman who *chanted* their opposition to the Sandinista regime. These briefings are really getting bizarre, I thought. Finally, "Constant Menace" Menges came in from the NSC with his own mantra of "the commies are coming, the commies are coming."

At the February 29 meeting the just-released Kissinger Commission Report (see chapter 8) is the main agenda item; as one of the Commission's lead consultants, I'm one of the speakers. My job is to explain the background of the Commission and its recommendations for aid, democracy, human rights, development, as well as security. I'm seated onstage next to Geraldine Macias, a nun who's introduced as leading the opposition to the Sandinistas. Also speaking is Colonel Earl J. Young who has his own model of counterinsurgency, learned in Vietnam, that he's applying in El Salvador. I think, "Poor El Salvador"—and, by extension, the rest of Latin America; they're always being used as guinea pigs for supposedly "global" models that have little relevance to their situation. Jackie Tillman, functioning as Constantine's deputy, presides: it's disorganized and almost incoherent.

At the March 7 meeting Arnaud de Borchgrave puts in a repeat performance on how to defeat global terrorism and counterinsurgency. Arnaud is a very sharp fellow, even if he is too conservative for my taste; the problem is, he knows little about Latin America and his solutions, derived from the study of KGB operations in Eastern Europe, are way too heavy-handed to work in the small, under-institutionalized countries of Central America. Next Jackie Tillman comes on stage to inform us that the U.S.-based Committees in Solidarity with the People of El Salvador (CISPES) is a "communist front" under the direction of Isabel Letalier, widow of the assassinated (in Washington, D.C.) Orlando Letalier of Chile. Well, I know from my own town of Amherst and my lecture tours around the country that there are CISPES groups in many cities and university communities made up of "old Lefties" from the Vietnam anti-war protests as well as radical students; but communists, no.

According to the agenda, Jackie is supposed to urge the group to get behind the Kissinger Commission recommendations. But, either by design or just incompetence, she never gets around to that. Instead she spends the time giving us an update on El Salvador and Nicaragua. However, as usual she doesn't have her facts straight and therefore relies on guesswork and her own strongly held ideological views—a disastrous combination. I put my hands over my eyes again in disbelief at the sheer incompetence of people in the White House. Jackie is above all else loyal to Jeane but one would hope at these levels for at least a minimum level of knowledge and facts.

At the March 14 White House meeting the principal speaker was Stanley Levchenko, a former Soviet intelligence officer. He told us how, under the guidance of the Central Committee of the Communist Party, the Soviets plant false stories in the Western press. He said he worked closely with Georgi Arbatov, head of the America Division of the Soviet foreign service, and with Novei Press, the propaganda network. The Soviets, he informed us, had the largest intelligence machine anywhere in the world. Not all of it, he said, was under the KGB; in addition, it operated through a variety of fronts. All this was fun to observe and interesting information, but it had little to do with Central America.

The next week we returned to Central America/Caribbean themes. Today, for the first time, the White House had metal detectors installed in the Executive Office Building. They were way too sensitive and caused long delays; in my case, after discarding keys, coins, belt, and metal-spined calendar, they were set off by a silver pen that I keep in an inner pocket. Faith Whittlesley welcomed us, this time on behalf of President *and* Mrs. Reagan, implying that she speaks in their name. The agenda always lists Faith as chairing the meeting even when she's away—another lesson for me in Washington self-promotion.

The speakers today are Marco Revelo, bishop of Santa Cruz, El Salvador, who comes dressed in his full bishop's habit, and Eugenia Charles, prime minister of Dominica. Revelo tells us the Church is not aligned with the government, the guerrillas, or the political parties; its interests, he says, are only in social justice. Prime Minister Charles is more impressive: learned, articulate, politically balanced; she's the leader who notified the White House about the deteriorating situation in Granada and was a lead voice globally in support of the U.S. intervention. The prime minister also provided a fascinating glimpse of what it's like to govern a tiny island and the difficulties of being taken seriously or listened to.

At the next White House meeting in early April I arrive early and therefore have a chance to gossip with friends and colleagues from our group before the meeting. I'm stunned by what I hear! I thought these were *all* hard-core, right wing ideologues, but it turns out there are many very smart, thoughtful, and quite centrist people here. First, none of them believe the heavy-handed message delivered constantly by Faith Whittlesley, Jackie Tillman, or Constantine Menges. They tell me the hard line doesn't work with their groups: the Administration has been saying this ("the commies are coming, the commies are coming") for three years now and the public hasn't bought it. It's time for a more sophisticated analysis.

Second, they are equally frank about the speakers they've been hearing. Like me, they have no use for Jackie whom they perceive as disorganized, confused, and not up to the job. Similarly, they think of Office of Public Liaison director Faith Whittlesley as intellectually unqualified for her position. They don't think much of the new Latin America guy at the NSC, Ray Burkhardt, whom they perceive as a nonentity chosen so he would not get in the way of the real decision makers: Jeane, her cohort, and the president himself. They *do* think Constantine is up to the job intellectually but he needs a real Latin America scholar or experienced foreign service officer to serve as a check on his more flamboyant inclinations. Wow! What an indictment! These were exactly my thoughts all along but I had been reluctant to express them out loud among this group. Now it turned out they shared my views.

The meeting itself is relatively calm. Faith Whittlesley gets an unexpected hand as she comes in. Bill Perry, formerly of CSIS, gives us a preview of the upcoming El Salvador election: he thinks the guerrillas will get less than 10 percent of the vote while Christian-Democrat presidential candidate Duarte may come close to the 50 percent needed to be elected outright. My AEI colleague Howard Penniman defends the electoral procedures vigorously, insisting that the Salvadorans had written their own electoral laws, that the election was their own show, and that the United States was not manipulating the process. He also defended the Salvadoran military, under strong criticism at that time for human rights abuses, by saying it helped prevent attacks on citizens, protected the electoral process, and thus preserved democracy.

The April 25 meeting featured two speakers. Ramiro Guardian, vice president of the Supreme Council of Private Enterprise (COSEP), the main business group still functioning in socialist Nicaragua, reported on human rights violations by the regime, the decline of pluralism in the country, and how difficult it was becoming for business to operate. At the same time, the Sandinistas were cementing their control over the country by expanding the army, *quadrupling* the size of the government bureaucracy, stifling opposition voices in the press and radio, and extending state control over the economy.

The second speaker, John Norton Moore of the University of Virginia Law School, was hired by the White House to provide it with *post hoc* rationalizations for its Granada intervention. I was learning this often happened in the think tank world as well: the government made a policy decision, and then it looked to us to justify a decision already carried out. Was that how scholars mainly influenced policy, I thought? Not so much by presenting policy options and alternatives but by bolstering one side or another in internal bureaucratic battles, in preparing congressional testimony for them, or by giving them arguments and rationalizations they can use in convincing others. That's what Moore, for a hefty fee, had done: prepared a seventy-page paper offering legal arguments under international law to justify Granada.

The next meeting I attended was in June; this time, Constantine was the main speaker. With a Ph.D. in government from Columbia, Constantine actually knows a lot about Marxist theory as well as the Soviet Union; the question always was, how much of this is relevant to Central America. He provided a long disquisition on the USSR and its relations with Cuba as well as information on how various European socialist parties and the Socialist International were helping radical left movements in Latin America. But to my considerable surprise, since that was not done in those White House gatherings, Brian Latell of the CIA, who really knows Cuba, took Constantine on. He insists Cuba has changed, has gone through stages, is not so monolithic as Constantine portrays. In private after I query him, Brian tells me he's high enough up that he doesn't have to worry about disagreeing with the White House. He also reports privately that when Constantine was at the CIA, he was always trying to proselytize for his views, selected out only those intelligence facts that supported his views, and was not an analyst seeing all sides but a fanatic (hence the unflattering designation "Constant Menace") only interested in pushing a particular (his own) line.

On a research trip to Europe, I skipped the next few White House meetings, returning for the August 1 session. Robert Reilly, previously the assistant to Faith, was now introducing himself as "special assistant to the president" as she had done; not having read the *Washington Post* for a few weeks, I must have missed the announcement that she was leaving. Bob introduced Bishop (later Cardinal) Miguel Obando who was now calling the Sandinistas "totalitarian." Senator Denton, a Vietnam veteran and former prisoner of war, told us that he saw Central America as an extension of Vietnam; what happened there, he said, is now occurring close to home. It was all orchestrated by the Soviet Union, he insisted, with Cuba serving as its local proxy. Well, there was some of that; but if he thought that was the only thing going on in Central America, he was mistaken.

My last meeting on August 29, 1984, with the White House group was a doozie, long and involved. First, Bill Doherty spoke, realistically but too negatively for this group, on the trade union movement in Central America. Bob Reilly tried to put a good face on Doherty's comments by saying the AFL-CIO had a superb track record in supporting democracy, but there were many questions and even catcalls from the audience on Bill's not-very-Reaganesque presentation. Then Bruce McComb, of Freedom House and my nemesis from the Kissinger Commission hearings, talked at length about the evils of Cuba and Nicaragua, how wonderful El Salvador was, and the widespread support throughout the hemisphere for the U.S. intervention in Granada. As a serious scholar, I thought Bruce's presentation was way too one-sided even for this group, and I called him on it by asking several critical questions. I also noted that he was introduced as "Dr. McComb," when in fact he had no doctorate, and that he didn't correct the record. As the recipient of a hard-earned doctorate, I objected to that too, but only in a whispering campaign to those sitting around me. I think at this stage I was just plain tired of all the false statements, the strident ideology, the PR messages, and the flights from reality that were so much a part of these White House meetings.

* * * * *

After that August 29 meeting, which was also the week before the end-of-summer Labor Day weekend, the family and I headed back to Massachusetts and our nice house in Amherst, as well as my University of Massachusetts professorship from which, according to my dean, I'd been absent too long. We had already made arrangements to stay on at AEI on a half-time basis, commute weekly to Washington, and continue to run AEI's Hemispheric Studies Program. But I wanted to retain my professorship and the tenure that went with it. And, to be honest, I was a bit fed up with Washington at this stage and all its hypocrisy and grandstanding, and was eager to return to "real friends" and "real people" in Amherst. However I'd already made arrangements with AEI, if not yet U-Mass, to return to full-time work at the think tank within two years. That in fact is what we did, returning in the summer of 1986 and staying there two more years, then returning to Washington again for most of the 1990s.

The materials in this chapter are meant to show something of the circus atmosphere, the craziness that prevailed during this period in Washington, in Congress especially but in the White House as well. Congress in particular was dominated by partisanship, political posturing, hypocrisy, and such all-consuming concern for its members' reelection calculations that it could not be considered a serious actor on foreign policy. It was also becoming dominated by superficial "face men," handsome and thereby eminently electable but hardly qualified in my view for high elective office. In the course of my numerous contacts with the Congress and frequent testimony there, I became so disquieted by what I saw, heard, and experienced that I vowed never to testify again.

But at the White House it seemed to me that things were even worse. I could hardly believe how intensely ideological, how radically conservative, how divorced from reality the White House often was. I would sit at those White House briefings not believing what I was hearing half the time, but meanwhile writing everything down in my notebooks.

One likes to believe that at higher policy levels a more rational and realistic policy viewpoint prevails, and at some points and on some policies it did. But on others the true Reaganites, the ideological true believers, won out; and then there was almost certain to be trouble. Although I voted for President Reagan in 1984 (unlike 1980 when I'd voted for Jimmy Carter), I did so mainly because the Democrats looked even worse and, to be honest, I thought selfishly that my chances of returning to Washington and serving in a high policy position would be better under a Reagan Administration.

As this chapter makes clear, however, I was not part of "The Movement" and not at all a Reagan "true believer." And even when that fall I started my weekly commuting to Washington and then returned there full-time two years later, I never returned to those weekly White House briefings. Part of it was scheduling conflicts (the briefings were on the wrong day of the week for me) but a large part of it was disgust and disbelief at all I'd seen and heard: it was hard for me to believe that *my* government operated on such an ideological, nonpragmatic, and ill-informed level.

Chapter Eleven

On the Lecture Circuit: Doing Well by Doing Good

When you're at Harvard or AEI, you have many more opportunities to speak on the remunerative lecture circuit than you do at U-Mass. First of all, it's simply assumed that if you're at these institutions, you're at the top of your game, at the highest levels of the academic or think tank totem pole, a high-level member of one of the most prestigious institutions in America. Second, when you're at AEI, especially during the Reagan period, you're assumed to have insider Washington knowledge, a direct line to the White House and policy-making, and that you can convey these insider stories to your audience. For a handsome fee of course.

Neither of these assumptions is entirely false, but they are not wholly true either. When I was at Harvard (1979–1981) and AEI (1981–1987), my lecturing, writing, and consulting opportunities certainly increased; indeed they increased geometrically; but I was not any smarter or more intelligent than I had been before. So far as I could tell, it was mainly the Harvard and AEI stationery and institutional positions that made the difference, not any quantum leap in IQ or talent. Similarly with the notion that we at AEI had a direct pipeline to the White House: this was not entirely true either, although we were careful, since it enhanced our own prestige and standing, not to disabuse people of the notion that we had more power and influence than we actually did. And I and others from the Washington think tanks traded on these notions that we somehow had superior knowledge to enhance our lecturing possibilities.

Because of my AEI senior scholar position, I frequently got thrown together at dinners and receptions with people who were way beyond my usual economic and social level. For example, because he was on AEI's board of directors, I once at an AEI dinner party sat next to David Rockefeller, the then president of Chase Manhattan Bank. I didn't know if I had a lot to talk about with David Rockefeller but I knew my ex-boss from the Central America Commission, Henry Kissinger, had once worked for him, and Henry had been in the news that day as receiving $50,000 for one lecture. At the time (before Bill Clinton topped it), that was an astounding fee so I asked Rockefeller to explain to me why Kissinger got so much and my honoraria, on the rise but still more modest than that by quite a ways, was so little.

"Howard," he said, "you don't understand at all." David [note how quickly we're on first-name terms] went on to explain it this way. Kissinger, he said, had such great, high-level connections (from the Harvard Fellows Program, as well as from serving as National Security Adviser and Secretary of State); he also had pizzazz (not a word you expect to hear from David Rockefeller). So, he went on, if we at the CEO level hear from him just one new idea or one insight we didn't know about, it's worth every penny to us. Fifty thousand dollars at that level, he said, is small change compared to the profits Chase and others can make from just one critical insight or piece of knowledge we didn't know before.

When I was at U-Mass, I would occasionally receive a lecturing fee of $75–100. Most often I was asked to speak *gratis* and, if I asked about an honorarium, people were often surprised and aghast, assuming that as a professor at a public university, I was obliged to share my knowledge for free. I sympathized with some of these small student or faculty groups and often did provide my services for free, but over time, because they imposed on research and writing time, I turned down more and more of these requests. I also started turning down the frequent $25 and $50 lecture fees as too low.

When I got to Washington I discovered that the minimum fee for think tankers like me to appear at a group (several speakers) seminar or forum was $300. If you yourself were the principal or plenary speaker, the fee jumped to $500 or $1,000. If you spoke at a trade association or interest group, the fee was $1,000 or $2,000. At the most prestigious of these, the honorarium might be $5,000. Similarly with invited papers: if I wanted someone to contribute a paper or chapter to an AEI program or book, I would offer them $1,000, with a sliding scale sometimes taking the fee up to $2,500. My experience with academics was, even if they were ideologically hostile to AEI, I was *never* turned down for a book chapter contribution if I offered this kind of honorarium. In my own case, the most I ever received for an invited, thirty-page paper of this kind was $15,000. And, as far as invited lectures and presentations go, by my second year at AEI I was doing these two or three times a week. A nice way to supplement your income.

In the course of this experience I became, all false modesty aside, a pretty good public speaker and lecturer. At U-Mass I had been only a slightly above average teacher, used to delivering the usual, quasi-boring fifty-minute classroom lecture, and rarely deviating from that schedule; but after my Washington experience my teacher evaluations soared to the very top of the university's ratings. For one thing, instead of the usual fifty minute lectures, I learned to speak for one minute, two minutes, five minutes, twenty minutes, forty minutes or whatever time in whatever kind of forum or format. I also learned to speak, if the need arose, without any preparation, with minimum preparation from notes scribbled on a napkin, or from an outline prepared backstage.

Finally, I learned that lecturing is like theater: you have to entertain your audience as well as enlighten. This is a generation, after all, brought up on television, MTV, the internet, and the worldwide web; they need to be entertained all the time, and if you do not do that, your audience will tune you out or switch channels. So I learned how to tell jokes, to be a commanding presence on stage, to tell interesting insider stories, make a dramatic entrance, pause for dramatic effect, employ cadence and a softer or louder voice, prance around on stage, even stand on my head if needs be (not literally) to attract and keep my audience's attention. In short, I learned to game the system and provide good theater and entertainment. In the process I became a really good lecturer. And as the word got around, my lecture fees went up accordingly.

I also learned how to disarm hostile audiences. Whether abroad or domestically, sometimes I would speak in forums where 90 percent of the audience was opposed to what I had to say. In some of these the potential was present for violence. So I learned how to tell self-deprecating jokes, to reveal insider stores about the persons or policies the audience thought I was there to defend, to deflect criticism by talking about processes rather than policies. In all my lecturing experience, the only time I ever felt physically endangered was in Russia in 1992 when local communist officials stormed the stage, knocked me aside, and seized the microphone.

As a debater, I could be calm and reasonable or fierce and go for the jugular. And, depending on the audience, in the question and answer period, since I usually knew far more about the subject and had more inside knowledge than anyone else in the room, I was not above utterly destroying my questioners—but usually doing so politely so the questioner did not fully realize he had been devastated. I remember quite a number of these sessions on college campuses where in a debate format I would be pitted against the local campus expert, and leaving my foe utterly destroyed on the floor before the eyes of his own students. Sorry to do that and it's a bit outside my character, but if you want to play these games in the big leagues, that's what you'd better expect.

I have lectured at literally hundreds of colleges and universities here and abroad, and participated in even more hundreds, maybe thousands, of public forums, seminars, and debates. A partial list of these is included as an appendix to this chapter. Only some of the most noteworthy experiences are described in any detail here.

JEANE K AT HARVARD

One of my earliest experiences with the kind of highly politicized, hostile, even dangerous audiences I would myself encounter out there on the college lecture trail came even before I went to Washington. And I was not even the speaker. But I sure learned a lot in the process.

This occurred in the spring of 1981. I had by then received my invitation to join the foreign policy program at AEI, but I had not yet taken up the position or moved to Washington, and I still had my position and office at Harvard's Center for International Affairs (CFIA).

Meanwhile, Ronald Reagan had been elected and inaugurated in January of that year, and Jeane Kirkpatrick had taken up her position as U.S. ambassador to the United Nations. Hers was a very controversial appointment, especially because of her famous (or infamous) *Commentary* article on "Dictatorship and Double Standards" in which she seemed to be justifying authoritarian regimes and their human rights abuses. Actually that was not Jeane's purpose in the article but that's the label that stuck: anti-human rights. In the spring of 1981 Jeane had been invited to speak at CFIA.

Since I had by then been invited to join Jeane's staff, whether at the UN or at AEI, and was now presumed to be a part of the inner circle, I, naturally, wanted to get some private time with her when she came to Cambridge. I wanted to find out more about what she wanted me to do for her and where I would fit in the larger scheme of her office and network. So I called Jeane's office; she was not just amenable to the idea but eager to get together. She told me to arrange the schedule with CFIA.

But CFIA and Harvard saw a problem. Jeane was very controversial. Her article had raised all kinds of red flags. It seemed to justify the regimes of dictator Somoza in Nicaragua and the repressive military colonels in El Salvador, to say nothing of Pinochet and the Argentine and Brazilian generals. Already the Harvard student body was mobilizing in protest as were the street people of Harvard Square and the anarchist and other radicals around the Cambridge-Somerville area. Harvard and CFIA officials feared violence. They thought Jeane's visit would be a repeat of the Vietnam-era protests when students occupied CFIA, then housed in the famous "Mummy Musuem," and harassed and intimidated faculty.

So CFIA proposed a plan. I would meet Jeane at the airport in an official Harvard vehicle. The drive in from Logan would be my private time with her.

When we got near Harvard we would switch cars. I would stay in the official car, don a wig, slouch down in the seat, pretend to be Jeane, and drive up to the front door of CFIA where the protestors were. Then I would doff the wig, alight from the car, and walk into CFIA as my normal self. Meanwhile Jeane would be delivered in a second, private car to the back loading platform of CFIA and slip in that way.

The entire plan seemed ludicrous and paranoid to me. But then, I had been on leave from my university in 1969–1970 when the great Vietnam/Kent State protests had occurred, so I had limited experience of the nastiness, divisiveness, even violence occurring then, or now, on college campuses involving students, outsiders, faculty, and administrators. I turned CFIA down, avowing it was demeaning and beneath my dignity to wear a wig and almost certainly be photographed that way even if only through the car window for the *Harvard Crimson*. In the end, Harvard persuaded one of its students to play the "fake Jeane" in this masquerade, I got my private time with her anyway on the airport ride, and her speech to a small, private, CFIA audience went off without a hitch.

A LECTURE AT SWARTHMORE: OUTDRAWING THE FOOTBALL TEAM

Swarthmore College is one of the elite private colleges on the East Coast. Along with Skidmore, Vassar, Bryn Mawr, Sarah Lawrence, Barnard, and others, it forms one of a group of small, upper-middle-class, elite, prestigious, East Coast colleges. Swarthmore is located on the famous "Blue Line" (so named because it services blue-blood communities) that runs out from Philadelphia through its wealthiest suburbs. Except for a handful of affirmative action students admitted to Swarthmore to assuage white, liberal guilt over its wealth, the college is not ordinarily a place where the poor would send their children. Tuition, fees, and costs are in the "most expensive" category of $40–50,000 per year.

Yet it is at Swarthmore in the 1980s, among these wealthy, upper-middle-class kids, that one found a hotbed of anti-Reagan, anti-Jeane Kirkpatrick, anti-U.S. foreign policy sentiment. Arriving at this plush, manicured, well-endowed campus in the fall of 1983, I was reminded of Hampshire College in my own college town of Amherst, MA. The hairstyles on the boys tended to be long and shaggy, frisbee was the sport of choice, and there was a pervasive drug culture where the smells of marijuana wafted over the grass and out of the ivy-covered dormitories.

The main (and only) Latin America scholar at Swarthmore in those days was Kenneth Sharpe. Ken was a serious scholar and writer; but his politics, which he assiduously conveyed to his wealthy upper-middle-class students, were decidedly on the left of the political spectrum. Not alone in this respect, Ken believed that U.S. policy in Central America was terrible, he had no use for either Jeane or Reagan, and he was committed to advancing the Contadora peace process, a solution that I viewed as hopelessly unrealistic because it excluded the main actor, the U.S., from participation in the discussions. I was not exactly a fan of Reagan Administration policy—that's why I had signed on with the Kissinger Commission—but I also thought any plan that would try to eliminate the U.S. from an area where it thought major interests were at stake was bound to fail.

My field notes (vol. V, p. 95) are remarkably brief and incomplete about the Swarthmore lecture, and I do not remember all the details. I seem to remember that Marxist writer James Petras also gave a lecture as part of the series in which I appeared, and that left-wing scholar William LeoGrande of American University also put in an appearance. Morris ("Mo") Blackman of the University of South Carolina also appeared; Ken Sharpe moderated the session.

But there is one thing I remember clearly and proudly about this event. On a clear, crisp, sun-filled Saturday afternoon in the fall, Howard Wiarda's presentation on Central America outdrew, by actual count, the Swarthmore College football team playing at home on that same afternoon. Take that, you followers of football in the Big Ten or SEC: how many of you can say that your lectures ever outdrew the football team on a Saturday afternoon? Of course we have to admit: Swarthmore football is not exactly that of Michigan, Ohio State, Alabama, or LSU! Nevertheless outdrawing the football team on a Saturday afternoon, even if it is Swarthmore, has to be one of the great moments in my lecturing career.

TUSCALOOSA, ALABAMA

In the spring of 1984, I was invited to the University of Alabama in Tuscaloosa, Alabama, to give lectures on Latin America and U.S. foreign policy. I was invited by former colleagues and good friends from the University of Massachusetts, Philip Coulter, who had been recruited to be the chairman of the political science department at Alabama, and Harvey Kline, my collaborator and coeditor on the best-selling textbook in the Latin America politics field and himself destined to serve at various times as both chair of the political science department and director of Latin American studies.

It was exactly twenty years earlier, the summer of 1964, that I had last been in Tuscaloosa. That had been one of the scariest experiences Iêda and I had ever lived through. Other than seeing old friends Phil and Harvey and learning about the Alabama program, I think that was the main reason I wanted to return to Alabama: to see how much the town and campus had changed since that earlier experience.

In 1964 Iêda and I had been living in the Dominican Republic while I wrote my doctoral dissertation. Living there, we were completely cut off from news of the great civil rights movements of that time, including the bombings that killed the little girls in Montgomery, the freedom marchers, the Klan activities, the killings of the three civil rights workers, and the spectre of George Wallace standing in the "schoolhouse" door to bar entry to two black students to the University of Alabama.[1] We had arrived in Tuscaloosa purely by chance en route from the Miami airport to Kansas, where we'd been invited to give some lectures to Peace Corps training groups.

Unknowing, we had arrived in Tuscaloosa the day after macho actor Jack Palance had integrated the town's only movie theater, the BAMA. Everything and everybody was very tense. And there I was: an obvious Yankee, Michigan license plates, a beat-up car, a foreign wife. Not only were people not friendly to us, they were downright hostile. No one would wait on us in restaurants, we were glared at and made to feel uncomfortable, and the hotel, before the era of VISA cards, would not accept our check. Not able to pay the bill, we were hostages in Tuscaloosa. The next day, before we could check out, we had to go to a local bank, call our bank in Florida, and let the Tuscaloosa bank verify we had sufficient funds to cover the hotel bill. As soon as we had paid, we got out of town as soon as possible.

The Tuscaloosa of 1984 was very different from the Tuscaloosa of 1964. The town was much more prosperous. It was friendly and hospitable. As a university town Tuscaloosa, like every other university town I can think of, was far more liberal than the rest of the state. The town as well as the university has been successfully integrated; indeed my own assessment was that race relations there were more peaceful, harmonious, and easygoing than in the North. And the university itself was making great strides: defying the stereotype of a "southern university" of only two decades before, the University of Alabama, like the big flagship campuses in North Carolina, Florida, Georgia, South Carolina, Kentucky, and even Mississippi, was making enormous progress, seeking to bring itself up to the level of the great Big Ten universities.

My lectures went well: at the University of Alabama the students were far less radical, and quite a bit more polite, than at Swarthmore. Ed Mosely, the director of International Programs at Alabama, could not have been more hospitable. Tall, handsome, distinguished Eric Baklanoff, of Austrian background and, at Alabama, professor of economics and business and, like me, a specialist on Spain, Portugal, and Latin America, introduced me to his new wife, Joy, then a Ph.D. student in anthropology. Prof. Larry Clayton, then the director of Latin American studies, was extremely hospitable; he was a Central America expert and knew my work. Similarly with Prof. Victor Gibean: Victor had invited me to give one of my first professional papers some twenty years earlier at the Southern Political Science Association; now he and young Assistant Professor Barbara Chotiner, a former Zbigniew Brzezinkski student, were using my corporatism model for a comparative study of Great Britain and Peru. All-in-all, a very pleasant visit and with none of the political theater and confrontations of other lectures.

MINNEAPOLIS

The day after the Alabama trip I flew to Minneapolis at the invitation of the Hubert Humphrey Institute at the University of Minnesota. Harlan Cleveland, the Institute director and former Marshall Plan director, served as host and did the introduction; he was gracious and fair-minded.

I flew up with Richard Feinberg who would become President Clinton's Latin America adviser on the National Security Council. Feinberg was considerably farther to the left than I, but he was also a serious scholar and open to points of view besides his own, which cannot be said for all academics in the field. By this point I had debated Feinberg—as well as such Latin America luminaries as William LeoGrande, Bob Pastor, and Abe Lowenthal—so many times that we knew all of each other's lines. Richard and I joked about forming a "tag team" and taking our "show" (which is what it was) on the road—precisely what we were doing at Minnesota and in numerous other venues. Much of this was "theater" and I was getting pretty good at it; my journal notes from the Minnesota visit say, "May have been my smoothest-ever delivery."

There were some hostile questions from this audience, unlike Alabama. After all, this is Hubert Humphrey (for whom I had voted in 1968), Walter Mondale, and the Minnesota Farm-Labor Party country; it was also a hotbed, which I'd not known before, of radical-Catholic politics sympathetic to liberation theology in Latin America and to the left-wing Christian Democrats who had joined the guerrillas in El Salvador and Nicaragua. But at the same time, this was the Minnesota of all those Swedes, Scandinavians, and Lutherans which meant most of the discussion was polite and respectful even where there were differences of viewpoints. At the end of the day I pocketed a handsome honorarium and flew back to Washington—just in time to attend my daughter's fathers-daughters banquet at Hood College. Isn't it amazing what modern jet aircraft enables you to do: to Minnesota and back all in one day and with lunch, lecture, a program, and then reception and dinner back in D.C.

MICHIGAN/CHICAGO

Two days after the Minnesota trip I was off again, this time to Michigan and Chicago. Michigan was old home territory for me: I flew into Detroit, rented a car, and went quickly to Ann Arbor and the University of Michigan where I'd gotten my undergraduate degree. I had friends and family (an uncle and aunt, younger brother of my father) there and spent the morning and had lunch. In mid-afternoon I drove from Ann Arbor to East Lansing and Michigan State University, about an hour away. When I was in college and working summers on a private road crew, we had resurfaced every street in East Lansing so I knew the town well. I also knew the campus well because as a fifteen-year-old high school sophomore I had won a scholarship to attend MSU's summer journalism school for high school newspaper editors—an experience that taught me a lot about editing and writing and that, in retrospect, I now think of as one of the major formative learning experiences of my career. But as a later U-M alum, we learned to look down on the "cow college" (a land-grant university with an ag school) down in East Lansing, even though it was widely conceded MSU had prettier coeds than did the more intellectual U-M.

My lecture was held in the Kellogg Center (named after Michigan's big cereal company), a large hotel/conference complex. I was surprised to find over three hundred persons in the audience. The audience was loaded for bear because I was booed, hissed, and shouted down on several occasions. It was pretty rough treatment; at one point I was afraid I would not be able to finish my speech and that the students might storm the stage and seize the microphone. I'm pretty good at disarming hostile audiences but I have to confess I was surprised at the reception at MSU. You might expect such hostility and politicization in activist Ann Arbor but not in moo-U East Lansing. I blamed it on the leftist faculty in the political science and Latin American studies departments at MSU, who had clearly politicized their students at what had once been a conservative, fraternity-dominated campus. At least they had the good grace to take me to dinner. But I was not unhappy to leave the campus.

The next morning I drove on to Grand Rapids, Jerry Ford's hometown and mine, where my father still lived. I visited the recently completed Ford Museum—very tasteful and interesting—and Calvin College, where I had friends and colleagues from high school days. Calvin, a first-rate liberal arts school, was the college of the Dutch-American Christian Reformed Church and a part of my own ethnic heritage as well—although at seventeen I had refused to go there and opted for the prestigious University of Michigan instead.

I expected Calvin to be conservative like its parent religious denomination, but when I visited the Political Science Department and my old high school teacher Jimmy De Borst, who had gotten a Ph.D. at Michigan and now taught at Calvin, I discovered Calvin was no longer so conservative. Its faculty and students had also been caught up in the conflict over Central America, were deeply troubled by U.S. policy there, and, similar to their Catholic counterparts, were intrigued by liberation theology and Latin America's left-wing movements. Quite a change from the conservative, even reactionary, culture, school system, and religious tradition that I too had been a member of thirty years earlier.

From Grand Rapids I drove down to Chicago, actually to its suburb of Wheaton, Illinois. Wheaton was the name both of the community and a college located there, both of them very conservative politically and evangelical (Baptist) Christian religiously. In short, Wheaton was much like Grand Rapids—or at least what I remembered of the city where I grew up.

At Wheaton my host was political science professor and chair of the department Mark Amstutz. Mark was very sharp and later rose to be a leading figure both in the political science profession and evangelical college circles. The audience was very polite and respectful but at this ultra-conservative college (no drinking, dancing, movies, or pre-marital sex—at least in those days) I detected the same attitudes as at Calvin: great skepticism of U.S. policy, strong questioning of our place in the world, and strong sympathy toward reform and even guerrilla movements whom the Reagan Administration had declared to be our enemy. In *all* these religious schools (members of the Coalition of Christian Colleges—CCC), I was discovering, a generational as well as a profound political transformation was taking place since I had grown up in the bosom of that tradition in the 1940s and 1950s. These colleges and religious bodies were far more liberal than they'd once been, were far more critical of U.S. policy, and were far more conscious of Third World social justice issues and the groups, including left-wing ones, that championed them.

U CONN/OHIO STATE

In early May 1984, we flew up to Hartford for a program sponsored by the up-and-coming University of Connecticut. Our host for dinner was Paul Goodwin, who a decade earlier had been a graduate student in history at U-Mass. The other dinner guest was Susan Kaufman Purcell who had been a policy planner in the Jimmy Carter Administration but had since moved way to the right, much like the neocons. Susan told us there was no longer a place for conservatives or even moderates (how we both thought of ourselves) in academia, that she, even with a great publications, teaching, and policy record, had been unable to find a teaching position, and that she saw her future career opportunities as limited only to the conservative think tanks—RAND, Hoover, AEI, etc. I thought, "How sad this is, and a devastating commentary on the biases in U.S. higher education."[2]

Our public lectures and debate the next day were held in the beautiful, gold-domed Connecticut State House in downtown Hartford. The audience consisted of city and state officials, members of the general public, as well as students and academics, and was thus more balanced and diverse than most academic audiences. Susan and I made up one of the panels and complemented each other nicely. As compared with Susan, I came off as a centrist, which is how I had always viewed myself—except on university campuses. She was much more supportive of Reagan Administration policy than I, backed U.S. policy in El Salvador, and supported aid to the Contras in Nicaragua. Susan was tough and articulate in stating her views, but in heavily Democratic New England her positions were not popular.

The other panel consisted of Bob Leiken, a former Maoist turned neocon, and Walter LeFever, a left-wing diplomatic historian from Cornell. LeFever knew the history well even if it was all anti-American and one-sided, while Leiken knew the Central America situation on the ground much better. I was struck in listening to LeFever how monolithic his presentation on U.S. policy was: the U.S. did this, the U.S. did that. That did not at all conform to my view shaped over the preceding few years in Washington of how policy worked. Rather than talking of U.S. policy as if it were singular and monolithic, my view was that you needed to specify what agency (State, Defense, CIA) was carrying out the policy, what faction (neocons versus more traditional conservatives) was talking, and whether it was Jeane Kirkpatrick or George Shultz who was in charge. And that implied a far more complex view of policy-making than the LeFever view. But for now I kept these opinions to myself because I already knew I would myself be debating LeFever later on.

From U-Conn we drove up to our home base in Amherst to spend a weekend seeing friends and inspecting our house, which was then rented. On Monday Iêda took the train back to Washington while I went on to Ohio State University for another lecture on Central America. Columbus was also "old home territory" for us: we had spent a year here in 1969-70 as a visiting fellow at the Mershon Center for Education in National Security Affairs. I spent some time driving through our old neighborhood, the Park of Roses, and along the Olentangy River before settling in at the Holiday Inn on the edge of campus.

My host at Ohio State was Doug Graham of the Agricultural Economics Department—very pleasant. We had lunch with Howard Gauthier, director of Latin American studies at OSU, military historian Allan Millett, a colleague from my Mershon Center year, and Richard Gunther of Political Science. Richard was a Spain specialist: he and I would disagree over the years over our interpretations of Spanish politics, with he emphasizing institutional changes and I stressing the importance of political culture and continuity.

My lecture was standing-room-only, over two hundred persons, very serious and attentive. No posturing or ideological harangues here. The questions were very good, the discussion excellent. I wondered why the audience at Ohio State was more civilized than some others I'd experienced recently: was it the Midwest, was there something about OSU that I didn't know, or was it the fact that the Latin America faculty here tended to be centrist and scholarly rather than ideological and rabble-rousing? I still don't know the answer to that question.

KENTUCKY

In the fall of 1984 I was back on the lecture circuit, beginning in October at the University of Kentucky in Lexington. This was the first time since junior high that I had been in bluegrass country; with all the horse farms, the area around Lexington was spectacularly beautiful. Prof. Ken Coleman was my host; his wife Mary Sue would go on after a meteoric rise to be president of the University of Iowa and then of my alma mater, the University of Michigan. A friend and collaborator on our AEI Iberia-Latin America project, Rick Salisbury, drove three hours to hear my presentation, and former graduate student Adalberto Pinelo came down from the University of Northern Kentucky to attend.

This was a major conference; Ken Coleman was trying to build up Latin American studies at Kentucky. The other speakers were Carl Gershman, president of the National Endowment for Democracy; Prof. Mitch Seligson from the University of Pittsburgh; and former Costa Rican president Daniel Oduber. In addition to lecturing, you always learn a lot on these expeditions either for future use or for your storehouse of cocktail party gossip tidbits. From Gershman I learned about the new NED grants program; from Seligson I learned that Jim Malloy, a leading scholar at Pitt for many years, was "flaking out"; and from Oduber I learned that because of U.S. interventions in Grenada, Nicaragua, and El Salvador, he considered the entire inter-American system (Rio Treaty, Organization of American States, Inter-American Defense Board) to be dead. What would substitute for it? There is nothing so far on the horizon, he said.

My lecture was again on Central America but my notes contain not a single word about that. That's because the lecture was now routine; it was the news and gossip from my colleagues that was more interesting.

ST. JOHNS/ST. BENEDICTS

A couple weeks after returning from Kentucky, I traveled up to Minneapolis for the second that year. My destination was St. Cloud, Minnesota, two hours north of Minneapolis and not all that far from the Canadian border. If you think Minneapolis is cold in the winter, St. Cloud is even colder; this area is also a center of Sioux Indian settlements and reservations.

My destination is St. Johns University and its sister institution, St. Benedicts. St. Johns is also a Benedictine monastery school; it was founded in the mid-nineteenth century to service the Minnesota German-Catholic community, many originally from western Pennsylvania, living in St. Cloud and along the upper Mississippi River. Both St. Johns and its women's branch are fine institutions; for Minnesota Catholics like Senator David Durenberger (whom I had met and before whose subcommittee I had testified) this is the place to go: very intellectual, high SAT scores, difficult to get into, rigorous training.

It surprised me a little that St. Johns and St. Benedicts are still a thriving monastery and convent. In this day and age, the idea of the monastic life has little appeal for most of us. I stayed in the abbey with the monks; no women or student visitors allowed. There is prayer time, a daily mass, and times for singing and contemplation. The rooms are quite Spartan with a hard bed, no radio, no TV, and religious icons on the walls. This is not the Hyatt or Sheraton.

The students here are well dressed, upper-middle-class, very midwestern. I see no blacks or other minorities on campus, though I may have missed a few. The most striking feature is that they're all Catholic and, more than that, heavily indoctrinated in the U.S. Bishops Conference's doctrines of peace, justice, and liberation theology. They're all nice kids but very naïve and uninformed. The faculty, all on the left, has fed them only one side of the story. I'm reminded of my trip to Calvin and Wheaton of only a few weeks back; we live in such a secular age and with such secular academic disciplines and policy discussions that it's unusual these days to find students and their institutions so religiously oriented.

The debate pitted me against Walter LeFever, whom I'd met before at U-Conn. Unfortunately the student organizers had not informed me of the debate format before we got to the auditorium. I had thought it would be my usual lecture on Central America for which I was well prepared; the unexpected debate format left me no time for adequate preparation. It was patterned after the Oxford Union debates: each of us got a certain time for presentation and rebuttal, we both were assigned student assistants, someone kept the clock and pushed a buzzer if we went over, and the student audience then voted for a winner. I put on a good show but since this is a "peace campus," the outcome was preordained: the LeFever position won by two hundred something to one hundred something. I considered it a moral victory, especially when I heard that my AEI colleague Michael Novak had been here a few weeks earlier to debate the nuclear freeze (he was against it) and had lost—and even been booed—by a wider margin than I.

Walter and I actually had a quite civil debate and we left as good friends. We shared the limousine ride back to Minneapolis and then the plane ride to Hartford. He had been the chair of the history department at Cornell when the big blowup over black power and armed black students on campus occurred in 1969-70. To my surprise, LeFever said he had sided with the conservatives including my friends and AEI colleagues (and former Cornell professors) Alan Sindler and Walter Berns. He told me Berns had been a wonderful teacher at Cornell and had now, like Jeane Kirkpatrick, brought scores of his former students to Washington and into government, all steeped in the neoconservative ideology. LeFever also told me the story of James Perkins, the then president of Cornell, who had been forced to resign over this episode. Perkins was a Quaker and committed to peace; the black students learned to manipulate him; and when their illegal actions clearly called for a police response, Perkins was unable because of his religious beliefs to make the call.

ROLLINS COLLEGE, FLORIDA

Two weeks after my St. Johns appearance I was en route to Orlando, Florida, for a lecture, classroom presentation, and media interviews at Rollins College. We rode a weather front all the way down the East Coast with severe bouncing of the airplane—definitely a white-knuckle flight. Those handsome honoraria for the lecturing that I receive are nice but when the weather is awful like this and you think you might not make it, you wonder if they're worth it.

Rollins is located in Winter Park, a beautiful suburb of Orlando that, with its clean streets, lakes, and Spanish-style houses, reminds me of Santa Barbara. Orlando and Winter Park are very conservative communities; my hosts at Rollins, Pedro Pequeño and Luis Valdés, are Miami Cubans and similarly conservative. In fact my problem at Rollins is just the opposite of that at Swarthmore, Michigan State, St. Johns, and other campuses: for the students, the faculty, the community, and the Orlando media, I'm not conservative enough! Orlando has an active branch of the right-wing John Birch Society and they are present when I give my talk.

The lecture, before an audience of 250, goes very well. There are quite a few "townies" present as well as students. Everyone is very polite and there isn't a single dissenting voice or hostile question. As a visiting "dignitary" from Washington, I'm on the evening news and do a one-on-one interview with Randi Harrison, foreign affairs correspondent for the *Orlando Sentinel.* He tells me the paper is so rich that, bucking national media trends to less international coverage, he was made a full-time foreign affairs reporter concentrating mainly on Middle East and Latin American news. Meanwhile hosts Pedro and Luis, both second-generation Cubans, fill me in on the politics and changes in the Cuban exile community—now considerably more pluralistic and less hostile to Fidel than is true of the older generation.

I felt comfortable at Rollins: this was more of a representative cross section of America than was true on most university campuses. I was told by my hosts that even my AEI neocon colleague Mark Falcoff, who usually feels threatened and even paranoid when surrounded by liberals, felt comfortable here. Nobody, he sensed, was out to get him. Rollins even made a play for me to settle there and teach part time when I'm ready to retire. Winter Park *is* beautiful; I could think of far worse places for retirement.

LAWRENCE, KANSAS

Kansas in the mid-1980s had two conservative senators, Bob Dole and Nancy Landon Kassebaum, daughter of Alf Landon who had been the losing Republican candidate against Roosevelt in 1936. Kansas was the heart of the heartland, farm country, a historically conservative state. But that leaves out Lawrence, the home of the University of Kansas and, like many university towns in the South and Midwest, a hotbed of radicalism and anti-Americanism in an otherwise conservative state. I was not prepared for what I found there.

Among the faculty my two closest friends were Lester Langley and Charles Stansifer. Lester was a prominent diplomatic historian who had written extensively on U.S. policy in Latin America. His analysis of Central America was that we can't win, but we can't lose either, and we can't quit the game. Therefore we were "stuck" in Central America (it sounds like Iraq today) with no honorable way out. Lester went on to argue that rather than the current crop of Central American strongmen and colonels being "our SOBs" (as Roosevelt had famously said of former Nicaraguan dictator Anastasio Somoza), in fact we are theirs—i.e., we are "prisoners" of the corrupt regimes we have chosen to support. This analysis seemed to be way out of line with what I knew of Washington policy and policy-making; Langley angered me even more, however, by using a story I had told him in confidence and in a private conversation in one of his books. At least (and thank goodness) he didn't include my name as the source of the story.

Stansifer was the director of Latin American studies at Kansas and, I had thought, a balanced, levelheaded person. But he had just come back from an election observer mission to Nicaragua where he had pronounced the recent, rigged Sandinista electoral victory as "fair and free." He and his fellow delegates, from the left-wing Latin American Studies Association, had arrived at that conclusion by looking only at the relatively brief election campaign itself, not at the Sandinista intimidation, monopoly of media time, harassment of opposition candidates, and state control of all instruments of government including the electoral commission that had occurred *before* the actual campaign began. I told Charles I was very disappointed in his whitewashing of the Sandinistas this way.

When I got to the auditorium where the lecture was to be held, I was in for more surprises. It was a large auditorium and completely full—about five hundred persons in the audience. As I walked onto the stage I immediately noticed that the first fifteen rows were packed with persons wearing the red Sandinista armband. They had arrived early to claim all the best seats and intimidate those (me) who didn't follow their line. "Howard," I said to myself, "this is not going to be a friendly audience."

My opponent this time in the debate that was to be held was Carlos Timmerman, the Nicaraguan ambassador to the U.S. He received a standing ovation when he walked onto the stage; I did not. Timmerman had brought an entire entourage from the Nicaraguan embassy with him to Kansas, all of whose transportation costs the university had paid for. It seemed like everything about this "debate" was stacked against me. I couldn't help but notice that of Timmerman's aides, one was black and another Mesquito Indian, probably the first time that either of these two minority communities had been represented in the Nicaraguan foreign service. Cynical me immediately thought that they were there mainly to appeal to American student audiences hung up on guilt over "racism," because in actual fact in Nicaragua both these minority groups were opposed to the Sandinista government.

After all this, our debate was almost anticlimactic. Whenever Timmerman spoke, regardless of how wrong or inane it was, the audience applauded. Whenever I spoke, there were catcalls, boos, and hisses. But as indicated earlier, I'm used to hostile audiences and how to disarm them, so I gave a very straightforward, factual, non-ideological presentation about Central America and how U.S. foreign policy worked, from which the audience could actually learn something. It must have worked because at the end I too got a smattering of applause, though not as large as the Nicaraguans'.

HARVARD

It's fitting that we begin this chapter (with the Jeane Kirkpatrick story) and end it at Harvard. For it was from my position at Harvard (and that all-important Harvard stationery) that I was recruited by Jeane to go to Washington and AEI, and to Harvard (as well as to U-Mass) that I would return after my first three-year stint at the Institute. I was given office space as well as the position of Senior Associate at Harvard's Center for International Affairs; in this capacity I lectured, wrote, and participated in the Center's vigorous academic and policy activities.

By this time, after several years in Washington and as an insider at AEI, I was beginning to organize my ideas for a book on American foreign policy, as I had seen and experienced it. I saw the American political system, since Vietnam and Watergate, as fragmenting, dividing, and polarizing. Moreover foreign policy was increasingly dominated by domestic political considerations, not a measured weighing of non-partisan rational interests. Almost all of our institutions—interest groups, public opinion, parties, the Congress, the media, even think tanks—reflected and reinforced these deep divisions. I worked up an outline which became the basis of one of my Harvard presentations and which later blossomed into a funny, jaded, cynical, best-selling textbook on American foreign policy.[3]

Lots of things as usual were going on at Harvard at this time. One of my best friends, Jorge Domínguez, a leading Cuba expert, had been accused by a young female faculty member in the Government Department of sexual harassment. I do not know precisely what happened between the two, nor do I want to know, because both of them, as well as Jorge's wife, were friends of mine. I do know, however, that women's groups in the Cambridge area were mobilizing to make this a *cause celebre*; at the same time, in the early eighties, Harvard was not yet organized institutionally to deal with sexual harassment cases. It had no machinery for doing so, no rules or legal procedures, no systematic way to deal either with victims' complaints or to protect the rights of the accused.

In this context, after numerous hearings, marches by the women, and administrative deliberations, I thought Domínguez got off rather light with a mild slap on the wrist: he was prohibited for a period of years from serving on graduate student thesis committees, he could not serve on department administrative committees, and he lost temporarily his office at CFIA. Frankly, all but the last of these could be considered blessings in disguise (none of us in academia like to serve on all these committees), and even the last penalty was soon negated when Domínguez not only got his CFIA office back but was eventually named director of the Center.[4]

The other big event of this period was the offer to me of a research position at Harvard. The offer came from my friend and colleague Sam Huntington who asked if I would be interested in heading up a new program the Center was organizing on comparative political culture. Well, this was precisely my research area and there was a $500,000 grant to fund the project. But there were several problems involved: (1) it was only a one-year appointment, initially; (2) it was not a tenured faculty slot; (3) I couldn't conceive that U-Mass, after allowing me to be away three years at AEI, would give me another year's leave of absence; and (4) if I was going to move, I wanted to move back to Washington and to AEI to influence policy, not to Cambridge for another academic job.

So I turned the position down. Can you imagine: *I turned down a job offer at Harvard!!!* The decision seemed clear-cut at the time; in retrospect it might have been foolish. Because in academia one-year positions often have a way of turning into permanent ones; non-tenured slots can become tenured ones; it may be that U-Mass would have granted me that leave (I didn't even try); and, as for the fourth reason above, what better position from which to move into Washington policy-making (think Mac Bundy, Henry Kissinger, Zbigniew Brzezinski, Joseph Nye, Graham Allison, *many* others) than from a Harvard base. In fact, I did go back to AEI, to Washington, and my career blossomed; but it may still be that the decision not to take the Harvard offer was one of the biggest mistakes of my life.[5]

* * * * *

I learned a lot out on the lecture circuit during my AEI years, as well as it being very remunerative. In the preceding pages I've recounted only *some* of the colleges and universities I visited during this period, to say nothing of the numerous forum, seminar, and lecture presentations I made in Washington, D.C. To tell the story of all these would require another full book; interested readers may have to be content with exploring my journal notes and the archive cataloged at the Richard B. Russell Library of the University of Georgia.

Among other things I learned:

- a lot about other colleges and universities that I visited.
- a lot about academic colleagues and competitors.
- a lot of gossip about friends and acquaintences.

I also learned:

- how far to the left most college faculty had gone.
- how out of touch they were with the realities of Washington policy-making.
- how badly informed and even indoctrinated most of their students were.

In terms of my own lecturing ability I learned:

- how to be an engaging, dynamic, and amusing public speaker.
- how to disarm and neutralize a hostile audience.
- how to speak for any length of time on almost any subject[6]

All of this was extremely helpful in my future career both as a policy advocate and a public speaker and teacher.

APPENDIX: COLLEGE AND UNIVERSITY LECTURES

Aichi Prefectual University (Japan)
Air Force War College
American University
Army War College
Beijing University
Bowdoin College
Brown University
Calvin College (2)
Central European University
Chinese Academy of Social Sciences
Comenius University (Slovakia)
Defense Intelligence College
Dickinson College
Dosisha University (Japan)
Dowling College
Economics University of Bratislava (Slovakia)
Emory University
Emporia State University
Fashion Institute of Technology
Georgetown University
Harvard University (6)
Haverford College
Hebrew University of Jerusalem
Heidelberg University
Helmut Schmidt University (Germany)
Hofstra University
Inter-American Defense College
Kansas State University

Kean College
Kiel University (Germany)
Michigan State University
MIT
Mount Holyoke College
Nanzan University (Japan)
National Academy of Sciences (Hungary)
National Institute of Geography (Portugal)
Naval Postgraduate School
Nizhny Novgorod University
Northeastern University
Nova University (Portugal)
Ohio State University
Ohio University
Oxford University
Pennsylvania State University
Portland State University
Portuguese Center for the Study of Southeast Asia (2)
Pretoria University
Rollins College
School of the Americas
St. John's University
Stanford University
State University of New York
Stellenbosch University (South Africa)
Stiftung Wissenschaft und Politik (Germany)
Swarthmore College
Towson State University
Trnava University (Slovakia)
Tulane University
Universidad Catolica Madre y Maestra (Dominican Republic)
United States Air Force Academy
United States Military Academy (3)
United States Naval Academy (2)
University of Alabama
University of Arkansas
University of Bonn
University of Budapest
University of California-San Diego
University of Cologne
University of Connecticut

University of Delaware
University of Florida
University of Freiburg
University of Georgia
University of Hamburg
University of Illinois
University of Kansas
University of Kentucky
University of Kobe (Japan)
University of Maine
University of Miami
University of Minnesota
University of Moscow
University of Nebraska
University of Pittsburgh
University of Santo Domingo (Dominican Republic)
University of Singapore
University of South Carolina
University of Surinam
University of Tennessee
University of Texas
University of Tokyo
University of Valencia (4)
University of Vienna (2)
Vanderbilt University
Vassar College
Warsaw University (2)
Westfield State College
Wheaton College

NOTES

1. Wallace's grandstanding was in June 1963; the bombing of the 16th Street Baptist Church in Montgomery was in September 1963; and the spring and early summer of 1964 had featured more civil rights marches, police dogs attacking black demonstrators, and violence throughout the South. On June 21, 1964, only days before we arrived in Tuscaloosa, the three civil rights workers, James Chaney, Andrew Goodman, and Michael Schwerner, had gone missing. We had no knowledge whatsoever of these events. No wonder Tuscaloosa was so tense.

2. Susan had taught at UCLA and received tenure there before going into the Carter State Department; now she was unable to go back or to find another tenured

slot. I had a tenured full professorship at U-Mass, but if I were starting my career anew I doubt with my center-right views if I'd be able to land an academic position.

3. Howard J. Wiarda, *Foreign Policy without Illusions: How Foreign Policy Works and Fails to Work* (Boston: Little Brown, 1990).

4. While Harvard had little institutional machinery at that time to deal with the Domínguez case, when, a year later, another colleague, Doug Hibbs, faced similar charges, the full weight of the university came down on him. Hibbs was forced to resign his Harvard position, he was unable for a time to find another position, his research ground to a halt, and, in effect, his career was ruined.

5. Another doozy was the decision not to run for Congress from my home district in Grand Rapids (Jerry Ford's old district) in 1984 when I was offered the opportunity to do so. At that time I explored the possibilities briefly but Iêda was not enthused about the prospect, we had just bought a house in Washington, we had just put our kids in school there, we would have to establish residence in Grand Rapids, and, after twenty-five years away from the city, I was not well versed on local issues. But I was intrigued by the offer and, as at Harvard, am still not sure I made the right decision.

6. I recall one time, because the meal had been served so late, beginning my after-dinner speech after midnight, when the waiters were clearing (and rattling) the dishes, the room was hot and uncomfortable, most people (me included) had had too much to drink, and everyone, including my hosts, was eager to get home. But I had received an extra-large honorarium for this talk and, as a "good" Dutch Calvinist, was determined to give them their money's worth. So I went on and on with my prepared speech; I felt good about it but I don't think anyone else did. From this I also learned another lesson: keep it short, keep it light, keep it funny. Unfortunately I hadn't heeded my own good advice.

Chapter Twelve

Washington Adventures and Misadventures: Are We a Banana Republic or What?

I had spent three years, the years 1981–1984, full-time in Washington, on leave from my university and in residence at AEI. After two years, which is the normal limit for a leave of absence from one's university, I had applied for a third year's leave. In my letter to the political science department and the dean, I stressed that I was doing important policy work and needed the extra year to finish the projects on which I was working. To my considerable surprise (remember, even Henry Kissinger when he was national security adviser had had to resign his Harvard position after two years), the university granted my request. I suspected they were less swayed by my argument that I needed to finish some projects than by the sentiment, widespread in academia, that Ronald Reagan was a total disaster as president and anything I could do to help the situation deserved support.

At the end of the third year we again had to make a decision. AEI wanted me to stay on in a permanent capacity. But in the absence of any guarantee of permanence (tenure) in my AEI position, I was reluctant to give up a tenured full professorship in beautiful, bucolic, peaceful Amherst. At the same time, I didn't think my university would grant me still a fourth year of leave. That was reinforced when my dean called up and told me I had been away for so long that people, thinking it was vacant, had begun applying for my position. "Howard," he said, "it's time to come home."

So I worked out an arrangement both with my department and AEI. In the department the arrangement was that I would teach all my classes in the first two and a half days of the week, Monday–Wednesday noon. That way, with an early afternoon flight, I could be in Washington by 3:00, usually returning to Amherst the following Sunday afternoon. For my two and a half days per week in Washington (I usually worked on Saturdays besides), AEI paid half of my regular salary plus all my travel and hotel expenses. This way I could keep my tenured academic position while also retaining my AEI/Washington/think tank job.

We maintained this strenuous life for two years: the 1984–1985 and 1985–1986 academic years. It was very hectic: all those twice weekly (sometimes more) airplane flights, half the week spent in a hotel, and basically doing two full-time jobs at once. But because I loved Washington and my think tank work and life so much, my family and I were willing to do it. Plus, note, I was earning a lot of money: my full-time university salary, half my AEI salary, and able still to do remunerative consulting, writing, and lecturing. After these two years back in the teaching trenches at U-Mass, I applied for and was again granted—this time with a bit more reluctance—another two-year leave to return to AEI, 1986–1988.

I recount this chronology for several reasons: first, to keep the story straight; second to indicate how long I stayed at AEI (1981–1988); and third to show how much I enjoyed Washington social and political life. Even when I went back to teaching half the week in Amherst, I kept my Washington office, kept all my Washington contacts and commitments, and maintained an active, vigorous schedule of political activities, writing, lecturing, and social engagements. In fact, despite the commuting, I don't think I slowed down at all from my energetic Washington activities even while holding down a full-time job somewhere else.

This chapter tells some of the stories of these activities. It covers the entire period 1981–1988 at AEI. Quite frankly, there are so many stories to tell that I have to be very selective in the ones I choose for inclusion. But I do want to include a sample to provide both a feeling for the life we led at AEI, and to convey the sheer fun and joy of doing policy work at one of the nation's premier think tanks.

SENATOR JOHN EAST AT AEI

One of the first major programs at AEI when I first got there in 1981 was a debate we sponsored between Senator John East of North Carolina and former attorney general (under Lyndon Johnson) Ramsey Clark, whose father Tom was a member of the Supreme Court. Many of us, especially AEI's constitutional scholars Bob Goldwin and Walter Berns, thought Ramsey was not too sharp and had gotten his position because of his father. Senator East, my wife Iêda, and I had all been graduate students together in political science twenty years earlier at the University of Florida. I knew things about East that no one else knew.

John East had been an obscure college professor teaching at East Carolina State University in Greenville. He was an ultra-conservative. In 1980 he had entered the Republican primary in North Carolina and won. No one gave him a ghost of a chance in the general election. But they had underestimated conservative sentiment in North Carolina and that the traditional hold of the Democratic Party on statewide offices in the South was about to be broken. With the aid of North Carolina's other conservative senator, Jesse Helms, and riding the conservative coattails of Ronald Reagan, East captured not only the Republican primary but then, to everyone's great shock, also won the general election.

John East had been a marine in the Korean War. In the war he had had both his legs blown away by a grenade. When we knew him as a fellow graduate student in the early 1960s, he had already been confined to a wheelchair for nearly ten years. But he never complained and his mind was sharp as a tack. East was widely thought of by his teachers and fellow graduate students as one of the smartest people in the program. As an ex-marine, he was also tough as nails.

East had an all-A record in the graduate program—except for one course. That had been taught by Prof. William ("Wild Bill") Carlton, who called himself a socialist and was an unabashed liberal—unusual in the early 1960s before our university campuses became radicalized. Carlton was an excellent and entertaining teacher (hence his "Wild Bill" nickname), except for the fact that he made no secret of his own politics in the classroom and expected the students to share his liberal beliefs. East refused to do so and in one graduate seminar even had the effrontery to argue and disagree with Carlton. That of course is what learning is all about and what good students are expected to do. But not with Carlton: he punished East by giving him a B in the seminar, purely on political grounds. Iêda was also in that seminar (she earned an A); all the other students knew East's work and knew that he too deserved an A. But he did not receive it, penalized for his political beliefs.

When we saw East at AEI, he was very happy to see us. We resumed our acquaintance and saw him socially from time to time. The AEI production that night was a lavish affair: our media adviser Heather David filmed it for national television, we published a transcript of the debate, there were drinks and *hors d'ouvres*. East was so much smarter than Clark and mopped the floor with him in the debate. It was for us a very friendly and pleasant evening; of course we were pleased to see our fellow grad student doing so well.

This story has a sad ending. Because of the pain from his body, complications of a thyroid disorder, and being confined for so many years to a wheelchair, East was forced to take stronger and stronger medicines as well as painkillers. He suffered depression as well as physical pain. His condition deteriorated both physically and mentally. Before the end of his first term, although after he had announced that he would not run again, in June 1986 he took his own life. The Senate had lost one of its undoubtedly smartest members.

CONFRONTING A GUERRILLA: JONAS SAVIMBI

Living in Portugal in the early 1970s, we had became fascinated by the fact of Portugal being the last colonial power in Africa, with vast territories there many times the size of Portugal itself. I was so interested in Portugal's colonial situation that, even though not an Africanist, I wrote up a research project that would have taken me to Angola, Mozambique, and Guinea-Bissau, received the assurances of funding for it, and prepared to go. But then the Portuguese revolution of 1974 occurred, Portugal granted a precipitous independence to its colonies, and Marxist national liberation movements took power in all its former colonies. My travel plans had to be scrapped; it was not until thirty years later that I finally got to Portuguese Africa.

In Angola the Marxist movement that seized power was called the Popular Front for the Liberation of Angola (MPLA). It was not only Marxist, but it was also corrupt, incompetent, and unable to pacify the country. Angola was, after all, still a tribal and ethnically divided society; the MPLA controlled the main cities but it did not control the tribal hinterland.

The main opposition group was UNITA (National Union for the Total Independence of Angola) headed by Jonas Savimbi. Savimbi was of a distinct ethnicity from that of the MPLA leaders; he also controlled a part of the country rich in diamonds (as in "Blood Diamonds"), which gave him an independent financial base. Although Savimbi once called himself a Marxist, he was also a nationalist and was therefore latched onto by some conservative American groups because he opposed the MPLA government and its Soviet and Cuban sponsors. He received assistance and armed backing from the white *apartheid* regime still in power in neighboring South Africa. One of those who backed him was Jeane Kirkpatrick.

So when Savimbi came to Washington for interviews with the Reagan Administration, he was also invited to AEI to give a talk. I rode up and down in an elevator with him. Even though he had a large entourage of well-armed bodyguards (not exactly necessary at AEI), I noticed he kept looking back over his shoulders even in the elevator. I surmised that if you've been living as a guerrilla out in the bush for as long as Savimbi had, you're probably constantly looking over your shoulder to see who might be sneaking up on you next. I similarly concluded that if you've been a guerrilla for over twenty years as Savimbi had, probably no other form of employment will be suitable for you.

Savimbi had received medical training and was a very intelligent man. At AEI he had interesting things to say. He argued for a unified Angola (under his control, of course) as distinct from the ethnically divided one that I suggested. He told us that Angolans despised the Cuban troops sent to bolster the MPLA regime. There was tension between the Cubans and not only his UNITA group but also with the very MPLA the Cubans had been sent to support, including some firefights. The Cubans lived in better houses, had better guns, and more perks than did the Angolans. Interestingly, Savimbi informed us that at first the Cubans had sent white and light-skinned troops; then they switched because of racial sensitivities to black troops who, however, had proved reluctant to shoot other blacks (Savimbi's forces); and now had switched back to light-skinned troops again.

I found Savimbi to be bright, quick, and engaging. Whether I would be willing to put the weight of the United States behind him in a civil war in Angola was, however, another matter. But in those pre-1989 days, recall, the Cold War was still hot, and one of the places it was hottest was in southern Africa.

THE LEFTIES AND BIANCA JAGGER

I tried to get along not just with the right-wingers at AEI and in the Reagan Administration, but with the lefties as well. In the Latin America field, that meant befriending the Reverend Joe Eldridge and all the radical Marxists, Catholics, progressives, and social-democrats clustered under the umbrella of the Washington Office on Latin America (WOLA).

I invited Joe to lunch at our plush AEI dining room, along with others of my friends and colleagues. The next day I heard about it negatively from AEI's big guns Howard Penniman, Kirk Kirkpatrick, and even Jeane herself. They viewed Eldridge and WOLA as not only being on the wrong side (pro-guerrilla groups, strongly critical of U.S. policy) in Central America but, through their frequent congressional testimony, as poisoning the political atmosphere for U.S. policy in Congress and in Washington generally. My own view of WOLA was more benign.

On several occasions that first year, I was invited up to WOLA gatherings on Capitol Hill. WOLA occupied space in a building owned by the Methodist Church, just across from the Capitol. That helped explain their effectiveness: to testify before Congress, all they had to do was roll out of bed, cross the street, and they were in the Capitol. WOLA was a phenomenon familiar in Washington of a church-related group that was far more radical than its denominational membership, in this case the Methodists whose members had voted overwhelmingly for Ronald Reagan in 1980. But WOLA had Catholics as well as Protestants among its leaders, including ex-nuns, ex-priests, and former and current ministers.

I was more amused than appalled by WOLA's tactics. Most of the secular-oriented priests, nuns, and ministers (ex as well as current) who worked for it would never be caught dead wearing their clerical collars or habits on the streets of Washington. But when they walked the halls of Congress and called on congressmen, they always wore their clerical garb. First, because that got them in to see the congressmen quickly; second because congressmen could not very well kick someone wearing a clerical collar out of his office; third because when they talked in the hushed tones of the confessional, the clerical collar made them even more effective. WOLA had as one of its agents a former nun named Heather Foote, an expert on human rights in Latin America, who was so knowledgeable on the subject, yet so pretty and soft-spoken, that several congressmen confessed to me they had fallen in love both with her and her message.

Compared to AEI, WOLA is very low budget. Its receptions are more like a university-based anthropology department get-together—wine, crackers, and cheese—than a high-powered Washington group. Attendees are mostly young, enthused, idealistic, inexperienced interns, as distinct from the K Street "suits" that I'm used to. The room is crowded but this is not "my crowd"—too young, too recently come to Washington. In my "banker's suit," I feel out of place and twenty years older than everyone else. I only know a half dozen other people in the room.

The guest on this particular night is Guillermo Ungo from El Salvador. He's the head of the Social-Democratic Party in El Salvador, which has a nice ring to it but consists (only a slight exaggeration) mainly of Guillermo, his wife, and other family members and hangers-on. He's a nice man—slight, soft-spoken—but has no chance in the often-violent rough-and-tumble of Salvadoran politics. Since he and I are the most senior people at the reception, we are quickly introduced and have a nice chance to talk. I conclude that he's naïve not only in the ways of Washington but also of El Salvador.

The real celebrity at the party is Bianca Jagger, and I'm also introduced to her. She's the Paris Hilton of her time: famous only for being famous. Nicaraguan by birth and now operating as an agent of the Sandinista government, she had spent time in London where she'd met and married rocker Mick Jagger. That was her only claim to fame. Now separated (or divorced?) from Mick, she was currently dating Senator (and former student of mine) Chris Dodd. Bianca was very thin with skinny legs and hollowed-out cheeks; she looked pale and maybe anorexic. To me she wasn't attractive at all. But then, maybe there was something there that I didn't know about.

MEETING BILL MIDDENDORF

I met Bill Middendorf for the first time only a few months after joining AEI. Bill was our ambassador to the Organization of American States and a true Reaganite conservative, one of the first high-level "true believers" I'd met. For most of my AEI/think tank/academic friends, even if they supported Reagan and the conservative revolution, did so with strong reservations.

But Bill was a died-in-the-wool conservative, an enthusiast for the cause. He was also Dutch like me and, also like me, a Frieslander, from one of Holland's most northern and rock-ribbed Calvinist provinces. However, Bill's family was Catholic—unusual in northern Holland—not Calvinist; and instead of emigrating to western Michigan where many of the Dutch immigrant Calvinists settled in the 1850s–1880s, his had migrated to Catholic Baltimore in the 1830s. The family had done well in business and banking; Bill was a big donor to the Republican Party. That's how he had been named ambassador to the Netherlands by President Richard Nixon in 1969 and now ambassador to the OAS by President Reagan.

Middendorf had the worst syntax I'd ever heard—worse than Eisenhower or George W. Bush, if one recalls the mispronunciations and malapropisms of their press conferences. Bill could not complete a sentence without getting so tangled up in the English language that you completely lost the point of what he was trying to say, or else you started to laugh, which was even worse since Bill was an important person and close to Reagan (who also mangled his sentences sometimes). I often wondered, to myself of course, how Middendorf had become so rich (was it inherited wealth?) and come so far (money and connections), given his all-too-obvious limitations. But he certainly dressed impeccably, and, with his gray hair and expensive suits, looked like he should be a senator or ambassador.

Scott Palmer, the director of the Latin America Program at the State Department's Foreign Service Institute, told me that Middendorf had been by far the worst student in the special ambassador's class. "He learned absolutely nothing," said Scott; "nothing sank in." And he was even worse in the Spanish language class. Despite twelve weeks of intense language training, he could not speak or understand enough Spanish to get by even on social occasions. And when he spoke it, it came out even more fractured than his English, which was bad enough.

But Bill always liked me (1) because we shared a Dutch background, and (2) because he recognized I knew far more about Latin America than he did. At first he tried to recruit me for his OAS staff, and later he sought to bring me on as a special adviser; but I couldn't imagine giving up my plush AEI position to work for such an ill-informed person. But I was always polite and respectful to him

(I'm sure, in Middendorf's experience, this was not always the case), even while resenting that his wealth seemed to me to have been a product of inheritance and I was a firm believer in merit.

But my friendship (if you can call it that) eventually paid off, because in 1985–86 when Bill was named by Reagan to chair a Presidential Task Force on Economic Justice (see chapter 9), he as well as Jeane Kirkpatrick lobbied for me to be named a member. Those efforts worked and I was appointed to the commission by President Reagan. And, recall, that is among my main claims to be able to carry the title of "Honorable."

GENERAL VERNON WALTERS: *MACHISMO* IN THE FALKLANDS

In the spring of 1982, my program at AEI, as part of a monthly program we had initiated, hosted General Vernon Walters. General Walters was an institution in Washington: a veteran of World War II, fluent in a couple dozen languages, serving as a translator for presidents and others, named special ambassador by Reagan, and, still in the future, ambassador to the UN succeeding Jeane. Walters was articulate, quick on his feet, and wonderful at providing policy briefings. In addition he *looked like* a general, barrel-chested and forceful, a definite presence. Some of us thought he was over the hill and far overrated, glib and anecdotal rather than analytical; nonetheless it was a real *coup* to get him for our program.

Walters's presentation went well, a real *tour de force* of global problems. The audience was very high-level: Senator J. William Fulbright, ex-CIA director Richard Helms, NSC official Ray Cline, diplomat William Hyland, about 100 movers 'n' shakers from the foreign policy establishment. The media was also present in considerable numbers. My boss, Bill Baroody, wanted to introduce him but I handled the discussion—one way of becoming known in Washington. Walters covered the world in thirty minutes and said something besides—no mean feat. Among the many *bon mots*:

- the 700,000 Cubans in the U.S. have a bigger GNP than the ten million on the island
- there are lots of studies of transitions from authoritarianism to democracy but none of post-communism because it has never [as of 1982] happened.
- *bukia* is the Arabic word for not being in a hurry; it carries none of the urgency that the Spanish word *mañana* does.

Of all the things that Walters says, however, the one the media picked up on was his comment that the recently commenced Falklands/Malvinas War [which pitted Argentina against Great Britain] was a "silly little war" that involved *machismo* on both sides and that, apropos Prime Minister Margaret Thatcher, "women have a machismo problem as well as men." The following day my phone rings all day from journalists trying to confirm that quote. I try to downplay the quote by emphasizing Walters's larger message, but unfortunately that became the lead headline from our program. Late in the day I hear from Secretary of State Al Haig's office that the secretary is upset and views such comments as hurting his efforts at negotiations. Well, then, if that's how you feel, blame Walters, not me.

Finally at 6:00 that evening I get a call from John Chancellor, the respected anchor of NBC news. No intermediaries, just him and me. He's about to go on the air and wants to know about "the *machismo* business." Is it possible, he asks, for a woman [Mrs. Thatcher] to practice *machismo*? He's very polite, deferential, and really wants to know. I sigh, and try to explain to him the cultural roots of machismo, that machismo stands for honor, grandeur, dignity, as well as sexual and political power, and not just opposition to women. But he gets it all wrong: in his editorial on the news that night he goes back to Elizabeth I, the Spanish armada, the Argentine military opposition to Perón's wives Evita and Isabel, and now Margaret Thatcher to argue that the Argentine military "has a problem with women."

This is sheer nonsense. Elizabeth I was a tough, able monarch; her actions against the armada had nothing to do with the fact she was a woman, though it may have influenced Philip II's decision to attack England. Evita and Isabel were opposed by the Argentine military maybe in part because they were women but mainly because they were incompetent and/or had little constitutional authority to govern. And Margaret Thatcher opposed Argentina's takeover of the Falklands not because she was a woman but because she refused to bow to armed aggression.

Chancellor got it all wrong; the next day we talked again and that night he corrected himself. As we talked more, Chancellor asked how come I knew so much about this. I replied that was my specialty and that's why I get paid as I do. He told me that was "neato" and he would put me in his rolodex of informants. The episode taught me how poorly informed even high-level journalists are and how they can get a story completely wrong.

CONFLICTS IN THE ADMINISTRATION

The Falklands/Malvinas War also stoked controversies within the Administration. Secretary of State Al Haig quickly, automatically, and in knee-jerk fashion sided with Great Britain, our traditional ally, in the conflict. In doing so, Haig was reflecting the traditional Eurocentric view of the American foreign policy elite and the Council on Foreign Relations.

But Jeane Kirkpatrick was of a different stripe. She was a product of the 1960s' emphasis on developing nations. Her doctoral dissertation had been on Argentina. She sympathized with Argentina and empathized with Third World aspirations. Without making this a public dispute, it was clear that inside the Reagan Administration, Jeane was the only person who sought to understand the Argentine point of view.

As a quasi-insider, I watched the dispute with rapt fascination, because I was also, like Jeane, a student of and sympathetic to the Third World, and I had long been critical of the Eurocentric focus of American foreign policy. To both Jeane and myself, this dispute was more than a brief shootout between Great Britain and Argentina; it was also a test of U.S. policy. In the United States, Latin America had long been viewed as a second-rate area, hardly worthy of serious U.S. attention. But Jeane, with my vigorous support, had been lobbying with President Reagan and within the administration both to give Latin America more attention and to elevate it in U.S. priorities. She wanted a special regional policy for Latin America, but Haig opposed that as well.

Argentina-Great Britain was the immediate issue but larger stakes were also involved. I met with Jeane several times during this period: we both understood that we were going to lose this battle and that Haig (and Great Britain) would win; nevertheless we wanted to make the point, which ultimately triumphed in the George H.W. Bush Administration (NAFTA, the Washington Consensus) that Latin America was of rising importance, deserved special attention, and was becoming increasingly *interdependent* (trade, oil, investment, tourism, drugs, immigration, natural gas, markets, labor supplies, etc.) with the U.S.

Jeane had other disputes in those days. I witnessed one on the White House lawn. Mary McGrory, whose columns in the *Washington Post* had become increasingly more strident, one-sided, and shrill, approached Jeane at an outdoor White House ceremony seeking to pose a series of questions on Central America. McGrory's recent columns had been more and more critical of Jeane, unfairly so, so on the lawn Jeane told her she had lots of answers but didn't want to share them with McGrory. In the course of this mini-tempest I learned from Jeane's friends that McGrory had once had an affair with John F. Kennedy. Meow, meow!

As part of Jeane's network I also learned of other contretemps, none of which so far as I know were publicized at the time. In the spring of 1982 Jeane was scheduled to receive honorary degrees from both St. Anselm's College (Catholic, to please Bill Baroody) and Franklin and Marshall University. In both places the faculty had asked her to withdraw or be disinvited because she was allegedly responsible for "thousands" of deaths in Latin America. This was sheer nonsense. There were also protests at Jeane's home university, Georgetown, over plans to award her another honorary degree, but she was a tenured faculty member and refused to even consider withdrawing her name from nomination. These were all foretastes of a much larger controversy that would blow up later at Smith College, the nation's most prestigious women's college (see below).

FUND-RAISING

I didn't *have* to do fund-raising at AEI in these early years because to that point the Institute was so rich it didn't need its scholars to do so, but occasionally I pitched in just to help out. So when Bill Baroody asked me to meet with rich Mrs. O'Donnell and a representative of the O'Donnell Foundation from Dallas, I was happy to do so.

Mrs. O'Donnell showed up at AEI in a limousine with driver that she had rented for the entire duration of her stay in Washington. Clearly there was money here that was above my level. She was accompanied by Carolyn Bacon from the foundation that bears the O'Donnell family name. Ms. Bacon was much sharper, informed, and with-it than was Mrs. O'Donnell. I took them to lunch in AEI's elegant dining room; Bill Baroody stopped by our table to press the flesh. They were interested in Mexico and immigration issues but were not well informed about either and very vague about the Foundation's priorities. I did my best to be charming, enthusiastic, and to get them interested in funding our program but it was an uphill battle.

In his follow-up letter to husband Peter O'Donnell, however, Bill Baroody asked for funding for AEI's trade policy project, not for Latin American studies. To me this was completely irrational. If I were the O'Donnells and had come all the way to Washington to discuss Latin America and then got a letter back talking about trade, I'd think AEI was incompetent and couldn't get its ducks in line. To my knowledge, we never did get any money from the O'Donnells. And the incompetent way it was handled was typical of the AEI development office. To this day I've never met a development officer that I thought was competent at bringing scholars and big donors together.

MISS TEXAS NATURAL GAS

Joann Herman was a bleached bottle blond from Texas who had a shape like Brigitte Bardot. She had a walk that emphasized all her curves and made men pay attention. At one point she won a beauty contest and was named "Miss Texas Natural Gas." How would you like to go through life known as "Miss Texas Natural Gas"? She was what my mother would call a "floozy."

On the basis of her undoubted assets, she married a man fifty years her senior, who died shortly thereafter. Think Anna Nicole Smith—but with brains! Joann inherited all of his considerable wealth. Every charity and cause in the world—including the Washington think tanks—were after both Joann and her money.

At one point she came to AEI. She was dressed like a tart, not in the conservative, professional suits that most Washingtonian women wear. Jim Abellera, a young, handsome, Naval Academy graduate who worked on security studies at AEI, was designated as her escort. Walking the hallways, she caused quite a sensation. I was designated as Abellera's backup.

And it turned out, Jim got sick or had another obligation for part of that day. So I was asked to escort her to a public AEI event that afternoon, a speech by ambassador and former SEC chairman Arthur Burns. I remember it was a big event with a long aisle and lots of people. AEI wanted Joann to sit in front, in the VIP section. She grabbed my arm as we walked down the aisle. It looked pretty intimate; all eyes turned to watch Joann on parade. She could sashay with the best of them. I was a little embarrassed by all this; I'm sure my ears turned red. Colleagues later teased that we made a "nice-looking couple." I'm glad Iêda wasn't there.

Later I escorted Joann to Bill Baroody's office. In the process I discovered she wasn't a bad kid—now there's a familiar theme!—but was not well-educated and felt way out of place at AEI. In addition, she hated Hispanics and blamed them for rising crime in Texas and the mugging of her own son—so much for my efforts to get money from her for our Latin America program. I don't believe the other programs at AEI were any more successful. The next day she flew back to Texas; I never saw her again.

That is, until one day I was perusing at Borders the book by George Crile called *Charlie Wilson's War*. And there was Joann in many of the pictures, with her story filling some seventy-five pages of the book. It turned out that, after AEI, Joann had gotten interested in Pakistan, in Congressman Wilson, and in his 1980s efforts to use Pakistan and the Taliban to drive the Soviets out of Afghanistan. Joann had gone to Pakistan with Wilson on numerous occasions where then dictator Muhammed Zia-ul-Haq, and half the Pakistan cabinet, had fallen in love with her. Joann did have undoubted charms; her money, instead of going to AEI, was being used to bankroll the Taliban! Now they have made a movie out of *Charlie Wilson's War*; Julia Roberts plays Joann.

THE MAKING OF A PRESIDENT: GENERAL BANZER OF BOLIVIA

In November 1983, I was sitting in my AEI office when I received a call from Ed Derwinsky from the State Department. Derwinsky was then, I believe, undersecretary of state and the third-ranking person in the department. He told me that former Bolivian president (and dictator) Hugo Banzer was in town and wanted advice on how to set up a think tank. Would I receive him in my office at AEI and tell him about think tanks?

I refused. For one thing I'd had a parade of visiting firemen that week and needed to get some work done. For another I knew General Banzer's record; during his term as president, there had been widespread human rights violations and Banzer had ruled as an authoritarian dictator. Third, I strongly suspected—correctly as it turned out—that Banzer didn't really want to establish a think tank as we know it; he wanted to establish, since political parties were banned at that time in Bolivia, a front for his political activities, call it a "think tank," but use it to serve as a base for the reelection campaign he was already planning.

Within two minutes of my refusal, I got a call from Bill Baroody. Derwinsky had gone over my head. Bill indicated that as a favor to the State Department and Derwinsky, I should see Banzer. So I agreed.

What was going on here? At that time (1983), Bolivia seemed about to disintegrate—again. The president was quasi-senile, planeloads of Bolivian leftists were going to the Soviet Union and Eastern Europe, labor leaders were calling for a revolutionary government, Trotskyite miners were demonstrating in the streets against the administration of President Siles Suazo. The U.S. Embassy in La Paz, under Ambassador Coors, was alarmed at the leftward tilt and the potential for instability. With all our attention devoted to Central America at that time, no one at high levels was paying attention to Bolivia. The State Department was looking for someone to lead the country back to the center-right. General Banzer seemed to be "our" man but in the context of the 1980s and the general swing to democracy in Latin America, we wanted him in power through democratic elections, not a *coup d'etat*.

I was pleasantly surprised when I met with General Banzer. He had a very quick and sharp mind. He was not at all loud and blustery as you expect Latin American generals to be, but polite, self-effacing, and deferential. Yet also very lively, animated, and enthused. I liked him a lot despite his inglorious past and found him very *simpático*. I especially liked the fact that he didn't try to bullshit me: he saw right away that I knew that all this talk of a "think tank" was just a façade to disguise the fact he was using it to launch his political campaign.

But we went through the motions. I gave him the grand tour of AEI. I showed him the research, publications, finance, and administrative offices. All the while, since I already had experience of advising other Latin American presidents on how to set up a think tank, I was telling him how to adapt the U.S. model to Bolivian realities and his own goals, which were to use his "think tank" much like a political party and as a base for his election campaign but not to overtly call it that. Banzer and I, to both of our surprise, got along very well; we understood each other.

He returned to Bolivia and set up his "research institute." We continued to be in touch mainly through his supporters who frequently traveled to Washington, and I continued to advise him on his think tank-cum-political party. Much to everyone's surprise, he ran a democratic campaign, won a fair election, and served out his term as a democratic leader with a good human rights record. As the chief "king-maker" and to some degree responsible for his successful campaign, I received an invitation to his inauguration. I couldn't go but I sent him a congratulatory cable. Unfortunately he developed a terminal cancer while in office and died prematurely shortly thereafter.

THE *NEW YORK TIMES* AND PLAGIARISM

A month after the Banzer meeting I was out in San Diego for a high-level meeting on the future of Latin America. All the big academic names were there: Abe Lowenthal, Riordan Roett, Peter Smith, Susan Purcell, Robert Wessin. The program's sponsor was the *San Diego Union*; it had invited local business and policy leaders as well as major newspaper writers and columnists such as Alan Riding and Tom Wicker of the *New York Times*.

It was a very prestigious gathering; our role as academics was to provide the journalists with new ideas and insights that they might draw on for their columns. It hardly needs saying that the food, the hotel accommodations, the beaches and parks of San Diego, and the intellectual discussion were all first-rate. Tom Wicker seemed to be especially intrigued by my presentation, which dealt with the conceptual failures in U.S. Latin America policy.

Imagine my surprise and shock, then, when I found that in his January 9, 1984, column in the *Times*, Wicker had taken his entire argument from my presentation. It was almost word for word and argument for argument. Moreover since my presentation at San Diego had been based on a formal paper I'd prepared for publication elsewhere, I had the entire argument set down in black and white. Another word for what Wicker had done, even high school writers learn, is plagiarism. And this from one of the most prominent journalists and columnists in the United States. And in the *New York Times*, our most respected and only national newspaper.

What to do? At first I considered the idea of just letting it go, forgetting about it. But I'm a writer and a scholar; in these fraternities, plagiarism is an unforgivable sin. So I called Wicker up (as distinct from his bosses) at the *Times*; he took my call immediately. I asked why he had used my materials without permission or acknowledgment. I didn't say the word plagiarism but it was clearly hanging there in the air. Wicker started to mumble almost incoherently, managed to get out an apology, and then mumbled some more about how he was pressed for time, didn't mean to do it, it was an accident. Frankly, I've heard these same excuses dozens of times in my career from students I'd caught cheating; I didn't expect it from one of the country's leading and prize-winning columnists.

I was tempted as this stage to go to his superiors. But eventually Wicker blurted out that he'd be happy to print an acknowledgment to my work at the end of his next column. That he did in a brief paragraph that attributed the problem to "oversight." I didn't believe that for a minute: I think Wicker was lazy and dashed off his column with my paper open and in front of him, perhaps thinking I'd never see his piece. But at that stage I was inclined to let it go: he *had* apologized, *had* acknowledged my work in his column, and what purpose would have been served by taking it to his superiors? I could have made a federal case out of it and likely ruined his career, but I chose not to do that. Did I make the right decision?

EDUCATING AL GORE

In January 1984, we traveled down to colonial Williamsburg in Virginia. It's a beautiful drive and a beautiful city, a replica of a colonial village but a lively city (William and Mary University is here) at the same time. Not a dead relic but a vibrant, interesting place.

We were here to provide a briefing on foreign policy for all the freshman congressmen, senators and representatives. The aim was to bring the entering class up to speed on foreign policy issues but to do so in a beautiful setting outside of Washington and its distractions. AEI and the Brookings Institution teamed up to do this every two years, with Brookings providing the Democratic perspective and AEI the Republican. We and the new congressmen spent the weekend together in Williamsburg.

I was teamed up on a panel with Bob Pastor from Brookings and Amb. Jim Michel from the State Department as moderator. Bob had been Jimmy Carter's principal adviser on Latin America on the National Security Council; Michel was a deputy assistant secretary on Inter-American affairs. Michel was very boring (a State Department career does that to you), but Bob and I went at it with gusto, vigorously airing out the partisan divide over Central America. At the end of the session we got a standing ovation from the congressmen who said it was the best panel of the weekend.

Two of the "students" stand out in my mind. One was Al Gore, the newly elected senator from Tennessee. There was nothing that made Gore exceptional at this meeting; he remained silent all during the seminar presentation and did not say a word in the discussion that followed. We all considered him a dolt who had won his seat by inheriting it from his father. Of course at that time we did not know that he would go on to be vice president in 1992 and win the popular presidential vote in 2000.

Another congressman present, Paul Henry from Michigan, was especially interesting to me. In the spring of 1983, because I was on television a lot concerning Central America issues, I had received a call from Republican Party officials in Michigan asking if I were interested in running for Congress from my hometown of Grand Rapids, Jerry Ford's old district. It was flattering to be asked and I considered it seriously. I even flew to Grand Rapids for a few days, talked with party officials (it's a predominantly Republican district), met with the big money folks (mainly the Amway Corporation whose officials had been the ones who'd contacted me), and tested the waters. But I'd not lived in Grand Rapids since I was seventeen, we didn't have a residence there, I didn't know the issues or the people, and name recognition would be a problem. Plus the incumbent, who was stepping down because of cancer, had waited until the last minute to announce both his disease and his decision not to run in the hope that his son would then inherit the seat. But that left me little time to prepare for the primary and the general election. In addition, Iêda was opposed because we'd just moved to Washington, just put our kids in school, and didn't want to go through all that disruption of moving the family around all over again.

I was ambivalent because at the time I was very happy with my AEI job, loved the writing that I was able to do, was enamored with my position as policy analyst (quite a bit of power but no responsibility), and wasn't sure I was cut out to be a congressman. I'm too impatient, do not suffer fools easily, and tend to speak my mind regardless of the political fallout. When I decided not to run, Calvin College political scientist Paul Henry stepped into the race and won handily. Paul was very bright, made an excellent congressman, and was being groomed for higher things within the Republican Party. Unfortunately he developed a brain tumor and died in his early forties, thus tragically cutting short a promising career. I was pleased that weekend in colonial Willamsburg to become acquainted with him.

SMITH RICHARDSON AND THE CONSERVATIVE FOUNDATIONS

The big foundations that bankrolled the conservative revolution of the 1970s and 1980s were the Bradley Foundation, Olin, Scaife, and Smith Richardson. The Ford, Mellon, McArthur, and Rockefeller foundations had been funding liberal causes for decades, but now the conservative foundations and their funding of groups like AEI, the Hudson Institute, the Heritage Foundation, and others had reached a level of parity. We at AEI were the beneficiaries of all this largesse, and what a windfall it was.

But the conservative foundations were often quite particular about how they spent their money. Richard Scaife, the Pittsburgh parking lot king, and beer mogul Joseph Coors preferred to give their money to the far-right Heritage Foundation. For them, AEI was too liberal! We did get a little money from Scaife but I know Bill Baroody was always disappointed that he couldn't get more from the real conservatives.

Two impresarios of the conservative foundations *cum* think tank world were especially important during this period. Michael Joyce was the executive director of the Bradley Foundation, located in Milwaukee. Les Lenkowsky was a neocon who floated between New York and Washington, was very close to Joyce, and gave advice to all the conservative foundations regarding which think tanks and which projects and individuals in them to fund. I didn't particularly like either one of them but I had to hold my tongue for fear of a funding cutoff. I thought Joyce was too self-important, made arbitrary and often ill-informed decisions about which projects to fund, and controlled way too much money for any one man with limited knowledge and background. Lenkowsky was similar: he thought of himself as an intellectual, he interfered in the internal affairs (by telling us whom to hire and fire) of the think tanks with which he dealt, and he favored his own friends and cronies over a more objective evaluation of projects. You can probably guess that my program and I were not among those favored by either of these individuals.

During my time at AEI we were probably closest to the Smith Richardson (no hyphen; Smith was his first name) Foundation, although we did get grants from Scaife, Olin, Bradley, as well as the Mellon, Tinker, Texaco, Brazil-Invest, and other big foundations. I recall several times traveling up to New York to meet with foundation officials. At Smith Richardson the executive-director was Devon Gaffney, sister of Frank Gaffney who in Washington has his own defense policy think tank. We got along well with Devon, although in some parts of the conservative foundation world the neocons already had such a stranglehold that I sometimes designated my assistant Mark Falcoff, himself a neocon in ways that I was not, to make the approach instead. We were very successful in our fund-raising efforts at AEI, raising over a half million dollars for our program in three years. But that was not enough, ultimately, to save either our program or AEI.

An interesting phenomenon was under way by now, already apparent even in the early-to-mid-1980s. That involved a generational and ultimately an ideological shift in the leadership of the big conservative foundations. The founding fathers of these big foundations had usually been, like Scaife or Coors, tough, crusty, self-made men. They had made money the old-fashioned way—they earned it—and they were very suspicious of big government and very conservative in their ideology. But their children or even grandchildren (think Stuart Mott of the once-conservative Mott Foundation) frequently felt guilt complexes over their inherited wealth, and when they took over tended to give to liberal causes and not to conservative think tanks like AEI. In my program we were already beginning to see the effects of this generational shift; by the late-1980s this factor would be one of the several financial nails in the almost-coffin of AEI.

DISPUTES OVER POPULATION POLICY

As scholars, my wife Iêda and I have both done serious research and published on population issues, focused on third world areas. Ours is a moderate position: we see excess population as a problem in many developing areas, increasing unemployment, doing environmental damage, retarding development, often adding to misery and poverty, and potentially producing instability and revolution. On the other hand we do not see increasing population as the world's most pressing problem, superseding other issues, and producing absolute calamity (as in a famous, overwrought book at the time, *The Population Bomb*, by Paul Ehrlich).

But this position was too moderate for my AEI colleague Ben Wattenberg, one of the Big Guns at the Institute. Running against the prevailing grain, Ben favored unchecked population growth. He denied that there was a population problem and urged an end to all population control programs. His argument was that population growth added to economic development and was good for the globe as well as individual countries. His position was called, after the Reagan economics policy, "Supply-Side Demographics." The other catchy slogan associated with Ben's position was "Capitalism is the best contraceptive."

I thought Ben's position was wrong and totally irresponsible, but I was content to let him have his say, crazy though it was. That was in keeping with AEI's motto of "the competition of ideas in a free society." The trouble was that Ben complained to Bill Baroody and Vice President Tait Trussell about *my* position on population. He wanted me silenced so that his would be the only and official position at AEI. He wanted the Institute to have only one population policy stance and his would be it. That did not sound like "the competition of ideas in a free society" to me.

The issue caused some tense moments at AEI. Ben was angry that I would not defer to his position, especially since he was more senior and better known in Washington than I. Even though I thought his position silly and ridiculous, I was willing to hear him out, but he wanted to deny free speech for mine. Several of AEI's senior economists also thought Ben's argument was ludicrous and sided with me. On the other hand, the strong Catholics at AEI (Baroody himself, Michael Novak), who constituted a powerful voice within the Institute and were generally against all abortion, "family planning," and birth control programs, were sympathetic to Ben, even while uncomfortable with the notion of "supply-side demographics."

Eventually I went to see Trussell. I told him that Ben's position on population was making AEI a laughing stock on the outside, that his position could not be allowed to be the official AEI position (that violated the "competition of ideas" motto of Bill Baroody Sr.), that the AEI economists were opposed, and that Ben's position on population had already cost my program a large grant from the Mellon Foundation. But Tait was a weak reed; he did not want to take on Wattenberg either. He did, however, carry my message to Baroody where the arguments that AEI was becoming a laughing stock, that it violated his father's motto, and that it cost us a grant (AEI was already feeling a financial squeeze) carried weight. The resolution (which I considered a victory) was: Ben would continue to write his thing, I would continue to write mine, and there would be no official AEI position on this or any other issues. However the dispute cost me the long-term enmity of Wattenberg and, I've heard, came within a whisker of costing me my job.

THE MOONIES AND RALPH REED

In the mid-1980s I contracted with the Global Economic Action Institute (GEAI) to edit a book on development successes and democracy in the third world. The main case studies were Costa Rica, Hungary, Ivory Coast, and Malaysia so the project required me to acquire expertise on three countries that I didn't know well (Hungary, Ivory Coast, and Malaysia; Costa Rica I already knew well)—countries whose development I have followed closely over the years. I was not a completely independent actor in doing this small book: GEAI had given me a partially completed manuscript drafted by some of its own personnel and advisers that had a strongly pro-democracy, pro-free market slant. The draft was way too strident and conservative for me but I could certainly support a moderate democracy/free market position. My assignment from GEAI was to take this draft, rewrite it, and convert it into prose that academics, think tankers, and policy experts could support. A handsome honorarium was involved.

So I took the draft, started from word one to rewrite, toned down the more ideological language of the original manuscript, and introduced a tone into the report that was social-scientific and academic. The report forced me to do considerable new research; it also got me thinking seriously not just about analyzing development in the Third World but, for the first time in a policy sense, how to achieve development. Some twenty years later I would return to these themes in my own, single-authored book on the developing nations where the main subject was what works in development and what doesn't.[1]

I was about halfway through the project before I came to realize that GEAI was a front for the Rev. Sun Myung Moon's Unification Church. This was a "Moonie" project and I was working for the "Moonie Church." I hadn't realized this before since all the officials I'd dealt with at GEAI, as well as the individuals who'd done the first draft, were all Americans. What to do? Rev. Moon, he of the karate chop delivery, the mass marriages (in the thousands in a football stadium) of his followers, and some truly bizarre religious and political beliefs, was not my favorite fellow. I didn't want to sell out my academic reputation; on the other hand, the money was good and I had been assured of complete academic freedom. So I finished the project, it turned out to be a respectable monograph, and it was published by GEAI, even though, fearing for my reputation from being associated with the Moonies, I asked that my name not be listed as author on the front cover.

In the course of doing this project, I got invited to several Moonie events in the Washington area. One was a large, annual Moonie reception for all its friends and hangers-on at the luxurious Marriott Hotel in downtown Washington. Iêda and I were amazed to find over 2,000 people present, the cream of Washington society and politics. We were also invited to other Washington Institute (another front for the Unification Church) sponsored seminars and policy forums; there I was surprised to find such luminaries as intellectual Richard Rubenstein, former Kissinger aide Hal Sonnenfeldt, philosopher and editor Morton Kaplan, and political boy wonder, then head of the Republican Young Americans for Freedom, Ralph Reed. All of these were friends or acquaintances of mine from Washington policy circles; I was as surprised to find them at a Moonie event as they were to find me. Rev. Moon had certainly bought himself access and influence in Washington; I assumed that, like me, they were all on the Unification Church payroll.

JEANE KIRKPATRICK AT SMITH

In the spring of 1985 Jeane Kirkpatrick was invited to come to Smith College to give a talk and receive an honorary degree. Since I also lived (Amherst) in the Pioneer Valley where Smith (in Northampton) was located only seven miles away, Jeane asked my advice on what she would be getting into there. I told her there would be protests (like Cambridge, the Amherst-Northampton area has a considerable radical, Trotskyite, Marxist subculture) but no threats to her personal security.

But Smith, bowing to the political pressures of some of its radical faculty and students, cancelled the invitation. Smith is supposed to be one of the leading, if not *the* leading, women's colleges in the U.S.; for it to buckle and cave to political pressures was shameful. This was a flagrant denial of free speech and an insult, whatever one's views of her politics, to one of the most articulate and accomplished women in America. To compound the sin, Smith lied about it, telling Jeane that it was concerned for her safety when in fact there was no security threat. This dispute also cost me a friendship with longtime colleague Susan Bourque, a professor of government at Smith who was a key policy advisor to Smith's beleaguered (and first woman) president, Jill Kerr Conway.

I learned more details about this sordid affair when I shared a plane ride up to Hartford with Meg Greenfield, editorial page director of the *Washington Post* and a member of the Smith College Board of Trustees. Meg, a Washington friend and colleague, told me that Smith's actions were even more despicable than reported. At first Smith tried to keep Jeane's appearance a secret—at a time when invitations had already been sent out and hundreds of faculty and students already knew about it. Then when the threat of protest arose, Smith panicked and sought to cancel the event. But Meg independently reported what I'd already told Jeane: there was no threat of violence and any disruptions could have been handled by campus and town security. But Conway was fearful of the bad publicity Smith would receive if Jeane's speech was accompanied by protests and disruptions; she called Jeane to revoke the offer even while Meg and the trustees were still deliberating the issue. On top of that, Conway refused to even read publicly the citation Jeane was to have received, instead offering to mail it to her. At that stage Jeane told her no thanks: you can keep your honorary degree and your citation. Knowing Jeane, I wouldn't be surprised if her language was even stronger, something to the effect of Stuff It!

This has to be one of the more shameful events in Smith College history. To deny free speech to one of the country's leading women who might well have become, if her husband had not gotten sick and she pulled out to care for him, the first woman president of the United States—and then to lie about the reasons besides—is a disgrace. Although Smith tried to cover this fact up, I learned later from my friend Meg that Conway's action in this case was one of the, maybe *the* principal reason, the college board of trustees voted a short time later to oust her.

JERRY FORD

Jerry Ford was one of our favorite people. I grew up in Ford's home district of Grand Rapids, I attended his campaign debates in high school, my uncle was a Ford campaign chairman in one of his early races, and he was my congressman during my formative years. In 1976 I was involved in Ford's presidential campaign (he failed to heed my advice on emphasizing experience in foreign policy over Jimmy Carter's inexperience—and he lost!), and after I joined AEI in 1981, now ex-president Ford was named a senior counselor and became very much involved in our think tank activities. Iêda and I had lunch or dinner with President Ford on several occasions in the 1980s; he knew my uncle Neil, me, and the Wiarda name.

We always found Ford to be extremely gracious, approachable, and friendly. Let me provide only two of many examples. One time we were at a large, AEI lunch at the Mayflower Hotel. Ford was the speaker and I rose to ask a question. For the audience's benefit I identified myself as "Howard Wiarda, Dutch, and from Grand Rapids." Ford responded, "Yes, I recognize a good Dutch name when I hear one"—the Dutch in western Michigan were, after all, the basis of Ford's constituency. But then he quickly turned to my AEI colleague Michael Novak who was moderating the discussion to assure him there were "lots of good Polish people in my district too." It was vintage Ford: nice, gracious, reassuring.

After he left office and had moved to Palm Springs, Ford continued his connection with AEI. We saw him from time to time; he visited AEI whenever he was in Washington and often relied on AEI for logistical support and intellectual firepower. One time I got a call from Ford asking if I would write a speech for him on U.S.-Mexico relations. I was happy to do it: Ford had done a lot for me and in Washington, when one of your mentors asks for a favor, you drop everything else and do it. So Iêda and I brainstormed and wrote what we thought was a great speech. We of course did this *gratis*, but much to our surprise a couple weeks later we received a check for $1,000.00, along with a gracious note from Ford thanking us for our services. Ford got $20,000–30,000 for his speech but, since we were expecting nothing, the thousand dollars was a nice little bonus.

CONFRONTING W.W. ROSTOW

Ron Scheman, a clued-in Washington lawyer and former OAS and Inter-American Development Bank official, had the great idea in 1987 of convoking a conference on the 25th anniversary of the Alliance for Progress, the historic assistance program for Latin America of John F. Kennedy. All the big wheels from the Kennedy era and the Alliance's main architects were there: economist Lincoln Gordon, speechwriter Ted Sorenson, historian Arthur Schlesinger Jr., presidential assistant Richard Goodwin, economist and former director of the State Department's Policy Planning Staff, as well as National Security Adviser W.W. Rostow, and me. Rostow, in his famous book *The Stages of Economic Growth*, had provided the intellectual arguments for the Alliance and had been one of its chief architects.

Because Scheman told me he wanted to publish a book from the papers presented, I had made the mistake of thinking this was a serious conference and not just a celebration of the Alliance. In my paper,[2] as well as in other writings, I was quite critical of Rostow and the developmentalist school of that time, arguing that it was Eurocentric, ignored national and regional cultural differences, that the conditions today were very different than those for earlier developers, and that Latin America would never exactly imitate the U.S. model. I said that the Alliance for Progress was killed not by Lyndon Johnson or Richard Nixon, which the Kennedyites like to believe, but that it was dead on arrival because the assumptions on which it was based were all wrong. In the meeting Linc Gordon was mildly critical of my paper but Schlesinger, a Kennedy apologist, was fuming. Apparently anyone who criticized his beloved Kennedy or its policies, let alone said its assumptions were wrong, had to be destroyed. Schlesinger launched a broadside attack that he also, unfortunately, made very personal.

More fireworks were to come. At dinner that night I was at the same table as Rostow, who had not been present at the earlier panel. My name, Wiarda, is an unusual one and sometimes hard to catch at first, and I don't think Rostow caught it when we were first introduced. So as we sat down Rostow was fulminating against "this fellow Wiarda who has written so many bad things about me." Whereupon I stood and said, "Mr. Rostow, I think I should *re*-introduce myself; I'm Howard Wiarda, the person you have been talking about." Whereupon—every hostess's nightmare—the entire room fell deathly silent.

After what seemed like an eternity but was in reality only a few seconds during which some icy glances were exchanged, we sat down again and Rostow and I had a long talk. I told him I was willing to meet him halfway, which was half more than most of my academic colleagues were willing to grant.

For Rostow's books and policies had argued that economic development would inevitably and universally give rise to democracy, middle classness, and stability just as it had in the U.S. and Europe. But in Latin America and elsewhere in the Third World, development had given rise not to democracy but to authoritarianism. The correlations—development, democracy—did not at all correlate. So Rostow was completely wrong in the short run. However I was willing to concede that in the long run—Latin America is today far more developed *and* democratic than it was twenty-five years ago—the Rostow approach might still be correct.

On that basis we parted, not exactly as friends but at least we understood each other. However I don't think Rostow ever forgave me for the effrontery, and from a then-junior scholar besides, of criticizing his work.

MEETING THE STARS

In the fall of 1986 we moved back to Washington, after a two-year hiatus in Amherst during which I had commuted to my AEI job. The two years in Amherst reestablished my bonafides there, which I thought was sufficient to qualify to apply for another two-year leave of absence. The leave was granted but this time not without some complaints from my colleagues. Meanwhile, now thinking that we would keep at least one leg in Washington permanently, we had taken the plunge and bought a house in the Maryland suburbs. It was a beautiful home, on four acres (which we later enlarged to ten), with a stream and a view, in the quaint little town of Brookeville. Brookeville's claim to fame was that it was the capital of the United States for one night, when the British burned the White House in the War of 1812 and President Madison was forced to flee. However local historians have discovered that while James went to Brookeville, Dolly went to McLean, leading to speculation that the Madisons had a "modern marriage" as early as 1812!

Being back in Washington enabled me to resume my lucrative lecturing schedule, which to be honest had not suffered overly during the time I commuted between Amherst and Washington. One of my first invitations was to attend and speak at a gathering of wealthy right-wingers from Tucson. Not my cup of tea politically but the fee for my talk was spectacularly high for me: $5,000.

My hosts even provided a first class ticket—not my usual way to travel but most welcome on this trip since the weather was terrible, the plane was bouncing around, and therefore the martinis that provided a certain calming influence were free. On the leg out my seatmate introduced himself as Señor López; he had a guitar in the overhead compartment. It took me about half the flight to figure out that this was Trini López the singer, who had had some spectacular hits a few years earlier that climbed high on the charts. He was just back from a tour in Brazil and told me he seldom sings anymore, devoting his time to golf and tennis. He was reading Kitty Kelly's *Sinatra* because, he told me, Frank Sinatra had helped him get started in the business and his first few records were cut by Sinatra's recording company. Born in Dallas, López was a *chicano* who no longer spoke Spanish, even though he made his living doing Hispanic music.

I had not been in Tucson before. The hotel was beautiful, surrounded by a spectacular golf course. The houses were in the Spanish style and the cactus as high as the houses. The conditions were desert-like but, because Tucson was more elevated, not "true desert" as around Phoenix. We took an evening tour of the old town and the "*misiones*"; dinner was at the Fuente, a Mexican restaurant but its diners were 100 percent Anglo. It was obvious Tucson was a very rich city; my friend and colleague Ed Williams from the University of Arizona told me it was also extremely conservative. Republican registration was rising, producing a succession of conservative senators: Barry Goldwater, Paul Laxalt (Reagan's Senate ally), John McCain, and John Kyl.

My audience the next day consisted of the richest-looking folks I'd ever spoken to before: all well coiffed, well tanned (real or artificial), and expensively dressed. Quite a number in the audience were ex-CIA or former midwestern bankers and businessmen who had retired to Tucson. But there was also a sprinkling of Hollywood stars who preferred Tucson to Malibu or Palm Springs for their retirement. I met former *Bonanza* star Lorne Green and his wife Nancy, twenty years younger than he and obviously not the mother of his children. She was flashy, rich, a "trophy wife," more political than he with her own right-wing newspaper. I perused a couple issues: it appeared to be the product of his money and her ego. Also present at one of my lectures were the parents (he a Union Carbide executive, she a former ballerina) of actress Linda Purl, who had leading parts in numerous movies and television shows, most famously (in my memory) in "Happy Days" and "Matlock."

One of many things that AEI did for its scholars was to put us in contact with people we would never have met if we had remained academic scholars. These included bankers like David Rockefeller, Paul Volcker, or Walter Wriston; CEOs like Potlach's Richard Madden or Enron's Ken Lay; and Hollywood stars like Charlton Heston or Lorne Green. It was fun to mingle with "the stars"; among other things, I learned that they often have the same (or more) family problems as the rest of us, the same biases and political hangups, and the same financial insecurities. What an eye-opener this all was for a midwesterner like me from Grand Rapids.

NOTES

1. Howard J. Wiarda, *Political Development in Emerging Nations* (Belmont, CA: Thomson/Wadsworth, 2004).

2. "Did the Alliance for Progress Lose Its Way? Or Were Its Assumptions All Wrong from the Beginning?" in Ronald Scheman (ed.) *The Alliance for Progress* (New York: Praeger, 1988), 95–118.

Chapter Thirteen

The Looming Crisis of AEI

When I first arrived at AEI in 1981 there were two things that impressed me more than any others. The first was the enormous amount of access, connections, and entrée that AEI and its scholars enjoyed at all levels of policy-making: the media, interest groups, and government. The second was the wealth and plushness of the place: the high salaries, that elegant AEI dining room, the wonderful benefits, the superb staff, the rich travel account, the unlimited telephone and copying privileges, my own secretary and research assistant. Compared to the threadbare facilities at my home university, at AEI I thought I was in scholar's heaven. My former university colleagues, and even counterparts at other less well-endowed Washington think tanks, were green with envy.

But in the mid-1980s the wheels started to come off at AEI. There had been earlier intimations of potential financial trouble but, among all the luxurious surroundings and the wonderful time I was having as a policy wonk, I chose to ignore the warning signs. By 1985, however, it was plain that there was bad trouble, and in 1986 AEI was in virtual free-fall. It came within a whisker of declaring bankruptcy and going belly-up. In the process, the president, Bill Baroody, was fired and the trustees had to take over. AEI went into receivership.

It's not unusual for Washington think tanks and other private sector groups to hit a rough patch, to go through financial hard times. What makes this financial crisis so interesting, however, is that it was accompanied by a virtual political *coup-d'état*. During my time there, AEI was conservative but diverse and pluralistic, with many moderate-to-liberal Republicans like me and a surprising number of Democrats. But now, in the midst of what was at first thought of only as a short-term money shortage, a political revolution was also underway at AEI. The Institute was taken over by a right-wing cabal that purged all the moderates, recruited the likes of Irving Kristol and Richard

Perle, and converted it into the neoconservative bastion that it is today. In the process, pluralism gave way to orthodoxy and AEI's older motto of the "competition of ideas in a free society" was reinterpreted to mean not healthy diversity *within* the Institute but only competition with other ideas emanating from *outside* groups.

EARLY INTIMATIONS OF TROUBLE

The first indication I received that everything at AEI was not quite what it seemed came during my first Public Policy Week in early December 1981. Public Policy Week was the time when the Institute showed off its scholars and their research work in a week-long extravaganza of seminars and presentations; it was very high-level and attracted leading congressmen, journalists, and government officials, not least because we were thought to be the brains behind the Reagan Administration. Public Policy Week was capped off with a formal dinner-dance on Friday evening attended by over a thousand guests and featuring a policy speech by no less than the President of the United States, Ronald Reagan.

I was there in my formal tux that I'd hardly worn since my undergraduate fraternity days (the jacket still fit me but we decided it was best to avoid potential embarrassment by purchasing new formal pants), while Iêda was wearing a new and spectacular dinner dress. I remember running into my AEI colleague and fellow Dutchman Marvin Kosters and his wife Bonnie in the receiving line and remarking socially how plush and luxurious this all was. To my great surprise Marvin responded that yes, it was nice but that I should not assume that AEI's financial condition was as sound as it appeared.

I was stunned by that retort. To that point, everything at AEI had seemed so lush and prosperous; I'd never heard even the slightest hint that things might be otherwise. When I saw Marvin the next week I asked him about his curious remark. He refused to elaborate on that point but in the course of our conversation did say that he thought it wise that I had chosen to hang onto my tenured university professorship. I agreed and filed the comment away, meanwhile thinking, because that's what my own eyes and ears were telling me, that Marvin must be mistaken. He was one of the country's leading labor economists, a veteran of the president's Council of Economic Advisers (CEA), and a leading light among AEI's stellar economics team; but at that time the thought went through my head that he must be overrated.

For the next six months I didn't hear, or think, much about a budget crunch. AEI was spending as much as ever; I saw no signs of a looming crisis. As a program head I did receive an occasional admonition or memo from Baroody's office to go easy on travel, overhead, and outside consultants; but I thought that was just the usual pleading that administrators engage in and none of us scholars took it seriously. Whenever I saw Bill he always approved everything I wanted to do in the way of travel, publications, etc., and I saw no signs of any cutbacks. From what I heard and observed, the other program heads and senior scholars went on spending as lavishly as I.

Then one night in early June 1982 at a dinner at Howard and Betty Penniman's house at which Jeane and Evron Kirkpatrick were also present, Jeane offhandedly remarked that "AEI might be going broke." As I recall, she dropped that bomb into the conversation without any preliminaries. Jeane was, of course, still in New York at the UN but maintained an office and staff at AEI; husband Kirk was in Washington at AEI, and both of them were closer to the power structure there than I. So this time I assumed the worries were valid. However, even then there was little follow-up.

The next week a lot of rumors were flying around AEI. Everyone seemed to be of the view that there were financial problems, but no one knew how severe they were. No one had access to Baroody and he wasn't telling the staff anything. Both my secretary and my research assistant had heard the stories and were worried because they assumed, correctly, if there were layoffs, staff would be the first to be let go but not scholars. At our luncheon "pub" (an unreserved table in the dining room where individual scholars could sit with other scholars for informal conversation) I mentioned Jeane's "going broke" phrase, which Marvin Kosters said sounded overly dramatic but couldn't be ruled out entirely. The trouble was no one had any clear facts.

In the next week more facts began to dribble out, after a budget review by AEI's central administration. We learned that the budget review showed almost all of AEI's income was going to fixed costs and overhead, leaving very little for research projects. Economist Rudy Penner reported that we were operating at budget but that a real crunch and cutbacks would come the next year. Ever the pessimist, Kosters, said he thought we were already operating at a deficit, though it was disguised. If he was right, cutbacks would be coming sooner rather than later. He said we should expect a memo from Baroody shortly after the upcoming board meeting on where we stand.

By the fall of 1982 it was clear that we were in some financial trouble, though the extent of the trouble was still unclear and we had no dollar amounts on which to make judgments. I noticed the slide in small things: publications were down from previous years; the in-house phone directory showed we were five persons less, by attrition, than the previous year; and one of our large copy machines was removed and not replaced. Baroody, preoccupied with financial matters, was moody and distant; he seemed unwilling to meet with scholars and program directors to lay out the facts and quell the rumors. A malaise was affecting the Institute that made it a more difficult place to work than in my first ebullient year there. Meanwhile, some of our scholars must have been talking on the outside, including to the press, because visitors to my office would ask me about the crisis and there was even a short article in the *Washington Post*.

On October 12 and 13 I had two meetings with Bill aimed at clarifying the situation. I needed to know if we should go ahead with several pending research projects and publications; since we were now thinking of buying a house in the Maryland suburbs, I needed also to know if my own job was secure. Bill assured me my own personal and institutional position was "protected," but he did ask me to hold off on some publications. When I told him that some big names (Sam Huntington, Lucian Pye, Stanley Hoffmann) were involved and it would affect AEI's reputation to cancel our obligations to them, he relented and told me to go ahead even while asking me to slow down the process. At this time and others, Bill was always cordial and friendly to me and told me he was impressed by my work and that at AEI I had "hit the ground running." Nevertheless, to me Bill seemed unusually preoccupied, not well served by a second-rate staff, especially Vice President Tait Trussell, and carrying all of AEI's burdens (including the powerful legacy of his father and AEI founder, Bill Sr.) on his own shoulders.

Bill's staff consisted of non-academics; but both he and they were often uncomfortable with the high-powered scholars at AEI. The staff, and Bill himself, came mainly out of public relations backgrounds; they had little sense of the research and scholarship side of the think tank. We scholars thought they were superficial and often not up to the job; behind our backs they were equally disparaging of the scholars. Meanwhile, Bill, following in his father's footsteps, ran the place like a Lebanese political party: centralized, secretive, top-down, and personalistic. Middle East expert Judith Kipper and I, as a Latin Americanist, used to joke that we were, because of our own research and area backgrounds, the only ones who understood how AEI functioned and how to operate in this environment. For example, while other program directors were wringing their hands over memos from the central office asking for cutbacks on travel and publications, I would immediately go to Bill personally, tell him AEI's credibility (following in his father's footsteps, Bill was very sensitive to this) would be damaged if we cut any of our obligations, and plead my case one-to-one. Bill *never once* turned me down.

In the spring of 1983, European specialist Joyce Shub was fired, the first scholar to be let go. The AEI rumor mill cranked up; people were suddenly fearful for their jobs. Heretofore, the only people let go had been lower-level clerical staff and that by attrition, but Joyce's departure was a considerable shock. In chasing down the rumors, however, I discovered there was less there than met the eye. Joyce had been fired not as a budget matter but because she had violated AEI's new rules about getting prior approval before making financial commitments to outside scholars and for publications. In doing so, she had violated Bill's trust (again the personalistic aspect) and, therefore, had to go. In contrast, I always got Bill's personal approval beforehand for any project I wished to carry out and *always* on that basis, despite grumblings from Vice President Trussell, had my projects approved.

Several other things were breaking in the spring of 1983 that led to major crises within AEI. First, the scholars discovered, because once a year we got a report on the matter, that AEI had not been making the deposits into our retirement accounts that, by contract, it was obliged to do. The AEI pension system, it needs to be said, was very generous, but that does not mean the Institute could unilaterally cancel its obligations, not make the contributions to the scholars' accounts, and on top of that seek to hide its actions from the scholars. The reverberations really hit the fan over this one and several scholars who had good connections there began going to friends on the Board of Trustees and demanding Bill's ouster. After that, the funds were quickly restored to the retirement accounts, but the episode left a legacy of distrust on the part of the scholars from which the senior staff, including Baroody himself, never recovered.

The next episode was at least equally dramatic and may have sealed Baroody's doom. Several of AEI's senior scholars who had endowed chairs—Mike Novak, Herb Stein, Ben Wattenberg, Jeane herself—discovered that the endowment funds that were supposed to support their positions had been drained of money to support AEI's general operating budget. They were sitting on empty or hollow chairs. I didn't have an endowed chair at AEI but these other persons did; they were highly influential; and they were fit to be tied. Now it really did hit the fan. Again they went to the Trustees with the even more insistent demands that Bill be fired. The issue was compounded by the fact that some of the Trustees—Bill Butcher of Chase Bank, Richard Madden of Potlatch Corporation, the Weyerhausers of lumber fame—were the same people who had established these chairs and donated the funds. It was *their* money. My understanding is that some of the senior scholars involved even threatened legal or criminal action against Baroody: to drain an endowed chair and use the funds for other than the purposes the donor intended could be considered fraud or even robbery.

As things were going from bad to worse during this period, Marve Kosters and I had a little wager on. For at the same time AEI was going through this internal crisis, it was also involved in a search for new quarters. The place at 1150 17th St. N.W., near the center of everything in Washington and only five blocks from the White House, where AEI had rented three or four floors, was getting cramped, crowded, and a bit shabby. In addition, real estate prices in downtown Washington were rising astronomically; it would be much better, including financially, if AEI rode this wave and owned its own building instead of continuing to rent.

So Baroody set up a task force to explore the possibilities. I hadn't been around AEI long enough to be a member of the task force but, since I had a background in construction, architecture, and building, Bill relied on me informally for advice. We visited a number of sites: a couple right in our neighborhood, one down on Pennsylvania Avenue midway between the White House and Congress, still another known as the "Portals" in Southwest where the 14th Street Bridge and the railroad trestle over the Potomac River empty into Washington, D.C. With Baroody and others, I reviewed the architectural plans for these buildings, either starting from the ground up or taking an existing building, gutting it, and completely renovating. AEI spent hundreds of thousands of sorely needed dollars, maybe millions, on site inspections, architectural plans, and interior design.

In the end, AEI decided to cancel all these plans and stay where it was. And that is what Marve's and my wager was all about. We said that if AEI went ahead with plans for the new building that would be a sign of the institution's vigor, good health, and a positive future. If, on the other hand, it opted not to go ahead, that would be a sign of a failed, dying, moribund institution; AEI did not go ahead.

AEI IN TROUBLE

What is going on here? How could an institution that to me seemed so plush and prosperous only a short time earlier so suddenly hit such hard times. The questions are especially poignant because intuitively one would think that, with Reagan and the Republicans in power and AEI seen as their brain trust, the money would be just pouring in.

To begin, one should not exaggerate the crisis. At its height in 1981–82 AEI had a budget of about $14–15 million. It then fell back over the course of the next three or four years to a budget of $10–11 million. That amounts to a 30 percent drop, an enormous amount for a small institution to absorb. But the shortfalls were spread over several years and it is not as though AEI ever went completely bankrupt or "belly up." In fact, it survived, albeit in shrunken form, with some of its scholars still there all during this period and new ones recruited as the budget picture gradually improved.

Second, there were a number of factors that led to AEI's decline. No one explanation is sufficient. Not all of it was mismanagement and financial shenanigans. Rather, it was a complex of causes not all of which we understood immediately but which, over time, the scholars as well as AEI leadership came to comprehend. Among the factors:

1. *Tax changes.* Under Jimmy Carter a tax reform had been enacted which made it much less financially attractive for business corporations, AEI's chief source of income, to donate to think tanks like AEI. But it took until the early 1980s for these tax changes to have their full effects on giving.
2. *The foundations.* Quite a number of the traditionally conservative foundations—Scaife, Smith Richardson, Olin, Bradley—were now in the hands of more liberal boards and family members and less willing to give to AEI.
3. *Changed donor priorities.* Many of our donors, especially wealthy individuals, discovered they received more glory and publicity by giving to the local opera, parks, or theater than by giving to AEI or Brookings and having to wait two or three years for these staid institutions to produce a "boring," six-hundred-page book with their name in it.
4. *Paradoxical politics.* AEI commissioned a survey to find out why some of its traditional business donors were giving less. We discovered that, feeling threatened, they gave more when Democrats were in power than Republicans. With Reagan in the White House they reasoned, "our guys are in power anyway, so why should we give to AEI?"
5. *Outflanked on the Right.* The rise of the Heritage Foundation in the 1970s and 1980s drew a lot of conservative money away from AEI. Especially big donors like Richard Scaife and Joseph Coors began giving far more to Heritage than to AEI.
6. *Outflanked on the Left.* Since the 1950s, AEI and the Brookings Institution had been strong rivals, Brookings on the left championing Keynesian economics and AEI on the right standing for the free market. But then Brookings appointed a Republican, Bruce McLaury, as its president and began drawing money from the center-right and the moderate business community to whom AEI had always looked for support.
7. *Designated gifts.* In the more ideological 1980s, many of our gifts came for designated projects. Whereas before, money had flowed into AEI to support the overall purpose and message of the Institute and could be used for general purposes, now more and more donations came to support specific programs, individuals, or ideas. I myself was "guilty" of that, raising over half a million dollars for my program. But that meant less and less money to support overhead and general operating expenses. And that is why Baroody dipped into the endowed funds and the pension money: since none of our donors like to support anything boring like overhead,

> Bill had less and less money available to support the central functions of AEI like electricity, maintenance, and equipment.

AEI continued to lurch along. I was so busy running my program that I hardly noticed any difference. We were asked to cut back a bit on publications but, whenever I had something that I really wanted to get out, I would go to Bill personally and he would always relent and approve. It was obvious we were not growing as fast as in recent years, and when people retired from or left the Institute they were not always replaced. We put on a few less programs and the fancy, expensive television shows, but that didn't affect us very much. No scholars were let go and very few staff. When Baroody's staff proposed that we close our elegant dining room, all the scholars got on their high horses and criticized the loss of jobs for the (mostly black) kitchen personnel. My salary continued to increase, and I still had plenty of travel funds. So for a considerable period, 1983–1985, the "great financial crisis" at AEI, to me at least, was more superficial than real.

In September 1985, I had a long private meeting with Baroody. He was as always extremely cordial to me and looked none the worse for wear despite the batterings of late from scholars and the board. He told me optimistically that AEI was in between a full-fledged crisis and what he called a "seasonal curve" in giving. Even at this date he was saying there would be limits on what we as a public policy institute could do but no dismantling of our programs. He was hopeful about a task force (my friends and supporters Kirk and Penniman were both on it) he had recently established to examine costs and priorities. He would not cancel any publications to which we'd already made commitments. Thank goodness, because I had a whole string of publications in the works; every one of them eventually got published.

He went on to thank me for my fund-raising efforts but insisted that future grants would have to come with 40 percent (about the standard university rate) designated for overhead. However, Bill's conception of "overhead" included money to pay the scholars' salaries, or a portion thereof. Oops! Heretofore, our salaries had been paid entirely out of the general AEI budget: "hard" money. Now if salaries were to be paid out of "soft" grant money, it put all of the scholars at risk. We were going to have to raise money not only for our projects, publications, and overhead but also to cover our own pay. For now, we were able to fend off that proposal, but a little later a similar proposal would be advanced that threatened the permanence of all but the most senior scholars. On the whole, it was a good meeting with Bill, but the potential for additional trouble lay just down the road.

Bill also told me about changes in the development office. AEI had long had a development office to help it raise money, but now the staff at that office was being beefed up. I've noticed this at other think tanks and institutions with which I've been associated over the last twenty years: there's such an emphasis on private fund-raising that over time that office comes to rival or surpass the size of the scholarly staff. The tail begins to wag the dog. And I've never yet met a development office that I thought was good at its job. Their idea is to send out a letter to the Fortune 500 companies asking for money; but in a think tank, university, or research institute the key is to match up specific scholar research interests and projects with specific donor project interests.

Most development offices don't know how to do that because they don't understand the worlds of research and ideas and how to put scholars and donors together on those levels. In our talk, Bill indicated to me that, despite paying hefty salaries, he had been disappointed in the development office's results. Among the development staff there at AEI, only Marguerite McAuliff had the intellectual acumen to make the linkages outlined above, and that was because she was very smart and a Ph.D. student in government at Georgetown. But she was too young and junior to have a large effect on the AEI budget shortfall.

In December 1985, I had another long talk with Baroody and his new assistant, young Naval Academy graduate Jim Abellera who had formerly been in AEI's national security studies program. By this time we all knew that cuts were coming; the Scholars' Task Force as well as the AEI central administration had been quietly doing its work. Other scholars and program directors were also meeting individually with Bill and his staff. I had already been told by Kirk and Penniman that there would be cuts in travel funds, copying, telephone, computers, publications, and business expenses. But these were not enough; there would also be cuts in personnel, up to 20 percent. By my count that meant thirty persons (of our then total staff of 150) would have to be let go. In addition, there would likely be some consolidation of programs, and AEI scholars would have to move out of their narrow research specializations and be willing to write and speak on a variety of topics of interest to donors and the "consumers" of our "products." Note the business model language now being introduced into our work for the first time.

Bill had also told me that, when pink slips were handed out, they would be by seniority: last hired, first fired. That meant, according to the schedule devised by the front office, that my research assistant Janine would be able to stay but new secretary Louise Skillings (Pam had left to raise a family) would have to go. It also meant that, while my position was secure (I hope it was based on more than seniority), Mark Falcoff would have to be let go. In the face of the abundant rumors flying around AEI, I was obliged, sorrowfully, to convey these decisions to the parties affected. But I also met immediately with Bill, Jim, Baroody's aide Liz Prestridge, and personnel director Gabrielle Hills to make a special plea on behalf of Louise and Mark. She was such a good secretary, I argued, that even if I had to lose her, she should be retained by AEI and installed in the central administration; "maybe she could fix the mess up there," I said. The central office was impressed with that self-sacrificing argument; Lousie stayed, at least for now. But Mark, I was told, would have to make the case for himself on the basis of his own credentials and fund-raising.

In that December meeting, Baroody indicated to me that AEI was already coming out of its crisis and better than expected. He told me the board meeting of the week before had been "tough," with his own job at stake; but he had survived and his proposed budget had not been completely "zapped." He said AEI's income was still at $12 1/2 million, down by two-and-a-half million from the earlier high. Neither he nor I knew at the time that it still had another two-and-a-half million or more to fall.

At that meeting I told Bill that he could count on me to help with the institute-wide restructuring that he and the task force were considering. I thought of myself as close to Bill, a friend as well as an employee, and sympathetic in light of the tough patch (his marriage had also recently broken up) he was going through. I told him that I would be well-qualified and happy to work on general foreign policy and not just Latin America, to serve as editor of AEI's *Foreign Policy and Defense Review*, and to help in reorganizing foreign policy studies at the Institute. Of course, in offering to work in these capacities I was usurping Robert Pranger's position as director of foreign policy studies. Pranger was not very effective and many of the scholars wanted to see him go, but he was a longtime friend of the Baroody family, Senior and Junior, and given the family-based loyalties at AEI, was hard to dislodge—although we did eventually succeed. I also suggested to Bill the three-part division of AEI magazines that was adopted for a time under the reorganization: one on economics, one on America and American social and political affairs, and one on foreign and security policy.

The next few weeks were frantic as everyone at AEI scrambled for advantage and position. We all realized the cuts were imminent; the question was, which programs were most vulnerable and could they be saved? We were not quite at the stage of "every man for himself" but not far from it. My Latin America program was, of course, vulnerable because Latin America had *never* counted for much in U.S. policy considerations (see chapter 5), or among AEI's other senior scholars. I met with Marve Kosters who told me (was this a hint?) that it was fortunate I had retained my tenured professorship in Amherst. He said that AEI had too many "arcane" programs in "peripheral areas" and that AEI could not afford separate programs in Europe,

Asia, the Middle East, and Latin America. Even his own "Center for the Study of Regulation," a hot AEI/Reagan Administration policy topic, was slated to be folded into a broader, umbrella economic policy program.

Howard Penniman, like Marve a member of the task force and, therefore, a reliable source of information, told me decision-making on AEI's restructuring was slow because a lot of deals were being cut. He informed me, not unexpectedly, that quite a number of senior people did not think Latin America important enough to keep it as a separate program, but he had fought to save it and apparently succeeded, albeit in reduced form. He confirmed that our staff would be reduced and our research budget cut way back to $10,000, not enough to do any publications or major projects. But, Howard brightened, he thought AEI would survive, that it could be a significantly reduced think tank operating on a much lower budget, and that, after a year of austerity, publications and other activities would be on the rise again.

This was really quite stunning news. Although I'd had earlier intimations of the ways the winds were blowing, now I had confirmation and from a trustworthy source who was on my side in these internal debates. But the bad news kept coming. For one thing, we learned the foreign policy and area studies programs were being cut proportionately more than the sacrosanct economic studies program which, to be fair, had always been AEI's basic bread-and-butter. Then, Jim Abellera came out with new criteria for publications; we would go ahead only with those for which we had a clear, *legal* (as distinct from political or moral) obligation. That left me in a bad position because I had at that time seven publications in various stages of the pipeline of which I could show a legal obligation for only one. But, bureaucratic infighter that I am, I went to work on Baroody and the central office on this, arguing that AEI's reputation was on the line, and I'm proud to report that eventually all seven came out. A few had to be postponed temporarily but none was cancelled. Meanwhile, with all this AEI uncertainty, we kept postponing our decisions on whether to go ahead with our house purchase or, alternatively, to start planning our return to Massachusetts.

Right after the holidays I met with Bill again in early January 1986. He was cordial as usual but with slumped shoulders and looking pale and morose in ways that I had never seen him before. I didn't know that, literally as we spoke, the budget axe was already falling on some programs and colleagues down the hall. I showed Bill a grant proposal to the National Endowment for the Humanities (NEH) that I had prepared, but he was, for the first time, uninterested in the proposal, only when the money might start coming in. I wanted to get his approval for the special issue of the *Foreign Policy and Defense Review* that we'd prepared on southern Europe (Greece, Italy, Spain, Portugal), but he said that he couldn't deal with that until after personnel and reorganization changes had been made. I tried to talk about my salary for the coming year and, since I was on leave without pay from my academic position, the need for a two-year contract; but Bill didn't want to talk about that either. Not a very satisfactory meeting. The one positive thing he did say is that we should have no fear about AEI folding; "we will be there," he said.

Meanwhile, in other parts of the building pink slips were already being delivered. Denis Doyle, head of AEI's education policy program and a good friend, came tearing into my office to tell me that Marcia Levine, the subdirector of his program, had just been let go as had most of his staff. Denis said the central office had decided to dissolve his whole program; he was hopping mad and said he had been lied to and misled. Later that afternoon I heard that three recently hired black secretaries, each of whom had families to feed for which they were the only provider, had been fired under the "last hired, first fired" rule. The travesty was that they had quit other jobs to come to AEI but at a time when the decision had already been made to let clerical staff go. Next I heard that Marve Kosters' Regulation Program, as earlier remarked, had been abolished, folded into the umbrella Economic Policy Studies Program. That was a shock because deregulation under Reagan was such a hot issue and AEI had led the way on it, because Marve was himself serving on the task force that made the decisions about cutbacks, and because he was one of the leading economists in the country. When I heard what happened to Marve's program, I knew immediately it would be just a matter of time before the distinct area programs (Asia, Europe, Middle East, Latin America) would be similarly folded into a single, less expensive unit to run foreign policy programs. I would continue to fight and lobby strenuously but the handwriting for my program was already on the wall.

As the pink slips continued to be handed out that week, more and more complaints came in—and not just from those fired—about Bill's and the Institute's management. From various sources of office scuttlebutt, I heard that Bill was drinking heavily, that he was taking Valium to stay calm, and that he had retreated for long hours to his club to avoid the unhappiness at AEI. From Kosters I heard the complaint that Bill was unable to confront problems directly and deal with them, that because of all his political, family, and personal loyalties he avoided tough decisions, only nibbled around the edges of the issues, and out of loyalty kept some people on who plainly should have been let go. We also heard that Bill was refusing to share budget data even with his own vice president or the task force deciding on the firings and reorganization, so life-and-death decisions on whom should be let go and what programs axed were being made in the dark, without the information to make them responsibly. Meanwhile, some of the most senior scholars at AEI were still steaming about Bill dipping into their endowed chair funds and his nonpayment into their pension accounts, and they were talking again to the board about removing Bill himself.

On January 13 we had a big, important senior staff meeting, the most substantive one since I'd been at AEI. Baroody presided; all the big guns were there. He said he was looking for greater scholar input in decision-making, both in setting priorities and fund-raising. He told the area program directors (me, *et al.*) that he would deliver a single budget figure for foreign policy to us and *we* would decide how to divide it. Among the several programs he said he was imposing a cap on all publications and new initiatives until the financial situation was clearer. From now on, he said, all outside grant proposals had to include an overhead charge of 43 percent. All the program directors would now be charged with raising their own "core budget" to carry out their research and publications; no longer could they count on support for projects from the central administration. Finally, Bill announced that the budget for the coming year would be \$11 1/2 million, down another million from the year before (and from what he'd told me only a week earlier) and down \$3 1/2 million from what it had been only three years earlier.

All the scholars at AEI understood the financial constraints we were operating under, so there was less hostility to Bill's announcements than might otherwise have been the case. My sense was that the scholars and program directors had for the past few months been more concerned about the uncertainty and the inability of Baroody's administration to make decisions so that they could plan their lives and programs than they were about the cuts themselves. So at the staff meeting few people spoke up. Jack Meyer, head of health policy studies, said we could live with the cap on publications and new initiatives for a short time but warned that the best scholars would leave if they had to spin their wheels for very long. Denis Doyle said the 43 percent overhead figure was too high; he doubted that foundations or the federal government would fund our program at such a rate. That was about all the discussion there was in open forum; the real fireworks would come a week later at our Arleigh House retreat.

After the meeting, of course, the hallways were abuzz with people talking and gossiping privately and in ways they didn't want to do in an open forum. I used the opportunity to poll my colleagues on whether we should go ahead with our house purchase, since that would give me a reading on whether they believed AEI would survive or not. Mike Malbin thought we should rent for another year; Jack Meyer said AEI looked very "iffy" to him and that he didn't think we'd hit bottom yet; Denis Doyle thought, given the uncertainty, that we'd be "crazy" to buy now; Bob Goldwin said he'd wait for a while because he was still worried about what we *didn't* know. In contrast, Norm Ornstein said we should definitely go ahead because our program had such a good reputation, while both Marve Kosters and former congressman (from Ann Arbor) Marvin Esch said we should do it because, even if AEI fails, my own reputation in Washington was so high that I'd have no trouble landing a position elsewhere. How nice of them! And that's eventually what we did: we bought the house even in the midst of all this uncertainty.

Tensions ran high during the next week. Walter Berns told me he was very unhappy with Baroody and AEI, that he was thinking of taking his Olin money and moving on. Bob Goldwin was similarly unhappy: he had had a big fight with Bill over plans to close his program on constitutionalism just when the U.S. was about to celebrate the bicentennial of our own constitution. Meanwhile, the scholars were mobilizing and had formed their own Scholars' Committee; sparks flew when Baroody said that he would appoint its chair. Faced with widespread protests, Bill relented; the scholars then elected economist John Makin as their chair. At the same time, the scholars were demanding data on the AEI budget that the central administration had refused to provide, leading to more gossip and insinuations that there must be something to hide.

My sense was that AEI was poised on the verge of a full-scale revolt; either that or a nervous breakdown. Things seemed to be moving toward a climax: a majority on the Scholars' Committee now wanted Bill to go and even his strongest defenders to that point (Mike Novak, Herb Stein) were now neutral. There was also strong talk of boycotting the upcoming retreat, but in the end most of the senior scholars decided to attend to give the administration one last chance to explain itself. If it did not do so satisfactorily, then the scholars were prepared to meet on their own, without Bill or the central office, to decide AEI's future directions. What had begun as a budget crisis, therefore, was now rapidly becoming a referendum on, and perhaps a challenge to, the Baroody presidency of AEI.

THE ARLEIGH HOUSE RETREAT

On January 20–21, 1986, in the midst of this red-hot internal crisis, the entire AEI "family" transported itself to Arleigh House in rural, horse-country Virginia. Our group included Bill Baroody and his senior staff plus all the program heads and scholars, about seventy-five persons. Arleigh House is a beautiful, former private estate now converted into a plush retreat and convention center with just enough room for medium-sized groups like ours. It has a pool, walking trails, a wonderful conference facility, superb dining, and individual, hotel-like rooms for all the guests. AEI chartered buses to take us there, but some of us preferred to drive in case we needed to get away early.

One might wonder why in the midst of its greatest financial crisis ever AEI would rent this entire conference facility at the cost of tens of thousands of dollars just for us for the whole weekend, but Bill argued that it was important to get away from the hothouse that is Washington and was AEI in those days to a more relaxed atmosphere where we could dress casually, unwind, and eat and drink informally together. Many of the scholars, however, felt that the fate and future of AEI, if it had one, was at stake at this meeting.

We gathered on that Saturday morning in the main Arleigh House conference room. A fire was burning in the large stone fireplace; we were all dressed casually in sweaters. Bill and his senior staff, who all looked like they'd been primed for this event, sat on one side of the room, the scholars in a semicircle on the other. It looked like we were prepared for confrontation.

Bill, looking nervous, began the meeting by welcoming us and attempting a few light remarks. He then launched into a history of AEI, some of which was new to us. He said that Glen Campbell, the then-president of the Hoover Institution, had been at AEI before moving to Palo Alto. David Abshire and Richard Allen, before founding CSIS, had also been at AEI; Bill Sr., had continued to pay their salaries even after they started CSIS. AEI, Bill said, was the granddaddy of the center-right think tanks and the incubator of serious conservative ideas in Washington, D.C.

Bill went on to say that in 1970 AEI had only fourteen scholars and a budget of $1 million; now it had seventy scholars and a budget of about $12 million. In 1976 there were ten research centers; now there were twenty-four. Bill's point was not just to review this past history, however, but to use that to begin to lead into his main points. He said that funding had recently "leveled off" but that we continued to develop new programs. He himself had approved projects for which the Institute had insufficient funds, and he took full responsibility for that. He also said that with twenty-four programs functioning largely autonomously, there was not enough coordination between them or setting of priorities. Now, however, AEI could no longer afford to operate that way. That is how he explained the new role of Robert Pranger, AEI's director of foreign policy studies and a Baroody family friend, whom many of us thought ought to have been the first person to be fired. Instead, Pranger was elevated to the position of vice president where he would oversee grant proposals, program activities, and the enlarged development office. Since Pranger had such an unfriendly personality and was roundly disliked by the scholars, I couldn't see how he could be successful in this new position. My notes written at the time say, "A Big Mistake."

Bill then went on to review the budget numbers which most of us had never seen before. Actually, Bill confessed he was not a budget person and when AEI was flourishing had never paid the numbers much attention, but now that the crisis was here he was forced to do so. First, he indicated that, while AEI had short-term debts (amounts unspecified) that were covered by a line of credit designed to keep the cash flowing and expenses paid on a regular basis, it had no long-term debts. Second, he indicated that, while AEI was still projecting revenues of that year of $13.4 million, they were budgeting for only $12.5 million, of which they intended to spend only $11.5 million as a way to build up reserves and begin to refurbish the endowment funds that had earlier been drained. Third, Bill gave us for the first time a breakdown of the budget: 58 percent went to salaries and benefits; 14 percent went for rent; and a whopping 25 percent would have to be used to make the cuts and fill the accompanying obligations of the various programs that had already been targeted. That sounded crazy to me: spending one-quarter of your income just to make the cuts that were designed to save you money.

Bill went on to say that his fundamental mistake was that he had faith that, as AEI programs multiplied in the early 1980s, revenues would rise to match the new activities. He blamed the problem largely on targeted funding by outside donors that left the central office without the general funds it needed to operate. Hence, when revenues flattened and even started to contract, he was forced to face the crisis that was now upon us. That was why he was now expanding the development office, to bring in more revenue and quickly. He said that, in the recently completed round of budget and program cuts, his priority had been to shave programs but not personnel. But when that proved insufficient to match the severity of the shortfall, he had been forced to cut personnel, albeit only at the staff level. He had insisted that no scholars be cut. While we were all cheered by that announcement, we had to be worried by Bill's next comment that he was hopeful the cuts already made would do it, that a second round would not be necessary.

While we scholars had previously heard stories that the preceding month's Trustees' meeting had been a knock-'em-down, drag-it-out affair, now we began to hear confirmation. The Trustees, almost all of whom were smart, able CEOs of big corporations, had been appalled at AEI's sloppy accounting and budgetary practices. Now they were being asked to pony up another $100,000 each, in addition to that same amount that was the price of their being on the board, to bail AEI out of the hole. There was much *sturn n drang* at the December board meeting over this request as well as AEI's ongoing budget woes. Eventually the Trustees went along with paying the supplement, but they insisted on two things in return: first, that AEI reform its budget procedures to bring it more in line with a business model; and second, that AEI accept one of their own employees, Jim Hicks of Dow Chemical (Midland, Michigan, my old home territory), as a new vice president put in charge of AEI spending and with the power to bring discipline to the Institute budget.

Poor Jim, he was capable and a nice guy but he was no match for AEI's clever, inside-the-beltway scholars.

I believe Bill did himself a service by laying out all this information and coming (mostly) clean on our budget difficulties. Ultimately, that would not be enough to save his job, but for now at least he had bought some time and disarmed the scholars who were out for his hide. I immediately noticed that the temperature in the room went down; what had looked like it might degenerate into a real confrontation now turned, for the most part for the next two days, into a civilized discussion. We were all in this together; AEI's fate was also our fate.

The discussion that followed, therefore, was spirited but not confrontational. Jack Meyer was the first to speak up. He said he didn't think the culprit was targeted funding by our donors but the fact AEI had changed, it had won the battle for free market economics, and now was oriented toward specific projects that donors and scholars were interested in. Bill had his new financial director, Pranger, answer for him, who angrily insisted the money and positions all belonged to AEI, not to any individual scholar or program. Oops, so much for a peaceful, nonconfrontational meeting.

Denis Doyle said that, with his budget and staff cuts, he was unable to deliver the report his sponsor had paid for. Bill got into the act on this one, responding that we would fulfill our commitments but that they might need to be postponed temporarily.

Mike Novak, who had earlier been a strong Baroody supporter until he learned his endowed chair had been emptied of funds, now showed that he was still on his side. He asked, wherein lies the crisis? He didn't see that there was a crisis. Pleased with this softball question, Bill agreed that the crisis might be exaggerated. He went on to say that he thought we could avoid a second round of cuts. That answer pleased the scholars but it's likely that Bill knew otherwise even as he expressed it.

Jim Abellera, not a scholar but part of Bill's administrative team, suggested we go back to the 1970s AEI model in which the central administration controlled all the funds; there were few established programs; and the scholars were there only on a one- or two-year period to complete a specific project and then left. All of us assumed Jim was a stalking horse for the central office and that what he said was what Bill wanted to do. Bill himself then followed up with a long, disjointed discourse on how good the scholars at AEI had it, in contrast to Brookings where "every minute" of the day had to be accounted for and the scholars had "no choice" in the subjects they were assigned to research. We *did* have it good at AEI but Bill's case was not helped by his misrepresentation of the situation at Brookings that many of our scholars, having participated frequently in seminars there, knew well.

Norm Ornstein, a Democrat and also a Baroody supporter, next issued a plea for flexibility as the planning at AEI went forward; he argued that we had to be free to bring in new people and to respond to new policy issues. Then Ben Wattenberg offered a thoughtful comment: we long had an ideal situation, he said; management raised the money and hired people, while the scholars did their own thing. It was a "brilliant theory of management." But now we're at a crossing point: the administration wants greater top-down control while the scholars want participatory democracy. Can we reconcile those two tendencies? Bill responds obliquely that he wants to maintain the "ad hoc nature" of AEI while moving toward greater central oversight.

We then took a break for an elegant lunch, thanks to Arleigh House. The discussion didn't resume until 2:00, enabling me to go to my room and write down my thoughts on the morning session:

1. Bill has smoothed over some of the earlier bitterness and criticism; the scholars are less hostile than earlier in the week.
2. Bill, Pranger, and Abellera are all pointing toward a clearer sense of mission and greater central direction and coordination.
3. Many of the scholars are not yet reconciled to that view; they want *absolute freedom* to do their own research. I may be one of the few willing to compromise with the administration on this, seeing my role as doing general foreign policy and not just Latin America/Southern Europe.
4. Having survived the first round of cuts, I should be careful in what I say and not antagonize anyone. Be prudent; don't criticize Bill; let others take the lead with the administration. Be a survivor!
5. AEI, from the presentations here, has a future and is not going broke. Better news than expected; hope it's true. That means *I* have a future here, too.

Our discussions resume in the afternoon. Some of it is charged, testy. John Makin presses for a clear answer as to how much of the grants we bring in will go into the AEI general fund and how much will be retained by the individual programs or scholars. Bill refuses to be pinned down but says he's searching for a model somewhere between "ad hocracy" and the RAND Corporation, which sets the agenda for all its employees' research. Denis Doyle asks for more specific budget details that Bill refuses to divulge; Denis also asks Bill point blank if there will be future staff cuts and Bill now responds "it depends," an answer different from in the morning session. I can feel the air being sucked out of the room.

Bob Goldwin complains, "AEI was flourishing"; he asks, "What went wrong?" He attributes our problems not just to the changed nature of the funding but to "bad management" of the funds that did come in. That sounds like a provocation to me, but Bill responds calmly that he wants to remain true to the AEI history and mission while also "tightening up" the administration. Pranger, now on the administration side, says the whole purpose of the present reorganization is to achieve greater management control of the budget since we'd reached a point where budget requests from the scholars and their programs were $4 million more than the Institute was taking in. "It was out-of-hand."

Bill and Pranger both report that there is a strong sense on the Board of Trustees that we need to cut back on the number of programs, do fewer things but do them well. Well, of course, but how to do that given AEI's great expansion of programs over the years and the commitments already obligated? There is no answer. Both administrators insist the greatest need now is general funding for the central office. But they admit that, even with a scaled-down Institute, there will not be enough funding to cover the costs. So the second priority is area-wide funding to cover general expenditures. A third priority, they say, is support for research activities already underway; and only fourthly and last will they be looking for funds for new projects. That sets off a sound of discussion among the scholars who correctly surmise *all* the money coming in will go to administration and none will be prioritized for research.

Five minutes later another "bomb" drops when Baroody admits there are priorities among the main programs. We'd all known or suspected as much but now for the first time we received confirmation. The Economic Policy Program, AEI's historic strength, was the #1 priority; it also received the lion's share of the program budget, about 40–45 percent. Next came the American Politics Program at around 25 percent. Social Programs (housing, education, health) was in third place at 15 percent while the international/foreign policy programs were last at 12 percent. Obviously, this rank ordering did not auger well for the future of the social and foreign policy programs at AEI, and in the just-completed cutbacks of the previous week they had been the hardest hit.

Along with the cuts and priorities, Bill Baroody reports the Trustees also want a clear statement of purpose, of mission goals. Again a laudable sentiment but how do you do that in an AEI that is now so diverse and with so many programs that it resembles a small university? But from the Trustees' perspective that *is* the problem: too much diversity, too many programs. Marve Kosters says you can't set a mission statement down in stone; it needs to be defined by the issues. Marve Esch, the ex-congressman, agrees, says we shouldn't spin our wheels for six months devising a strategy but should let the scholars go out and find the hot issues and write about them. That's what we do best, he says, to general applause of the scholars but to the consternation of the front office people.

Bill wants each program to establish its own advisory board and the sooner the better. That suggestion also comes from the Trustees. Not only to give advice and direction to the various programs but also because such boards can help the program raise funds, or the members themselves contribute as a condition of being named to the board. We're asked to come up with lists of wealthy people in our research area. As the day and the discussion wind down, we're starting to get the impression that AEI is so desperate for a quick infusion of funds that it will do almost anything to get the money coming in.

By now it's 5:00 p.m. and I'm ready for a beer. But after washing up and roaming down to the Arleigh House bar, the only person I find there is Bill's hard-nosed assistant, Liz Prestridge, not my favorite person to have a drink with. Liz is quite cynical about the meeting. She says hostilely that the scholars have been "put in their place." But why this hostility; does she reflect Bill's own view of the day's discussions? She goes on to say that, while there is anger here among the scholars, there's been no serious criticism of management, its structure, or its plans. Since Liz is vindictive, I have to bite my tongue not to respond to that, meanwhile wondering what she thinks she's been listening to all day if it wasn't criticism.

Dinner that evening is a sumptuous repast; we're all cordial to each other and talk informally and with good cheer after the hard day's discussion. But the next morning we get our marching orders:

1. There will be unit as distinct from individual program budgets from now on.
2. Our program budget, for Latin America, will be handled by the unit director for general foreign policy.
3. The unit director will give us specific targets and tell us how much we can spend.
4. New projects will require "trade-offs" (cancellations) of other projects.
5. There must be better communications between program directors and unit directors.

Next came directions regarding the timetable:

1. We would be going on a two-year budget basis. (I assumed management believed that would be the length of the crisis.)
2. We would now follow a calendar year budget process.
3. In the next two months all program directors will need to prepare two budgets: one for the "short year" of July 1–December 31, 1986, and the other for the full calendar year, January 1–December 31, 1987.

4. The budget process would be an instrument for forcing all program directors to set priorities.

There was still more to come, mainly from financial vice president Pranger:

1. An admonition: We *must* bring the budget down.
2. We must raise $1.5 million more than the stated budget for replenishment purposes.
3. We're looking for funding for each of the four units (economic, political, social, foreign affairs).
4. We must move away from targeted funding. That seemed unrealistic to me because more and more donors want to designate where their money goes.
5. The consolidation of programs into four units is closely tied to future fund-raising goals.

As we start to wind up, Bill and his staff make some final points:

1. We *do* need a mission statement—for AEI and for each unit and program in it.
2. Donors will need to be involved in our programs and activities.
3. We're now the center of the political spectrum among Washington think tanks, where Brookings used to be, and Bill wants to keep it that way. We pay a price financially, he says, because we're not so ideological as the Heritage Foundation but, to general cheers, "we don't want to become another Heritage."
4. Bill insists our present shortfall is only temporary. "We're not about to go under." He assures us there are adequate funds "to get through the year." I *guess* that's reassuring.
5. Pranger reports he's raised over a million dollars in the past few months from foreign sources. But they're interested in our *domestic* programs—e.g., on deregulation—not our foreign policy studies.
6. Ben Wattenberg counters by remarking how understaffed he thinks we are on foreign policy. He wants to increase international studies but make it "feisty" and neoconservative. Says he wants a "hard edge" and "passion." My friend, Marguerite McAuliff from the development office, chimes in her agreement: "That's what motivates people to donate."

My notes written at the time say that today's discussion was much more positive and constructive than yesterday's. Yesterday, I wrote, we got all our negative and critical comments out; today was much more devoted to concrete planning and was future-oriented. I thought Bill's message in this wrap-up session was also more positive and did wonders for morale and our individual and collective self-confidence.

On that basis, on the Wednesday following the retreat, we went ahead and took the plunge. We plunked the money down to make a commitment on a house purchase. After all this agony, discussion, and debate, we did it! It was a lovely house on four acres, which we soon expanded to ten, in Brookeville, northern Montgomery County. Two things were operating here: a commitment to stay permanently in Washington, and, on the basis of the Arleigh House retreat, faith that AEI and my job there would survive.

In the long term, the house purchase worked out extremely well. But in the short term it was a very risky proposition. For one thing, AEI's financial situation turned out to be considerably more precarious than we'd been led to believe at the retreat; thank goodness I'd held onto my tenured professorship. For another, I should have paid more attention to Ben Wattenberg's concluding remarks. I should have been keeping track not just of the financial situation and the number of people being let go, but also *who* was being fired. For the fact was, had I looked more closely, that it was mainly moderates and centrists like me who were being let go. Already the neocons at AEI were plotting and moving to consolidate their power and force the moderates out. Over the course of the next year that process would be completed. And Bill Baroody and I would both be among the casualties.

Chapter Fourteen

AEI in Collapse: A Farewell to D.C.

After the January 1986 retreat at Arleigh House, it looked like AEI might be on the way back. Bill Baroody presented a more optimistic picture; we now had more information and knew more about the budget situation; and the antagonism that had grown between the scholars and the central administration had been mitigated. On the basis of this more optimistic feeling, we had gone ahead and made a commitment on a Washington house.

But in the next few weeks this mood of hope and optimism again turned sour. The budget turned out to be in far worse condition than Bill had let on at the retreat. He and his senior staff, it was now acknowledged, had repeatedly lied to us. Meanwhile, after saying these practices had ended, Bill had continued dipping his fingers into the pension fund and the endowed chairs. Indeed, on that front the news was even worse than before: not only was he dipping into those funds but he was also using for general AEI budget purposes the money its scholars had designated out of their own salaries to be set aside as added contributions to their retirement funds. That was *our* money, not just endowment funds; it was out of *our* pockets. If the first act of taking money from the pension and endowment funds was not criminal, then this surely was. I think the words for it are theft, fraud, robbery. When I got wind of this latest AEI act of desperation, which if not criminal certainly appeared so, I knew immediately that it would be unforgivable and Baroody would have to go. Some of the Big Guns like Herb Stein went directly to the Board of Trustees and now demanded that Baroody be fired.

THERE'S TROUBLE IN RIVER CITY

Immediately after the Arleigh retreat and contrary to the optimistic message we'd received there, new cuts and freezes were announced. For instance, the central administration froze the funds that we'd planned to use to print a new edition of our program brochure. Since the printing costs for that were under a thousand dollars, I knew that AEI was really scraping bottom.

Next, the senior staff decided to indefinitely postpone the special issue of the *Foreign Policy and Defense Review*, with me as guest editor, we had prepared on changing strategic policy in the Mediterranean. This was also relatively inexpensive, but I felt obliged to write to my contributors and explain the delay. One of those contributors was Harvard's Robert Putnam, about to make it big with his "bowling alone" thesis, whom I considered a good friend. What I got back from Putnam was one of the nastiest, ugliest, most arrogant and hectoring letters I've ever received in my life. He proceeded insultingly to lecture me on my obligations, etc., etc., as if it were my personal fault that AEI was running out of money and as though I didn't understand what our obligations were. We did manage to publish the *Review* a few months late, thanks to my negotiations with Baroody's staff, but I don't think I've ever forgiven Putnam for writing such a stupid, insulting letter.

I next heard from my colleague, Mark Falcoff, the subdirector of our program, that he'd landed another job at the NSC. Mark was on the first list of people let go by AEI so I was happy he had landed on his feet, not only finding a job but a good job. He'd be succeeding Constantine ("Constant Menace") Menges at the NSC and working with Jackie Tillman and Ray Burckhardt. Mark has a fine mind, knows Latin America (in contrast to these others), and is a wonderfully sharp and provocative writer, even though he sometimes sticks the knife in too far and twists it unmercifully. Mark and I, with our very different backgrounds, styles, and political orientations, had nevertheless made a fine pair at AEI, elevating our program to the very top ranks of Latin America programs in Washington, D.C. I wished him well and was genuinely sorry to see him go, even while knowing that with his quick tongue, sarcastic repartees, and disdain for administrative work and political correctness, he was miscast in this White House position. True to prediction, Mark lasted only a few months there. But at least he'd landed a job; other AEI top people including, as we shall see, Bob Pranger and Bill Baroody himself were not so lucky.

Mark's departure would mean more of the workload would now fall on my shoulders. But with the budget cutbacks, our program was largely suspended for the spring and fall anyway. And, since Mark was a neocon, it also meant politically that I, as a centrist, would no longer have a buffer to shield me from attacks by AEI's neocon right wing. But at the time I was just happy to have survived the first round of cuts and didn't fully see until it was too late how vulnerable I'd become to an ideological challenge. Amidst all this continuing uncertainty, we closed on our Washington house, even while Kirk Kirkpatrick, Austin Ranney, and Howard Penniman were all telling me to hang onto my tenured professorship.

I spent the next two weeks ("spring vacation") in Amherst and Cambridge. While I was gone, much of the roof fell in at AEI. Immediately upon returning I was briefed by Kirk and Marve Kosters. Among the items:

1. The budget situation was continuing to deteriorate.
2. Another 20–25 people, including scholars as well as staff, would have to be let go. This would be Round Two.
3. Entire programs would have to be abolished.
4. The Academic Advisory Committee (made up of scholars, the successor of the earlier Task Force) had voted that Latin America be one of the programs to be abolished.
5. AEI was deeply in debt and may by now have exhausted its credit.
6. AEI had not been paying its bills; in effect, that had been another line of credit.
7. AEI might have to go back to its core strength, the Economic Policy group, and let *everyone* else go.

This was the factual stuff; meanwhile at the gossip level the reports were even worse. First, that in the midst of this crisis, AEI was continuing to hire new people who, in Kirk's view, were not good. Kirk went on to tell me that he and Jeane, who by now had stepped down from her UN position and was a powerful voice at AEI and with the Trustees, had decided Bill was a "terrible" manager; that he could not make decisions and, when he did, made the wrong ones. Meanwhile, Marve Kosters told me that Bill's family situation had similarly disintegrated: that he had *several* girlfriends, that his wife had known about the cheating and had put up with it for a time, but as the children grew up and his philandering got to be too much, she kicked him out. He was now living in a room at his club. To me, this was starting to sound like King Lear: not only was there a storm raging outside at AEI but there was a storm raging in his heart and soul as well.

When the board met again on April 21, the news was even worse. The financial situation was far more catastrophic than we'd anticipated even in our worst scenarios; drastic action needed to be taken. The board was now insisting that all debts had to be paid by June 30, including obligations to endowed chair contributors. The board had also approved a budget for the Institute for the coming year of $10 million. What had happened to the budget Bill had presented to us at the retreat only three months earlier of $13.5 million? Was it a complete fabrication? My job, my program, and the decision we'd made in good faith on the basis of that earlier meeting to buy the house looked extremely precarious. Had the numbers Bill had presented us then been a complete pack of lies? And did he and his senior staff know it was false at the time it was presented to us? The evidence was accumulating that the answer was "yes" to both those questions.

The board, in collaboration with senior management, now unveiled an elaborate and clearly unworkable personnel plan to "save" the Institute. To begin, fifteen to twenty persons were to be "riffed" or let go. The pink slips were to go out within forty-eight hours, in contrast to the earlier "Christmas massacre" of the previous December that had dragged out for two weeks while Bill dithered over the list. My assistant Janine was on this list. A second category of personnel was to be "challenged." That means they were given until December 31 to raise the funds for their own salaries. But since it often takes a long time to devise and write a project and get funding for it, and since funding agencies like to support projects but not administrative costs or personnel, this short time frame seemed totally unrealistic to me. My secretary Louise was unaccountably put in this category; presumably I would be the one to raise the money to cover her. But Louise was a very smart lady as well as a superb secretary; she surveyed not just the financial situation but also the darkening mood at AEI and decided to leave before the guillotine came down. She landed a better job.

The third and highest category was called the "core." I was given that designation. That was encouraging for future job stability—except it soon trickled out that there were two kinds of "cores." The "real core" consisted of the economics team plus such prominent scholars as Jeane, Mike Novak, and Ben Wattenberg. They were permanent; their jobs were not in jeopardy. But then there was what was called the "flexible core." I was part of the latter group. That meant we were core scholars but could still be let go at some future date. However, we were told that was highly unlikely.

These designations of "challenged" and "core" were closely related to the budget situation. If the AEI budget stayed at $10–11 million, the persons listed as challenged would be kept on. If the budget sank to about $7 million, only the core would be kept. These budgetary numbers made it all sound rather mechanical, but what about the ideological and political housecleaning that some rumors said were in store?

Meanwhile, in trying to gather up more information I learned that Bill was having trouble deciding between Middle East experts Hal Saunders (a former diplomat) and Judith Kipper (journalist and Baroody favorite) as to which was core and which was challenged. I learned further that to save more money the administration was consolidating major units still more, going from four to three: economic, foreign policy, and now a combined social and political policy program. Still one more disturbing sign was that the Olin Foundation, a major AEI funder, had decided, on the basis of consultations with AEI scholar and Baroody enemy Walter Berns, to withhold funding until Baroody was removed. Ouch! That really tightened the screws. If any more of our big funders did that, we'd be sunk.

Among the casualties in this round of cuts was my friend Mike Malbin, a political party expert. My assistant Janine was also riffed. Another friend Denis Doyle was "challenged" but given only two months to raise outside funds for his program, which was tantamount to being fired. Up and down the corridors, more people were getting pink slips; those challenged were scurrying around seeking advice on how to raise money, which many of them had never done before. AEI adjunct scholars and those with various kinds of fee arrangements were let go almost to a person. Meanwhile, in the central office (Abellera, Pranger, Ed Somensato, Prestridge), where many of us thought the first housecleaning ought to take place, the staff remained intact. None of Bill's own people were fired.

In the weeks after this second round of cuts (by now the staff in two rounds of cuts had been reduced from 150 to 105), AEI was alive with rumors, uncertainty, and horror stories. All this upheaval was terribly upsetting to the normal business and work of the Institute. As usual, I went around to all my friends and supporters, both to gather the latest intelligence and to build support for my own position. Howard Penniman told me the political studies programs had been so decimated by the cuts that he was now a director without anything or anyone to direct. Kirk Kirkpatrick, always clued in, said he was not sure AEI could survive. Almost all the "challenged" people were getting out: they either didn't think they could raise the money in the short time period they were given or else they reasoned, even if they could raise the money, why should they give 40 percent of it in overhead back to AEI? Why not keep it for themselves and form their own think tank?

Via the grapevine I learned another fact that was very disturbing. One of the big grants in the several-hundred-thousand-dollar range, that I had applied for on behalf of my program, had indeed been awarded to us. But AEI's central administration had never notified me of that fact and had instead put all the money in the general account. I thought that was highway robbery, akin to AEI emptying the endowed chair funds and taking the money that the scholars contributed to their retirement accounts—bordering on criminality. When, screaming (not literally) mad I went to see Kirk about this, he told me mine was not the only outside grant mishandled in this way. He also told me Jeane had concluded that Baroody had to go.

AEI seemed to be continuing on its downward spiral. Janine and Mark left; Louise, seeing the handwriting on the wall, told me she had accepted another job and would be leaving soon. That left me, like Howard Penniman, as a program director without a program. I assumed that one of these days my program would be abolished and folded into foreign policy studies. With all these people leaving, the corridors at AEI, normally abuzz with news and activity, seemed dead or dying. And with all this empty space, AEI decided it could reduce the rent by having all of us occupy smaller offices. I was told to pack up my desk and papers and get ready to move. But AEI couldn't even get its act together sufficiently for that purpose. After being assigned on three different occasions to three different offices and wasting much research and writing time in the process, I ended up staying in the same place.

The spring of 1986 was a very frustrating time to be at AEI. There was a lot of uncertainty; everything was up in the air. Almost all the programs had ground to a halt; we were putting on none of the fancy dinners, television shows, book launches, and seminars and conferences that I remembered from my early years at AEI. The entire program was at a standstill. Except for me; as usual, I had a half-dozen projects I was working on simultaneously. If AEI funding and publications were drying up and everyone was nervous because their jobs were on the line, I kept plenty busy with consulting, textbook writing, and a big grant from the Twentieth Century Fund to write a major book on Latin America.

Besides, to the envy of my colleagues, I had a nice academic job in a lovely part of the country that I could always retreat to. Many of my colleagues, both those riffed and those now challenged, were coming to me asking, with all of AEI's problems, why do you even want to stay on here? The answers were complex: they mainly involved our new house as well as love of the Washington policy scene. But no longer AEI. Hal Saunders put it best: "You can undoubtedly stay on here if you want; the question is whether AEI will still be the kind of place you'll want to stay."

BAROODY OUT

I spent part of May and early June 1986 traveling, first up to Amherst and Cambridge and then to Europe and Latin America. After all the cuts of recent months, it might be surprising to hear that I still had money in my travel account. But that's how AEI often worked: what it took away with one hand, it gave back with the other. And for those few of us still left at the Institute, AEI could be very generous. I decided to use up my travel funds before they, too, disappeared. And without batting an eyelash, once I told him it was to fulfill the obligations of our grants, Bill Baroody approved the travel. That's also how AEI operated: if Bill liked you, he would try to do everything for you. When I came back the third week of June I was in for a big surprise.

On June 26 the beleaguered Bill Baroody resigned as president of AEI. The resignation was the result of all the problems we'd seen accumulating over the past year and more: bad management, criticism of him by several of AEI's Big Guns, the continuing financial crisis, inability to pay the bills the Trustees insisted had to be paid by the end of June, growing unease on the part of the Trustees who didn't want to be associated with a failed institution. But the most immediate cause was pressure from AEI's big funding agencies (Olin, Bradley, Smith Richardson, Chase Bank) who had all decided not to give more money until Baroody was removed. Faced with that kind of ultimatum, the Board would have no choice but to ask for Bill's resignation.

Things had come to a head that last week of June 1986, the occasion being the summer Board of Trustees meeting. Ordinarily, AEI Board meetings are happy and festive events—the Board treats all the scholars and spouses to dinner at a fancy place; there are big cigars and warm feelings all around—but not this time. On short notice, the Trustees' dinner for that evening was abruptly cancelled; an emergency staff meeting was held during the day. There was a lot of back-stage activity; AEI was alive with rumors but no one seemed certain what was happening.

Bill presided at the staff meeting. All his senior staff were there and all the scholars. He reviewed briefly the budget situation and offered a defense of his own policies. But then, unexpectedly, the meeting became quite dramatic. Economist Tom Johnson, who headed the Economic Policy Program, and political scientist Walter Berns suggested that Baroody resign. That kind of direct challenge to his authority had never happened before and certainly not in an open meeting. The room was in an uproar. The request caught Bill and his staff by surprise; he responded with Nixon-like bitterness, blamed it all on "back-stabbers," swore he would not resign, and stalked out of the room to the scattered, weak applause only of his own staff and a handful of diehard supporters.

The room was in turmoil; everyone was talking at once. Then Bill came back into the room looking like a lupine cat that had swallowed the canary. This time he was humble, gracious, and gave a moving speech. He had obviously had second thoughts; knowing the Baroody family system, I assumed Bill was fearful he would disgrace his father's memory if he resigned or was fired. He practically begged to stay on and said he would carry out necessary reforms. Apparently, even at this late date, Bill still thought that his emotional appeal would carry the day. He then walked out again and sequestered himself in his office. For the rest of the day he was said to be in intense meetings; some of us thought he might be having a nervous breakdown.

Meanwhile, the Board of Trustees was convening and was scheduled to meet formally the next day. The Scholars' Advisory Committee now had a representative who sat in on Board meetings and most of us also had friends among the Trustees; between these two sources we pieced together what happened next. Until two weeks earlier most of the Board had still supported Baroody. They had heard all the bad stories but were still unwilling to dump him. No one wanted to take the lead. But the steadily deteriorating finances, Bill's "unorthodox" accounting methods, the cutoff of money from our major sponsors, and now Bill's bizarre behavior began to tip the balance. Mike Novak reported to the Board that a poll of the senior scholars had resulted in an overwhelming vote of 19–1 against Baroody. Other scholars were contacting and meeting privately with individual Board members. At the Board meeting itself, incoming chair Bill Butcher of Chase Manhattan Bank announced he would not serve as chair if Baroody stayed on.

The Board meeting of June 25 was a real donnybrook. Bill apparently hadn't realized his position had severely deteriorated among Board members as well as scholars. Seventeen members of the Board, the largest number ever, were gathered for the meeting. Even David Packard, of Hewlitt-Packard, who rarely attended Board meetings anymore, came. It was an emotional meeting, not least because in Bill Baroody's view, his *family* honor was at stake. Outgoing Board chairman Richard Madden of the Potlatch Corporation tried to offer a compromise formula under which he and Bill would share AEI executive responsibility for a year, but the rest of the Board had gone beyond that by now. And none of the Board wanted AEI to fail on their watch. Bill was asked for his resignation; a day later he formally agreed to go.

All these dramatic, internal happenings now began to spill out and become matters of external knowledge. At the conservative Heritage Foundation and Hoover Institution, other scholars and officials were making jokes about AEI, saying that the formerly high-flying Institute had gotten its comeuppance and had received what it deserved—meanwhile trying to steal some of our personnel away. Then, in a bombshell article in the style section of the *Washington Post* on June 26, writer Sidney Blumenthal, a future Clinton speech writer, aired out all the dirty linen. He said that AEI had failed not just because of administrative mismanagement but also because it had abandoned its conservative base in favor of a centrist position. Since I considered myself a centrist, I was cheered by that news—except for one thing. Reading between the lines of Blumenthal's article, it was clear that most of his information was coming from the neocons at AEI, and that they were using these leaks to the press as part of a strategy to steer AEI back in a neocon direction or perhaps take over the Institute for themselves. In other words, the crisis at AEI was not just financial and managerial any more; it was also ideological. The Blumenthal article stimulated letters back to the *Post* and a debate within AEI if he was correct in his interpretation or not. Was a neocon coup d'etat underway?

THE MCCRACKEN INTERREGNUM

Even if the possibility of a neocon takeover was real, it could not happen immediately, because at its June meeting the Board named Paul McCracken as acting president and created a search committee to find a new permanent head. Paul McCracken was a member of the Board and had been one of the first economists appointed by Bill Baroody Sr., to AEI's crack economic team; he had also been a member of the Council of Economic Advisers. He was a traditional financial conservative but not an ideological neocon. Even more important from my point of view, he was a longtime professor of economics at my alma mater, the University of Michigan, had been chairman of the economics department when I was there, and was a member of my uncle Jerry Wiarda's Presbyterian Church in Ann Arbor. I was overjoyed at the McCracken appointment: I didn't know him well, only a little, but as a practitioner of patronage politics myself, I assumed all these old school and family connections would serve me in good stead. I couldn't conceive of ever being let go by Paul McCracken—and I wasn't.

My friend Marve Kosters filled me in on what he thought would happen next. He said that McCracken would move cautiously on any further program or staff cuts and reorganization. At the same time, AEI would not go back to what it was before: a high-spirited bevy of highly individualistic scholars. Instead, the new centralizing, consolidating, more top-down administration introduced by Bill Baroody but never fully implemented would stay. The search for a new president, Marvin said, would also be careful and deliberate. There would be a search committee; McCracken himself would serve as chair. Bill Butcher, newly installed as chairman of the Trustees, said the search might take a year and not to expect drastic changes in the meantime.

AEI scholars were generally pleased at the McCracken appointment. The attitude around the Institute was upbeat. McCracken was seen as very solid, a good Presbyterian, honest, and cautious. He himself told us any major reorganization would be left to his successors. His goal, he said in a staff meeting shortly after his appointment, was to preside over a smooth transition, do some fund-raising, keep things on an even keel, and prepare the ground for his successor. At these reassuring words, the scholars breathed a collective sigh of relief. Some of us were reminded of the Nixon resignation of twelve years earlier: to use some of the language from that period, AEI had been exhausted and paralyzed for almost two years; now it appeared our long institutional nightmare was over.

Not much happened in the next two months. Recall that the dramatic Board meeting at which Baroody had been let go was at the end of June, but in July and August most AEI scholars, like the rest of Washington, are away. They travel, do research, and go off to summer homes to write. Hence, the summer months within the Institute are like the summer doldrums at sea: no wind but the threat of ferocious fall hurricanes to come. Paul McCracken soon discovered there was red ink all over the place—much worse than had been anticipated. Meantime, virtually the only funds coming in were from the companies and foundations of the members of the Board of Trustees who, practically alone, were keeping AEI afloat. McCracken had also made a mistake in my view in retaining all of Baroody's office staff—Abellera, Pranger, Prestridge—and, even worse, following their advice. The AEI administration continued to be attracted—still another mistake, I thought, but understandable since McCracken had been recruited to AEI during that period—by the 1970s model of a lean, spare institute staffed mainly by core economists and with others brought in on a temporary basis only for short-lived projects.

Returning to AEI at the end of the summer, I discovered that very little had changed. The financial situation had continued to deteriorate. Paul McCracken, true to his intentions to not undertake major reorganization until a successor had been named, was not doing much, spent most of his time at his home in Ann Arbor, and refused to make the decisions that most of us thought were necessary. I thought Paul, who was very pleasant personally, was not fully aware of and had underestimated the problems at AEI, and had accepted the job thinking he could do it part-time. He was not, in my view, demonstrating good political skills, in the sense of schmoozing, meeting with people, and balancing contending forces, and he was not at all adept at fund-raising. It all looked quite precarious to me.

I met again with my best sources—Kirk, Penniman, Kosters—to get a sense of which way the winds were blowing. Already the names of potential presidential possibilities were being bandied about. One possibility was McCracken himself, but he was now elderly, not attuned to Washington politics, preferred Ann Arbor over D.C., and told us he had no interest in the presidency on a permanent basis. Another possibility was Alan Greenspan, the future, long-time, oracle-like Federal Reserve chairman. But this was before Alan's appointment to the Fed; he was in between jobs and might have made a good president. The fear among the scholars, however, was that as president he would be too top-down as compared with the scholar-dominated AEI of the recent past.

A third possibility and one being actively courted and promoted by some of the scholars was Irving Kristol. Irving was the self-proclaimed godfather and founder of the neoconservative movement. It was he who had famously defined a neoconservative as a "liberal who had been mugged by reality." Like nearly all the neocons, Irving had started off in the 1930s way on the left (in his case, communist, Trotskyite), and then in the 1970s, disillusioned by the McGovernite campaign, the Democratic Party's move to the anti-war left, and Jimmy Carter's presidency, had moved way to the right. Irving was a splendid writer, a well-known public intellectual, with a razor-sharp mind and wit. He reminded me a lot of Mark Falcoff, or maybe it was vise versa. His ascendancy to the presidency of AEI would cause headlines to be flashed, as well as eyebrows raised, all over the country.

Kristol's candidacy was being championed by the neocons at AEI, including Jeane, Walter Berns, Mike Novak, and Bob Goldwin. Others, such as Howard Penniman, Kirk Kirkpatrick, and most of the foreign and economic policy teams were opposed. I was one of those opposed. I had met Irving on several occasions and found him to be not only bright and witty but also arrogant, condescending, highly ideological, and not very committed to a diversity of ideas, especially those that differed from his own well-established beliefs. Second, he had no administrative experience; I couldn't imagine him as a good manager. A third criticism was that he had no track record as a fund-raiser, precisely what AEI needed at this time. Finally (and this was my formulation), if Kristol was so mistaken as to be mesmerized by communism in the 1930s, why should we trust his judgment now as any better than then? In the end, these arguments carried weight and a compromise was reached: Kristol was named a Senior Fellow at AEI, a position in which his intellectual acumen and talents as a public intellectual could be used, but he was passed over for the presidency.

As we came back to Washington after the Labor Day holiday, a new round of staff cuts was in the wind. This would be the third set of riffs since the previous December. It included persons who had, by earlier criteria, been "challenged"—that is, asked to raise their own funds—but were now being let go because they'd not raised sufficient amounts or quickly enough. The new list included *both* Middle East experts Judith Kipper and Hal Saunders, education specialist Denis Doyle, and political analyst Norm Ornstein. The new list was curious to me for two, maybe three, reasons. First, it included some of the best-known scholars and analysts at AEI; Norm Ornstein, for example, was the most quoted ("Mr. Quotemeister") pundit in all Washington, D.C. Second, it was interesting for whom it did not include, especially the administrative group around Robert Pranger whom I considered second-rate and with nowhere near having the merit or stature of those mentioned above. And third, and maybe most important, the list did not include me.

The AEI that I came back to in September 1986 was not the same AEI I remembered from earlier, happier days. The pizzazz was gone. There was no longer any sense of intellectual excitement. McCracken was mostly an absentee president. The place wasn't run right from an administrative perspective; it still had all the wrong ways of doing things and the wrong people—Pranger and the central office staff—left over from Baroody. There was a depressing, hang-dog expression about the place. Everyone expected the guillotine to drop again—not exactly good for morale.

Although McCracken was putting off any major reorganization until a successor could be named, he did make some modifications in the earlier procedures. He told us that he didn't see any difference between the "core" and the "challenged" categories of personnel, that *all* the programs were expected to raise their own funds. Since my program already had big outside grants (Mellon, Smith Richardson, Tinker), I didn't see that change as an immediate threat to my position. But I could see it becoming a problem in mid-1987 when several of the grants would run out. But even then, I reasoned, while my program on Latin America might be dissolved and incorporated into foreign policy studies, my own personal position would be secure based on both merit and fund-raising. How naive this turned out to be.

In early October the new AEI brochure came out. It afforded the first overview of the Institute as a whole since the cuts of the previous ten months. In looking through it, I counted only seven big names: Jean, Arthur Burns, Kristol, Mike Novak, Herb Stein, Alan Walters (the architect of Margaret Thatcher's privatization), Ben Wattenberg. In addition, I counted fewer than ten additional persons whom I considered serious scholars. The other persons listed in the brochure were mainly acting, visiting, or adjunct, or they were already on the way out the door. That meant a total of fewer than twenty what I would call serious, first-rate writers, analysts, and scholars. AEI to me looked very thin—a shadow of its former self.

The situation at AEI was bad enough that I now began seriously to look at other job options. Actually, I'd preliminarily begun a job search sometime earlier but this time I was serious about it. Among think tanks, IPS on the radical left and the Heritage Foundation on the right were both too extreme for me, so that left Brookings and CSIS as possibilities. CSIS was already reducing its Latin America program so that possibility was out; at the Brookings Institution I met with John Steinbrenner, its foreign policy director, who in effect told me he didn't think Latin America was important enough for his think tank to pay attention to it.

The university scene was not much more hopeful. I contacted American, Catholic, Georgetown, George Washington, George Mason, and the University of Maryland about the possibilities of joining their faculties. Maryland had no positions open while Catholic U was going through an upheaval in its political science department that led to its best scholars leaving. George Mason was a new university with such ad hoc procedures and academic units that it couldn't decide where I might fit. Georgetown was a strong possibility and I explored it seriously, but it already had John Bailey, Sam Mujal-Leon, José Sorzano, and, of course, Jeane as its Latin America scholars, and in the end the position never materialized.

At AU the dean, Louis Goodman, had gotten his appointment thanks in part to a recommendation letter I'd written on his behalf full of exaggerations and hyperbole; but when I now turned to him in *my* time of need, he was not only unhelpful but also dismissive. I was sufficiently angered by this cavalier treatment and the ingratitude it demonstrated that over the next few years I practiced the sage Washington advice of "don't get mad, get even": I connived to kill both some job possibilities and some grant applications that Goodman and AU sorely wanted.

That left George Washington University as my best possibility. I met with professors Cynthia McClintock, Harvey Feigenbaum, and Peter Klaren, the chair of the political science department, and Elliott School Dean Myron (Mickey) East. All were longtime friends; they were all enthused about the prospect of my joining them. As always, however, the question was where the money would come from. Meantime, I was still hanging on at AEI. So I put GW on hold for a few months, but shortly after the first of the year we got serious again, and a number of fortuitous circumstances then came together to make it possible.

In mid-October, seeking clarification on what we should be doing, I was also meeting at AEI with Jim Abellera and the central administration. It was a wide-ranging discussion. Among other things, Jim reported it was difficult to get the economics group, secure in their position as indispensable core staff, to cooperate with other entities at AEI. He told me the development office was badly organized and run, had too many projects and too few staff, projects were ignored or allowed to slide, and it was not raising sufficient funds.

He mentioned, apropos the presidential search, that our Trustees were all mainstream Republicans. They were presently looking at former Federal Reserve Chairman Paul Volcker as a possible president, but Irving Kristol had been rejected as too ideological. Jim further informed me that AEI was still struggling to come up with a mission statement on which everyone could agree, despite Trustee pressure to "get our act together." Finally, Jim told me, with regard to the specific reasons I went to see him, that AEI had to broaden its base of support at all costs to find new funding sources, and that until it did so no new appointments could be made or projects undertaken. Thank goodness I have my own writing projects; otherwise, the message seemed to be that we should spin our wheels even though on full salary until the budget situation was resolved. This made no sense at all.

In any uncertain climate like that prevailing at AEI in the fall of 1986, gossip and rumors fly around that are difficult to verify. First, I heard from two sources (adjunct scholar Robert Nisbett and director of personnel—she of the wiggle—Gabrielle Hills) that over the summer, at the time of the earthshaking Trustees' meeting, AEI was "absolutely broke" and on the verge of going under. Only the action of the Trustees, who quickly raised or pledged $1.5 million, saved the sinking ship. Next, I learned that Bob Pranger was out as vice president—long overdue in my view—and was returning to his position in foreign policy studies; oops, not good. In his place Pat Ford from the PR side of AEI was being elevated to vice president: Pat was bright and hardworking but he had no background in scholarship. We were also informed that for the first time in a long time AEI was back in the black with an income of $10 million and expenses, after all the cutbacks, of $9 million.

After the fact (and his departure) we also learned more about Bill Baroody's stewardship, or the lack thereof. We learned, for example, that the various efforts to find a new building for AEI may have cost upwards of $3 *million*, not the "mere" $400,000 we'd been led to believe, including a whopping penalty fee for pulling out of a signed contract. This and other capers had piled up legal fees similarly in the millions. Meanwhile, the bills from Baroody's expensive clubs, memberships, and travels were still coming in. Apparently Bill had traveled all over the globe and was in the habit of taking his friends and cronies, including women friends, with him, all expenses paid. Jim Hicks, the businessman still trying to restore order to the accounts, told me he and McCracken could do almost no planning because they had no idea what big bills were still outstanding and about to land on their doorstep.

I was getting ready to write off AEI as completely dysfunctional. Hal Saunders, who'd accompanied Secretary of State Kissinger on his Middle East shuttles, had tried to raise funds for his writings on diplomacy and the peace process, but the AEI development office sat on his proposals to the Ford and Rockefeller foundations for so long that all momentum was lost. Norm Ornstein told me that he'd been put on "challenge," then told to leave, and now was welcomed back again; he was meantime sitting on an offer from Brookings. Judith Kipper left but not without getting a friend to write up her story in the *New York Times* that made Judith come out smelling like a rose while AEI was cast in the worst light. On my floor it appeared to be complete chaos with offices being emptied, boxes piling up, people moving in and out, and no rationality or coherence so far as I could see amidst the disorder.

In mid-November I went off on a two-week lecture/conference tour that, in the balance, proved to be the wrong time to be away. First I went to Chicago to give a lecture there, next to Portland, Oregon, for a lecture at Portland State University, and then back to Amherst, Massachusetts, for dinner with visiting President Raúl Alfonsín of Argentina at Chancellor Joe Duffey's residence, and then a program with Alfonsín. The next day I visited my former "home," the Political Science Department, where I received a warm reception and noted that the department seemed to be in good shape, with new faculty members coming in and a new chair. An early snowstorm in New England forced cancellation of my flight to New York, but I managed to catch a train from Springfield into the city and from there a cab to the Barbizon Hotel.

I was in New York for a Council on Foreign Relations conference on "The Reagan Doctrine"—if there was one. Robert Kagan, Larry Eagleburger, Jeane Kirkpatrick, Ed King, and I were among the speakers; it was a fascinating and spirited session. But I need to skip over that substance for the sake of continuing the story of AEI that was now building to a crescendo. I used the opportunity of my New York visit to meet with both James Morris of the Mellon Foundation and Martha Muse of the Tinker Foundation. Both were among my main program sponsors at AEI. But both of them had heard the rumors, had an image of AEI as falling apart, not doing anything substantive, and disintegrating. Under those conditions, they said, they could not continue their support. And these were our friends! When I met with Jeane privately later in the day, she too was pessimistic about AEI.

Back after the Thanksgiving holiday, I found AEI ready to implode. Rumors were flying around like paper airplanes. Jim Abellera told me when I reported on my New York foundation conversations that the Trustees were aware that the view of AEI on the outside was that it was moribund. He shared my view that there were too many people on the staff who were not cooperating with the new reform efforts or with the central administration. Things were spinning out of control. At the same time, mindful of the points I'd made repeatedly about the dangers to AEI's reputation if commitments and publication obligations are not lived up to, Jim to my great surprise released sufficient funds for *all* the publications I'd scheduled, including two of my own books, to come out.

Public Policy Week that year, as usual the first week of December, was a tense time. One of the sessions featured prominent economists Barry Bosworth, George Eade, and Beryl Sprinkel reporting on the good prospects for the American economy. Meanwhile, the session's sponsor, AEI, was going broke. The irony was not lost on the assembled guests. I must have been asked a hundred times that week: How is AEI doing? And this question from people who were our sympathizers, who wished us well and wanted us to succeed.

THE DÉNOUEMENT

In the midst of Public Policy Week rumors had begun to swirl around that the Trustees had made a choice. The formal announcement of a new president came shortly thereafter.

The choice was Christopher DeMuth. DeMuth had a law degree from the University of Chicago, which made him acceptable to the economists at AEI, most of whom had their Ph.Ds from Chicago's conservative, Milton Friedman-dominated economics department. His specialization as a lawyer was deregulation, which similarly endeared him to AEI's economists who had led the charge in the Reagan Administration against excessive government regulation. DeMuth's most recent position had been as a lecturer in Harvard's John F. Kennedy School of Government where he taught a course on regulatory (actually, *de*-regulatory) law.

Now, as a serious academic I always worry about people whose title is "lecturer"; that usually means a part-time position and one that only lasts a year or two. Similarly, with the Kennedy School: it has a fine reputation for turning out practically oriented MA students in public policy but, based on my experience at Harvard before going to AEI, it is not a center of research and scholarship. I never saw DeMuth's curriculum vitae but I subsequently learned he only had a couple of modest articles on deregulation published in popular magazines—not encouraging for an institution dedicated to serious writing and scholarship. Nor did he have any administrative or fund-raising experience or record. Plus—and this was the most telling indictment—I had never heard of him before! What kind of qualifications were these if he was going to rescue AEI?

The next thing I heard was that DeMuth was a neocon. This surprised me: I had heard, and based on the earlier names that had been floated, that the Trustees were looking for a good administrator and a good fund-raiser, not an ideologue. Nor were the Trustees themselves very ideological; for the most part, they were Jerry Ford Republicans, not Reaganites. So how suddenly and without the name ever surfacing before did they settle on this complete unknown with a strong ideological stripe as the choice? No one among my friends at AEI knew the answer to that, and those who did presumably know the answer weren't talking.

To this point DeMuth with his University of Chicago law and deregulation background had been mainly an economic conservative. He was a Reaganite on such political-economy matters as deregulation but his ideas on other political issues were either unknown or unformed. He had an agenda but he had no "feel" for politics or public policy. And he had no international or foreign policy experience whatsoever. To remedy these gaps in his knowledge and consciousness, I soon heard, DeMuth had already been taken under the wings of and was being tutored by Jeane on foreign policy and Irving Kristol on domestic social and political issues. I didn't worry about Jeane on that score but Irving Kristol as his mentor? That was dangerous; it meant a complete neocon triumph at AEI.

In one version of this story I heard that DeMuth's appointment was all part of an earlier political deal, or a coup d'état if you prefer. That instead of Kristol coming to AEI as president, with all that job's difficult administrative and financial burdens, he would come as senior fellow. But the condition was that Kristol would either choose or get to mentor the new president. I don't know for sure if DeMuth came as Kristol's "discovery" or if he was discovered by someone else and brought to Kristol for tutoring. Either way, it seemed to me like a bad idea.

In the week after Public Policy Week—dubbed the "Second Annual Christmas Massacre," the first having occurred exactly a year earlier—the axe started to fall once again. This would be the fourth large cut in personnel in the last twelve months. Terry Hartle of the education policy program was the first to be let go. Senior economists Tom Johnson and Gottfried Haberler were also "retired." Since DeMuth would want to bring in his own front-office staff, Liz Prestridge, Roger Labrie, Ed Cutler, Ed Somensato, and Larry Foust were on the chopping block. So, without Baroody's protection, was Bob Pranger. The list was said to include twenty to thirty persons. Everyone was scrambling to find out who was on or not on the list, or to save their jobs.

My own program and position seemed increasingly precarious. I had known for a long time that my Latin America program was likely to be incorporated into a single foreign policy studies unit. After all, my entire staff and research collaborators had been by now let go; I was left standing as a one-man program. But I had always assumed, and been repeatedly told by the AEI powers-that-be, that even if my program was abolished, I would be kept on as a scholar on merit grounds. Then from personnel director Gabrielle Hills I heard the disturbing news that merit was no longer the criterion for deciding who stays or who gets cut because by this stage only the meritorious were left. And from vice president Jim Hicks I heard that McCracken, the Trustees, and now DeMuth had reached consensus on a new AEI model. In this new model (1) the message would be "sharper" (i.e., neoconservative), (2) foreign policy studies would be downgraded, and (3) there would no longer be permanent, lifetime slots at AEI, only short-term appointments of two to three years. None of these plans augured well for my position or my permanence at AEI.

As usual when things looked troubled and I needed trustworthy advice, I went to see Howard Penniman and Kirk Kirkpatrick. Together they related the story of Howard's own saga. On Friday morning he was on "the list" to be let go; the news quickly traveled up and down the corridors. But by Friday p.m. he was off the list, leaving Howard not sure where he stood. In front of me, he asked Kirk if he should go see McCracken or DeMuth to resolve the issue. Kirk advised, no; let *them* make the move to fire you. He argued that there's no reason to force the issue; let them come to you. Plus, he said, the front office is so "screwed up" that if you don't say anything, they may forget they fired you and you can stay on forever! Unhappily, it didn't work out that way: not only was Howard let go but AEI cancelled his prestigious "At the Polls" book series with the Duke University Press, leaving seven volumes and dozens of contracted contributing authors in the lurch.

On my situation Kirk was uncertain. He said, confirming my earlier suspicions, that my Latin America program would certainly be abolished as a separate program. He also said that I had angered the economists at AEI by insisting in an earlier public presentation that the Third World debt was a political more than an economic issue. He informed me further that he "thought" my name had been, along with Penniman's, on the fourth and most recent list of persons to be axed, but he said he'd also heard it had later been removed. He promised to check with Jeane, who he informed me was taking over Pranger's old position as director of foreign policy studies. I got the feeling from this meeting that Jeane and Kristol were essentially running AEI at this stage, guiding DeMuth whom Irving was now happily referring to as "my boy."

The next day, true to his word, Kirk stopped by my office. He told me I had been on the list but that Jeane had intervened to take me off. So it looked like I would be staying. I breathed a big sigh of relief. Reassured, I immediately called up DeMuth's office to make an appointment to see him. Other than the usual pleasantries in the hallways, I'd not yet talked with him in any depth. We had all been waiting for the proverbial other shoe to drop. When it didn't, or apparently not in my case, I thought this was a good time to become better acquainted.

Before going in, I devised an elaborate plan. First, with Jeane, knowing that she wanted to write about her political and UN experiences and not do administrative tasks, I volunteered to her and Kirk that, as a good administrator, I would handle the day-to-day administrative tasks of AEI's foreign policy program, leaving her free to do what she wanted to do. I laid it on thick, telling both her and Kirk that they could count on me to be loyal

(Jeane's requirement of staffers above everything else), that I was a good program administrator (Kirk could attest to that), and that politically (she was still contemplating a presidential or, with Jack Kemp, a vice presidential bid at this time) I was a strong Jeane supporter.

Second, with DeMuth, my plan was to, first of all, thank him for keeping me on; second, to offer some suggestions, nothing very controversial, about AEI—the need for scholar input on decisions, the need to honor our commitments to authors, etc.; and third, to provide him with some of my thoughts about foreign policy studies, obviously in conjunction with Jeane's ideas. But my journal notes written a day or two before the meeting show that, even with Kirk's reassurances, I was still apprehensive. They say quite clearly that if the vibes from DeMuth were negative, I was prepared to (1) withdraw my comments, (2) write a tell-all novel about AEI, or (3) go back to Amherst the following fall.

The fateful day was December 17, just before the Christmas break. I went upstairs to the president's office to see DeMuth. He was cordial but not very friendly, but then he had never been known to be warm and *simpático*. I started off with my thank-you, then got barely one sentence into my spiel about foreign policy studies at AEI when he interrupted, "Oh, by the way," he said, uncordially, "you're on the list to be let go." I almost fell out of my chair. I'd never been fired in my life—except once twenty-five years before when, as a college student working summers, I'd angered my boss for urging that the road crew on which we were toiling fourteen to sixteen hours a day be unionized. Despite Gabrielle's warnings, I'd still thought merit (mine!) would prevail. And I'd had Kirk's assurance that I'd been removed from the list.

I immediately stopped my little speech about helping AEI, helping Jeane, and bolstering foreign policy studies at the Institute. What was the point of going on? But even though I was in shock, I still managed to settle two issues before leaving the office with as much dignity as I could muster. First, I asked him about the discrepancy between what he had just told me about being on the list to be let go and what Kirk had said that I'd been removed from it. The answer, DeMuth said, was that there were two lists, a and b. The a list was of people to be terminated immediately. The b list was for people who would be terminated later. DeMuth told me he had been through the files and seen that I had grants from Tinker, Pew, Mellon, and Smith Richardson—all of which concluded the following summer. So I would not be formally terminated until my grants ran out and I'd had a chance to finish the projects under them. Thus, although I'd survived four cuts, the fifth one got me.

That response also answered my other question. I would stay on at AEI at full salary through the summer of 1987. I could keep my office, use the dining room, have access to all the facilities, and retain full benefits. My responsibilities would be to finish the studies called for under my grants (they were already done but I didn't tell DeMuth that) and prepare any final reports that were due the granting agencies. And even after August 31, I could stay on as an adjunct scholar at AEI but with no pay. So this was it. I had been let go. But as "severance packages" go, this one was pretty generous: I would stay on the payroll for another eight-and-one-half months. So it was mainly my ego that was affected: I was crushed, angry, and quite bitter.

AFTERWORD

I immediately called Iêda from my AEI office. I told her I'd been fired. She was very sympathetic, which helped. But I'm not one to go out and drink myself into a stupor after such devastating news. Already we started planning what our next moves would be. I had been granted a *two*-year leave of absence from my university and this was still only the first year. Should I use the next eight months to try again to persuade Jeane and AEI to keep me on? Should I explore other grant and teaching opportunities in the Washington area? Or maybe both of these strategies at once? And if neither of them worked out, should we prepare as a fallback to move back to Amherst? And then what would we do with our Washington house? Within a few minutes of my encounter with DeMuth and having gotten over the shock, all of our analytical wheels were turning again.

I spent the next eight months at AEI. I was disappointed, even bitter at some moments at the treatment I'd received, but in some ways this was idyllic. I no longer had any administrative responsibilities and could devote full time to research and writing. I no longer had to worry, strategize, and plot over the internal politics at AEI; that was now settled. I kept my office there, had the use of all facilities, and could entertain guests at that still-superb AEI dining room. I still had some projects and reports to finish up for our several outside grants, but those were pleasurable to write and mostly they involved my own books.

I made a few desultory attempts to see if I might still stay on at AEI. But mainly I'd resigned myself to moving on at the end of the summer and so these were half-hearted efforts. I met first with Jeane; at this point, she and I were the only two foreign policy experts left at AEI. Jeane was friendly and hospitable as usual; but it was plain she had her own agenda; she didn't want Latin America or any other area specialists but instead intended to write and lecture on global issues, and she told me she didn't really need any administrative help. I also met with Chris DeMuth, who was actually friendly this time, but again it was clear there was no future for me at AEI. I had a couple of telephone conversations with Trustee Dick Madden with whom I was particularly close and whose daughter I had helped get into Georgetown; but it was not appropriate, nor did I even want to ask, that he interfere on my behalf.

AEI's financial situation didn't improve much but at least the deterioration of the previous year had been arrested. Plus, at this stage it was operating with only a skeleton staff and a small core group of scholars, so there was actually now some money to begin to rebuild and bring in new scholars. Immediately I noticed a pattern to the new hires: it was solidly neocon. Richard Perle, once known as the "Prince of Darkness" because of his opposition to any and all arms control agreements, was brought in to head the new defense policy program. Joshua Muravchik, a former Jeane grad student and also a neocon, was hired to do foreign policy analysis. Constantine Menges (remember, "Constant Menace") was a person whom most of Washington thought of as a disaster as a foreign policy analyst, but for some reason Jeane liked him and so he was brought onboard as well.

From her UN staff Jeane brought in Allen Gerson, another neocon who had been the tough-minded counselor to her UN mission activities. For shorter stints she had Chuck Lichtenstein also from her UN staff, and José Sorzano, another former Jeane graduate student and UN staffer. Much to my surprise, she also brought back Mark Falcoff, who had formerly been my assistant at AEI and was another neocon. That appointment led me to recall that, when I was chosen back in 1981 to head AEI's Latin America program, I was favored by Kirk Kirkpatrick and the search committee but Jeane had favored "the other candidate," who turned out to be Mark. The new team also included foreign policy analyst Owen Harris, and looming over this whole neocon scene was Irving Kristol. I now began to think that maybe it was good for me to be leaving AEI; I didn't think I could feel comfortable or get along with this new crowd. There were too much orthodoxy and too many "true believers" for me.

As these appointments were being made, I had my own future to think about and what I would do. To be honest, I didn't suffer at all from being let go at AEI; though I was angry and disappointed at first, I was probably better off *not* being associated with AEI in the future. In any case, I now had eight months to explore other possibilities and remained for all that time on full salary. I also had a large, two-year, very generous *individual* (not through AEI) grant from the Twentieth Century Fund to write a book on *The Democratic Revolution in Latin America*,[1] with sufficient funds to tide me over for another full year, if necessary, without the AEI salary. In addition, I could go back to my university teaching position if I wanted at any time.

But I wasn't ready for that quite yet. I still had that second year of my leave. I was planning to write a book on American foreign policy,[2] and I was still enamored of Washington. So I began to explore other possibilities. Irony of ironies, I think it was my ongoing AEI affiliation and stationery that got me some new opportunities. One thing that came through was another large grant from the U.S. Institute of Peace, then still run by and (dare we say?) for more conservative scholars. Second, Iêda and I received, thanks to Elliott School Dean Mickey East, appointments to teach for a year as visiting professors at George Washington University—she replacing Cynthia McClintock and teaching her Latin American politics courses, and me replacing Burt Sapin and teaching his foreign policy courses, which forced me to think seriously about and organize the book (actually, two) mentioned above.[3] Finally, I applied for and received an appointment as the Thornton B. Hooper Scholar in National Security Studies at the Foreign Policy Research Institute (FPRI) in Philadelphia. FPRI was the minor league of think tanks compared to the majors in Washington, and for that reason among others they were overjoyed to have a senior scholar from AEI join them. But that is a whole 'nother story.[4]

NOTES

1. Published by Holmes and Meier for the Twentieth Century Fund (New York, 1990).
2. Published as *Foreign Policy without Illusion: How Foreign Policy Works and Fails to Work in the United States* (Chicago: Little Brown/Scott-Foresman, 1990).
3. The second volume, a companion to the one noted above, was a reader: Howard J. Wiarda (ed.), *On the Agenda: Current Issues and Conflicts in U.S. Foreign Policy* (Chicago: Little Brown/Scott Foresman, 1990).
4. A companion volume on FPRI is forthcoming.

Chapter Fifteen

AEI Reborn and Reconstituted

Being let go at AEI was a terrible shock to me. It was not just that I had been let go but also that I had never before been associated with an institution that went downhill so far so fast. AEI in the winter and spring of 1987 was in very bad shape: the president had been deposed; the new president was a cold fish; many of its best scholars had left; the physical plant (carpeting, offices, etc.) had deteriorated. Compared to the prosperous, glorious years of the early 1980s, AEI was just a shadow of its former self.

Nor was I happy with the new directions in which AEI already seemed to be going. I thought the unknown Chris DeMuth, lacking administrative and fund-raising skills, with no knowledge of foreign policy, and with a hard, even prickly personality, was the wrong choice to be president. I thought he was just the face of what I perceived to be a neocon coup already under way.

Irving Kristol seemed to be one of the powers behind the throne, and Jeane, the other. I knew Jeane was tough and a hard-liner but in my conversations and work with her over the years, she had always been pragmatic, helpful, and reasonable. But now I thought Jeane's more ideological side was coming out. I was surprised when Richard Perle, Constantine Menges, Joshua Muravchik, Mark Falcoff, and other neocons were recruited for the AEI foreign and defense policy program, while I was shunted aside. To me, this change represented the triumph of a single orthodoxy at AEI in an institution that had long prided itself on a diversity and pluralism of ideas, and that had even employed "the competition of ideas in a free society" as its motto. More than that, it was the *wrong* orthodoxy.

I had been let go in December 1986–December 17 to be exact—but I still had another eight-and-one-half months to go before my contract would be terminated. I spent a good part of that time on my own writing projects, finishing up some reports for the donors to our program, and exploring other job possibilities in the Washington area. I thought hard about my career and whether I wanted to stay in Washington or return to Amherst, and whether I was suited to the hard politics of D.C. or the more contemplative research and writing life of academia. For at some levels I loved Washington, at others I found it hypocritical, mean, excessively partisan, and downright nasty. But was academia really any different? Yes, I decided, the stakes are much lower.

I had landed on my feet after being let go at AEI, but others were not so lucky. I had my Twentieth Century Fund grant, a visiting professorship at George Washington, a fellowship year at FPRI in Philadelphia, and my tenured position in Amherst to return to if and when I pleased.

But others who had labored for AEI for years often found themselves shuttling from job to job, scrambling to keep up appearances, and often having no job at all. He was never my friend at AEI but when I subsequently ran into Bob Pranger, for example, on the streets of Washington, I felt sorry for him. His clothes were tattered; he needed a haircut; he looked scraggly and unkempt; and he had, so far as I could tell, no regular job. His was a sad case. Years and even decades later, persons like Denis Doyle, Judith Kipper, Joyce Shub, Tom Johnson, and others were still angry and bitter about their AEI experience of being let go.

But the saddest case by far was Bill Baroody himself. I had always liked and gotten along well with Bill, even while recognizing his administrative and managerial limitations. He had always treated me well and come through for me and my program; more so, I suspect, than for some other programs. After he was fired by the AEI Trustees, he could not find another job. AEI's troubles had been described in detail in the newspapers, as had been Bill's mistakes and his firing. Washington is really a small town where everyone knows everyone else's business, history, and family situation. In Bill's case not only were his managerial faults well known but so were the financial shenanigans mentioned earlier. No company or agency would touch him with a ten-foot pole. Plus, his marriage had broken up and his wife and (large) family had disowned him.

Occasionally I would see Bill, by himself or with a date, at some Washington social gathering. Without his wife to take care of him he looked like Pranger—terrible: poorly dressed, bad haircuts, disheveled. It wasn't long before I realized he was also seriously sick, because he both looked bad and was wearing an oxygen tube. His condition deteriorated rapidly and he died in 1991. I'm convinced, knowing the importance of family to Bill and his well-established sense that, by failing at AEI, he had disgraced his father, that, along with his physical maladies, he died of a broken heart. Iêda and I went to his funeral at the Meronite Christian Church in the Washington suburbs. A handful of Bill's former personal staff and loyalists were there: Isabel Davidov, Marguerite McAuliff; but almost none of the scholars that the Baroodys, father and son, had brought to AEI. It was a very sad occasion in more ways than one.

AEI AND THE GEORGE H. W. BUSH ADMINISTRATION

The relations of AEI and the George H. W. Bush Administration, 1988–1992, were far less close than they had been with the Reagan Administration. About thirty AEI scholars had gone into the Reagan Administration versus only a handful who had gone to work for Bush. Ideologically, too, many AEI scholars felt close to Reagan. They were part of the "Reagan Revolution," and they saw their ideas on privatization, deregulation, and the like being implemented into policy. George H. W. Bush also sensed this: he was less close to AEI and its scholars, relied less on them, and kept his distance from AEI far more than had his predecessor.

Actually, this split within AEI had been present from the moment I arrived there. AEI had long been divided between its more pragmatic and its more ideological wings. The more pragmatic wing, identified with the Richard Nixon-Jerry Ford-Henry Kissinger-Mel Laird-George H. W. Bush wing of the Republican Party, included Robert Pranger, Herb Stein, Denis Doyle, Jack Meyer, John Makin, and myself. Not least, it also included—and that was one reason for his downfall—Bill Baroody Jr. The more ideological conservatives—some of whom were products of the Goldwater campaign of 1964, others were more recent converts via the neocon route—included Bill Baroody Sr.; Marvin Kosters; Jeane; her husband Evron, in his later years; Ben Wattenberg; Mike Novak; and Mark Falcoff. Astute readers will note it was the first group that was mainly depleted in the great purge of the mid-1980s, while the latter group was not only kept on but augmented after Bill Jr. was fired with the addition of such neocons as Irving Kristol, Richard Perle, Constantine Menges, Josh Muravchik, and others.

There had long been bad blood between the two groups. Remember, George H. W. Bush had been a main *competitor* of Reagan in the primaries and for the 1980 Republican presidential nomination, before Reagan chose him to balance the ticket as his vice presidential running mate. During the campaign and even after the election, the priorities and even the staffs of the two candidates did not merge very well. On policy matters they remained poles apart: I remember during Reagan's first term when Jeane was at the UN her complaining mightily that Bush was a weak reed and did not strongly enough (or at all) support Reagan Administration policy on the Soviet Union, Central America, and other issues.

Then, when Jeane returned to AEI from her UN position, a mini-boomlet presidential campaign was launched on her behalf for the 1988 nomination. I'm not sure how many people remember that Jeane was a serious possibility during this period to become the first woman president or vice president. Jeane was tremendously popular in quite a few quarters for her fiery, 1984 Republican convention speech (especially her criticisms of what she called the "Blame America first crowd"). She was admired for her strong positions at the UN; and she was thought of as a tough-minded woman. In the mid-1980s, "Jeane K for President" lapel pins were popping up all over. Close to Congressman Jack Kemp, a former NFL quarterback who was also conservative and a part of the AEI family, Jeane was mentioned prominently as a possible Kemp vice presidential running mate or as the first woman secretary of State or national security adviser in a future Kemp Administration. I was myself part of a group of close friends that gathered at Jeane's summer home in LeBaux, Provence, France, to plan strategy for what we assumed would be a Jeane K presidential campaign in 1988.

As we know, none of this worked out: Jeane took herself out of the race (mainly to support her ailing husband); Kemp failed in his bid to get the nomination; and George H. W. Bush got the nomination and was elected the forty-first president of the United States. But it was a close call and the outcome had Jeane stayed in might have been different. With Jeane out of the race, I felt free to join the 1988 Bush foreign policy advisory team, to whom I felt much closer ideologically and in a policy sense. Meanwhile, once Jeane dropped out, quite a number of the neocons moved over to support Bob Dole, not Bush. And with the moderates at AEI now mainly purged and the neocon takeover in full swing during the course of 1988, relations between AEI and the newly elected Bush Administration were bound to be tense. Both the neocons and the Bushies have long memories and sharp swords.

But Bush was, after all, a Republican and he had laid claim to the Reagan legacy, so conservative criticism of him was generally muted and kept behind closed doors. In addition, the 1989–91 period—precisely the term of Bush's presidency—was the time when the Soviet Union was collapsing, the Berlin Wall came down, and Eastern Europe was liberated from Soviet control; and the deft way Bush and his foreign policy team handled these earth-shattering events was widely applauded including by conservatives. But neocons at AEI continued to see Bush as wimpy, not fully committed to their causes, and unwilling to include their members in his Administration; and they continued to press their agenda. Mostly they did so through Vice President Dan Quayle's office where Bill Kristol, a Harvard Ph.D. in government and son of the legendary Irving, was chief of staff. But they had little direct access to high levels of the Bush Administration, and in Secretary of State James Baker and National Security Adviser Brent Scowcroft they were faced with persons in power who didn't want the neocons around.

Largely muted during Bush's first year in office, conservative criticism of him began to grow during 1990. David Keane, chairman of the American Conservative Union, got it right when he said, "Conservatives tend not to be overly impressed with the Bush policies, but not upset enough to say they're angry." He went on, "If someone is viewed as ideologically oriented or a movement conservative, they're viewed pejoratively by most people at the White House." He then summed up, "You could characterize conservative views as lukewarm support with some low-level grumbling."[1]

During the 1988 election and throughout his term, Bush was widely criticized for his lack of vision. Remember "the vision thing," as Bush himself put it? The criticism came not just from Democrats but also conservative Republicans. Irving Kristol in 1990 decried the "intellectual vacuum within the Republican Party" and predicted a "decade of continuous frustration."[2] Conservatives Paul Weyrich, Pat Buchanan, the Heritage Foundation, Pat Robertson, and the Moral Majority all weighed in with criticisms. For on such issues as abortion, gay rights, and religion in the public domain, Bush was known not to share conservative views.

The White House was well aware of these criticisms and assiduously cultivated conservative support. It appointed Douglas Wead, an evangelical Christian, as special presidential assistant to liaison with conservative groups. Not wanting to lose this constituency for the upcoming 1992 reelection campaign, the Bush White House was usually very careful to return telephone calls from conservative groups and leaders. At an April 26, 1990, gathering of two-hundred-odd conservative leaders in the Executive Office Building (the same group whose meetings I had attended regularly under Reagan), Bush credited conservatives with helping him win the presidency in 1988, reminded them of his support for a cut in the capital gains tax, and said he supported a constitutional amendment allowing prayer in public schools: all issues close to conservatives' hearts. Bush was also personally solicitous of conservative leaders and especially Republican congressmen, sending them notes and returning their phone calls. And unlike the more ideological conservatives, the congressmen were practical politicians: they understood that President Bush was their leader; he would be the candidate in 1992; and they had nowhere else to turn.

These contending ripples within the Republican Party and among conservatives continued to bubble along but without their producing major rifts or an explosion until the Iraq War of 1990 (which would then be repeated even more viciously in the second Iraq War of 2003). There had, of course, long been differences between the several factions: fiscal conservatives, religious conservatives, "movement" conservatives, traditional conservatives, and neocons. The differences were not just political but also religious, personal, ideological, and ethnic. Hence, when Bush attacked Iraq in 1990 to drive Saddam Hussein's forces out of oil-rich Kuwait which they had just occupied, traditional conservative (and future presidential candidate) Pat Buchanan, who had been nurturing these ideas for some time, voiced the inflammatory suspicion that U.S. policy in the Middle East was dominated by persons who were more concerned with defending Israel than by a hardheaded defense of *U.S.* national interests.[3] The neocons, many of whom were Jewish and had favored the U.S. action against Saddam, were outraged and accused Buchanan of thinly disguised antisemitism. The battle was on, and it would be nasty.

Buchanan's position and that of many traditional conservatives was that, with the Soviet Union vanquished and the Cold War over, the United States should reduce some of its international obligations. Without a major enemy or even a serious potential one anywhere on the radar screen, Buchanan and others said, the U.S. no longer needed to be the policeman or fireman of the world. This was not an isolationist position—although that's what Buchanan was accused of—but an argument for prudently reducing our international commitments in a time of peace.

Specifically, Buchanan argued that, with the Soviet Union gone, we no longer needed so many NATO forces in Europe. Nor should the U.S. be expected to carry the full burden ("Where are our allies?") for putting out brush fires or engaging in expensive nation building throughout the world. Above all, Buchanan warned, we should not engage in crusades—will-o'-the-wisps—to use the National Endowment for Democracy and other agencies to bring democracy to countries that are ill-prepared for it. That chord struck especially close to the neocons since they had been instrumental in creating the NED in the early 1980s and were already beginning to fashion a larger plan to bring democracy to the Middle East in ways they believed would advance *both* U.S. and Israeli interests.

Both neocons and traditional conservatives, for the most part, supported the U.S. invasion of Iraq in the early 1990s. Traditional conservatives could support the invasion because it was in defense of an ally (Kuwait), punished aggression (Saddam's), was in defense of U.S. interests in the Middle East (oil), and was a hardheaded defense of U.S. national security interests. The neocons also supported the invasion for these and other reasons, including the spread of democracy and that striking a blow against Saddam also removed a threat to Israel. But then Bush stopped short of ousting Saddam, content to roll back the Kuwait invasion, destroy Saddam's army, but not invade Baghdad with its attendant expected large-scale loss of life, both ours and theirs. To this, the neocons, especially Richard Perle, Jeane, Charles Krauthammer, Bill Kristol, and Josh Muravchik, were outraged: they wanted a more muscular demonstration of U.S. power, the ouster of Saddam, and a democratic Iraq. There is evidence the neocons carried over their disappointment and this agenda into their advocacy for the Second Iraq War beginning in 2003. And in President George W. Bush, who seemingly had his own oedipal and other reasons for trumping his father's accomplishments in Iraq, they found a leader with whom they could work, or manipulate.

At AEI by this time the foreign policy team had become entirely a neocon team. Headed by Jeane, it included Perle, Muravchik, Allen Gerson, Menges, Falcoff, and Mike Ledeen. Irving Kristol also kept a hand in on foreign policy; his son Bill, though having his own center and magazine (*The Weekly Standard*), had his office in the same building as AEI and often hung out there. Paul Wolfowitz, Charles Krauthammer, Robert Kagan, Les Lenkowski, and other neocons were there frequently and participated in AEI programs.

Curiously, much of the rest of AEI was not neocon. The economic team left over from the Baroody administration was not necessarily neocon although it was dedicated to conservative, free-market principles. President Chris DeMuth as well as senior scholars Ben Wattenberg, Bob Goldwin, and Mike Novak were neocons on most issues, but one would be hard-pressed to say such pragmatic and centrist political analysts as Norm Ornstein, Bill Schneider, or Karlyn Bowman were neocons. AEI was *more* a neocon institution, especially on foreign policy, than it had been under Baroody Jr., but it was not monolithically so.

In the early 1990s AEI was still having a hard time attracting new money. It was not close to the Bush Administration, so that was one problem. Its Board of Trustees was mainly Jerry Ford-George H. W. Bush, middle-of-the-road Republicans, not ideologues, and certainly not neocons, so that was a second problem. Third, many of AEI's former donors, both conservative foundations and business corporations, were down on the Institute, didn't fully trust it after the managerial-*cum*-bankruptcy crisis of the late 1980s, and only slowly and then in a more limited fashion came back to financing AEI. Another problem was the new president, DeMuth, seen as cooly analytical but not exactly a warm, fuzzy, back-slapper (in the form of Robert Strauss) who would be good at fund-raising. Only slowly and over several hard years did AEI begin to pull out of its earlier financial troubles and begin to approach the budgets it had in the early-to-mid-1980s. It took until 1995, seven years after the meltdown, for AEI to reach again the level of a $15 million budget that was approximately its size during the earlier glory years.

THE CLINTON ADMINISTRATION

There isn't a lot to say about the AEI neocons and the Clinton Administration. In general, they were opposed to his policies. They viewed Clinton much like they viewed Jimmy Carter: soft, wimpish, morally bankrupt, insufficiently committed to the spread of democracy, so political as to have lost all ethical compass. It's safe to say that on both domestic and foreign policy Bill Clinton was not viewed as one of AEI's favorites. Some of AEI's more ideologically oriented conservatives found Clinton so sleazy, so slimy, so repugnant, that they almost got sick thinking about him. And, of course, his wife was seen as even worse: not just an extremely liberal activist but probably a closet socialist.

AEI scholars were, therefore, amazed when Clinton adopted many of their positions and, to be fair to both camps, applauded him when he did. Most of the Clinton policies AEI could support emerged from Clinton's (and Dick Morris's) famed "triangulation" when he was able to secure enough Republican as well as centrist Democrat votes to get his proposals through Congress. These included such AEI inspired economic policies as a balanced budget, even budget surpluses, and a business climate hospitable to investment. They also included his steps toward welfare reform, greater deregulation in some areas, privatization, and his proclamation that the era of big government was over. AEI scholars took these Clinton policies as evidence that their program had truly triumphed, that they were not limited just to the period of the Reagan Revolution but had become genuinely bipartisan. If now both Republicans and Democrats accepted the AEI agenda, that was really something. As a result, AEI's budget recovery now began to increase at a faster pace.

One of the most interesting aspects of the AEI-Clinton relationship was the strenuous effort put forth by the neocons to secure high places in the new administration.[4] This may appear strange and awkward on first glance (and turned out that way in the end) because, ideologically, AEI and the Clintons seem so far apart. But Clinton had assiduously wooed the neocons during the 1992 election campaign and, still hating the moderate Bush so intensely, some prominent neocons helped in his campaign. Let us not forget also that many of the neocons were still Democrats; not all of them went the Jeane Kirkpatrick route of changing over to the Republican Party. The neocons had been courted before the election on Clinton's behalf by Senator Joe Lieberman (D-CT); they had also worked with the Democratic Leadership Council to give Clinton a centrist image. Having assisted in the campaign, therefore, the neocons naturally enough wanted to be rewarded afterward with positions in the Clinton White House.

But such appointments were not forthcoming, which made them even more hateful of Clinton and solidified over time their gravitation toward the Republican Party. Ben Wattenberg was the leader of the group that had worked for Clinton's election, but he came to feel that moderates and conservatives were unwelcome in the new administration. Josh Muravchik was another AEI neocon who had supported Clinton and had pushed to be named assistant secretary of state for human rights, but that appointment was not forthcoming. The neocons tried to get such friends and sympathizers as Penn Kemble appointed director of USIA, Congressman Dave McCurdy as secretary of defense, Congressman Steve Solarz as undersecretary of state, human rights advocate Richard Schifter to head a new post as undersecretary for democracy and global affairs, and academic/think tank experts Michael Mandelbaum and Will Marshall in high policy planning positions. None of these appointments ever materialized.

The foreign policy neocons' early criticism of Clinton was that he failed to intervene initially to stop human rights abuses in Bosnia, abandoned his campaign pledge to stop the forcible repatriation of Haitian refugees, and failed to get tough with China's rulers on democracy or establish, as promised, Radio Free Asia aimed at the mainland. The criticisms were strong enough that Clinton National Security Adviser Anthony Lake and Deputy Sandy Berger met with the neocons to assure them their concerns were being listened to and they would be considered for appointments in the administration. But to the neocons' chagrin, none of these high policy positions came through; all they got were a couple of low-level slots, none of them at policy-making levels.

The neocons' pitch was that the administration should be open to "all" shades of opinion in the Democratic Party. But that was precisely the rub. Having supported Ronald Reagan in the 1980s, the neocons had not endeared themselves to Party regulars. Many Democratic loyalists who had been battling the Republicans for so long and were hurting from being out of office for twelve years did not trust the neocons. They had not struggled in opposition as the regulars had. The regulars considered the neocons as traitors. Why should we now give positions to disloyal people, they asked. So under Clinton the neocons were pretty much shut out in the cold.

Rejected for policy positions in the Clinton Administration, the neocons returned to a more familiar role as critics of society as well as administration policies. Arguably, they had more influence by operating from the outside than they would have as insiders. Much of the Administration's logic, argument, and policy proposals for balanced budgets, fiscal responsibility, and a pro-business stance came out of the AEI "playbook," specifically *Regulation* magazine of the 1980s. So did the ideas for welfare reform, deregulation, and social security reform.

As a foreign policy specialist, I have long been amazed that the Democratic Clinton Administration, with many socialists and social-democrats in its ranks, basically accepted all the main features of the Republican Bush Administration "Washington Consensus" for the developing nations: free trade, democracy, open (capitalist) markets. All of these were AEI, neocon, and Republican ideas. And yet, bereft of ideas of their own, with no alternatives available, and with the evidence accumulating that these policies worked, the Democrats rolled over and embraced a wholly Republican agenda. Wonder of all wonders!

An early indication of future neocon foreign policy came with the publication of Charles Krauthammer's oft-cited *Foreign Affairs* article, "The Unipolar Moment." With the collapse of the Soviet Union and no other challenger likely to emerge anytime soon, Krauthammer wrote, the United States should take advantage of the moment and assert its hegemony on the world. The proposal was truly breathless, both for its audacity and for its global reach. In Krauthammer's view, that meant the U.S. should be willing to impose democracy on non-democratic Third World regimes, champion global capitalism and free markets, and be willing to use American military might to enforce these policies as well as stamp out local brush fires (at that time Iraq, Haiti) where they occur. It was truly an agenda for a muscular America foreign policy; it was also foolhardy.

By this time (the early 1990s), I had left AEI, returned to Amherst and Cambridge for a time (1988–1991), and then went back to Washington (1991–1996) as professor of national security policy at the National War College. There, I was tracking as well as heading up a project on rethinking U.S. strategic policy in the post-Cold War era.[5] We read Krauthammer in our courses, but the students and I considered him too extreme and unrealistic. We treated his muscular global interventionism ("do everything") at one end of the spectrum of post-Cold War policy agendas, and isolationism ("do nothing") at the other end. The students, other faculty members, and I considered Krauthammer's agenda as way too ambitious, unaffordable financially, likely to break the armed forces, and with little support among the public which had no desire to continue serving as the world's policeman or fireman.

Of course, at the National War College, none of us was isolationist either. Rather, we favored all but unanimously a middle course not all that far from what earlier had been called the "Weinberger" (after the former secretary of defense) and now was called the "Powell" (after the then-current secretary of defense) doctrine. And that called for *selective* U.S. interventions rather than a global crusade, the advancement of democracy *where the chances of success were good*, and the prudent use of military force *where our national interests were affected*. We thought this was a sensible and quite centrist policy;

little did we know that the extremist Krauthammer policy would, after September 11, 2001, actually succeed in the later Bush Administration as *the* basis for policy.

Meanwhile, AEI and the neocons began preparing for the 2000 election. The Republican candidate in 1996, Bob Dole, was a traditional Republican par excellence and not a neocon; he despised them and the feelings were generally mutual. Plus, Dole was uninspiring and had no chance against Clinton so why waste time on him? Much better, the neocons figured, to plan for the long term. A key step came in 1995 when Bill Kristol launched his magazine, *The Weekly Standard*, with Rupert Murdoch (Fox News) and conservative foundation (the usual suspects) money. The *Standard*, with Kristol and Fred Barnes as editors, quickly became the bible of the neocon movement. Kristol hired another young neocon foreign policy writer, Robert Kagan, to be one of his contributors. In the magazine's pages, Kristol, Kagan, Krauthammer, and others began beating the drums for a U.S. military buildup, a stronger diplomacy, and U.S. military intervention in Bosnia, Iraq, and, eventually, Iran. With the founding of the *Standard*, even though their offices were in the same building, Kristol began spending more time at his magazine and less at AEI.

A particularly important development was the organization by Kristol in 1997 of the Project for the New America Century (PNAC). At the time, I saw PNAC as a new generation, new iteration of the old Coalition for a Democratic Majority (Ben Wattenberg, Jeane Kirkpatrick, House Speaker Jim Wright, Senator Scoop Jackson, and others) that I had been close to twenty years earlier. Kristol served as director; other members included virtually the entire neocon establishment who would, not coincidentally, lead us into the Iraq War:

Elliott Abrams	Bruce Jackson
Gary Bauer	Donald Kagan
William Bennett	Robert Kagan
Jeb Bush	Zalmay Khalizad
Dick Cheney	I. Lewis Libby
Eliot Cohen	Norman Podhoretz
Midge Decter	Dan Quayle
Paula Dobriansky	Peter Rodman
Steve Forbes	Stephen Rosen
Aaron Friedberg	Henry Rowen
Francis Fukuyama	Donald Rumsfeld
Frank Gaffney	Vin Weber
Mark Gerson	George Weigel
Fred C. Iklé	Paul Wolfowitz

Well, there you have it. A few surprise names on the list: Gary Bauer, Jeb Bush, Paula Dobriansky, Steve Forbes, Zalmay Khalizad, Dan Quayle. And a few surprising omissions: Irving Kristol, Jeane, Doug Feith, Constantine Menges, Richard Perle. But, examined closely, this is basically the group that brought us the Iraq War. It is a hawkish government-in-waiting.

In its 1997 Statement of Principles, PNAC announced that American foreign and defense policy was adrift. Echoing Krauthammer's "Unipolar Moment," it said that the U.S. was the world's preeminent power and should use that power to shape a new century favorable to American principles and interests. Its ideology was American greatness and nationalism and the willingness to use American power to project these. It advocated prudence in the use of that power (abandoned in Iraq) but then went on to advocate U.S. global leadership, the maintenance of peace and security in *all* global areas, and the advancement of democracy and human rights worldwide. Specifically, it argued for:

- significant defense spending increases
- strengthening ties to democratic allies and challenging regimes hostile to U.S. interests and values
- promotion of worldwide political and economic freedom
- preserving and extending an international order friendly to U.S. security, prosperity, and principles

The manifesto, again reminiscent of the kind non-McGovernite Democrats issued in the 1970s, ended with a call for a "Reaganite" policy of military strength and moral clarity, which it viewed as unfashionable but necessary.

Not all of these PNAC signatories were members of AEI, of course. But a good many of them were or had been at one time or another. Or they were members of what I will call the "neocon network," the web of conservative think tanks, study groups, and interest lobbies that had been organized, often under AEI auspices, in the 1980s and 1990s. Of the twenty-eight names on the list, I knew, had met, or had worked with at AEI twenty-four of them.

Meanwhile, AEI itself had continued to expand, bring in new faces, and grow its budget from the devastating years of the late 1980s. My AEI 2000 (reporting on the year 1999) *Annual Report* shows such new and prominent scholars as Allan Meltzer, Leon Aron, Lawrence Lindsey, Lynne Cheney, Dinesh D'Souza, Hillel Fradkin, Jeffrey Gedmin, James Glassman, Michael Ledeen, Charles Murray, in addition to such old-timers as Jeane, Ben Wattenberg, Bob Goldwin, Marve Kosters, Norm Ornstein, and others. Paul Wolfowitz was now a member of AEI's Council of Academic Advisers; future UN ambassador John Bolton was senior vice president; Newt Gingrich was a senior fellow. There were new programs in financial markets, international trade, telecommunication, Asian studies, and trans-Atlantic relations. At the same time, and financing all this, AEI's budget had now increased to $19 million—as against only $16 million in expenditures. That was $4 million above the mid-Clinton 1996 budget and *double* what AEI's budget had sunk to in the crisis years of a decade earlier. Note also that AEI continued to operate in the black, with a $3 million surplus. Some of this surplus was used to pay off debts still lingering from the 1980s; some of it was used to build up the Institute's endowment for a rainy day. Never again, after the disastrous Baroody experience, would AEI allow itself to operate in the red, on the basis of deficit financing.

AEI AND BUSH II

When George W. Bush won the presidency in 2000, it was, at AEI, like the Reagan victory of 1980 all over again. A *score* of AEI scholars, adjunct fellows, and hangers-on were recruited into the new Bush Administration—and at very high levels. The AEI "Glory Days" of the 1980s were back again. Look at that list on page 289; it is a veritable who's who of the new administration and especially its foreign policy. Dick Cheney was elected vice president meant to lend foreign policy gravitas to the new president's inexperience in that area. Donald Rumsfeld was secretary of defense; Larry Lindsey was chair of the Council of Economic Advisers; Elliott Abrams went to the NSC where his portfolio included democracy and the Middle East; Paul Wolfowitz was deputy secretary of defense; Paula Dobriansky, undersecretary of state. Eliot Cohen joined Condi Rice's staff; Zalmay Khalilzad became ambassador to Iraq; and John Bolton, ambassador to the UN. Richard Perle was named chairman of the Defense Policy Board, while Peter Rodman and Doug Feith were also at Defense with a direct pipeline to Wolfowitz and, hence, the secretary, his close friend the vice president, and on into the Oval Office. Except for the State Department where Colin Powell was installed (at least through the first term, when Condi Rice took over), it was almost a complete AEI/neocon takeover of foreign and defense policy.

Conspiracy theories abound about how this all occurred. Was this a neocon plot? Did the so-called Israeli lobby orchestrate an internal coup d'état? Was the entire Iraq War aimed at protecting Israeli as distinct from U.S. interests? How could such a misconceived foreign policy as in Iraq be explained? Since I have these prior AEI connections, my friends in academia, the Washington policy community, and colleagues abroad are constantly asking me to explain how this happened. Sometimes, if they're close friends, they refrain from asking, assuming that it's too embarrassing for me to answer.

Actually, there are two questions that friends and colleagues, who tend *overwhelmingly* to be liberal democrats, pro-Al Gore, anti-Bush, and anti-war, want me to answer. The first is: How could a person of Mr. Bush's obviously quite limited abilities and knowledge, especially on foreign affairs, get nominated and elected in the first place? The second is: How could Bush have gotten us into such a disaster as the Iraq War? And was it all an AEI/neo-con conspiracy? I think I know the answers to both these questions.

To answer the first question about Bush's nomination and then election, we need to go back to 1998–1999. The earliest presidential preference polls were just beginning to come out which showed that in a match-up Bush would beat Vice President Al Gore, the presumptive Democratic Party nominee, by twenty percentage points. No other potential Republican candidate, including Senator John McCain, the other leading candidate, showed that wide a margin.

To the Republican establishment, of which I count myself a member since I was in on some of the early campaign strategy meetings, that was all we needed to know. Republicans had been chafing for eight years under Bill Clinton, were appalled at the Monica Lewinsky affair, despised Al Gore and thought him boring, and wanted above all else to return to power and all those juicy political positions from which they'd been deprived since 1992. All they wanted to do was defeat the Democrats. None of us cared much who the Republican candidate was; we just wanted to *win* and reoccupy the executive branch. And here we had this governor down in Texas who carried an honorable name, whose father was deeply respected, who had a good record, and who, above all, could beat Gore by twenty points.

None of us at the time looked very closely at Bush Jr.'s limited educational background, his arrogance and cockiness, his intensely held religious beliefs, or his lack of experience in foreign affairs. None of that mattered if he could beat Gore. So the Republican establishment prior to any of the primaries rallied around Bush. Word went out to state and local party chiefs that he was the man. McCain was discredited and defeated in the primaries. In the Republican think tanks, intellectual salons, and foreign policy gatherings that I frequent, the word was "Yes, he's inexperienced in foreign policy but the Cold War is over. There are no current threats (this was before 9/11), and if he ever gets in trouble, he can count on his father and his father's foreign policy advisers (us!) to bail him out."

What chutzpah on our part! Worse than that, it never happened. For when Bush *did* get in trouble in Iraq, he did not consult the Republican establishment nor his father's foreign policy team (I'm talking here of the James Baker, Brent Scowcroft, Larry Eagleburger, moderate, centrist, "adult" wing of the party of which I also count myself a member); he didn't even, famously (remember

Bush saying that he would consult only with his heavenly father), consult his own father. In fact, the pragmatic wing of the Republican Party was purposely cut out of the decision-making. And the rest, as they say, is history.

Now, let us take up the second related question. Did a small cabal (all the persons listed on page 289) of AEI/neocon thinkers and policy makers conspire to have Bush attack Iraq, even though Iraq seems to have been quite peripheral to U.S. security interests and the war on terrorism? And, even more controversial, was this group motivated more by a desire to advance Israeli interests as distinct from those of the U.S.?

Obviously, this is very loaded and controversial stuff. There are land mines everywhere. Nor do I claim to have all the answers. Let me try to sort through the information and provide what I know. Let us begin with some stipulations:

1. This group, through its magazines, think tank affiliations, and media and policy connections, is very influential—far beyond what its small numbers would indicate.
2. The group is disproportionately (relative to the general population) Jewish, but more than half are not. Moreover, just as the Irish are interested in their homeland Ireland, Italians in Italy, and yours truly in The Netherlands, it is perfectly natural and acceptable for the neocons to be interested in the fate of Israel.
3. The key policy players on the list—Dick Cheney, Don Rumsfeld—are more traditional conservatives than they are neocons. Both had only a distant relationship with AEI. Or with Israel.
4. Among this group, both neocons and others, there was a strong belief, going back to the first Gulf War, that Saddam Hussein had to go, that Bush I had made a mistake in 1991 in not going on to Baghdad and ousting Saddam then. In this the neocons differed strongly from the Bush I-Baker-Scowcroft-Eagleburger position.
5. Among both Jewish neocons and the more traditional conservatives on the list, the sense was strong that Israel must be defended at all costs. And that U.S. and Israeli interests in the Middle East were closely integrated and inseparable. There were strong historic ties to Israel, many religious conservatives saw Israel's dominance in the Holy Land as part of a biblical imperative, Israel was seen as our best (and only?) true ally in the Middle East, plus it's universally viewed as good domestic politics to be supportive of Israel. When I first went to AEI in 1981, I quickly absorbed three profound injunctions:
   a. America cannot be evenhanded in the Middle East; it will always tilt toward Israel.

b. Never cross the Israeli lobby (as Senator Chuck Percy had done—and was roundly defeated in the next election, a lesson that all then-congressmen and others absorbed).
c. While the Israelis can often be SOBs, the Palestinians are worse!

6. Cheney and Rumsfeld, both of whom, going back to the 1970s, I had considered Jerry Ford, Mel Laird, Richard Nixon centrist Republicans, had gravitated over the decades to a more hardline position. In Washington this is variously attributed to creeping old age, hardening of the arteries, their private sector experiences, or even Mr. Cheney's pacemaker. Recall Brent Scowcroft's comment, "I don't know Dick Cheney any more." It did not take much neocon advice, let along arm-twisting, especially after 9/11, to get Cheney and Rumsfeld to go to war in Iraq.
7. And then there is Mr. Bush: inexperienced in foreign policy, not knowledgeable about Iraq or the Middle East, absolutely dependent on his advisers, both military and civilian. But he is also firm in his often uninformed convictions, unwilling to take advice from his father or his father's advisers (the Baker-Scowcroft team, perhaps hapless Colin Powell as well, outmaneuvered by Cheney-Rumsfeld), and perhaps looking, oedipally, either to outdo his father on Iraq or avenge Saddam's attempted assassination of his father. Remember, too, that his brother Jeb Bush, governor of Florida, whom he trusted, was also among the original PNAC signatories.
8. I doubt if there was some vast conspiracy involved. The neocons had no particular leverage over or influence on the president. Rather, I think there was a convergence of interests. Both Jewish and non-Jewish members of the PNAC, for their own reasons, had a common interest in both defending Israel and attacking Iraq. Nor, given their common interests, would they see any conflict between U.S. and Israeli interests. Especially after 9/11 there was not a lot of daylight between the neocons and the traditional conservatives on these issues.
9. President Bush, not knowing much but having strong convictions, did not need much persuading to attack Iraq. He probably really believed there were weapons of mass destruction there and that Iraq was connected with Al Qaeda. So, at the time, did most of his key advisers, including Colin Powell. Bush was ready to attack Iraq, to outdo his father, to defend U.S. interests as he saw them, to show his manliness and military-strategic prowess. What the neocons did was to give him a logic, a justification, a theory (the spread of freedom and democracy) for what he was ready to do anyway. He didn't require much convincing. Instead, he was ready to do it; all he needed was a rationalization.

And that, recall, is precisely how we began this consideration of think tank influence in Washington, D.C. For rarely do the think tanks present new policy options to policy makers. Rather, what they do is provide rationale and justification for what policy makers have already decided to do. I believe that's what happened in the Iraq case.

AEI and the neocons wanted regime change not just in Iraq, however. Theirs was a far larger, more ambitious plan to bring democracy to the entire Middle East. "Benevolent world hegemony" is what Bill Kristol and Robert Kagan called it. The plans included regime change in Iraq, Syria, Iran, and eventually even Saudi Arabia; democratization would be strongly pushed in Lebanon, Jordan, and Egypt. The plans were breathtaking in their audacity and scope. And they were sold as being good for both Israel and the United States. One can easily see how the neocons and more traditional, large-power nationalists like Cheney, Rumsfeld, and Bush could come together on this agenda, especially after 9/11 divided the world into, as the president put it, "those who are with us and those against us."

Long before the U.S. actually went to war in Iraq, the *Weekly Standard* and the PNAC had quite precisely spelled out the agenda and plans for the U.S. policy. Knowing who the members of the PNAC were, reading what they'd written, and seeing their positions in the Bush Administration, no one should be surprised at what happened after 9/11. You can find it all on the PNAC's website! There is a list of all their memos, op-eds, and letters to the Bush Administration, on a range of issues from Bosnia and Kosovo to Iraq and Iran. Kristol, Krauthammer, David Frum, Perle, Kagan, and others of the neocons were quite clear and explicit in what they wanted to do, not just in their writings but in speeches around Washington and abroad. The difficulty is not in finding plans and indications of what, precisely, the neocons wished to do; instead, the difficulty is that people in the foreign policy establishment, moderates and centrists like me, and our European allies never believed the Bush Administration would be so foolish as to accept these grandiose plans and attempt to carry them out.

Before going too far with this train of thought, I ought to make clear what my own position is. First, I never believed Saddam Hussein had weapons of mass destruction seriously capable of threatening the U.S., Israel, or other allies. I may be the only person in Washington, Republican or Democrat, who did not accept the early intelligence on this. It's not that I had any special access to some alternative intelligence; it's simply that his acquiring WMD made no sense logically. Saddam was a thief, a kleptomaniac, and he was raking in millions of dollars in graft from the UN's oil-for-food program; why would he risk all that and even his own continued rule for the sake of acquiring WMD? It made no sense.

Second, while I'm all in favor of democracy for Iraq and the Middle East (who would not be?), I don't think it's possible to bring, let alone impose, democracy there in the present circumstances. In this instance, as a specialist in developing nations, I do have some expertise. The odds of achieving democracy in Iraq or Afghanistan are about the same as winning the lottery—actually, worse. You cannot make a successful policy on the basis of such low odds or, in Mr. Bush's case, on simple, God-given faith that it will all work out. Here is why the policy had no chance of success:

1. These two countries have no history of democracy.
2. Their political culture is not supportive of democracy.
3. Their middle class is too small to support democracy.
4. Their socioeconomic indicators (per capita income, literacy, etc.) are too low to support democracy.
5. Countries racked by civil war cannot simultaneously build democracy.
6. Countries organized on the basis of tribe, clan, and ethnicity cannot create democracy.
7. Countries torn by religious or sectarian violence, and where each group has its own militia, cannot build democracy.
8. Countries occupied by a foreign power are poor candidates for democracy.
9. Countries lacking institutions (bureaucracy, army, political parties) have almost no chance of democracy.
10. Countries with weak or nonexistent civil society are poor candidates for democracy.

Readers would be bored with a methodological discussion, but here, briefly, is how a social scientist like me would approach the subject and do the math. Let's say the odds of a country with (criterion #1) no history of democracy becoming democratic are one in twenty—not good odds. Then, if we also stipulate that the odds of a country lacking a democratic political culture becoming democratic are also one in twenty, the odds become steeper because two criteria come into play. In fact what happens is the denominator is multiplied (1/20 x 1/20) so the odds are now one in four hundred.

Then as each of our ten criteria are introduced, and assuming for the sake of simplicity the odds for each are also approximately one in twenty, the denominator continues to be multiplied until the odds are one in ten trillion, two hundred forty billion. One does not have to carry this to absurdity to see my point. The odds of succeeding are impossibly difficult. You can't base policy on such long odds. The cost-benefit figures don't add up. And, of course, for a policy to be sustained, it must also show success, or at least the possibility of achieving such. Iraq and, even less so, Afghanistan don't even come close in these respects. Why didn't Cheney, Rumsfeld, or at least Condi with her international relations academic background understand this?

When the Administration, belatedly, began to realize its democracy-building efforts in Iraq were not working, either well or as fast as it had anticipated, it turned to a new strategy. That was to rebuild the Iraqi armed forces and police so they could keep order and stability once the U.S. forces left. But I'm saddened to report (I get no pleasure out of seeing my views vindicated on Iraq), again based on overwhelming historical and social science evidence, that strategy is unlikely to be successful either. Without going into too much detail, here are the main reasons; our analysis takes three cuts:

1. Historical. In the 1920s the British similarly tried to bring a form of democracy to Iraq and to create a centralized, non-political police and armed forces. In these efforts they failed. With their skills at colonialism, if the British couldn't succeed then, why should we think we can succeed now?
2. Comparative analysis. We know a lot about U.S. efforts in earlier occupations—Cuba, the Philippines, Nicaragua, the Dominican Republic, Haiti, Guatemala, Panama, Vietnam—to create an apolitical, national, non-sectarian, non-partisan police and military to keep order after the U.S. military forces leave. *None* of these, that I know of, has ever been successful. Why should we think we could be successful in Iraq?
3. Iraq society. See again the ten indicators listed on p. 296. Among all these factors, perhaps the most telling relating to the military are those that indicate Iraq is riven by tribal, ethnic, religious, and sectarian divisions. Why would we think those divisions would not be reflected in the military forces we are trying to create? If our goal now, having largely abandoned the democracy goal, is to get out of Iraq as quickly as possible by leaving behind a national and non-partisan policy and military that can keep order after we leave, I don't see, given what we know about Iraqi society, how that could be possible. I, too, wish it could be true, just as I wish Iraq were a democracy, but sound policy cannot be based on wishful thinking and by excluding from consideration a great deal of social science knowledge and understanding built up over the last fifty years.

As the Iraq War thus began to turn sour, and as it became apparent the objectives set forth could not be achieved, AEI and the neocons began to back away from the very war they had earlier justified, rationalized, and even beat the drums for. Two positions emerged. The first of these sought to place the blame on Bush, Rumsfeld, or the Defense Department. Since no one in Washington can ever admit he/she is basically wrong, the strategy is to shift the blame for mistakes made to someone else, in this case the president and his advisers. Neocons like Ken Edelman, Richard Perle, and others argued that the problems in Iraq were the result of the *execution* of the war by the White House and the U.S. armed forces. Perle was quoted as saying, "If I'd known the U.S. was going to essentially establish an occupation, then I'd say, 'Let's not do it.'" Edelman said, "This didn't have to be managed this bad. It's just awful." In other words, the main thrust from the neocons was that the war was a sound idea, just badly executed. And if that were the case, the main persons to be blamed were Bush, Rumsfeld, or General Tommy Franks, for bad war planning and management.

But one or two of the neocons were intellectually honest enough to raise the other alternative: that the problem may not have been the execution of the war but its original conception. Josh Muravchik of AEI raised this possibility when he said, "All of us who supported the war have to share some of the blame." He went on, "There's a question to be sorted out: whether the war was a sound idea but very badly executed." And, if the neocons were wrong, he said, "They should admit their mistakes and openly discuss what went wrong." Muravchik, who unlike Kristol has considerable background as a foreign policy expert, had the courage to at least raise the possibility that the basic justifications for the occupation were mistaken. The other neocons played "the blame game," shifting the responsibility away from themselves and toward Bush and Rumsfeld. My own view is that both responses are correct: the war was badly conceived as explained above *and* it was badly executed by Rumsfeld, Tommy Franks, and Occupation Coordinator L. Paul Bremer.

An even bigger neocon heavyweight to weigh in on the debate was Francis Fukuyama. Author of *The End of History* and *Trust*, Fukuyana was a major thinker.[6] He was also, unlike most of the neocons, trained in historical sociology and comparative politics. So he knew the writings referred to earlier by Rostow, Lipset, Pye, Huntington, and others on the political, cultural, and socioeconomic prerequisites of democracy. Hence, he was, like me, skeptical of the Iraq War from the beginning and became even more so as the war dragged on. In effect, Fukuyama has by now resigned his neocon membership. What made his critique so devastating is that he attacked not just the execution of the war but its basic premises. In other words, it was not just Bush-Rumsfeld execution that was bad but the neocon assumptions going in as well. For his pains, Fukuyana was viciously attacked by Krauthammer and other neocons because he struck at the entire neocon ideology and belief system.[7]

Where do AEI and the neocons go from here? One would think that after the massive and disastrous failures of their Iraq policy, a little humility would be in order. The miscalculations were enormous: there were no weapons of mass destruction; Saddam was not allied with Al Qaeda; the Iraqis did not welcome the American occupation with garlands of flowers; democracy is not working; Iraq and Afghanistan are failed states. The war has been enormously costly in lives, injuries, horror, money, and destruction; it was organized and advocated by people lacking either Middle East knowledge and experience or military understanding, let alone children in the military, a sore point with many.

But in Washington you never retreat or admit you're wrong. So the neocons have come back full strength. First, as a strategy, they have disowned their own war. Both Richard Perle and AEI scholar Frederick Kagan, among its chief architects, have now distanced themselves from the war they helped design and set in motion. Second, they have laid the blame elsewhere, mainly on Rumsfeld and the Defense Department but no longer on President Bush, since they thought they might still need him to approve other appointments and favors. Third, they have brutally gone after such critics as Fukuyama, disagreeing not only with his arguments but also seeking to undermine his credentials as a scholar and destroy him personally. Fourth, they have tried to change the subject by going on to new causes: Max Boot and other neocons want the U.S. to slay more dragons in Iran and Syria; the neocons have strongly attacked the U.S. nuclear agreement with North Korea; and poor White House counselor Harriet Miers had to suffer neocon attacks on her intellectual capacities when she was nominated by Bush to the Supreme Court—attacks that were so strong and nasty that Miers had to withdraw her name. No, this is not a group that is about to become contrite about its mistakes, apologize for them, or hide its lights under a bushel.

The neocons still have a lot of things going for them. First, they are solidly embedded not just at AEI but in other think tanks as well: Freedom House, the Hudson Institute, the Foreign Policy Research Institute, and others. Second, they have access to major funding: Rupert Murdock, the conservative foundations, businesses, and private individuals. Third, the neocons have ready access to the media: talk radio, FOX News, op-ed pages, the mainstream media as well as cable news, the *Weekly Standard*. The neocons, fourth, continue to be rich in intellectual creativity. That plus the ability to influence policy are what attracted me to AEI in the first place. Think of the BIG ideas (not just Iraq) that this group has been responsible for: government downsizing, social security reform, deregulation, welfare reform, big-government conservatism, health care reform, democracy building, human rights, free trade, open markets, and much more.

No other group within the Republican Party has such a font of ideas, such a vast network to get broad exposure for their plans, or the ability—as in the Iraq War case—to provide rationalization and justification for decisions that policy makers want to make, and thus themselves have a hand in shaping that policy. And don't forget one other advantage: the neocons, like Hillary or maybe Madonna, have an extraordinary ability to reinvent themselves. So if they were wrong on Iraq, we should not at all underestimate their ability to disown their own war and go on to other policy issues. For, as *The Economist* magazine put it,[8] the Republican Party, and the Democrats, too, need intellectual "fuel" to keep them going. And the neocons "have no rivals around when it comes to supplying that fuel."

Much of that fuel still comes from AEI. During the Bush presidency and six years of Republican administration, 2000–2006, AEI has executed a quite remarkable recovery. In 2004 AEI reported revenues for the previous year of $24.4 million, expenses of only $19.5 million, net assets (including endowed chairs) of $55.4 million, a parallel increase in media exposure for AEI scholars as well as attendance at AEI conferences. The 2006 *Annual Report* showed a whopping increase to $37.9 million in revenues (about *triple* what it was when I was there), expenses of only $21.4 million, net assets of $69.3 million, with investments income covering fully 22 percent of its budget. This represents a remarkable turnaround since the dark days of the 1980s and even the slow-growth period of the 1990s.

A dark cloud is the fact that during this period my mentor and discoverer, Jeane Kirkpatrick, was eased out of her position as vice president for foreign and defense policy studies at AEI in circumstances that left Jeane feeling unhappy and used. She was replaced in that position by Danielle Pletka, a Middle East and terrorism expert who had come up through the ranks via Senator Jesse Helms's staff. But Pletka was not a scholar nor was she a neocon so there was, and remains, considerable tension between her and others at the Institute. Nevertheless, the foreign and defense policy program at AEI was growing; it received a 20 percent budget increase over the previous year; it was doing many new things; and it had even resurrected the program on Latin America studies for which I had been brought to Washington twenty-five years earlier.

AEI continued to attract new and top-notch scholars and writers: Cristina Hoff Sommers, John Yoo, Jeremy Rabkin, Michael Rubin, Gary Schmitt, Charles Murray, Leon Kass, Revel Marc Gerecht, Frederick Kagan, David Frum, and others. A particularly important catch as a critic of Islam was Ayaan Hirsi Ali, the remarkable, Somali-born, former member of the Dutch parliament, who joined AEI as a resident fellow in 2006. It also attracted as speakers and fellows top policy-markers: Congressmen (Newt Gingrich), Supreme Court justices (Antonio Scalia), the secretaries of state and defense. And don't forget that every year at its annual dinner the president of the United States himself feels obliged to show up on the AEI doorstep and deliver a major speech. That by itself may be the single best indicator of the Institute's ongoing influence and success.

NOTES

1. *New York Times* (June 22, 1889), B7.
2. *Time* (May 19, 1990), 17.
3. Patrick J. Buchanan, *Where the Right Went Wrong: How Neoconservatives Subverted the Reagan Revolution and Hijacked the Bush Presidency* (New York: St.Martin's Press, 2004).
4. *Washington Post* (March 15, 1993), A17.
5. Howard J. Wiarda, *U.S. Foreign and Strategic Policy in the Post-Cold War Era* (New York: Greenwood Press, 1995).

* Justification for this conclusion has been provided by AEI neocon foreign policy analyst Joshua Muravchik. Muravchik has written that neither liberal internationalism nor traditional conservatives had an answer to the challenge of terrorism. But neoconservatism did. Its answer was democracy. He said, "If democracy had shown its potency in discouraging war elsewhere [Russia, Eastern Europe], it stood to reason it could also be a cure to terrorism in the Middle East." Muravchik went on to say, "This latter extrapolation, admittedly, was just a hypothesis, but *Bush embraced it because it was the only strategy on offer*." In short, we went to war in Iraq on the basis of an "extrapolation" and a "hypothesis." And Bush adopted it because it provided a rationalization, apparently the only justification available, for what he, Cheney, and Rumsfeld intended to do anyway. (*Washington Post*, November 19, 2006, B3.)

* I have a theory about Condi in this regard and would love to see her academic transcript from graduate school at the University of Denver to back up my hunch. I think Condi was likely trained as a Soviet or Russian area specialist. I suspect she lacks a broad background in comparative politics/developing areas. Therefore, she may not have been trained in the developmental theory and analysis used above. The one person in the Administration who might have saved us from the Iraq folly, for this as well as other bureaucratic and political reasons, was unable to do so.

6. Francis Fukuyama, *America at the Crossroads: Democracy, Power, and the Neoconservative Legacy* (New Haven: Yale University Press, 2006).
7. *Washington Post* (March 28, 2006), A23.
8. *Economist* (September 18, 2004), 43.

Conclusion

AEI had emerged in the 1960s and 1970s as the leading conservative alternative to the Brookings Institution. In those years it mainly stood for balanced budgets, a conservative economic policy, and a free-market economic approach as compared with the Keynesianism of Brookings. When the Republicans were in power (Eisenhower, Nixon, Ford), AEI's market economics as well as the economists from the Institute were dominant; when the Democrats were in power (Kennedy, Johnson) Keynesianism was triumphant.

By the late 1970s AEI had begun to rapidly grow its budget and to expand its staff into nontraditional activities. Bill Baroody Sr., AEI's president during this period, took the lead in these expansion efforts, which were continued by his son Bill Jr. One of the areas into which AEI expanded was foreign affairs. I was part of the wave of new hires brought on during this period with the goal in mind of expanding AEI's foreign policy expertise.

AEI's rise in the 1970s and 1980s was part of a broader Washington phenomenon: the emergence during this time of a full spectrum of "think tanks" that grew as influential as interest groups and political parties in formulating Washington policy. With AEI and Heritage on the right, Brookings and IPS on the left, CSIS in the center, and Hoover and Hudson out there in the hinterland, the think tanks cut across the full range of political views and presented alternative policy options.

We used to kid ourselves that the think tanks did the government's thinking for it, and that perspective was not all that far from the truth. Among other things, we wrote speeches and prepared testimony for government officials, worked on federal budget issues, did the background and historical research that government agencies were often unable to do, prepared the studies on which much public policy (health care, social security, deregulation, Central

America, etc.) was based, and presented the options papers to policy makers that often led to official government action. AEI scholars not only did this policy background work but, beginning with Ronald Reagan, sent over thirty of its personnel into government to help carry out the new policies.

AEI had begun as a quite traditional, conservative, Republican think tank. But beginning in the late 1970s it received an infusion of neocon ideas and personnel. Most of the neocons had been liberal Democrats in the 1960s but had become quite disillusioned with the Democratic Party, first by George McGovern's anti-war, peacenik campaign of 1972, and then by Jimmy Carter's naivete and romantic idealism, 1976–1980. The neocons had helped found the Committee on the Present Danger that sought to impress on President Carter the need for a stronger foreign policy vis-à-vis the Soviet Union. When those efforts failed, and then such neocon heroes as Senators Henry ("Scoop") Jackson, D-WA, and Daniel Patrick Moynahan, D-NY, decided to forego the 1980 presidential election campaign, quite a number of the neocons went over to the Republican Party—and to AEI.

When I arrived at AEI in the spring of 1981, a few months after Reagan's inauguration, it was a very exciting place to work. A large number of AEI scholars had gone into the Administration at high levels; AEI ideas on deregulation, privatization, and economic and governmental reform were dominating the agenda; and everyone assumed AEI (since Reagan was presumed to be incapable of doing so) was running the government. Internally, AEI during this period was a wonderful place to work, with great salaries and nice perks, a marvelous dining room, ready access to media and government officials at the highest levels, and a sense of excitement that we were changing the world. There was also, within AEI, a real belief in its motto, the "competition of ideas in a free society," and a nice balance between neocons and more traditional conservatives.

In this context I flourished as a scholar and writer. With wonderful staff and facilities and only a minimum of administrative responsibilities, I produced numerous policy papers, memos, scholarly articles, and books and book chapters on Latin America, American foreign policy, the developing nations, Spain and Portugal, international relations, and comparative politics. It was the most prolific period of my life. The dean at my university once told me, "Howard, every time you sneeze it gets published."

Plus, in the process I learned an awful lot about Washington politics and policy-making. That explains the early chapters in this book on the Washington think tanks and their role in policy-making, how policy-making on Latin America is shaped heavily by cultural and societal biases toward that area, and how the overall process of American foreign policy-making works and fails to work. Using the knowledge built up and the inside access I had through my AEI affiliation, I wrote in the mid-to-late 1980s a pioneering, and quite cynical, book on American foreign policy. The book argued that American foreign policy was driven *overwhelmingly* by domestic political considerations as distinct from rational calculations of the national interest, a message that at that time many academic colleagues wished not to hear, even while their students waxed enthusiastic over the many insider anecdotes and stories related in the book.[1]

Subsequent chapters in the present book tell the story of what it was like to live in Washington during this period, to be at AEI, to be involved as an insider in the policy process, to go down to the White House, up to the Congress, or over to the State and Defense departments or the CIA on a regular basis. In this book I have tried to convey not just the substance of policy but also the personalities involved, their (and my) foibles, the climate and atmosphere in which we operated, the petty backstabbing that goes on, the sheer incompetence of many of the people involved, and the way policy influence works. What a ride this was!

The chapters in this book deal with the issues I knew best and participated in personally. For during much of this period I kept a private journal of the meetings I attended, the people met, and the conflicts—petty and otherwise—generated. For this reason the book may contain information on White House meetings, policy initiatives, and the process of foreign policy-making never revealed before. Hence, the chapters on the role of AEI in formulating the initial Democracy Initiative that later became the much-celebrated National Endowment for Democracy, my role as lead consultant to the National Bipartisan (Kissinger) Commission on Central America, and the near-comic-opera politics of the Presidential Task Force on Economic Justice meant to bring Employee Stock Ownership Programs (ESOPs) to Central America. Hence, also what I regard as the fun as well as interesting chapters or subchapters on AEI efforts to found a conservative international, my role as "official" U.S. representative to INTAL (the Institute for Latin American Integration), and our travels (and travails) at home and abroad lecturing on U.S. foreign policy. And what other than cynical conclusions could one reach after reading the chapters on the White House Public Outreach weekly meetings, testifying before Congress, or consulting gigs with State, Defense, and the CIA.

I was at AEI during the "glory years" of the early-to-mid 1980s; in this book I have tried to convey both the policy excitement of that time and the sheer fun we had as participants in the process. For many people believed at that time that AEI was basically running the policy shop in the government and was the font of all its policy ideas, and naturally, since it enhanced our own power and prestige, none of us wished to disabuse the press, the public, lobbyists, and even government officials of that notion. For most of the

1980s, encompassing two presidential elections and the two presidential terms of Ronald Reagan, AEI enjoyed unprecedented access and influence and became known as one of the most powerful institutions in Washington.

But then came the decline and eventual denouement. I had heard the rumors that AEI's financial condition was precarious as early as the winter of 1982, but most of AEI's scholars, myself included, caught up in the glories and importance of our role, chose to ignore the early warning signs. The fact that the AEI administration, to pay for the general operating budget, had been dipping its fingers into the endowment funds, skipped payments into our retirement accounts, and was using grant funds for purposes other than what was set forth in the proposals was extremely worrisome; but even then most of us assumed AEI would pull out of the slide OK. Hence, it was only in the mid-to-late 1980s when programs were cut back or abolished, publications curtailed, and, in round after round of staff cutbacks, personnel let go that we realized how serious the crisis was.

At the time I believed that AEI's crisis was mainly financial and administrative—and maybe it was. That is, for a variety of reasons that had to do with changes in the tax laws, changing donor preferences on giving, competition from other worthy recipients (museums, orchestras), etc., AEI's revenues began to decline. They went from near $15 million at one point in the early 1980s down to under $10 million at the height of the crisis in 1986-87, a 33 percent drop that no institution could possibly absorb. At the same time, when things got tough, AEI president Bill Baroody proved to be a weak reed, a terrible administrator, and totally incompetent as a financial manager.

Along with the financial *cum* administrative crisis, however, a number of political agendas were also being served. As wave after wave of AEI scholars were let go as part of the financial pruning, the new scholars brought in tended overwhelmingly to be neocons. Especially in the foreign affairs area, such new, or renewed, appointments as Richard Perle, Michael Ledeen, Constantine Menges, Mark Falcoff, Joshua Muravchik, Elliott Abrams, Allen Gerson, to say nothing of the movement's guru, Irving Kristol, were all in the neocon tradition. The fact that Jeane Kirkpatrick, after her UN experience, was now directing AEI's Foreign and Strategic Studies Program, made the neocon takeover complete. It was a veritable neocon coup d'état. The new appointments were sold to the AEI Board of Trustees as providing greater and needed "bite" as well as focus to the program; I'm not sure the Board realized at the time that it was buying into a full-fledged political/ideological agenda as well.

Context is everything; we need to understand what was happening at that time, including scenarios that *didn't* work out. For one thing, Jeane herself was enormously popular with a large part of the public, was contemplating a run for high office, and had not discouraged a Jeane-for-president boomlet that emerged during the 1984-87 period. For another, Congressman Jack Kemp, who was also an AEI associate and a conservative, was thinking seriously of challenging Vice President George H. W. Bush for the Republican presidential nomination in 1988. If Jeane had run and won, we would have certainly had an all-neocon foreign and defense policy team; if Kemp had run and won, he would certainly have appointed Jeane and her team to high positions. Either way it would have meant a neocon takeover of foreign and defense policy not unlike what occurred after George W. Bush won in 2000.

But things did not work out that way—at least at first. When George H. W. Bush was elected president in 1988, he brought in a foreign policy team from the pragmatic, traditional, realist wing of the Republican Party (Brent Scowcroft, James Baker, Colin Powell, Dick Cheney) and, as we have seen, kept the neocons at arm's length. Then, when Bill Clinton was elected in 1992 and reelected in 1996, despite neocon efforts to portray themselves as Democrats all along and, therefore, deserving of high positions in his administration, he similarly kept the neocons out and marginalized, not disapproving of Democratic Party leaders portraying them as turncoats and traitors. During that twelve-year interval, 1988-2000, both the neocons and AEI as their primary haven were largely excluded from the political process, marginalized, and kept out of high government positions.

Meanwhile, the neocons had not been standing passively by but were already formulating plans for a comeback. With the founding of the *Weekly Standard*, the organization of the Project for a New American Century (PNAC), and with funding assured from some of the major conservative foundations, AEI and the neocons were churning out a steady stream of op-eds, position papers, and memos critiquing the administration (Clinton's) and setting forth their own expansionist vision for the future. A new generation of neocon journalists and analysts—Charles Krauthammer, Bill Kristol, Robert Kagan—all either affiliated with AEI or closely associated with its intellectual currents, provided new ideas and intellectual firepower.

When George W. Bush was elected president in 2000, AEI and the neocons were rehabilitated and received a new opportunity to influence policy. I see the 2000 election as largely giving the neocons the opportunity for a high policy role that they would have received in 1988 had the Jeane Kirkpatrick or Jack Kemp political campaigns proved successful. In 2000 the neocons were particularly successful in having their members serve in the Defense Department and on Vice President Richard Cheney's staff. The names are by now quite familiar to us: Richard Perle, Paul Wolfowitz, Lewis ("Scooter") Libby, Elliott Abrams, Peter Rodman, Douglas Feith, Bill Kristol, Charles Krauthammer, Robert Kagan, and Fredrick Kagan remained outside of government, but they provided the intellectual firepower and the cheering section for the neocon agenda.

I am already on record as indicating what I think happened in the fateful decisions—and for which the neocons will always be remembered, if not held accountable—to go to war in Iraq. I think that after 9/11 Secretary of Defense Donald Rumsfeld, Vice President Richard Cheney, and President George W. Bush himself were already convinced that they would attack Saddam Hussein and go to war in Iraq. In this they were persuaded either by earlier neocon arguments, by their own convictions, or, in the president's case, some combination of desire for revenge for Iraq's efforts to assassinate his father, the wish to complete his father's unfinished business in Iraq, or to go down in history and successfully win a second term as a "war president."

In any case, based on my policy experience in Washington and years at AEI, I think what happened is that the neocons provided legitimation and rationalization ("bringing democracy and freedom to the Middle East") for what the Bush-Cheney-Rumsfeld team wished to do regardless. It is not, as has often been alleged, that the neocons led us by surreptitious means into this fateful war, but that they provided the logic, the arguments, and the idealistic motivation ("toppling of tyranny," "freedom and democracy") that justified what the Bush Administration wanted to do anyway.

The question now is: Will this disastrous Iraq War discredit AEI and the neocons? Or will they emerge unscathed? My prediction is that not only will AEI and neoconservatism survive the Iraq War fallout but also that they will quickly emerge again as a major voice on the national scene.

First, one might expect, given the inglorious failures in Iraq, that the neocons might show a little contriteness and for a time at least withdraw into silence. But the neocons have never been known as wallflowers; I see no sign that they are repentant or that they intend to give up the fight. Among neocons, only Joshua Muravchik—and then only briefly—has been brave enough to state publicly that maybe the assumptions of the Iraq War and the supposed ease of building democracy there were wrong from the beginning.

Instead, the preferred strategy has been to blame someone else. The assumptions going into the war cannot be wrong for that would be to challenge fundamental AEI and neocon ideas; far better, from the neocon viewpoint, to shift the blame onto someone else's shoulders for their *execution* of the war. Candidates include former Secretary of State Colin Powell, former NSA and former Secretary of State Condi Rice, the United States military or its generals, the provisional authority and Ambassador Paul Bremmer, or President Bush. All of these have been given responsibilities for the failures of Iraq in one form or another, but political considerations are also involved. It may be politically dangerous, or the accusations may come back to haunt you, if you blame Powell, Rice, the U.S. military, or the president. But the generals (Tommy Franks, now safely retired) or the CPA head (Bremmer) are fair game. In any case, one understands the strategy: blame the executioners of the strategy and not the strategy itself, for that would be to cast doubt on neocon first principles, and that will not do.

Over in the Bush Administration, meanwhile, pragmatism and realism were supposedly in the air and the neocon agenda ignored and forgotten. Rumsfeld is gone; Wolfowitz is gone; Feith is gone; Libby awaits sentencing; and Cheney's health is precarious. Francis Fukuyama and other neocons have defected from the ranks, while some longtime AEI scholars (including Jeane Kirkpatrick and the present author) believe the assumptions underlying the Iraqi War effort—that we could bring democracy to countries that were woefully unprepared for it—were wrong from the beginning. Condi Rice, who was never a neocon, had now apparently rediscovered her realist intellectual background and was carrying out a more pragmatic policy from her new perch at State. For a time it seemed like the "adults"—James Baker, Brent Scowcroft—in the form of the Iraq Study Group, might recapture the levers of foreign policy influence, but that did not happen. Meanwhile, the greatest neocon of them all, President Bush, remained in power and showed no sign of surrendering any of his authority, either to a Democratic Congress or to the realists even within his own administration.

In mid-July 2008, four months before the election, Chris DeMuth stepped down as president of AEI. DeMuth had served as president for twenty-two years, restoring AEI's financial health and, under Bush II, its foreign policy influence as the most listened-to think tank in Washington. DeMuth was, reportedly, tired after over two decades as president; he also wanted to write more and do other things besides leading AEI. He was replaced as president by Arthur C. Brooks, 44, a business and government professor at Syracuse University. Brooks is a vigorous scholar and had worked at AEI; he was said to represent a change at AEI to a new and younger generation. For at least some of the scholars written about in these pages are now starting to pass from the scene, and AEI is recruiting new scholars with new ideas. AEI is still identified with neoconservatism but that no longer means automatic adherence to the Reagan principles of the 1980s. While some AEI scholars are critical of George W. Bush's "big government conservatism," others applaud that approach. Still others are looking for a new public philosophy for America for the twenty-first century. In the foreign policy arena, even though Iraq has not gone as hoped, the neocons at AEI still remain committed to a vigorous defense of U.S. democracy initiatives and a muscular foreign policy with regard to North Korea, Iran, and other issues and areas.

Do not expect AEI or the neocons, therefore, to slink ashamedly out of town or to hide their lights under a bushel. American public opinion is remarkably fickle and short-term; the neocons have taken a few lumps; they are reassessing their assumptions, and in a few weeks the criticisms of them will be largely forgotten. Already the same faces appear on television talk shows and familiar names appear in the op-ed pages denouncing the North Korea nuclear deal, speaking out on Lebanon and Hezbollah, calling for sanctions against Syria, and, as if the Iraq War were not enough, calling for military action against Iran. It seems almost as if Iraq never happened or that it would go away and neocon responsibility for that failure would disappear.

At the same time, in both Republican and Democratic think tanks and election campaigns, there is talk of a new realism. The Bush Administration was said to have abandoned at some levels the freedom agenda advanced by one-time Russian dissident Natan Sharhansky, a Bush favorite, while at the Democratic New America Foundation the scholars are weighing such rallying slogans as "ethical realism" or "neo-Wilsonianism." But this will not do: America has *never* been able to function with a Kissingeresque, strictly realist foreign policy that ignores the plight of peasants in Central America, blacks in South Africa, Jews and Baptists in the former Soviet Union, genocide in Bosnia, or starving, diseased children in sub-Saharan Africa. Rather, America and American foreign policy have always functioned best when they were able to combine and reconcile—as in World War II—hardheaded realism and pragmatism with idealistic democracy and human rights concerns. Undoubtedly that reconciliation will happen again, sooner rather than later, in American foreign policy. And when it does, AEI and its primary group, the neocons, stand ready to provide both the toughness and the political savvy that is necessary, and the spotlight on democracy and human rights issues for which they have long been justly famous and which resonates clearly in the American body politic.

NOTE

1. Howard J. Wiarda, *Foreign Policy without Illusion* (Chicago: Little Brown/Scott Foresman, 1990).

Index

About the Author

Howard J. Wiarda is Dean Rusk Professor of International Relations and founding head of the Department of International Affairs at the University of Georgia. He is also a senior associate at CSIS and a senior scholar at the Woodrow Wilson Center in Washington, D.C. Over the past 25 years, he has divided his time among the academic, policy, and think tank worlds. He has been visiting scholar/research associate at the Center for International Affairs at Harvard University; resident scholar and founding director of the Center for Hemispheric Studies at the American Enterprise Institute for Public Policy Research; visiting professor at MIT, Georgetown, and George Washington Universities; course chairman at the Foreign Service Institute of the Department of State; lead consultant to the National Bipartisan (Kissinger) Commission on Central America; Thorton D. Hooper Fellow in International Security Affairs at the Foreign Policy Research Institute; and professor of national security affairs at the National Defense University.

A prolific author, Dr. Wiarda has written or edited over 70 books and is the author of over 300 scholarly articles, book chapters, op-eds, and congressional testimonies. Some of his best-known books include *American Foreign Policy* (HarperCollins, 1996), *Development on the Periphery* (Rowman & Littlefield, 2006), *Introduction to Comparative Politics*, 2nd ed. (Harcourt, 2000), *European Politics in the Age of Globalization* (Harcourt, 2001), *Latin American Politics and Development*, 6th ed. (Westview, 2006), Civil Society (Westview, 2003), *Political Development in Emerging Nations* (Wadsworth, 2004), Policy Passages (Praeger, 2002), *Comparative Democracy and Democratization* (Harcourt, 2002), and *Corporatism and Comparative Politics*

(M.E. Sharpe, 1997). He is a graduate of the University of Michigan, holds M.A. and Ph.D. degrees from the University of Florida, and an M.S. degree from the National Defense University. He has been a post-graduate scholar at Harvard and Ohio State Universities, and he holds an honorary doctorate from Nizhny Novgorod State University in Russia.

www.ingramcontent.com/pod-product-compliance
Lightning Source LLC
Chambersburg PA
CBHW051254200926
51612CB00001B/39
* 9 7 8 0 7 3 9 1 2 8 8 3 1 *